PATERNOSTER BIBLICAL MONOGRAPHS

The Authenticity of 2 Thessalonians

PATERNOSTER BIBLICAL MONOGRAPHS

The Authenticity of 2 Thessalonians

Daniel W. Macdougall

Copyright © Daniel W. Macdougall 2016

First published 2016 by Paternoster Press

Paternoster Press is an imprint of Authentic Media
PO Box 6326, Bletchley, Milton Keynes MK1 9GG

authenticmedia.co.uk

The right of Daniel W. Macdougall to be identified as the Author of this Work
has been asserted by him in accordance with the Copyright, Designs
and Patents Act 1988.

*All rights reserved. No part of this publication may be reproduced, stored in a retrieval
system, or transmitted, in any form or by any means, electronic, mechanical, photocopying,
recording or otherwise, without the prior permission of the publisher or a license
permitting restricted copying. In the UK such licenses are issued by the Copyright
Licensing Agency Ltd, Barnard's Inn, 86 Fetter Lane, London, EC4A 1EN.*

British Library Cataloguing in Publication Data
A catalogue record for this book is available from the British Library

ISBN 978-1-84227-840-6
978-1-84227-898-7 (e-book)

Typeset by Daniel W. MacDougall
Printed and bound by Lightning Source

PATERNOSTER BIBLICAL MONOGRAPHS

Series Preface

One of the major objectives of Paternoster is to serve biblical scholarship by providing a channel for the publication of theses and other monographs of high quality at affordable prices. Paternoster stands within the broad evangelical tradition of Christianity. Our authors would describe themselves as Christians who recognize the authority of the Bible, maintain the centrality of the gospel message and assent to the classical creedal statements of Christian belief. There is diversity within the constituency; advances in scholarship are possible only if there is freedom for frank debate on controversial issues and for the publication of new and sometimes provocative proposals. What is offered in this series is the best of writing by committed Christians who are concerned to develop well-founded biblical scholarship in a spirit of loyalty to the historic faith.

Series Editors

I. Howard Marshall	Honorary Research professor of New Testament, University of Aberdeen, Scotland, UK
Richard J. Bauckham	Professor of New Testament Studies and Bishop Wardlaw professor, University of St Andrews, Scotland, UK
Craig Blomberg	Distinguished Professor of New Testament, Denver Seminary, Colorado, USA
Robert P. Gordon	Regius Professor of Hebrew, University of Cambridge, UK
Stanley E. Porter	President and Professor of New Testament, McMaster Divinity College, Hamilton, Ontario, Canada

PATERNOSTER BIBLICAL MONOGRAPHS

Acknowledgments

Throughout our time in Aberdeen and the years following our time there, we have been very aware of God's providential care in supplying our needs and in providing many individuals who have assisted in making this work possible.

First, I would like to express my gratitude to Professor I. Howard Marshall, King's College, the University of Aberdeen, who was always very patient and gracious in all of his dealings with me. His insight and breadth of reading made him an ideal thesis supervisor.

Second, I want to express my gratitude to our parents, Daniel and Phyllis MacDougall and Robert and Laura Moolenaar. Their generosity and loving support gave me the opportunity to study.

Third, I would like to thank all those at Paternoster for their help and patience in this process.

Finally, I want to thank my beloved wife, Barb, who with her loving encouragement and patience and work is not only my partner in life but as well in this work. She, more than anyone else, has made this work possible and readable.

Contents

Abbreviations	xi

Chapter 1 The Debate about the Authenticity of 2 Thessalonians 1
The Debate about the Doctrine of 2 Thessalonians 1
   Doctrine and the Disputers 1
   Doctrine and the Defenders 6
The Debate about the Literary Character of 2 Thessalonians 8
   The Literary Character and the Disputers 8
   The Literary Character and the Defenders 11
The Debate about External Attestation to 2 Thessalonians 30
Conclusion 30

Chapter 2 External Attestation to 2 Thessalonians 31
Middle Second Century 32
The Apostolic Fathers 33
Polycarp 35
   Citations of 2 Thessalonians in Polycarp's Epistle 36
   The Life of Polycarp 45
   The Integrity of Polycarp's Epistle to the Philippians 47
   Polycarp and the Terminus ad Quem *for 2 Thessalonians* 61
External Attestation and the Authenticity of 2 Thessalonians 62

**Chapter 3 Tradition in 2 Thessalonians: Terminology
and Identification** 63
The Terminology of Tradition 64
   Words Found in 2 Thessalonians 64
   Words Not Found in 2 Thessalonians 74
   Evaluating the Terminology 83
The Identification of Tradition in 2 Thessalonians 84
   Tradition in 2 Thessalonians 2 85
   Tradition in 2 Thessalonians 3 87
   Tradition in 2 Thessalonians 1 87
   Conclusion on the Identification of Tradition 93
Tradition in the Undisputed Pauline Epistles 94
   The Identification of Tradition in 1 Thessalonians 94
   The Identification of Tradition in 1 Corinthians 119
Tradition and the Authenticity of 2 Thessalonians 135

Chapter 4   Doctrinal Content of 2 Thessalonians 141
Eschatology 141
   2 Thessalonians 2:1-12 142

Contents

The Eschatological Parallels to 2 Thessalonians	171
2 Thessalonians and Apocalyptic Literature	175
Eschatology and the Problem of Authenticity	178
Imitation	180
The Concept of Imitation	181
The Character of Paul Presented in 2 Thessalonians	190
Conclusion on Imitation	197
Christology	198
Transfer to Jesus Christ of Attributes Traditionally Ascribed to Yahweh	199
Absence of the Cross and Resurrection from the Christology of 2 Thessalonians	200
The Titles for Christ in 2 Thessalonians	201
Conclusion on Christology	207
Soteriology	207
Grace	208
Faith	211
Conclusion on Soteriology	213
Doctrine and the Authenticity of 2 Thessalonians	213
Chapter 5 The Literary Character of 2 Thessalonians	**215**
The Overall Structure of 2 Thessalonians	215
Rhetorical and Epistolary Analyses of 2 Thessalonians	215
The Structure of 2 Thessalonians and the Disputation by Wrede	218
Sentence and Internal Structure of 2 Thessalonians	232
Embeds	232
A-B-A Pattern	234
Scalometry	235
Vocabulary and Stylistic Features of 2 Thessalonians	238
Word Ratios	239
Stylistic Peculiarities	240
Connectives	243
Independent Vocabulary and Grammatical Features	244
Stylo-statistical Analysis	246
Further Vocabulary Analysis	249
Literary Character and the Authenticity of 2 Thessalonians	251
Conclusion	**253**
Bibliography	**255**
Index of Ancient Sources	**271**
Index of Authors	**287**

Abbreviations

Primary Sources

1 Clem.	1 Clement
2 Clem.	2 Clement
4 Bar.	4 Baruch
4 Macc.	4 Maccabees
Ant.	*Jewish Antiquities* (Josephus)
Ascen. Isa.	*Martyrdom and Ascension of Isaiah* 6-11
Att.	*Epistulae ad Atticum* (Cicero)
B. Bat.	*Baba Batra*
Barn.	*Barnabas* (epistle of)
Ber.	*Berakot*
Dial.	*Dialogue with Trypho* (Justin Martyr)
Did.	*Didache*
Diogn.	*Diognetus* (epistle to)
Gos. Pet.	*Gospel of Peter*
Haer.	*Against Heresies* (Irenaeus)
Herm. *Mand*	Shepherd of Hermas, *Mandate*
Herm. *Sim.*	Shepherd of Hermas, *Similitude*
Herm. *Vis.*	Shepherd of Hermas, *Vision*
Hist.	*Historiae* (Tacitus)
Hist. eccl.	*Ecclesiastical History* (Eusebius)
Ign. *Eph.*	Ignatius, *To the Ephesians*
Ign. *Magn.*	Ignatius, *To the Magnesians*
Ign. *Phld.*	Ignatius, *To the Philadelphians*
Ign. *Pol.*	Ignatius, *To Polycarp*
Ign. *Rom.*	Ignatius, *To the Romans*
Ign. *Smyrn.*	Ignatius, *To the Smyrnaeans*
Ign. *Trall.*	Ignatius, *To the Trallians*
Jdt.	Judith
Jub.	*Jubilees*
LXX	Septuagint
m. 'Abot.	Mishnah tractate 'Abot
Mart. Ascen. Isa.	*Martyrdom and Ascension of Isaiah*
Mart. Isa.	*Martyrdom and Ascension of Isaiah* 1-5
Mart. Pol.	*Martyrdom of Polycarp*
MT	Masoretic Text
NT	New Testament
OT	Old Testament
P. Oxy.	Oxyrhynchus Papyri
PGM	Greek Magical Papyri
Pol. *Phil.*	Polycarp, *To the Philippians*

Abbreviations

Praescr.	*Prescription Against Heretics* (Tertullian)
Pss. Sol.	*Psalms of Solomon*
Sib. Or.	*Sibylline Oracles*
Sir.	Sirach/Ecclesiasticus
T. 12 Patr.	*Testaments of the Twelve Patriarchs*
T. Dan	*Testament of Dan*
T. Levi	*Testament of Levi*
Vit. Apoll.	*Vita Apollonii* (Philostratus)

Secondary Sources

AB	Anchor Bible
ACNT	Augsburg Commentaries on the New Testament
AnBib	Analecta Biblica
ANCL	Ante-Nicene Christian Library
ANTC	Abingdon New Testament Commentaries
ATANT	Abhandlungen zur Theologie des Alten und Neuen Testaments
AThR	*Anglican Theological Review*
BECNT	Baker Exegetical Commentary on the New Testament
BETL	Bibliotheca Ephemeridum Theologicarum Lovaniensium
BHT	Beiträge zur historischen Theologie
Bib	*Biblica*
BibS(F)	Biblische Studien (Freiburg, 1895-)
BJRL	*Bulletin of the John Rylands University Library of Manchester*
BNTC	Black's New Testament Commentaries
BTN	Bibliotheca Theologica Norvegica, Oslo
BZAW	Beihefte zur Zeitschrift für die neutestamentliche Wissenschaft
CBQ	*Catholic Biblical Quarterly*
CNT	Commentaire du Nouveau Testament
ColT	Collectanea Theologica
CQR	Church Quarterly Review
DRev	*Downside Review*
EKKNT	Evangelisch-katholischer Kommentar zum Neuen Testament
ETS	Erfurter theologische Studien
EvQ	*Evangelical Quarterly*
ExpTim	*Expository Times*
FF	Foundations & Facets
GNS	Good News Studies
HNT	Handbuch zum Neuen Testament
HTR	Harvard Theological Review
IB	*Interpreter's Bible*. Ed. G. A. Buttrick et al. 12 vols. New York, 1951-1957.
IBC	Interpretation: A Bible Commentary for Preaching and Teaching

Abbreviations

ICC	International Critical Commentary
IDB	*The Interpreter's Dictionary of the Bible.* Ed. G. A. Buttrick. 4 vols. New York, 1962.
IDBSup	*The Interpreter's Dictionary of the Bible: Supplementary Volume.* Edited by K. Crim. Nashville, 1976.
IVPNT IVP	New Testament Commentary Series
JBL	*Journal of Biblical Literature*
JGRChJ	*Journal of Greco-Roman Christianity and Judaism*
JSNT	*Journal for the Study of the New Testament*
JSNTSup	Journal for the Study of the New Testament Supplement Series
JSOT	*Journal for the Study of the Old Testament*
JTS	*Journal of Theological Studies*
KD	*Kerygma und Dogma*
LCC	Library of Christian Classics. London, 1953-.
LCL	Loeb Classical Library
MNTC	Moffatt New Testament Commentary
NA^{26}	*Novum Testamentum Graece*, Nestle-Aland, 26th ed.
NCB	New Century Bible
NIBC	New International Bible Commentary
NICNT	The New International Commentary on the New Testament.
NIDNTT	*New International Dictionary of New Testament Theology.* Edited by Colin Brown. 4 vols. Grand Rapids, 1975-85.
NIGTC	New International Greek Testament Commentary
NIV	New International Version
NovT	*Novum Testamentum*
NovTSup	Supplements to Novum Testamentum
NTAbh	Neutestamentliche Abhandlungen
NTS	*New Testament Studies*
NTTS	New Testament Tools and Studies
OTP	*Old Testament Pseudepigrapha.* Edited by J. H. Charlesworth. 2 vols. London, 1985.
PG	Patrologia graeca. Edited by J.-P. Migne. 162 vols. Paris, 1857-1886.
PW	*Paulys Real-encyclopädie der classischen Altertumswissenschaft.* Edited by K. Ziegler. Stuttgart, 1952.
RHPR	*Revue d'histoire et de philosophie religieuses*
SBL	Society of Biblical Literature
SBLDS	Society of Biblical Literature Dissertation Series.
SBLSP	*Society of Biblical Literature Seminar Papers*
SE	*Studia evangelica 4*
SFEG	Schriften der Finnischen Exegetischen Gesellschaft
SNTSMS	Society for New Testament Studies Monograph Series
SP	Sacra Pagina
SPAW	Sitzungsberichte der preussischen Akademie der Wissenschaften
ST	*Studia Theologica*

Abbreviations

StPatr	Studia Patristica
Str-B	Strack and Billerbeck, *Kommentar zum Neuen Testament aus Talmud und Midrasch*. 6 vols. Munich, 1922-1961.
TBei	*Theologische Beiträge*
TDNT	*Theological Dictionary of the New Testament*. Edited by G. Kittel and G. Friedrich. Translated by G. W. Bromiley. 10 vols. Grand Rapids, 1964-1976.
TNTC	Tyndale New Testament Commentaries
TSK	*Theologische Studien und Kritiken*
TynBul	*Tyndale Bulletin*
TZ	*Theologische Zeitschrift*
TZTh	Tübinger Zeitschrift für Theologie
UBS^3	*The Greek New Testament*, 3rd ed. United Bible Societies, 1983.
VCSup	Vigiliae Christianae Supplements
WBC	Word Biblical Commentary
WMANT	Wissenschaftliche Monographien zum Alten und Neuen Testament
WUNT	Wissenschaftliche Untersuchungen zum Neuen Testament
ZBK	Zürcher Bibelkommentare
ZNW	*Zeitschrift für die neutestamentliche Wissenschaft und die Kunde der älteren Kirche*
ZTK	*Zeitschrift für Theologie und Kirche*
ZWT	*Zeitschrift für wissenschaftliche Theologie*

Chapter 1
The Debate about the Authenticity of 2 Thessalonians

Before the very end of the eighteenth century, the authenticity of 2 Thessalonians was never debated. Throughout the church fathers it is quoted as from Paul, and it is never classed with any of the letters debated in the early church.[1] Since about 1800 the debate has gradually grown as more scholars have come to adopt the view that Paul did not write this letter. Today the debate continues with a growing number of those skeptical about its origin, yet also a significant number of defenders of authenticity. Thus it is not as disputed as the Pastoral Epistles or Ephesians, nor as accepted as the seven 'undisputed' letters of Paul (Rom., 1 and 2 Cor., Gal., Phil., 1 Thess. and Phlm.). Throughout this debate, two primary areas have become the focus: 1) the very different eschatology found in 2 Thessalonians, and 2) the literary relationship of 2 Thessalonians to 1 Thessalonians. Other secondary issues have arisen from both disputers and defenders of authenticity.

In order to understand the debate it is necessary to review the arguments presented by both the disputers and the defenders of authenticity. Only those scholars who present a new reason for disputing or defending the authenticity of the epistle or who have greatly influenced the direction of the debate will be examined.

I. The Debate about the Doctrine of 2 Thessalonians

A. *Doctrine and the Disputers*

1. Eschatology and the Disputers

Virtually all the disputers of authenticity have thought that the eschatology in 2 Thessalonians is significantly different from that in 1 Thessalonians. Some have thought that 2 Thessalonians is a correction of a misunderstanding of the first epistle or is a commentary on the first epistle;[2] others have seen it differing

---

[1] In this book, the word 'epistle' and the word 'letter' will be used interchangeably. Unless otherwise noted, Scripture citations of words and small phrases are my translations; all longer quotes are from the NIV.

[2] William Wrede, *Die Echtheit des zweiten Thessalonicherbriefs untersucht* (Leipzig: Hinrichs, 1903), pp. 41-46; John A. Bailey, 'Who Wrote 2 Thessalonians?', *NTS* 25 (1978-79), pp. 132-37; Glenn S. Holland, *The Tradition That You Received from Us: 2 Thessalonians in the Pauline Tradition* (Tübingen: Mohr Siebeck, 1988), p. 90.

from or even correcting the first epistle;[3] and others have seen the second letter as a replacement or refutation of the first epistle.[4] In 1 Thessalonians, the second coming of Christ is usually viewed as imminent[5] and sudden, whereas in 2 Thessalonians it is viewed as delayed,[6] preceded by signs,[7] impeded,[8] and

---

[3] J. E. Christian Schmidt, 'Vermutungen über die beiden Briefe an die Thessalonicher', in Wolfgang Trilling, *Untersuchungen zum 2. Thessalonicherbrief* (ETS 27; Leipzig: St. Benno, 1972), p. 159.

[4] Adolph Hilgenfeld, 'Die beiden Briefe an die Thessalonicher, nach Inhalt und Ursprung', *ZWT* 5 (1862), pp. 249, 262-64; Heinrich J. Holtzmann, 'Zum zweiten Thessalonicherbrief', *ZNW* (1901), pp. 93-108; Willi Marxsen, *Der zweite Thessalonicherbrief* (ZBK; Zürich: TVZ, 1982), p. 35; Andreas Lindemann, 'Zum Abfassungszweck des Zweiten Thessalonicherbriefes', *ZNW* 68 (1977), pp. 35-37, 39; Franz Laub, 'Paulinische Autorität in nachpaulinischer Zeit (2 Thes)', in *The Thessalonian Correspondence*. (ed. Raymond F. Collins; Leuven: Leuven University Press, 1990), pp. 404-06; Frank Witt Hughes, *Early Christian Rhetoric and 2 Thessalonians* (JSNTSup 30; Sheffield: JSOT Press, 1989), pp. 82-85.

[5] J. E. C. Schmidt, 'Vermutungen', p. 159; Wrede, *Echtheit*, pp. 41-42.

[6] F. C. Baur, *Paul, the Apostle of Jesus Christ, his Life and Work, his Epistles and his Doctrine: A Contribution to the Critical History of Primitive Christianity* (ed. E. Zeller; trans. A. Menzies; 2 vols.; London: Williams & Norgate, 1875), p. 92. Baur's later writing, in which he changes his views, 'The Two Epistles to the Thessalonians: Their Genuineness and Their Bearing on the Doctrine of the Parousia of Christ', can be found as Appendix III (pp. 314-40) in the 1875 edition of Baur's work *Paul*. See also Holtzmann, 'Thessalonicherbrief', pp. 103-108; Herbert Braun, 'Zur nachpaulinischen Herkunft des zweiten Thessalonicherbriefes', *ZNW* 44 (1952-53), pp. 152-56; Wolfgang Trilling, *Untersuchungen zum Zweiten Thessalonicherbrief* (ETS 27; Leipzig: St. Benno, 1972), pp. 91-92; Harold E. Littleton, 'The Function of Apocalyptic in 2 Thessalonians as a Criterion for its Authorship' (PhD thesis, Vanderbilt University, 1973), p. 169; J. A. Bailey, 'Who Wrote 2 Thessalonians?', pp. 132-37.

[7] Hilgenfeld, 'Die beiden Briefe', pp. 246-59; Paul Wilhelm Schmidt, *A Short Protestant Commentary on the Books of the New Testament*, (ed. P. W. Schmidt and F. von Holzendorff; trans. F. H. Jones; 3 vols.; London: Williams & Norgate, 1884), vol. 3, p. 66; Georg Hollmann, 'Die Unechtheit des zweiten Thessalonicherbriefs', *ZNW* 2 (1904), p. 30; Willi Marxsen, *Introduction to the New Testament* (trans. G. Buswell; Oxford: Blackwell, 1968), pp. 37-45; Marxsen, *Der zweite Thessalonicherbrief*, pp. 32, 107-17; Gerhard Krodel, '2 Thessalonians', in *Ephesians, Colossians, 2 Thessalonians, The Pastoral Epistles* (Proclamation Commentaries; ed. J. Paul Sampley et al.; Philadelphia: Fortress, 1978), p. 75.

remote.[9] Although some of the disputers do not see the eschatology of the two letters necessarily contradicting,[10] they all think the eschatology of the second epistle moves the parousia further into the distance[11] or at least beyond what is said in 1 Thessalonians.[12] When interpreting the two letters, the disputers usually argue that in 1 Thessalonians, death is described as an exception before the parousia, whereas in 2 Thessalonians the near expectation of the parousia is lost.[13] This loss of near expectation of the parousia and the listing of signs allow the reader to identify at least a general timetable in 2 Thessalonians: 1) now is the time of restraint; 2) then there will be a rebellion or time of apostasy; 3) after this will be the revelation of the man of lawlessness; then finally 4) Jesus will appear.[14] Therefore the present time calls for patience and faithfulness.[15]

Most disputers describe the eschatology of 2 Thessalonians as more apocalyptic than 1 Thessalonians.[16] However, some would use the terminology opposite this,[17] saying that the conceptual world of apocalyptic was the view of Judaism, early Christianity, and Paul, and that 2 Thessalonians with its delay of the parousia and chronological scheme is later and anti-apocalyptic.[18]

The disputers are not unified in their identifications of various ideas in 2 Thessalonians 2. J. E. C. Schmidt identifies the explicit error being argued against by the author of 2 Thessalonians as the belief that the parousia is imminent (2:2).[19] Later on, Marxsen identified the errorists as gnostics.[20] However, the overwhelming number of disputers and defenders are agreed that the explicit error mentioned in 2:2 concerns whether the day of the Lord has already arrived.[21]

---

[8]Wrede, *Echtheit*, p. 41-46.
[9]Laub, 'Paulinische Autorität', pp. 407-11.
[10]Baur, *Paul*, pp. 90-93; Wrede, *Echtheit*, pp. 41-46.
[11]Braun, *'Zur nachpaulinischen Herkunft'*, p. 155.
[12]Wrede, *Echtheit*, pp. 41-46.
[13]Peter Müller, *Anfänge der Paulusschule, Dargestellt am zweiten Thessalonicherbrief und am Kolosserbrief* (ATANT; Zurich: TVZ, 1988), p. 84.
[14]Hughes, *Early Christian Rhetoric*, p.58. See also Krodel, '2 Thessalonians', p. 95; Littleton, 'Function of Apocalyptic', pp. 51-54.
[15]Hughes, *Early Christian Rhetoric*, p. 54; Holland, *Tradition*, pp. 87-88.
[16]Hollmann, 'Unechtheit', pp. 32-33, says neither Paul nor Jesus had an apocalyptic viewpoint.
[17]Lindemann, 'Zum Abfassungszweck', pp. 36-41; Littleton, 'Function of Apocalyptic', pp. 51-54.
[18]Littleton, 'Function of Apocalyptic', p. 111.
[19]J. E. C. Schmidt, 'Vermutungen', p. 159.
[20]Marxsen, *Der zweite Thessalonicherbrief*, p. 54; Marxsen, *Introduction*, p. 39.
[21]Friedrich H. Kern, 'Über 2. Thess 2,1-12: Nebst Andeutungen über den Ursprung des zweiten Briefs und die Thessalonicher ', *TZTh* 2 (1839), pp. 147, 149;

In the early years of the dispute, many disputers identified the opponent (2:3-4, 6-10) with the *Nero redivivus* myth,[22] but since the beginning of the twentieth century this identification has been dropped in favor of a more generalized identification with the antichrist.[23] The disputers have varied in their interpretation of the restrainer (2:6-7), frequently identifying it with the Roman emperor and with the Empire,[24] or more recently, with God and his will.[25] Some have updated the terminology with respect to emperor and empire to that of secular governments and rulers,[26] while others believe this information is simply unknowable.[27]

Probably the most difficult phrase for the disputers to interpret is that the man of lawlessness will 'sit in the temple' (2 Thess. 2:4). The earlier disputers interpret the word 'temple' literally and so date 2 Thessalonians near the fall of Jerusalem,[28] or they identify the temple with Christianity in general.[29] Others have believed this statement is an earlier piece of tradition that was incorporated into 2 Thessalonians without editing[30] or that it is a symbolic action based on apocalyptic terminology.[31] There is no real unanimity on all these identifications.

Trilling, *Untersuchungen*, pp. 124-27. Krodel, '2 Thessalonians', p. 76, would still define the error described in 2:2 as the belief that Christ's parousia is imminent. Holland, *Tradition*, p. 48, makes a unique distinction between the day of the Lord, the parousia, and the day of the Lord Jesus Christ and believes only the first of these (the 'day of the Lord') has arrived.

[22]Kern, 'Über 2. Thess 2,1-12', pp. 175-92, 200, 206-207; Baur, *Paul*, p. 324; Hilgenfeld, 'Die beiden Briefe', p. 252; Hollmann, 'Unechtheit', p. 36.

[23]J. E. Frame, *A Critical and Exegetical Commentary on the Epistles of St. Paul to the Thessalonians* (ICC; New York: Scribner's Sons, 1924), p.41, says that since the work of Gunkel, Bousset and Charles, this identification is no longer made.

[24]Kern , 'Über 2. Thess 2,1-12', pp. 175-92, identifies the emperor as either Vespasian or Titus. See also Baur, *Paul*, p. 324; Hilgenfeld, 'Die beiden Briefe', p. 252; Hollmann, 'Unechtheit', p. 36.

[25]Holland, *Tradition*, p. 111; Müller, *Anfänge der Paulusschule*, p. 50.

[26]Earl J. Richard, *First and Second Thessalonians* (SP 11; Collegeville, MN: Liturgical Press, 1995), pp. 338-40.

[27]Beverly R. Gaventa, *First and Second Thessalonians* (IBC; Louisville: John Knox Press, 1998), pp. 113-14; Victor Paul Furnish, *1 Thessalonians, 2 Thessalonians* (ANTC; Nashville: Abingdon, 2007), pp. 156-57.

[28]Kern, 'Über 2. Thess 2,1-12', pp. 175-92, 200, 206-207; P. W. Schmidt, *Commentary*, pp. 68-74.

[29]Hilgenfeld, 'Die beiden Briefe', p. 253.

[30]Wrede, *Echtheit*, pp. 96-98, 104-108, 112. Hollmann, 'Unechtheit', pp. 36-37, says either the phrase is figurative or the writer forgot to deal with it.

[31]Richard, *Thessalonians*, p. 329.

The Debate about the Authenticity of 2 Thessalonians

2. Other Doctrines and the Disputers

The disputers identify a number of other doctrinal emphases in which they believe 2 Thessalonians differs from the undisputed letters of Paul: tradition, imitation, Christology, and soteriology.

The disputers state that tradition in 2 Thessalonians has become normative and is equivalent to witness, gospel, and truth.[32] According to them, this illustrates a later time period when orthodoxy is stressed, and the life and authority of the apostle Paul have become exalted as an example.[33] The only means of passing on this tradition is through an apostolic letter, like the pseudepigraphal 2 Thessalonians.[34]

Closely related to the topic of tradition is that of imitation. In the paraenetic section of 2 Thessalonians which addresses the idle/disorderly (3:6-13), the author stresses that one of the purposes of Paul's working hard was so they would imitate him in their daily lives. Some of the disputers link these idle/disorderly individuals with the ones who are causing the eschatological trouble in 2 Thessalonians 2,[35] while other disputers do not link them.[36] Yet, either way, most disputers believe this problem and the writer's manner of exhortation show that this is from a post-Pauline time, for in 1 Thessalonians 2:9 Paul says he worked hard in order not to be a burden to his hearers. Furthermore, they argue, when Paul stresses that his hearers imitate him, it is as he imitates Christ (1 Cor. 11:1; 1 Thess. 1:6).[37] The disputers believe the emphasis on the need to work also suggests a post-Pauline time, for the delay of the parousia must be explained.[38]

Concerning the Christology of 2 Thessalonians, most commentators point out that the terminology used to refer to Jesus in 2 Thessalonians almost always refers to Jesus as Lord (twenty-two out of the twenty-three times Jesus is mentioned) and that the characteristics normally attributed to God are explicitly being attributed to Jesus.[39] Furthermore, in contrast to Paul's normal practice, they point out that there is no explicit mention of the cross and resurrection.[40] From this lack of Pauline content and the different use of this terminology in

---

[32]Trilling, *Untersuchungen*, p. 113; Laub, 'Paulinische Autorität', p. 413.
[33]Hilgenfeld, 'Die beiden Briefe', pp. 243, 260-62; Trilling, *Untersuchungen*, p. 113; Marxsen, *Der zweite Thessalonichbrief*, p. 32; Müller, *Anfänge der Paulusschule*, pp. 234-37.
[34]Trilling, *Untersuchungen*, p. 116; Müller, *Anfänge der Paulusschule*, pp. 225-27.
[35]Holland, *Tradition*, pp. 52, 157.
[36]Hughes, *Early Christian Rhetoric*, p. 65.
[37]Hilgenfeld, 'Die beiden Briefe', pp. 261-62.
[38]Hollmann, 'Unechtheit', p. 35.
[39]Braun, 'Zur nachpaulinischen Herkunft', p. 155; Krodel, '2 Thessalonians', p. 83; Trilling, *Untersuchungen*, pp. 128-29.
[40]Trilling, *Untersuchungen*, p. 180; Müller, *Anfänge der Paulusschule*, pp. 38, 82.

reference to Jesus, the disputers conclude that the Christology is not that of the apostle Paul.

Some disputers view the soteriology of 2 Thessalonians as different from that in Paul's undisputed letters. The doctrine of justification by faith which is so explicitly expounded by Paul has been replaced by a works-righteousness.[41] The distinguishing mark of the Christian is no longer faith in Christ, but tribulation[42] and faithfulness.[43] Therefore, according to these disputers, even some of the most basic Pauline doctrines are contradicted by 2 Thessalonians.

B. Doctrine and the Defenders

Most of the defenses of authenticity in terms of doctrine have many similarities. First, the defenders believe the eschatological accounts of the two Thessalonian epistles are complementary, not contradictory,[44] for each epistle is discussing a somewhat different situation. Second, they do not see any contradiction between having preliminary signs of the end and yet having an unexpected arrival of the day of the Lord.[45] They usually point out that the eschatological discourses of the synoptic gospels display this same kind of tension. Third, they believe that the saying that the man of lawlessness is 'to sit in the temple' (2 Thess. 2:4), whether this is to be understood literally or figuratively, would not be written after AD 70 without further qualification.[46] Nor do they see 2 Thessalonians as very different from the undisputed letters of Paul concerning tradition, imitation, Christology, and soteriology. Thus, even though they do not agree on all the identifications in 2 Thessalonians 2, they do agree the letter was written by Paul.[47]

Robert Jewett presents the most innovative solution to the defense of the authenticity of 2 Thessalonians, and indeed, to the whole understanding of the

---

[41]P. W. Schmidt, *Commentary*, p. 67.
[42]Braun, 'Zur nachpaulinischen Herkunft', pp. 152-53.
[43]Holland, *Tradition*, p. 90, defines 'faith' throughout this letter as faithfulness.
[44]D. E. H. Whiteley, *Thessalonians* (New Clarendon Bible; Oxford: Oxford University Press, 1969), pp.13-15, is an exception who thinks the eschatologies of 1 and 2 Thess. do contradict but that this does not mean Paul is not the author of both letters.
[45]C. L. Mearns, 'Early Eschatological Development in Paul: The Evidence of 1 and 2 Thessalonians'(*JSNT* 27; 1981), pp. 137-57, sees that Paul further develops his eschatology, even between the two Thessalonian epistles.
[46]John A. T. Robinson, *Redating the New Testament* (London: SCM, 1976), pp. 17, 21, 53, bases his whole redating of the New Testament on the idea that the fall of Jerusalem is never mentioned, and explicitly, that 2 Thess. assumes that the temple in Jerusalem must still be standing.
[47]A detailed examination of different theological interpretations of both disputers and defenders will be given in later chapters.

Thessalonian epistles. He describes Thessalonica as an ancient community where the primary religion was the Cabirus cult. Cabirus, a figure who was worshipped at Thessalonica, had been murdered by his brothers and yet was expected to return to help the lowly and helpless, especially in the city of Thessalonica. This cult gave the native Thessalonians hope for a better day when all things would be transformed. However, according to Jewett, this cult became merged with the Roman cult and was 'coopted' by the Romans in Thessalonica, so that the common Thessalonian no longer had a part in the mystery cult of Cabirus. This created a religious vacuum which was filled by Christianity, which in its original form was a radical millenarianism. Because of the similarities with the Cabirus cult and the 'millenarian' expectations it created, there was a great deal of confusion among these new Christians. Jewett bases his model on other sociological studies of millenarianism.[48]

Jewett's model offers a unified approach to the problems addressed by both Thessalonian epistles. He defines the 'idlers' as those who are out-of-step, obstinate resisters of authority. They are a distinct group who are still part of the church, and are being supported financially by it, but they resist the work ethic, the sexual ethic, and the congregational leadership. They also sense that they are already participating in the divine reality.[49] This explains why they need instruction about the believers who have died (1 Thess. 4:13-18) and why they might have thought the parousia was already present (2 Thess. 2:2). Jewett believes these opponents were actually using 1 Thessalonians to support their error, and that is why Paul refers in 2 Thessalonians 2:2 to a letter 'as from us'.

Jewett also believes his model explains the theology of 2 Thessalonians. Jesus takes on the role of Cabirus and is the apocalyptic benefactor. Jewett links the emphasis on 'Lord' in 2 Thessalonians to the cult of Cabirus and stresses the political sense of many words in the letter.[50]

Because Jewett's model is based primarily on information outside of the Thessalonian epistles, that information must be evaluated to see if it really does present the picture Jewett presents. Helmut Koester has evaluated the archeological record for Thessalonica as 'spotty'.[51] Only two locations in Thessalonica have been excavated thoroughly (going back to about AD 300), and most of the information we have comes from a few monuments. Koester

---

[48] Robert Jewett, *The Thessalonian Correspondence: Pauline Rhetoric and Millenarian Piety* (FF; Philadelphia: Fortress, 1986), pp. 125-31, 162-78.

[49] Jewett, *Correspondence*, pp. 104-106, 175-76.

[50] Robert Jewett and Frederick Danker, 'Jesus as the Apocalyptic Benefactor in Second Thessalonians', in *The Thessalonian Correspondence* (ed. R. Collins; Leuven: Leuven University Press, 1990), pp. 486-98.

[51] Helmut Koester, 'From Paul's Eschatology to the Apocalyptic Schemata of 2 Thessalonians', in *The Thessalonian Correspondence* (ed. Raymond F. Collins; Leuven: Leuven University Press, 1990), p. 442.

does not doubt the importance of the Cabirus cult or its contact with the cult of Caesar, for there is an inscription that speaks of a priest of Augustus visiting the Cabirus sanctuary in Samothrace. In addition, from the third century a number of names of the aristocracy are associated with the cult and with a politarch who was the leader. However, this does not prove Jewett's claim that a 'cooptation' occurred in the first century or that Paul presented Jesus in terms based on Cabirus. We possess very little information about what the Cabirus cult actually believed, and there is no reference in either Thessalonian epistle to this cult. Furthermore, nearly all commentators have recognized the Old Testament coloring or allusions in 2 Thessalonians; these are clearly not based on the Cabirus cult. The author of 2 Thessalonians refers to his teaching as 'tradition', not as a reaction to a particular geographical or cultural setting. Therefore the basis for Jewett's situational explanation of the Thessalonian epistles is almost non-existent, and the model he presents does not match the picture given in the Thessalonian epistles themselves. Jewett's evaluation of the authenticity debate is very useful, his rhetorical insights interesting, but his unlikely solution does not support authenticity.

II. The Debate about the Literary Character of 2 Thessalonians

A. *The Literary Character and the Disputers*

1. Literary Dependence on 1 Thessalonians

Those who dispute the authenticity of 2 Thessalonians nearly always view 2 Thessalonians as literarily dependent on 1 Thessalonians.[52] This idea that the writer of 2 Thessalonians made extensive use of 1 Thessalonians goes back to some of the earliest disputers.[53] It was first expounded in detail by Holtzmann,[54] and soon after, expanded by Wrede,[55] whose presentation has influenced those who have followed him. The first third of Wrede's work attempts to show how extensive the parallels are between 2 Thessalonians and 1 Thessalonians. In many ways Wrede does not really change the information found in Holtzmann, but his argument is much more thorough and his presentation is much more convincing by showing in synoptic fashion the parallels. Wrede acknowledges that the main eschatological section (2:1-12) is not dependent on 1

---

[52]One disputer, Krodel, '2 Thessalonians', pp. 80, 85, is an exception when he states that the case for literary dependence has not been made, yet he believes the writer of 2 Thess. did possess a copy of 1 Thess.

[53]Kern, 'Über 2. Thess 2,1-12', p. 214. Baur, *Paul*, pp. 336-40, in his later article actually sees that 1 Thess. is dependent on 2 Thess. and that 2 Thess. is dependent on Rev. and the Corinthian epistles.

[54]Holtzmann, 'Thessalonicherbrief', pp. 97-104.

[55]Wrede, *Echtheit*, pp. 3-36.

Thessalonians.[56] The parallels, which both Holtzmann and Wrede include, cover about one third of the words in 2 Thessalonians.[57] Trilling sees Wrede's argument as the most important place to begin the discussion about authenticity. He adds further literary arguments to Wrede's arguments by listing stylistic peculiarities which he believes contribute to the case that 2 Thessalonians is non-Pauline.[58] Thus, according to most of the disputers, the writer of 2 Thessalonians made extensive use of 1 Thessalonians in the writing of his letter, but shows that he is a different writer by all the stylistic peculiarities he uses.

2. Letters

A second difficulty disputers have with the literary character of 2 Thessalonians is the manner in which the writer of 2 Thessalonians talks about letters (epistles). Four times the writer refers to letter(s) (2:2, 15; 3:14, 17), yet despite this emphasis on letters, the writer does not explicitly make mention of a previous letter to the Thessalonians.[59] Furthermore, most disputers take the statement in 2 Thessalonians 2:2 about 'a letter as from us' to mean that the writer believes there is a pseudonymous letter of Paul already in existence, and they argue that this is extremely unlikely during the life of Paul.[60] They think this possibility of a forged letter is strengthened because the writer mentions (3:17) the marks of authenticity found in all his letters.[61]

3. Tone

In terms of the character of 2 Thessalonians itself, the disputers stress that although its structure is very similar to 1 Thessalonians, with a number of clear parallels, the character of the letter is formal and official.[62] It is also very impersonal and solemn, with a tendency to make generalizations instead of specific applications. In fact, it sounds like a later ecclesiastical tract.[63] Thus they conclude that a later writer has imitated the overall literary form of 1 Thessalonians, with a very similar terminology, yet the letter is filled with non-Pauline characteristics.

---

[56]Wrede, *Echtheit*, p. 13.
[57]Frame, *Thessalonians*, p. 45
[58]Trilling, *Untersuchungen*, pp. 58-62
[59]J. E. C. Schmidt, 'Vermutungen', p. 159; Krodel, '2 Thessalonians', p. 85.
[60]Hollmann, 'Unechtheit', p. 38; Trilling, *Untersuchungen*, pp. 103, 105; Krodel, '2 Thessalonians', pp. 85-86.
[61]Marxsen, *Introduction*, pp. 42-43.
[62]Trilling, *Untersuchungen*, pp. 55, 63; J. A. Bailey, 'Who Wrote 2 Thessalonians?', p. 137.
[63]Trilling, *Untersuchungen*, pp. 58, 65, 71, 73, 104, 157.

4. Stylo-statistical Models

Certain disputers have tried to quantify some of the literary differences they have discerned between 2 Thessalonians and the undisputed letters of Paul. The earliest statistical models merely gave broad statistics focused on vocabulary, and even though there is some unusual vocabulary in 2 Thessalonians, on the whole the vocabulary looks Pauline and the number of unique words is not more than is to be expected in a letter of this size. In response to this, Trilling states that this fact is really meaningless to the authenticity debate.[64]

Kenneth Grayston and G. Herdan present two vocabulary tests.[65] The first test presents a ratio ('C') which is defined as: C = [(words peculiar to a chosen part) + (words common to all parts)] / (vocabulary of the chosen part). The only groups of epistles within the Pauline corpus that are not relatively close on the ratio C are the Pastoral Epistles and the Thessalonian epistles. The second test, called a 'bi-logarithmic type/token ratio', compares the vocabulary of a particular letter to the total text length of the letter (g = log V/ log N, where 'V' = vocabulary of a particular letter and 'N' = the length of the text). This information is then placed on a bi-logarithmic graph. Ten of the Pauline letters are very close to the constant ratio, while only the Pastorals are not close to the rest of the Pauline corpus.

A.Q. Morton has presented two stylistic tests[66] to determine the authorship of the Pauline epistles. His first test has to do with 'sentence length distribution'. Because this test requires a document to have at least fifty sentences, he was not able to include 2 Thessalonians, Titus, or Philemon in this test. The result of this test is that only Romans, 1 and 2 Corinthians, and Galatians are seen as Pauline. His second test, which includes all but Titus and Philemon (because they are too short), evaluates the relative frequency of certain connectives ['and' (καί), 'but' (δέ), 'for' (γάρ), 'if' (εἰ)]. This test yields similar results to the first test: only Romans, 1 and 2 Corinthians, and Galatians can be accepted as Pauline. Ephesians, Philippians, and Colossians are all isolated from each other statistically. In this test, 1 and 2 Thessalonians are grouped together as one letter, as are 1 and 2 Timothy. Even Romans, although genuinely Pauline, has been 'adapted from one addressed to another party', with the addition of approximately six or eight sentences in the first chapter.[67]

Daryl Schmidt adds a new dimension to the literary arguments against the authenticity of 2 Thessalonians in his examination of different syntactical

---

[64]Trilling, *Untersuchungen*, p. 66.
[65]Kenneth Grayston and G. Herdan, 'The Authorship of the Pastorals in the Light of Statistical Linguistics', *NTS* 6 (1959-60), pp. 1-15,
[66]A. Q. Morton, 'The Authorship of the Pauline Epistles', in *Literary Detection: How to Prove Authorship and Fraud in Literature and Documents* (Bath: Pitman Press, 1978), pp. 165-83.
[67]Morton, 'Authorship', pp. 180-83.

patterns in 2 Thessalonians.[68] He computes the complexity of sentences at the clause level. Each subordinate clause within a complex sentence is referred to as an 'embed'. One may speak of a total number of embeds within a sentence and also of the degree of complexity of those embeds, which Schmidt refers to as the 'depth of embedding'.[69] Schmidt's analysis of the thanksgiving in 2 Thessalonians 1 shows that it contains twenty embeds with a depth of embedding to level fifteen, 'the greatest degree of embedding in any thanksgiving section in the Pauline corpus'.[70] The only comparable levels of embedding are found in Ephesians (eighteen embeds to level thirteen), and Colossians (twelve embeds to level nine). The embeds in 2 Thessalonians are different from those in the undisputed letters of Paul in that they primarily use relative pronouns, whereas Paul more frequently uses adjectival pronouns to begin his embeds. In addition, Schmidt observes, the author of 2 Thessalonians also uses an impersonal approach in addressing his audience. Furthermore, Schmidt also sees grammatical peculiarities in 2 Thessalonians 2:1-12. These are not the same as in 2 Thessalonians 1 but concern how the sentences are connected, for a number of sentences begin without conjunctions (2:3, 5, 8, 9b, and 10), three sentences begin with 'and' (καί) (2:6, 8, 11), and one with 'for' (γάρ) (2:7). All of these features are atypical of the Pauline style of 1 Thessalonians. Thus, Schmidt believes 2 Thessalonians is clearly non-Pauline.

B. *The Literary Character and the Defenders*

The unique relationship of the Thessalonian epistles to each other has also been recognized by the defenders of authenticity. This relationship has been explained in a number ways.

1. Letter Order

The idea that 2 Thessalonians was written before 1 Thessalonians has a long history amongst both commentators and the defenders of authenticity.[71]

---

[68] Daryl Schmidt, 'The Authenticity of 2 Thessalonians: Linguistic Arguments', *SBL Seminar Papers, 1983* (SBLSP 22; Chico, CA: Scholars Press, 1983), pp. 289-96.
[69] D. Schmidt, 'Authenticity', p. 290. These embeds can be introduced by participles, infinitives or by a 'COMP-word' ('complementizer') such as 'who' (ὅς), 'because' (ὅτι), 'in order that' (ἵνα), 'just as' (καθώς), and 'as' (ὡς).
[70] D. Schmidt, 'Authenticity', p. 291.
[71] Hugo Grotius, *Annotationes in Novum Testamentum*, cited in F. F. Bruce, *1 & 2 Thessalonians* (WBC 45; Waco: Word, 1982), p. xxiv; T. W. Manson, 'St. Paul in Greece: The Letters to the Thessalonians', *BJRL* 35 (1952-53), pp. 428-47; Johannes Weiss, *Earliest Christianity*, (Gloucester, MA: Peter Smith, 1970), pp. 289-91; R. Gregson, 'A Solution to the Problems of the Thessalonian Epistles', *EvQ* 38 (1966), p. 77; J. C. Hurd, 'Second Letter to the Thessalonians', *IDBSup*, p. 901; J. C. West,

Wanamaker says, 'If it can be shown that a strong case exists for the priority of 2 Thessalonians, many of the problems associated with the relation between the two letters can be resolved'.[72] Since the question of the relationship between the two epistles is one of the major hindrances to accepting the authenticity of 2 Thessalonians, these defenders believe the case for authenticity is strengthened by reversing the order. However, upon careful examination, many arguments to reverse the order of the Thessalonian epistles do not prove a reversal; they only show that a particular argument could be read in another direction. To understand the weakness of this position, it is helpful to critique six of the major arguments for reversing the order of the letters.

1. Letters.[73] Those who reverse the order point out that the word 'letter', used four times in 2 Thessalonians, does not refer explicitly to 1 Thessalonians. Because Paul says in 1 Thessalonians that Timothy has just returned from Thessalonica, they postulate that Paul probably had sent a letter to the Thessalonians with Timothy, and 2 Thessalonians could have been that letter. While it is true that 2 Thessalonians does not refer explicitly to 1 Thessalonians, its references to letters of Paul show clearly that the readers know that Paul is a writer of letters, most likely because this is a second letter (especially 2 Thess. 2:15). Also, the situation addressed in 2 Thessalonians is further developed than that of 1 Thessalonians. The writer of 2 Thessalonians claims to know more of the situation at Thessalonica than Paul would have known when he first sent Timothy back to Thessalonica, possibly with a letter of inquiry, making it impossible to identify 2 Thessalonians with that letter.

2. Missionary Effort.[74] Others argue that 2 Thessalonians focuses on Paul's initial visit, whereas by the time of 1 Thessalonians more time has passed and a

---

'The Order of 1 and 2 Thessalonians', *JTS* 15 (1914), p. 69; Robert W. Thurston, 'The Relationship between the Thessalonian Epistles', *ExpTim* 85 (1973), p. 53; F. J. Badcock, *The Pauline Epistles* (London: SPCK, 1937), p. 47; Lyle O. Bristol, 'Paul's Thessalonian Correspondence', *ExpTim* 55 (1943-44), p. 223; W. Hadorn, 'Die Abfassung der Thessalonicherbriefe auf der dritten Missionreise und der Kanon des Marcion', *ZNW* 19 (1919-20), pp. 67-72; Edward Thompson, 'The Sequence of the Two Epistles to the Thessalonians', *ExpTim* 66 (1944-45), pp. 306-307; Paul Trudinger, 'The Priority of 2 Thessalonians Revisited: Some Fresh Evidence', *DRev* 113 (1995) pp. 31-35.

[72]Charles A. Wanamaker, *The Epistles to the Thessalonians* (NIGTC; Grand Rapids: Eerdmans, 1990), pp. 38-45.

[73]West, 'Order', pp. 73-74.

[74]John C. Hurd, 'First Thessalonians', *IDBSup,* p. 900. Hadorn, 'Abfassung der Thessalonicherbriefe', pp. 67-72, also reverses the order of the Thessalonian epistles and sees 1 Thess. being written three or four years later on Paul's third missionary journey. Badcock, *Pauline Epistles,* p. 47, also believes this passage requires more time to take place. See also West, 'Order', p. 71.

The Debate about the Authenticity of 2 Thessalonians

full missionary effort has begun. This, however, is an over-reading of 1 Thessalonians 1:8-9. The focus of those verses is on the Thessalonians' initial reception of the gospel and their conversion which has become known everywhere, not on a full blown missionary effort.

3. Desired Visit. [75] Some argue that Paul's words in 1 Thessalonians 2:18 ('once and twice') refer to a first visit, when he sent 2 Thessalonians, and to a second visit, when he is sending 1 Thessalonians. This, however, over literalizes an idiom that is simply used to say that he has often desire to visit. [76]

4. Persecution. Another argument has been made that persecution is still present in 2 Thessalonians but is past in 1 Thessalonians 2:14.[77] However, this argument for reversal assumes there was only one persecution, at the founding of the church. As well, the Thessalonians had been taught (in 1 Thess. 3:3) that persecution is to be expected; therefore it could still be continuing.[78]

5. The Idle. Some suggest that the more complete directions about the 'idle' in 2 Thessalonians show that this is the first time Paul addresses the problem in his letters.[79] This is merely speculation. More likely, the situation concerning the 'idle' has deteriorated from the time of the writing of 1 Thessalonians to that of 2 Thessalonians; in 1 Thessalonians 4:11-12 and 5:14, Paul gently gives some general warnings concerning work, whereas in 2 Thessalonians 3:6-13 these warnings have become severe rebukes.

6. Eschatology. To some it appears that the Thessalonians know more eschatology in 1 Thessalonians.[80] However, Paul's reminder of what the Thessalonians 'know' in 1 Thessalonians 5:1-2 refers, not to what was taught in

---

[75]West, 'Order', p. 71.

[76]The LXX (Deut. 9:13) uses this exact phrase but does not translate the Hebrew literally. Instead, the phrase emphasizes the idea of repeated obstinacy. The charge of being a stiff necked people has been made more than 'twice' (see Ex. 32–34). For a fuller discussion see Leon Morris, *The First and Second Epistle to the Thessalonians* (rev. ed.; Grand Rapids: Eerdmans, 1991), p. 88, n. 89.

[77]Manson, 'St. Paul in Greece', p. 438.

[78]I. Howard Marshall, *1 and 2 Thessalonians* (NCB; Grand Rapids: Eerdmans, 1983), pp. 91-92, states that persecution may still be continuing according to 1 Thess. 3:3.

[79]West, 'Order', p. 71; Trudinger, ' Priority', pp. 31-35.

[80]Manson, 'St. Paul in Greece', p. 443; Gregson, 'Solution', p. 77; Hurd, 'Second Thessalonians', p. 901. West, 'Order', p. 69, asks why Paul would revert to Jewish eschatology (2 Thess.) when the church was becoming more and more Gentile. Thurston, 'Relationship', p. 53, makes a further point along the same lines, stating that the two major theological points in 2 Thess. are faith and love, whereas in 1 Thess. this is expanded to faith, love, and hope because Paul has learned what they need. See also Badcock, *Pauline Epistles,* p. 47. Bristol, 'Thessalonian Correspondence', p. 223, also thinks the problem with the dead would take longer to happen.

2 Thessalonians or any earlier letter, but to information taught at the founding mission. No details about when the Lord will come are given in 2 Thessalonians; it only maintains that the day of the Lord has not yet come.

2. Audience

Another way some defenders have explained both the similarities and differences between 1 and 2 Thessalonians is to suggest that the two letters were actually written to different audiences at, or very near, the same time. They usually see 1 Thessalonians as written to the whole congregation, but suggest a variety of possible audiences for 2 Thessalonians: Jewish Christians,[81] a special circle in the church at Thessalonica,[82] the church at Berea,[83] the church at Philippi,[84] church leaders at Thessalonica,[85] or a particular house church at Thessalonica.[86]

Each of these explanations contains a number of weaknesses.

1. A number of these defenders require a textual emendation. However, there is no textual evidence for those emendations, and no one agrees on the emendation.[87]

2. The idea that 2 Thessalonians has more Old Testament coloring and a more solemn tone does not help to confirm or deny a particular audience. Ernest Best cites Lake, who argues that 'the extent of Paul's use of the O.T. is determined

---

[81] Adolf von Harnack, 'Das Problem des zweiten Thessalonicherbriefs', *SPAW* 31 (1910), pp. 560-78. Both Edward Thompson, 'Sequence', pp. 306-307, and Kirsopp Lake, *The Earlier Epistles of St. Paul: Their Motive and Origin* (London: Rivington, 1911), pp. 83-85, accept Harnack's arguments.

[82] Martin Dibelius, *Die Briefe des Apostels Paulus, II, an die Thessalonicher I, II, an die Philipper* (HNT; 3rd ed.; Tübingen: Mohr Siebeck, 1911), pp. 26, 34, 39; Dibelius, *A Fresh Approach to the New Testament and Early Christian Literature* (Hertford: Ivor Nicholson & Watson, 1936), p. 152.

[83] Maurice Goguel, *Les Épîtres Pauliniennes.* (vol. 4, part 1 of *Introduction au Nouveau Testament;* Paris: Ernest Leroux, 1925), pp. 335-37.

[84] Eduard Schweizer, 'Der zweite Thessalonicherbrief ein Philipperbrief?', *TZ* 1 (1945), pp. 90-105.

[85] E. Earle Ellis, 'Paul and His Co-Workers', *NTS* 17 (1971), pp. 437-52.

[86] A. J. Malherbe, *The Letters to the Thessalonians* (AB 32B; New York: Doubleday, 2004), p. 353.

[87] Schweizer's arguments in 'Philipperbrief?' that 2 Thess. was written to the Philippians as attested by Polycarp's use of 2 Thess. will be dealt with in ch. 2, but it is interesting to note that if there appear to be differences between 1 and 2 Thess., there are even greater differences between Phil. and 2 Thess. in terms of tone and areas of concern.

by his subject matter and not by his recipients'.[88] Thus tone has more to do with content than with audience. In addition, if the information in Acts 17 is historically accurate, then the largest group of converts at the founding mission was 'God-fearing Greeks' (Acts 17:4), who would be very familiar with the Old Testament.

3. The idea that Paul sent 1 and 2 Thessalonians at approximately the same time without receiving further information from Thessalonica does not fit the evidence in the epistles. In the previous section it was shown that 2 Thessalonians can most easily be understood as a development of the situation in 1 Thessalonians. Furthermore, there is no threat envisioned in 1 Thessalonians that corresponds to the false teaching spoken against in 2 Thessalonians 2:2. Therefore 2 Thessalonians requires the receiving of more information than was available for the writing of 1 Thessalonians.

4. Harnack believes the statement 'not all have faith' (2 Thess. 3:2) refers to the lack of faith by the majority of Jews at Thessalonica. This idea, however, ignores the context of the statement, for the author of 2 Thessalonians is requesting prayer for his continued gospel ministry and is not specifically talking about the Jews or about the Thessalonians. In addition, and most devastating to Harnack's position, it is impossible to conceive that Paul, who in Galatians said Jew and Gentile are one in Christ (Gal. 3:26-29), would tolerate the existence of a distinct Jewish group within the church and say nothing about this error to them.

Most who say that 2 Thessalonians was written to an audience different from 1 Thessalonians place a great deal of weight on use of the word 'firstfruit' (2 Thess. 2:13). However, many commentators prefer the reading 'from the beginning'.[89] Thus the very existence of a major piece of their evidence is

---

[88]Ernest Best, *A Commentary on the First and Second Epistles to the Thessalonians* (BNTC; London: Black, 1972), p. 39.

[89]The following commentators believe the phrase 'from the beginning' makes better sense: Walter F. Adeney, *Thessalonians and Galatians* (Century Bible; TC & EC Jack, 1901), p. 246; John W. Bailey and J. W. Clarke, 'The First and Second Epistles to the Thessalonians', (*IB* 11; New York: Abingdon, 1955), p. 331; Best, *Thessalonians*, pp. 312-14; James Denney, *The Epistles to the Thessalonians* (Expositor's Bible; London: Hodder & Stoughton, 1892), p. 343; Frame, *Thessalonians*, p. 280; William Hendriksen, *Exposition of 1 and 2 Thessalonians* (New Testament Commentary; Grand Rapids: Baker, 1955), pp. 187-88; Marshall, *Thessalonians*, p. 207; Marxsen, *Der zweite Thessalonicherbrief*, p. 89; Charles Masson, *Les Deux Épitres de Saint Paul aux Thessaloniciens*, (CNT 11a; Paris: Delachaux & Niestlé, 1957), p. 108; George Milligan, *St. Paul's Epistles to the Thessalonians* (London: Macmillan, 1908), p. 106; Morris, *Thessalonians*, p. 238; William Neil, *The Epistles of Paul to the Thessalonians* (MNTC; London: Hodder & Stoughton, 1950), p. 181; Beda Rigaux, *Saint Paul Les Épitres aux Thessaloniciens*,

questionable. When Paul uses 'firstfruit' in reference to the first converts in a particular location, he always qualifies the word with the place (see Rom. 16:5; 1 Cor. 16:15). The only place that might give Harnack some support is Romans 11:16, where Paul uses the term to refer to the Jews. The context, however, makes it clear that he is speaking about the relationship between Jews and Gentiles, and in no way does this section seem parallel to what is being discussed in 2 Thessalonians 2.

Of all those who attempt to define different audiences for the two Thessalonian epistles, Ellis (church leaders at Thessalonica) and Malherbe (a house church at Thessalonica) make the most plausible arguments. They do not make an unnatural division in the church, and it makes sense that a number of the first converts would become leaders within the church. The problem with Ellis's argument is that he makes an absolute identification of the term 'brothers' with church leaders in 2 Thessalonians. The term 'brother(s)' is used nineteen times in 1 Thessalonians. In only one instance does it clearly refer to one of Paul's co-workers, Timothy (1 Thess. 3:2); all other cases appear to be addressed to the congregation as a whole. The epistle itself is addressed to the 'church' (1 Thess. 1:1), and the book closes with the command to 'have this letter read to all the brothers' (1 Thess. 5:27). If this so clearly is the case in 1 Thessalonians, why should it not also be true in 2 Thessalonians, which is also addressed 'to the church'? Although Paul may frequently refer to a fellow worker as 'brother', it is a mistake to think this term was more restricted than the term 'Christian'.[90] Malherbe's argument that the two letters are to different house churches is plausible, but there is actually nothing in the text in either letter that suggests this.[91]

Paris: Gabalda, 1956), p. 682; Wolfgang Trilling, *Der zweite Brief an die Thessalonicher* (EKKNT; Zurich: Benziger, 1980), p. 121; von Dobschütz, *Die Thessalonicher-Briefe* (1909; repr., Göttingen: Vandenhoeck & Ruprecht, 1974), p. 298; Wanamaker, *Thessalonians*, p. 26; and Beale, *1-2 Thessalonians* (IVPNT; Downers Grove, IL: IVP, 2003), p. 227.

The following commentators prefer the translation 'firstfruit': Bruce, *Thessalonians*, p. 190; Dibelius, *Thessalonicher* (1911), p. 34; Gordon D. Fee, *The First and Second Letters to the Thessalonians* (NICNT; Grand Rapids: Eerdmans, 2009), p. 78; Jeffrey A. D. Weima, *1-2 Thessalonians* (BECNT; Grand Rapids: Baker, 2014), p. 550; Gene L. Green, *The Letters to the Thessalonians* (Pillar New Testament Commentary; Grand Rapids: Eerdmans, 2002), p. 326; and Malherbe, *Letters to the Thessalonians*, p. 427.

[90] See Phil. 1:14; 2 Cor. 8:23; 9:3, 5; 11:9; Gal. 1:2. See Wolf-Henning Ollrog, *Paulus und seine Mitarbeiter* (WMANT; Neukirchen: Neukirchener Verlag, 1979), p. 78, n. 93.

[91] The arguments used against the position held by Ellis can be applied to the position held by Dibelius in his third edition. It is clear that 1 Thess. is addressed to the whole church and is to be read to 'all the brothers' (1 Thess. 5:27).

The Debate about the Authenticity of 2 Thessalonians

3. Co-Authorship

Another way of explaining the differences and similarities of the two Thessalonian epistles, and of explaining their differences from the other Pauline letters, is to attribute the writing of these letters to one or both of the other co-senders.[92]

In considering the possibility of co-authorship, the question must be asked: what is really gained if this suggestion is accepted? This solution does not explain the literary relationship of 2 Thessalonians to 1 Thessalonians. Both letters claim the exact same authorship—Paul, Silas and Timothy—and therefore to say that Timothy or Silas had a greater hand in one epistle than the other is merely speculation. It is hard to believe that two close associates of Paul could be so different in theological outlook and presentation, as some have claimed. Prior's ideas of a variety of secretaries and co-senders of the Pauline letters make all bases for comparison impossible; furthermore, there is a high degree of conformity between at least some letters of Paul, even with the variety of 'helpers'.[93] The high degree of similarity between the letters with different co-senders makes it reasonable to assume that Paul was the primary author of all these letters. Selwyn's presentation about the use of tradition[94] is helpful, but one need not accept Silas as the primary author of the Thessalonian epistles or 1 Peter in order to say that the writers of these letters made use of preformed traditions. If these were available to Silas, they were also available to Paul.

---

[92]Friedrich Spitta, *Zur Geschichte und Literatur des Urchristentums* (Gottingen: Vandenhoeck & Ruprecht, 1893), pp. 112, 117, 118, 119, 124-25; and Karl P. Donfried, '2 Thessalonians and the Church of Thessalonica', in *Origins and Method: Towards a New Understanding of Judaism and Christianity. Essays in Honour of John C. Hurd.* (ed. Bradley H. McLean; JSNTSup 86; Sheffield: Sheffield Academic Press, 1993), pp. 132-34, suggest that 2 Thess. was written by Timothy, while F. C. Burkitt, *Christian Beginnings* (London: University of London Press, 1924), pp. 128-33; E. G. Selwyn, *The First Epistle of Peter* (London: Macmillan, 1946), pp. 17, 441-49, 382, and Bruce, *Thessalonians*, pp. xxxii-xxxiv, say Silas had a major role in both epistles. Robert Scott, *The Pauline Epistles* (London: T & T Clark, 1909), pp. 216-33, thinks that Silas (1 Thess. 4–5; 2 Thess. 1–2) and Timothy (1 Thess. 1–3; 2 Thess. 3) each wrote distinct sections in both letters. Michael Prior, *Paul the Letter-Writer and the Second Letter to Timothy* (JSNTSup 23; Sheffield: Sheffield Academic Press, 1989) suggests most of Paul's letters were co-authored (for evidence on 1and 2 Thess. see especially pp. 39-40, 48, 180-81).

[93]His co-senders and helpers include Tertius (Rom. 16:22), Sosthenes (1 Cor. 1:1), Timothy (2 Cor. 1:1; Phil. 1:1; Phlm. 1), Silas and Timothy (1 Thess. 1:1), and 'all the brothers' (Gal. 1:2—contrasted to Paul's own handwriting in Gal. 6:11).

[94]Selwyn, *First Peter*, pp. 17, 441-49, 382.

4. Close Literary Relationship

The strong similarities between the two Thessalonian epistles have been recognized by the defenders of authenticity. Zahn suggests that Paul may have made a first draft of each of his letters, which he kept, and then sent the final copy, as was the practice of Cicero. Zahn then suggests that Paul read over again the original copy of 1 Thessalonians before dictating 2 Thessalonians'.[95] Zahn's very brief proposal is certainly possible. His evidence shows that the practice of saving letter drafts did exist. However, Zahn's idea is simply unprovable: nowhere does 2 Thessalonians say, 'I just reread what I wrote to you'.

J. Graafen suggests that 2 Thessalonians presupposes the exact same situation as 1 Thessalonians; in fact, Paul does not yet know if the Thessalonians have received his first letter.[96] Reflecting back on the joyous letter he had just written a few days before, he wrote the more sober 2 Thessalonians and signed it with his own hand (3:17) as a psychological necessity.[97] Graafen overstates the difference in tone of the two letters. In 1 Thessalonians Paul does not appear to be overwhelmed with joy and lacking in objectivity, but instead, his tone seems very forthright as he defends his ministry (1Thess. 2:1-16), soberly warns the Thessalonians (1Thess. 4:7-8), displays genuine pastoral concern (1Thess. 4:13-18), and realistically admonishes his readers (1Thess. 5:12-22). The tone in 2 Thessalonians is also serious; it is the situation that appears to have changed. The very few days suggested by Graafen do not account for this. Furthermore, if it is only a few days later and a special closing of the letter is required to authenticate it, then why does not Paul remark on this very short period of time?

Colin Nicholl has recently expanded and developed some of the basic ideas found in Graafen.[98] Nicholl sees a single crisis in two stages affecting the church in Thessalonica, with 2 Thessalonians functioning as an appendix to 1 Thessalonians.[99] The gap of time between 1 and 2 Thessalonians could be as short as one or two weeks, and Paul does not yet know if they have received the

---

[95]Theodor Zahn, *Introduction to the New Testament* (trans. J. M. Trout et al.; Edinburgh: T & T Clark, 1909), vol. 1, p. 250, n. 6. See also Josef Wrzol, *Die Echtheit des zweiten Thessalonicherbriefes* (BibS[F] 19.4; Freiburg: Herder, 1916), pp. 79, 89- 90, 101, who basically accepts Zahn's proposal, but adds that Paul was not sure what had caused the eschatological agitation—his first letter or something else (2 Thess. 2:2, 15).

[96]J. Graafen, *Die Echtheit des zweiten Briefes and die Thessalonicher* (NTAbh 14; Munster: Aschendorff, 1930), pp. 18, 26.

[97]Graafen, *Die Echtheit*, pp. 47-52.

[98]Colin R. Nicholl, *From Hope to Despair in Thessalonica: Situating 1 and 2 Thessalonians* (SNTSMS 126; Cambridge: Cambridge University Press, 2004).

[99]Nicholl, *From Hope to Despair*, p.16.

first letter when he writes the second.[100] According to Nicholl, the primary problem in 1 Thessalonians is that some members have died and the new believers are ignorant about the future resurrection from the dead and consequently have become hopeless.[101] They are also fearful of the coming day of wrath.[102] Very shortly after writing the first letter, Paul receives more information about the Thessalonian Christians.[103] Persecution has caused them to think that God's judgment is unjust and that salvation has passed them by.[104] They have moved from 'nervous dread to perturbed despair'.[105] Paul, in 2 Thessalonians, reassures them that they have not missed the end time events and that persecution purifies them and prepares them for God's kingdom.[106]

Nicholl's work is helpful in showing some of the thematic links between the two Thessalonian letters and also in demonstrating that 2 Thessalonians is directed at a specific situation. However, there appears to be much more development between the letters than he acknowledges, which would require more time. Paul explicitly says in 1 Thessalonians 3:6, 'Timothy has just now come to us from you'. If a significantly different eschatological problem on the level described in 2 Thessalonians was going to occur in the next couple of weeks, Timothy should have at least had some hint of this and would have relayed this information to Paul. Yet there is not a hint of this in 1 Thessalonians. Although the eschatological sections (4:13-18; 5:1-11) are significant in 1 Thessalonians, they are not directed at the same problem seen in 2 Thessalonians at all. Nor are they the most important point of the letter, but rather, Paul's ministry at Thessalonica and his relationship with the new believers is the primary focus (2:13–3 :10). The same could be said about the problem with the idle. It appears to be a very minor problem in 1 Thessalonians, whereas it is addressed at length and in much stronger terms in 2 Thessalonians. Thus a far more likely scenario, if both letters are written by Paul, is the traditional understanding that there are at least a number of months between the two letters.

5. Redaction

According to Walter Schmithals, the contents of both Thessalonian epistles are derived from Paul and are authentic, but both letters are redactional

---

[100] Nicholl, *From Hope to Despair*, pp. 194-95.
[101] Nicholl, *From Hope to Despair*, pp. 112, 185.
[102] Nicholl, *From Hope to Despair*, p. 53.
[103] Nicholl, *From Hope to Despair*, p.193.
[104] Nicholl, *From Hope to Despair*, pp.142, 152.
[105] Nicholl, *From Hope to Despair*, p.188.
[106] Nicholl, *From Hope to Despair*, pp.133, 152.

compositions dependent on four letters from Paul to the Thessalonians.[107] The order and contents of the four letters are as follows:
Thessalonians A—2 Thessalonians 1:1-12 + 3:6-16
Thessalonians B—1 Thessalonians 1:1–2:12 + 4:3–5:28
Thessalonians C—2 Thessalonians 2:13-14 + 2:1-12, 15–3:5 + 3:17-18
Thessalonians D—1 Thessalonians 2:13–4:2.

His primary reason for dividing the letters is that he finds an introductory thanksgiving in 1Thessalonians 2:13 and typical closing phrases in 1 Thessalonians 3:11 and 4:1 and 2 Thessalonians 2:16. No longer are there two letters, each with two thanksgivings, but four letters, each with one thanksgiving, and the imitation of 1 Thessalonians by the writer of 2 Thessalonians is due to a similar pattern of redaction.

Schmithals's hypothesis presents numerous difficulties. First, his reasons for dividing the letters as he does are not valid. Bjerkelund has demonstrated that the 'typical' closing phrases isolated by Schmithals are regular parts of exhortative sentences.[108] Second, not only does the complexity of the solution make it improbable, but also the contents of the letters do not make much sense in the order in which he places them. Letter A is very brief, and with the heart of 2 Thessalonians torn out of it amounts to a thanksgiving with a few added exhortations. Letter C is especially complicated, and the links between the verses are very strange.[109] In letter A Paul gives a very severe rebuke to the idlers, isolating them from the community; in letter B he is much milder and deals with them as part of the community.[110] Yet these letters are all presumed to have been written in a very short period of time. The more carefully the four individual letters are examined, the less likely the solution appears.[111]

6. Rhetorical Analysis
Ben Witherington III, in his commentary on the Thessalonian epistles,

---

[107]Walter Schmithals, 'Die Thessalonicherbriefe als Briefkompositionen', in *Zeit und Geschichte* (ed. E. Einkler; Tubingen: Mohr Siebeck, 1964), pp. 295-315. This redactional hypothesis does not concern only the Thessalonian epistles; Schmithals also believes that six Corinthian letters have been redacted into two, three Philippian letters into one, and that Romans is also a composite of two letters. See also Best, *Thessalonians*, p. 46.

[108]Carl J. Bjerkelund, *Parakalô: Form, Funktion, und Sinn der parakalo-Sätze in den paulischen Briefer* (BTN 1; Oslo: Scandinavian University Books, 1967), pp. 109, 128-37. See also Jewett, *Correspondence*, pp. 33-34.

[109]Best, *Thessalonians*, p. 47; Jewett, *Correspondence*, p. 35.

[110]Jewett, *Correspondence*, p. 36.

[111]For a fuller discussion see: Best, *Thessalonians*, pp. 45-50; Marshall, *Thessalonians*, pp. 15-16, and Jewett, *Correspondence*, pp. 33-36.

stresses the importance of rhetorical analysis.[112] He emphasizes several points with reference to authenticity: 1) the two aims of deceiving the audience about authorship and yet trying to shape them morally in a Pauline manner are not rhetorically compatible;[113] 2) 'unlike some other genres (e.g., early Jewish apocalyptic works often attributed to one patriarch or another) it was not a regular part of the literary conventions for the letter genre to have a falsely attributed author', and 'the early church did not see pseudepigraphy as a harmless literary technique';[114] 3) the parallels between 1 and 2 Thessalonians can best be explained by what a rhetorician does 'when his discourse is not fully understood or its implications not fully taken and applied': he gives 'another discourse based on the first one, amplifying what has been said before but dealing with whatever problems which have arisen from the first discourse and also in the interim since it was delivered';[115] and 4) the difference in tone and expression between the two Thessalonians letters is best accounted for by the proper recognition of different forms of rhetoric: 1 Thessalonians is an example of an epideictic letter, and 2 Thessalonians is a deliberative letter.[116] An epideictic letter like 1 Thessalonians seeks to enhance knowledge, understanding, or belief. It reminds and celebrates what is true; it is either filled with praise or blame and is more emotional and inspirational.[117] Deliberative rhetoric like 2 Thessalonians seeks to change a practice or belief; thus it often stresses authority more than epideictic rhetoric does.[118] This analysis helps to explain why the letters are so similar and yet so different. It also opens up a comparison of 2 Thessalonians not only with 1 Thessalonians, but also with the other epistles in the Pauline corpus which are of similar rhetoric.[119]

7. Stylo-statistical and Structural Models

Statistical analysis of stylistic features has been used to defend some of the letters in the Pauline corpus, including 2 Thessalonians. Anthony Kenny has examined ninety-nine independent vocabulary and grammatical features of the Greek text to determine peculiarities and similarities within the New

---

[112]Ben Witherington III, *1 and 2 Thessalonians: A Socio-Rhetorical Commentary* (Grand Rapids: Eerdmans, 2006).
[113]Witherington, *Thessalonians*, p. 13.
[114]Witherington, *Thessalonians*, p. 13. See also Terry L.Wilder, *Pseudonymity, the New Testament, and Deception* (Lanham, MD: University Press of America, 2004).
[115]Witherington, *Thessalonians*, p. 29
[116]Witherington, *Thessalonians*, p. 21
[117]Witherington, *Thessalonians*, pp. 21-23.
[118]Witherington, *Thessalonians*, p. 34.
[119]Witherington, *Thessalonians*, p. 22. Witherington mentions 1 Cor. as another 'problem solving letter'.

Testament.[120] Using these tests he calculates the correlation between each epistle and every other epistle in the Pauline corpus. He then presents an order for similarity from the 'most comfortable to the least: Romans, Philippians, 2 Timothy, 2 Corinthians, Galatians, 2 Thessalonians, 1 Thessalonians, Colossians, Ephesians, 1 Timothy, Philemon, 1 Corinthians, Titus'.[121]

Kenny's work is valuable for its exhaustive format focusing upon characteristics of style. However, it must be used carefully, for Kenny does not include any larger grammatical stylistic categories. Nor does he deal with any theology in his study, but only with the letters as a whole. He does not remove quotes, citations, or any other material from the text, possibly affecting some of what he determines to be Pauline characteristics.

David Mealand reexamines Morton's test on the frequency of certain connectives by employing the use and position of four Greek particles ('and' [καί], 'but' [δέ], 'for' [γάρ], 'if' [εἰ]) at the beginning of sentences (first or second position) in order to see if this criterion distinguishes four letters, as Morton concludes (Rom., 1 and 2 Cor., Gal.), seven letters (adding Phil., 1 and 2 Thess.), or ten letters (adding Col., Eph., 2 Tim.) as from Paul.[122] He finds that 'if' [εἰ] is a poor discriminator, and 'for' [γάρ] has a great variety of usage among all the epistles. Mealand concludes that if the use of positional tests of this sort is valid, then a seven-epistle theory (which includes 2 Thess.) fares better than a four-epistle theory.

One of the most thorough examinations of style of the Pauline epistles is by Kenneth J. Neumann.[123] Neumann's goal was to discover which stylistic tests are statistically valid for determining the authenticity of the disputed letters in the Pauline corpus. He assumed six undisputed letters of Paul (Rom., 1 and 2 Cor., Gal., Phil., and 1 Thess.; Phlm. is too short to deal with statistically) and compared these known samples of Pauline writing with non-Pauline samples (Heb., *1 Clem.*, Ignatius, Philo, Epictetus, and Josephus) on the assumption that in order for a test to be valid for authenticity it must be able to distinguish known Pauline samples from samples known to be non-Pauline.[124]

---

[120] Anthony Kenny, *A Stylometric Study of the New Testament* (Oxford: Clarendon, 1986). The following is a summary of the tests used by Kenny (for a full list see Kenny, pp. 123-24): occurrences of 'and' and 'to be'; conjunctions and particles; prepositions; articles in various forms; nouns in various forms; pronouns in various forms; 'he, she, it' [αὐτός]; adjectives in various forms; 'all'; adverbs; and verbs in various forms.

[121] Kenny, *Stylometric Study*, p. 98.

[122] David L. Mealand, 'Positional Stylometry Reassessed: Testing a Seven Epistle Theory of Pauline Authorship', *NTS* 35 (1989), pp. 266-286.

[123] Kenneth J. Neumann, *The Authenticity of the Pauline Epistles in the Light of Stylostatistical Analysis* (SBLDS 120; Atlanta: Scholars Press, 1990).

[124] Neumann, *Authenticity*, pp, 20, 124, 130.

Before Neumann tested any of his samples, he removed portions which did not display the writer's own stylistic characteristics, such as all quotes, citations, salutations and pre-formed traditions.[125] He then used a sample size of 750 words, which consisted of two random samples each of 375 words. He lists seventy-one tests under six different headings: (I) Lexical Studies, (II) Morphological-Length Studies, (III) Syntactic-Length Studies, (IV) Morphological-Category Studies, (V) Syntactic-Category Studies, and (VI) Non-Grammatical Studies.[126] Neumann determined the six best, ten best and twenty-four best indices; he then combined them in a variety of ways to see which group of tests gave the most consistent identification of known samples.[127] From this he found that two groups of tests were the most consistent in discerning one author from the other.[128]

When Neumann examines the disputed letters (Eph., Col., 2 Thess.), he concludes, 'Colossians and 2 Thessalonians do not exhibit as many extremes as the Ephesian samples; whenever they are closer to other authors, they are usually not far from Pauline values. The overall picture, consistent with the results from discriminant analysis, is closest to a Pauline style'.[129]

In addition to his findings about the three disputed letters, Neumann has documented that many of the tests used previously—including syllable length, content-word length by vowels, syntactic length measures in general, dependent genitives, depth of clause nesting, strung prepositional phrases, verb-subject order, direct predication patterns, number of hapax legomena, and common conjunctions—are of no value in reference to the question of authenticity. The most effective index to distinguish between early Christian authors was the average number of letters in each word.[130]

Concerning 2 Thessalonians, Neumann's work neither proves nor disproves Pauline authorship. Because of the size of 2 Thessalonians, he does not remove any pieces of tradition and consequently may have committed the same error with regard to 2 Thessalonians which he was so careful to avoid with other documents. Therefore, in regards to the authenticity of 2 Thessalonians, Neumann's work in its present form is only of limited value.

Jerry Sumney has sought to develop a new understanding of the literary form of 2 Thessalonians.[131] Sumney notes that J. Hurd has recently defended the

---

[125] Neumann, *Authenticity*, pp. 127-29, 131 n. 52. Romans contains 19.1% of this material; Heb., 22.9%; 1 Pet., 25.3%; and *1 Clem.*, 36.4%.
[126] Neumann, *Authenticity*, pp. 120-23.
[127] Neumann, *Authenticity*, p. 163.
[128] Neumann, *Authenticity*, p. 194.
[129] Neumann, *Authenticity*, p. 211.
[130] Neumann, *Authenticity*, pp. 203-205, 214.
[131] Jerry L. Sumney, 'The Bearing of a Pauline Rhetorical Pattern on the Integrity of 2 Thessalonians', *ZNW* 81 (1990), pp. 192-204.

integrity of 1 Thessalonians by finding a pattern he refers to as 'the sonata form', or more simply, an A-B-A pattern. Sumney believes this same rhetorical pattern is seen in 2 Thessalonians 1:3–3:5 (1:3-12 = A, 2:1-12 = B, 2:13–3:5 = A'). Sumney concludes that (1) the A-B-A pattern gives a positive argument for the integrity of 2 Thessalonians; (2) 2 Thessalonians 2:13–3:5 is one section and should not be broken at 2:16 or 3:1; and (3) it is unlikely that a secondary author would repeat this Pauline rhetorical pattern.[132]

Sumney's parallels, however, are often weak or non-existent. The parallel between the beginning of the two thanksgivings (1:3; 2:13) has always been recognized, for 2 Thessalonians 2:13-14 does pick up the themes found in the first thanksgiving and in the first chapter, and the necessity to remain faithful in the midst of persecution (1:5-8) can be linked to obedience (2:15-17). This does not, however, prove an A-B-A pattern, but only shows that 2:13-17 is the closing of the first main section of the letter. Although there are some similarities between 1:10-12 and 3:1-5, they are not close enough or numerous enough to be identified as parallel. Nor do Sumney's parallels do justice to the words linking various sections. The beginning of 2 Thessalonians 2:15, 'So then' [ἄρα οὖν], clearly draws a conclusion from what precedes it. Furthermore, the introductory word of 3:1, 'Finally' [τὸ λοιπόν], makes a strong break in the argument. On the other hand, Sumney does show that the links between 2 Thessalonians 1 and 2:15-17 are 'certainly more substantial than the verbal similarities with 1 Thessalonians that Marxsen and Trilling note'.[133]

In 1995, Mealand produced a much more sophisticated model than his previous study.[134] He first removed clearly marked quotations and hymns, and then used a sample size of 1000 words. Because 2 Thessalonians has only 823 words and Titus has only 659, he multiplied their statistics to make it up to the sample size of 1000.[135] He used nineteen variables for his study.[136] Eventually, with discriminant analysis, six of the nineteen variables were chosen which were most helpful in identifying groups: word length, initial tau, 'for' [γάρ], relatives and indefinites, 'in' [ἐν] and 'not' [οὐ].[137] With reference to 2 Thessalonians he concludes his study by noting that 1 Thessalonians is more unlike the major letters of Paul than is 2 Thessalonians and that, based on discriminant analysis, 2 Thessalonians is to be classed with Paul.[138]

---

[132] Sumney, 'Pauline Rhetorical Pattern', pp. 202-203.
[133] Sumney, 'Pauline Rhetorical Pattern', p. 198.
[134] D. L. Mealand, 'The Extent of the Pauline Corpus: A Multivariate Approach', *JSNT* 59 (1995), pp. 61-92.
[135] Mealand, 'Extent of the Pauline Corpus', p. 64
[136] Mealand, 'Extent of the Pauline Corpus', p. 70.
[137] Mealand, 'Extent of the Pauline Corpus', p. 81.
[138] Mealand, 'Extent of the Pauline Corpus', pp. 82, 85-86.

Gerard Ledger also used cluster and multivariant analysis in 1995, but focused entirely on vocabulary.[139] He began his study by breaking the entire New Testament into 126 samples of 1000 words each. The only book under 1000 words that he examined was 2 Thessalonians, and he multiplied his results to make it comparable to other samples.[140] He used a total of twenty-nine variables concerning vocabulary: nineteen concerned the percentage of words containing a particular letter in the Greek alphabet,[141] nine concerned the percentage of words ending in a specific letter,[142] and the third category was the type/token ration (TTK). Because each sample has 1000 words, then there are 1000 tokens for each sample. The types are the number of different words in the sample; any different form of the same word counts as a separate type.[143]

He then examined multiple samples from Acts, Romans, 1 Corinthians, and Revelation using multivariate and cluster analysis and found these samples created three distinct clusters with one cluster having both Romans and 1 Corinthians, one for Acts, and one for Revelation. When he ran these tests on all the New Testament epistles, he found two defined clusters.[144] The first cluster consisted of Romans, 1 and 2 Corinthians, Galatians, Philippians, and 2 Thessalonians. The second cluster contained Colossians, Ephesians and Hebrews. The books of James, 1 and 2 Peter, 1 Thessalonians and 1 and 2 Timothy were all found at varying distances from the first cluster. He acknowledges that statistics cannot prove authorship, yet he concludes 'that 1 and 2 Corinthians, Galatians, Philippians, 2 Thessalonians and Romans seem to form a core Pauline group, but that the authenticity of all the remaining Epistles as Pauline works must remain doubtful.'[145]

There are a number of possible weaknesses with this study. First, it is focused entirely on vocabulary, yet particular topics or congregational needs may require a different vocabulary. Second, although explicit quotes are removed, no other traditional material is removed from the samples. Nevertheless, it is significant that 2 Thessalonians is more closely associated with the undisputed

---

[139] Gerard Ledger, 'An Exploration of Differences in the Pauline Epistles Using Multivariate Statistical Analysis', *Literary and Linguistic Computing* 10.2 (1995), pp. 85-97.

[140] Ledger, 'Exploration of Differences', pp. 86, 97. Thus he excluded from his examination the following letters: Titus, Phlm., 2 John, 3 John, and Jude.

[141] Because six of the letters in the Greek alphabet are rarely used, he combined these six letters into one test.

[142] Greek words only use a limited number of endings, so every Greek word ends with only one of nine letters.

[143] Ledger, 'Exploration of Differences', p. 86.

[144] Ledger, 'Exploration of Differences', p. 90. He excluded 1 John because the data could distort the more general results.

[145] Ledger, 'Exploration of Differences', p. 95.

Paulines than 1 Thessalonians is.

George Barr presents a statistical model called 'scalometry' which he uses to determine the authenticity and integrity of the letters of Paul.[146] His basic premise is that writers, including Paul, display distinct patterns in the length of their sentences. Barr's primary methodology is to graph the sentences, with the cumulative sum[147] of the length of each sentence on the vertical axis, and each sentence in order on the horizontal axis. The basic pattern revealed in the letters of Paul consists of longer sentences in the first portion of each letter followed by shorter sentences in the paraenetic section. When compared to twenty modern and ancient writers, the graph of 2 Thessalonians follows the distinctive pattern found in the undisputed letters of Paul, with the exception of 2 Corinthians, and also in the rest of the epistles attributed to Paul in the New Testament.[148]

There are, however, some weaknesses with Barr's methodology. Because Barr must adjust some of the sentences in some samples (not in 2 Thess.), it could be argued that his methodology was adapted to make his graphs work.[149] Furthermore, although Barr does remove some quotations, it is possible that he should remove many more items of preformed material. Finally, although his methodology does take into account where the sentences are in the letter as a whole, there still is an attempt to separate the statistical methods from exegesis.

Concerning 2 Thessalonians, Barr's methodology does show that 2 Thessalonians has integrity as a letter; it is not just a cut-and-paste based on 1 Thessalonians. This is clearly seen in that, even though the eschatological

---

[146]George K. Barr, *Scalometry and the Pauline Epistles* (JSNTSup 261; London: T & T Clark, 2004).

[147]The cumulative sum (S_i) is determined by three factors: the previous cumulative sum (S_{i-1}) of the preceding sentence; the length of the particular sentence (X_i); and the average length of all the sentences (X_{ave}) in the total sample. He uses the sentences which conclude with a full stop in UBS^3. The cumulative sum is found in the following equation: $S_i = S_{i-1} + (X_i - X_{ave})$. Thus for 2 Thess., there are 27 sentences containing 823 words. Therefore X_{ave} is $823/27 = 30.48$ or rounding it to 30.5. The graph always begins at (0, 0) and it always ends back on the horizontal axis. Therefore S_0 is a value of 0. The first sentence is 28 words long, so $S_1 = 0 + (28 - 30.5) = -2.5$. (See Barr, *Scalometry*, p. 28.)

[148]Barr, *Scalometry*, p. 94. He also believes that 1 Tim. and Titus have each had insertions.

[149]He does not remove all the quotes from Rom.; he combines short questions together when they are listed as a group in Rom., 2 Cor., and Gal.; and he ignores colons (p. 36). He also says that 1 Tim. and Titus have each had insertions. See Sean Adams, 'Review of *Scalometry and the Pauline Epistles*', *Journal of Greco-Roman Christianity and Judaism* 2 (2001-2005), pp. R31-34.

sections of 2 Thessalonians are found in the first portion of the epistle and the primary eschatological sections of 1 Thessalonians are found in the second portion of that epistle, the cumulative sum lengths remain appropriate for the pattern of Paul's epistles.

In all of the above listed defenses of authenticity, the most helpful are the rhetorical approach and some of the stylo-statistical approaches. The others are either of no real help or are simply too speculative. Thus what is needed is a more comprehensive approach which incorporates these two approaches.

8. Comprehensive Defenses

Over the years, commentators have given a variety of reasons for accepting the epistle as Pauline. One of the earliest defenses, by Wilibald Grimm,[150] is especially helpful in critiquing Baur for placing so much weight on arguments from silence.[151] Bornemann presents a very thorough early history of the disputers and defenders of authenticity,[152] then states that the similarities and differences between 1 and 2 Thessalonians can best be explained by a psychological understanding of the apostle. He suggests that Paul had waited anxiously to find out if the Thessalonians had remained true; having received the news from Timothy, he was overjoyed and wrote 1 Thessalonians. However, when he wrote 2 Thessalonians, Paul had mixed emotions, for persecution had intensified, false teaching was prevalent, and idleness had further developed, yet at the same time they were growing in faith and love.

Two strong defenses of authenticity were produced around 1900 by Milligan and Frame, both of whom examined the external attestation, the language and style, the doctrinal contents (especially eschatology), and the literary relationship of the letters.[153] Frame makes exhaustive categories to define vocabulary and phraseology differences and similarities, and he concludes that

---

[150]Wilibald Grimm, 'Die Echtheit der Briefe an die Thessalonicher: gegen D. Baur's Angriff vertheidigt', *TSK* 23 (1850), pp. 753-816. Wilhelm Bornemann, *Die Thessalonicherbriefe: völlig neu bearbeitet* (Göttingen: Vandenhoeck & Ruprecht, 1894), pp. 498, 519-28, lists other early defenders. Other than Grimm he particularly focuses on Pelt (1841, who specifically writes against Kern, stating that the Christian connection with the Nero myth only occurred much later), Westriks (1879, who gives an overall general defense), and Klöpper (1888, who gives a thorough defense, specifically focusing on the literary relationship).

[151]Grimm, 'Echtheit', pp. 784, 782.

[152]Bornemann, *Thessalonicherbriefe*, p. 516.

[153]George Milligan, 'The Authenticity of the Second Epistle to the Thessalonians', *The Expositor* 9 (1904), pp. 431-50. See also Milligan, *Thessalonians*, pp. lxxvi-xcii; Frame, *Thessalonians*, pp. 39-54.

the vocabulary and phraseology of both letters is Pauline.[154] Concerning the literary relationship, Milligan notes that less than one third of the content of 2 Thessalonians is parallel to 1 Thessalonians and that these parallels do not display a 'slavish copying by one man of another'.[155] The statistics gathered by these two commentators, especially those of Frame, have continued to form the basis for discussion.

The largest modern commentary and one of the most extensive defenses of the authenticity of 2 Thessalonians was done by Beda Rigaux in 1956. Rigaux presents a very strong cumulative case for accepting authenticity. He notes that the percentage of words in 2 Thessalonians also found in the four largest letters of Paul (86%) is higher than the percentage of words in 1 Thessalonians found in the four largest letters (82%).[156] One of Rigaux's contributions to the defense is his suggestion that the similarities of vocabulary and style between the two letters predate the first letter and that Paul uses clichés and an oral vocabulary. The sources of the parallels in the two letters are the kerygma, apostolic paraenesis and epistolary genre.[157]

In 1963, Jan Stepien wrote a thesis on the authenticity of the Thessalonian epistles.[158] It surveys the external attestation, the linguistic and literary characteristics of the letters, and doctrine.[159] He notes that there are two major obstacles to accepting the authenticity of 2 Thessalonians: its eschatology and its literary relationship to 1 Thessalonians. In discussing the literary relationship, he notes the tendency to focus either upon the differences or the similarities with 1 Thessalonians. Stepien presents a philological-psychological approach. He accounts for the similarities of the two letters by saying that it was natural to repeat phrases, especially formulas which were fixed before AD 50. Psychologically, this repetition was likely because only a few months had passed since the writing of 1 Thessalonians, and repetition is a habit of preachers. He accounts for the differences between the letters by a change in time and a change in circumstances. He attributes the impersonal tone to Paul's choice to omit the names of persons so that he might not chastise without necessity; consequently, the Old Testament comes to the fore.[160]

Although in recent years there appears to have been a shift of opinion against the authenticity of 2 Thessalonians, there nevertheless have continued to be well-reasoned defenses of the authenticity. Four relatively recent defenses have

---

[154]Frame, *Thessalonians*, pp. 31-32.
[155]Milligan, 'Authenticity', p. 439.
[156]Rigaux, *Thessaloniciens*, pp. 81, 83.
[157]Rigaux, *Thessaloniciens*, pp. 149-52.
[158]Jan Stepien, 'Autentycznosc Listow Do Tessaloniczan', *ColT* 34 (1963), pp. 91-182. I was assisted by Davorin Peterlin, who did an oral translation of Stepien's work.
[159]Stepien, 'Autentycznosc', pp. 94-136.
[160]Stepien, 'Autentycznosc', pp. 171-76.

The Debate about the Authenticity of 2 Thessalonians

been written by Best (1972), Kümmel (1975), Marshall (1983), and Malherbe (2000), all of whom believe that the disputers have overstated their case.[161] They recognize the similarity of the structure and themes of the Thessalonian epistles but note that this similarity covers only about a third of 2 Thessalonians and that the themes do not occur in the same order.[162] They note that the vocabulary is Pauline but that the style is a subjective measure because it changes with content. In fact, the personal concern of Paul shines through. In addition, Marshall points out that the disputers often focus on unusual items in 2 Thessalonians without recognizing the many unusual items in the undisputed Pauline corpus.[163] These defenders see no final conflict of eschatologies in the two Thessalonian epistles, for it is common for Jewish sources and the Gospels to place side-by-side the idea of an unexpected return and the appearance of preliminary signs.[164] They also raise a number of points to support an early date: (1) No other Pauline letters are used in 2 Thessalonians, except possibly 1 Thessalonians;[165] (2) 2 Thessalonians is not just a single issue tract but a real letter concerned not only with eschatology, but also persecution (2 Thess. 1) and work (2 Thess. 3).[166] (3) Christians are accepted by God on the basis of their belief (2 Thess. 1:10), not simply because they are Christians;[167] (4) Paul regularly used his authority; if the writer really wanted to stress 'apostolic' authority, why does he not refer to Paul as an 'apostle?'[168] (5) 'Lord' was used in ancient Christian prayers (see 1 Cor. 16:22);[169] (6) the problems are the same as in 1 Thessalonians, and we have no later references to loafers;[170] (7) the reference to the temple in 2:4 is most easily explained if the temple is still standing;[171] and (8) there is no evidence of any office-bearers in Thessalonica, which shows it still is an early date.[172] In short, a later date offers no advantages in explaining the epistle, only more difficulties.[173]

---

[161]Best, *Thessalonians*, pp. 37-59; W. G. Kümmel, *Introduction to the New Testament* (rev. ed.; trans. H. C. Lee; London: SCM, 1975), pp. 262-69; Marshall, *Thessalonians*, pp. 25-45; Malherbe, *Letters to the Thessalonians*, 349-74.

[162]Kümmel, *Introduction*, p. 267.

[163]Marshall, *Thessalonians*, pp. 32-34.

[164]Best, *Thessalonians*, p. 55.

[165]Marshall, *Thessalonians*, p. 43.

[166]Malherbe, *Letters to the Thessalonians*, pp. 351, 375.

[167]Kümmel, *Introduction*, p. 266.

[168]Kümmel, *Introduction*, p. 267; Best, *Thessalonians*, p. 55.

[169]Best, *Thessalonians*, p. 54.

[170]Best, *Thessalonians*, p. 57.

[171]Kümmel, *Introduction*, p. 267.

[172]Best, *Thessalonians*, p. 57.

[173]Marshall, *Thessalonians*, p. 45. Other brief defenses in commentaries include: David J. Williams, *1 and 2 Thessalonians* (New International Biblical

III. The Debate about External Attestation to 2 Thessalonians

Most disputers do not discuss the historical attestation to 2 Thessalonians. Kern mentions that 2 Thessalonians is attested in Clement of Alexandria, Tertullian, Irenaeus, and Marcion's canon.[174] Other disputers accept that the earliest witness is Polycarp, who knew 2 Thessalonians early in the second century.[175] Some other disputers believe the portion of Polycarp's letter *To the Philippians* which quotes 2 Thessalonians is from a later letter (about AD 135) of Polycarp that was conflated with an earlier letter of Polycarp's.[176] The disputers who discuss this believe this leaves a sufficient gap of time after the life of Paul, yet before a set collection of Paul's letters has been made, for pseudepigraphy like 2 Thessalonians to have arisen and to be accepted.

The defenders of authenticity also spend little time looking at the implications of the earliest witnesses to 2 Thessalonians. Rigaux's thorough examination of the external attestation leads him to conclude that the dates of the ancient attestation do not make pseudepigraphy impossible.[177] Best is hesitant to push a definite date for Polycarp's letter, but if there is a Pauline collection by early in the second century, then 2 Thessalonians must be dated significantly earlier.[178]

Conclusion

Thus there is a need to reexamine the question of the authenticity of 2 Thessalonians. This must take into consideration the earliest historical attestation and its implications, which so often are only mentioned briefly. We also must investigate the use and place of tradition, which frequently is assumed to be illustrative of a later time period. In addition, we must determine if the explicit mention and use of tradition in 2 Thessalonians is like Paul or not. Then we must reevaluate the doctrines found in 2 Thessalonians to determine if they are consistent with, complementary to, or contradictory to the doctrines in Paul's undisputed letters. In particular we will examine the eschatology, but also imitation, Christology and soteriology. Finally, the literary character of the letter needs to be explained in terms of both its peculiarities and its similarities with 1 Thessalonians as well as with the rest of the undisputed letters of Paul.

Commentary 12; Peabody, MA: Hendrickson, 1992), pp. 11-13; Green, *Thessalonians*, pp. 59-64; Beale, *Thessalonians*, pp. 29-31; Fee, *Thessalonians*, pp. 237-41; Weima, *Thessalonians*, pp. 46-54.

[174]Kern, 'Über 2. Thess 2,1-12', p. 210.

[175]Wrede, *Echtheit*, pp. 92-95; Braun, *'Zur nachpaulinischen Herkunft'*, p. 156; Trilling, *Untersuchungen*, pp. 20-21.

[176]J. A. Bailey, 'Who Wrote 2 Thessalonians?', p. 156; Holland, *Tradition*, p. 143.

[177]Rigaux, *Thessaloniciens*, p. 120.

[178]Best, *Thessalonians*, pp. 37-38, 56.

Chapter 2
External Attestation to 2 Thessalonians

Many modern commentaries on 2 Thessalonians and discussions of its authenticity either totally ignore or only briefly mention external attestation, often because it is believed that the historical testimony adds nothing of significance to the discussion. Yet a review of the attestation is important in order to understand how widely and how early 2 Thessalonians was accepted as Pauline and to show that the *terminus ad quem* for 2 Thessalonians is significantly earlier than most disputers of authenticity recognize.

The numerous early undisputed references to 2 Thessalonians are found in Eusebius, Cyprian, Origen, Hippolytus, Tertullian, Clement of Alexandria, and Irenaeus, and nearly all of these quotes are explicitly attributed to the apostle Paul.[1] In addition, virtually all of the ancient canonical lists include 2 Thessalonians,[2] including the earliest list, the Muratorian Fragment, which is usually dated sometime between AD 170 and 190.[3] Furthermore, the number of early copies of 2 Thessalonians testifies that the early church included it among the undisputed letters of Paul.[4]

---

[1] The best examinations of external attestation are found in Milligan, *Thessalonians*, pp. lxxvi-lxxvii; Frame, *Thessalonians*, p. 39; and especially Rigaux, *Thessaloniciens*, pp. 112-20.

[2] Cyril of Jerusalem (c. 350), the Cheltenham Canon (c. 360), Synod of Laodicea (c. 363), Athanasius (367), the 'Apostolic Canons' (c. 380), Gregory of Nazianzus (329-89), Amphilochius of Iconium (after 394), Third Synod of Carthage (397), Epiphanes (c. 315-403), Mommsen (c. early 4th), and Codex Sinaiticus (c. AD 350). Taken from Bruce M. Metzger, *The Canon of the New Testament: Its Origin, Development, and Significance* (Oxford: Clarendon, 1987), pp. 311-15, and Daniel J. Theron, *Evidence of Tradition* (London: Bowes & Bowes, 1957), pp. 119-23. The only early canonical list that does not include 2 Thess. is Codex Claromontanus (c. 6th century). Under the heading 'Epistles of Paul' it lists only ten letters, not including 1 Thess., 2 Thess., or Phil. (see Theron, *Evidence of Tradition*, pp. 122-23).

[3] Theron, *Evidence of Tradition*, p. 107. For arguments for a later date see Albert C. Sundberg, 'Canon Muratori: A Fourth Century List', *HTR* 66 (1973): pp. 1-41. For a refutation of Sundberg see E. Ferguson, 'Canon Muratori: Date and Provenance', *StPatr* 18 (1982), pp. 677-83.

[4] From NA^{26}: Codex Sinaiticus ('א') –fourth century; Codex Alexandrinus ('A') –fifth century; Codex Vaticanus ('B') –fourth century; Codex Bezae Cantabrigiensis ('D') – sixth century; 'F' –ninth century; Codex Boernerianus ('G') –ninth century; 'I' –fifth century; 'Y' –eighth or ninth centuries; uncial '0111' –seventh century; P^{30} –third century. See also Rigaux, *Thessaloniciens*, pp. 120, 282-95. For dates see *The Greek New Testament*, UBS^3, pp. xiv-xv.

Therefore, as Frame observes, 2 Thessalonians has been accepted by all sections of the church since the time of Irenaeus in the latter half of the second century.[5] Furthermore, none of the early Christian writers shows any knowledge of a time when it was not accepted.[6]

I. Middle Second Century

Although Justin Martyr, who wrote between AD 150 and 160, does not mention Paul by name, he uses the terminology of 2 Thessalonians to describe the events surrounding the return of Christ in his *Dialogue with Trypho*. In 32.4 he speaks of the 'man of sin' and in 110.2 he refers to 'the man of apostasy, who speaks strange things against the Most High'.[7] Therefore it appears clear that Justin knew of 2 Thessalonians and accepted its teaching.[8]

Two other writings of this approximate time also appear to make use of 2 Thessalonians. *The Apocalypse of Peter,* written sometime in the second century and mentioned in the Muratorian Fragment, describes (in the Ethiopic text) 'the deceiver which must come into the world and do signs and wonders to deceive'.[9] Most likely this comes from 2 Thessalonians 2:3-12.[10] The *Ascension of Isaiah,* a composite document, basically consists of two parts: the *Martyrdom of Isaiah* (chs 1-5), and the *Vision of Isaiah* (chs 6-11). The first part, which contains a Christian addition (3.13–4.2), was most likely composed near the end

---

[5]Frame, *Thessalonians*, p. 39.

[6]Three other early documents quote directly from 2 Thess., but because of the difficulty of dating them they are not usually included in most external attestation discussions. A letter ascribed to Anterus, who succeeded Pontianus as bishop of Rome (AD 236-7), is one of the pseudo-Isidorian forgeries. It quotes 2 Thess. 2:15-17; 3:1-3, 4 (See Irenaeus and Hippolytus in vol. 9 of LCL, pp. 247-248). In ch. 11 of the spurious *Epistle of Ignatius to the Antiochians*, 2 Thess. 3:10 is quoted, and in the longer recension of Ign. *Magn.* 9, this same verse is also quoted. See *Apostolic Fathers* (vol. 1 of Ante-Nicene Christian Library; ed. A. Roberts and J. Donaldson; Edinburgh: T & T Clark, 1876), pp. 465, 181.

[7]In Chapter 32.4 τὸν τῆς ἀνομίας ἄνθρωπον and in 110.2 ὁ τῆς ἀποστασίας, ὁ καὶ εἰς τὸν Ὕψιστον ἔξαλλα λαλῶν. The English translation is taken from *Justin Martyr and Athenagoras* (vol. 2 of Ante-Nicene Christian Library; ed. A. Roberts and J. Donaldson; Edinburgh: T & T Clark, 1867), pp. 127, 236. The Greek is taken from S. P. N. Justini Philosophi Et Martyris, *Dialogue with Trypho* (PG 6:544, 729).

[8]Rigaux, *Thessaloniciens*, pp. 118, 120. Frame, *Thessalonians*, p. 39, also lists *Dial.* 116.5 as a possible reference in Justin, but this is not so clear. See also Milligan, *Thessalonians*, p. lxxvii.

[9]M. R. James, *The Apocryphal New Testament* (Oxford: Clarendon, 1923), pp. 506, 512.

[10]Rigaux, *Thessaloniciens*, p. 118.

of the first century.[11] In the fourth chapter, it is said that Beliar will descend in the form of a man, he will accept sacrifice and claim to be the LORD, and he will have the power to do miracles. In addition, when the Lord comes with his angels, he will give rest to all those who have faith in him. This combination of items is found elsewhere only in 2 Thessalonians 1:7-8 and 2:4, 8-9; therefore whoever added this section must have had 2 Thessalonians.[12]

Marcion, who was expelled from the church at Rome about AD 140, had a canon that included ten Pauline epistles (not the Pastorals). Knox and many others suggest that this implies a collection of these ten epistles before the end of the first century. We also have copies of the Marcionite prologues which probably go back to the second century. There was just one prologue to both Thessalonian epistles, but it is universally accepted that Marcion's canon included both epistles to the Thessalonians.[13]

II. The Apostolic Fathers

The *Didache*, or *Teaching of the Twelve Apostles*, was composed by the early second century, or perhaps even earlier.[14] The final chapter contains an apocalyptic section with similarities to both 2 Thessalonians 2 and Matthew 24. Four themes appear in all three discourses: lawlessness, wickedness, deceit, and signs and wonders. The question is whether all the information found in *Didache* could have arisen from Matthew 24 or whether certain items make it

---

[11] M. A. Knibb, 'The Ascension of Isaiah the Prophet' in *OTP* (ed. J.H. Charlesworth; 2 vols; London: Darton, Longman & Todd, 1983-1985), vol. 2, pp. 143-49, says *Mart. Isa.* refers back to Nero's death (AD 68), yet it is referred to by a number of other fairly early documents (see *4 Bar.* 9.18, 20 and *Gos. Pet.*). Knibb (p. 149) says *4 Bar.* is 'a work attributed to the early second century', and *Gos. Pet.* is a 'work which dates from the middle of the second century'. See also W. O. E. Oesterley, *The Books of the Apocrypha* (London: Robert Scott, 1915), pp. 219-20.

[12] Rigaux, *Thessaloniciens*, p. 112, not only lists seven references in this chapter but also sees an allusion in 9.13 to 2 Thess 2:4. Knibb does not note any similarity in the ninth chapter. Best, *Thessalonians*, p. 38, says that the date of *Ascen. Isa.* is uncertain and that the references are not exact enough to assume knowledge of 2 Thess.

[13] John Knox, *Marcion and the New Testament: An Essay in the Early History of the Canon* (Chicago: University of Chicago Press, 1942), pp. 1, 3, 37, 55. The prologues can be found in Knox, Appendix I, pp. 169-71, in both Latin and English.

[14] Kirsopp Lake, *Apostolic Fathers* (LCL), vol. 1, p. 307. Robinson, *Redating*, p. 327, suggests the very early date of between AD 40 and 60. He also notes (p. 323) that J. P. Audet suggests dates of between AD 50 and 70 for the *Didache*. Jonathan Draper, 'The Jesus Tradition in the Didache', in *The Jesus Tradition Outside the Gospels* (vol. 5 of Gospel Perspectives; ed. David Wenham; Sheffield; JSOT Press, 1984), p. 269, suggests that it most probably must be dated before the end of the first century.

likely that 2 Thessalonians was known to the author. A number of phrases are found in *Didache* and Matthew but not in 2 Thessalonians;[15] however, what is important for our study is that the *Didache* shows an independence from Matthew at a number of points[16] and especially in the description of the evil adversary. Matthew refers to these opponents in the plural and in broad generalities, whereas in 2 Thessalonians and *Didache* the description focuses on a final individual adversary. Therefore, 2 Thessalonians and *Didache* either represent independent attestation of early Christian eschatological teaching, or *Didache* has made use of 2 Thessalonians.[17]

---

[15]These include the command to watch, for the hour the Lord comes is unknown (*Did.* 16.1; Matt. 24:42); the mention of false prophets (*Did.* 16.2; Matt. 24:11, 24); the promise that those who endure will be saved (*Did.* 16.5; Matt. 24:13); and a series of final signs: the sound of the trumpet (*Did.* 16.6; Matt 24:31), and the Lord coming on the clouds (*Did.* 16.8; Matt 24:30). For a more detailed comparison and analysis of the relationship of *Did.* 16 and Matt. 24, see Draper, 'Jesus Tradition', pp. 281-82.

[16]Draper makes note of this independence from both Matt. and Luke, and suggests that the gospel tradition was still in the process of formation at the time the *Didache* was written (p. 278).

[17]**Parallels of *Didache* 16 and 2 Thessalonians 2**

Didache 16	2 Thessalonians 2
deceit	
4 and then the deceiver of the world will appear as a son of God	4 Showing himself that he is God
καὶ τότε φανήσεται ὁ κοσμοπλανὴς ὡς υἱὸς θεοῦ	ἀποδεικνύντα ἑαυτὸν ὅτι ἔστιν θεός
signs and wonders	
4 the deceiver of the world . . . will do signs and wonders	9 the lawless one . . . with all miracles, signs and false wonders
κοσμοπλανὴς . . . ποιήσει σημεῖα καὶ τέρατα	ὁ . . .ἐν πάσῃ δυνάμει καὶ σημείοις καὶ τέρασιν ψεύδους
committing of sin	
4 he will do iniquities which have never ever occurred	4 he will oppose and will exalt himself over everything that is called God or is worshiped, so that he sets himself up in God's temple, proclaiming himself to be God
Ποιήσει ἀθέμιτα, ἃ οὐδέποτε γέγονεν ἐξ αἰῶνος	ὁ ἀντικείμενος καὶ ὑπεραιρόμενος ἐπὶ πάντα λεγόμενον θεὸν ἢ σέβασμα, ὥστε αὐτὸν εἰς τὸν ἑαυτὸν ὅτι ἔστιν θεός

Rigaux, *Thessaloniciens*, pp. 114-15, 120, sees as probable the use of 2 Thess. by *Didache*.

External Attestation to 2 Thessalonians

Ignatius, who was martyred in Rome between AD 108 and 117, wrote a series of letters on his trip to Rome. At the end of his letter to the Romans he says, 'in the endurance of Jesus Christ' [ἐν ὑπομονῇ Ἰησοῦ Χριστοῦ.].[18] This rather curious phrase is almost identical to 2 Thessalonians 3:5 [εἰς τὴν ὑπομονὴν Χριστου]. The Oxford Committee, however, gives this phrase only a 'd' rating, which means the phrase in question 'may possibly be referred to, but in regard to which the evidence appeared too uncertain to allow any reliance to be placed upon it'.[19] The problem with the phrase is first of all a difficulty with Ignatius's epistles as a whole. Commentators on Ignatius are generally agreed that Ignatius was greatly affected by the letters of Paul. However, Ignatius rarely gives exact quotes but instead feels free to express himself in his own way. This can be seen in the many 'd' ratings by the Oxford Committee concerning Ignatius. Furthermore, Ignatius uses the phrase as a closing, whereas the writer of 2 Thessalonians uses it as part of a prayer. Although these two uses do not necessarily contradict each other, neither does the different use strengthen the case that the source of the phrase is Ignatius himself. Furthermore, the phrase is somewhat different in Ignatius, having a different preposition, a different use of articles, and a changed name of Jesus. One could make a similar case that the phrase in Ignatius is based upon Revelation 1:9, 'and patience of Jesus' [καὶ ὑπομονῇ ἐν Ἰησοῦ]. Therefore, concerning Ignatius's use of 2 Thessalonians, all that can be said is that it is possible.[20]

III. Polycarp

In most discussions concerning the authenticity of 2 Thessalonians, the earliest clear witness to 2 Thessalonians is generally considered to be Polycarp's epistle *To the Philippians*. In such discussions, Polycarp's citations

---

[18] Ign. *Rom.* 10.3 (Lake, *Apostolic Fathers*, LCL).
[19] Oxford Society of Historical Theology, *The New Testament in the Apostolic Fathers* (Oxford: Clarendon, 1905), pp. 75, iii.
[20] Rigaux, *Thessaloniciens*, pp. 118, 115, also notes that both Shepherd of Hermas and *Barnabas* may have used 2 Thess. In Herm. *Vis.* 2.1.2; 3.4.3; 4.1.3, the phrases 'to glorify his name' and 'the name of God might be glorified' are used, and these are similar to 2 Thess. 1:12, 'the name of our Lord Jesus may be glorified in you'. The problem is that this is also an OT phrase found in Ps. 85: 9, 12 (LXX) and Isa. 24:15 and 66:5. 2 Thess. uses the verb ἐνδοξάζομαι (as does Isa. 24:1—LXX), while Herm. *Vis.* uses δοξάζω (as do Ps. 85 and Isa. 66). Therefore no weight can be placed on Herm. *Vis.* Also, *Barn.* 2.1 says 'the worker of evil himself is in power' [αὐτοῦ τοῦ ἐνεργοῦτος ἔχοντος τὴν ἐξουσίαν], using the word 'work' in reference to Satanic work, as does 2 Thess. 2:7: 'the mystery of lawlessness is already at work' [τὸ γὰρ μυστήριον ἤδη ἐνεργεῖται τῆς ἀνομίας]. Although the concept is similar, it is questionable whether there is a literary dependence.

from 2 Thessalonians are usually noted but not examined, and consequently most critics postulate a date for the epistle from Polycarp that is consistent with their presuppositions about the date of the formation of the New Testament canon. For example, John A. Bailey says that Polycarp probably cites from 2 Thessalonians 'about A. D. 115 (or 135 if we follow the dating advocated by P. N. Harrison)'.[21] However, as Bailey concludes his arguments he says the *terminus ad quem* for the writing of 2 Thessalonians is the writing of Polycarp's letter to the Philippians in AD 135.[22] Although Bailey is primarily concerned, not with an historical examination of the relevant information, but with arguments concerning internal criteria, a later *terminus ad quem* enables him to postulate a potentially later date—the last decade of the first century—for 2 Thessalonians. Philipp Vielhauer, on the other hand, would date Polycarp's epistle about AD 110,[23] and this forces him to postulate a date for 2 Thessalonians in the 80s.[24] As the Bishop of Gloucester has observed, if the testimony of Polycarp can be held to be about AD 140 instead of AD 110, it is 'rather innocuous'[25] and therefore adds little to the case for authenticity.

Therefore because Polycarp's *To the Philippians* is most likely the earliest witness to 2 Thessalonians, it is necessary to examine carefully this letter. This examination will show that Polycarp had 2 Thessalonians and cited from it. From these citations we shall see not only that Polycarp accepted 2 Thessalonians, but also that he viewed it as Pauline, and furthermore, that this was the view not only of Polycarp himself, but also of those who taught him. From this, we will establish a date for Polycarp's letter *To the Philippians*. This information, along with the rest of the external attestation, will serve to provide a *terminus ad quem* for 2 Thessalonians.

A. Citations of 2 Thessalonians in Polycarp's Epistle

1. The Manuscripts

There is no early complete Greek manuscript of the whole of Polycarp's epistle; in fact, the earliest Greek manuscript we possess is an eleventh century document (Cod. Vatic. Gr. 859).[26] Nine Greek manuscripts of the letter exist, all

---

[21] J. A. Bailey, 'Who Wrote 2 Thessalonians?', pp. 131-32.
[22] J. A. Bailey, 'Who Wrote 2 Thessalonians?', p. 143.
[23] Philipp Vielhauer, *Geschichte der urchristlichen Literatur* (Berlin: de Gruyter, 1975), p. 102.
[24] Vielhauer, *Urchristlichen Literatur*, p. 102.
[25] A. C. Gloucester, 'The Epistle of Polycarp to the Philippians', *CQR* 141 (1945), p. 3.
[26] Robert M. Grant, *Introduction* (vol. 1 of *The Apostolic Fathers: A New Translation and Commentary*; ed. R. M. Grant; 6 vols; New York: Nelson, 1964), p. 64.

derived from a common source.[27] The problem with each of these manuscripts is that they all combine a part of *To the Philippians* with part of the *Epistle of Barnabas*: the beginning of Polycarp's epistle through 9.2 is followed by *Barnabas* beginning at 5.7 and continuing to its conclusion.[28] Most likely at some point in the past some pages of a collection containing both documents were lost, and the documents were simply copied as they were found. For the remaining portions of the letter, we are therefore primarily dependent on Latin versions of the text. In addition, Eusebius (*Hist. eccl.* 3.36.13-15) contains most of the thirteenth chapter of the letter in Greek, and there are also a few quotations in Monophysite or semi-Monophysite writers of the fifth to seventh centuries.[29] From these documents Theodor Zahn and J. B. Lightfoot have each reconstructed a Greek text for the Latin portion of the letter.[30]

2. The Citations

Polycarp's epistle contains two possible citations from 2 Thessalonians, both in ch. 11, for which we have only the Latin text. Chapter 11 has to do primarily with Valens, a former presbyter of the church at Philippi, and his wife, who appear to have misused or misappropriated church funds because of their love of money (11.1). Polycarp expresses his deep sorrow about the situation and, having warned the Philippians about the danger of a love of money, advises them to seek after the couple in order to restore them into the church (11.4). The closing portion of 11.4 says:

Polycarp *To the Philippians* 11.4

Therefore be yourselves also moderate in this matter, and 'do not regard such men as enemies,' but call them back as fallible and straying members, that you may make whole the body of you all. For in doing this you edify yourselves.[31]	sobrii ergo estote et vos in hoc; et non sicut inimicos tales existimetis, sed sicut passibilia membra et errantia eos revocate, ut omnium vestrum corpus salvetis. hoc enim agentes, vos ipsos aedificatis.	Νήφετε οὖν καὶ ὑμεῖς ἐν τούτῳ, καὶ μὴ ὡς ἐχθροὺς ἡγεῖσθε τοὺς τοιτούτους, ἀλλ' ὡς μέλη παθητὰ καὶ πεπλανημένα αὐτοὺς ἀνακαλεῖσθε, ἵνα ὅλον ὑμῶν τὸ σῶμα σώζητε· τοῦτο γὰρ ποιοῦντες ἑαυτοὺς οἰκοδομεῖτε.[32]

---

[27]William Schoedel, *Polycarp, Martyrdom of Polycarp, Fragments of Papias* (vol 5 of *The Apostolic Fathers: A New Translation and Commentary*; ed. R. Grant; London: Nelson, 1967), p. 5.
[28]Schoedel, *Polycarp*, p.5.
[29]Grant, *Apostolic Fathers*, vol. 1, p. 64.
[30]Theodorus Zahn, *Ignatii et Polycarpi*, Leipzig: Hinrichs, 1876; J. B. Lightfoot, *The Apostolic Fathers* (5 vols; London: Macmillan, 1885), part 2, vol. 2.
[31]Pol. *Phil.* 11.4 (Lake, *Apostolic Fathers*, LCL).

The phrase 'do not regard such men as enemies' appears to be taken from 2 Thessalonians 3:15, which in the Greek text reads και μη ὡς ἐχθροὺς ἡγεῖσθε τοὺς τοιτούτους, and in the Vulgate, *et nolite quasi inimicum existimare*. Because the Greek text of Polycarp is a reconstruction, to compare it to the Greek New Testament may be inappropriate. A comparison with the Vulgate shows that the Latin text of Polycarp is not based on the Vulgate but is a good translation of a Greek text. A number of differences can be seen between Polycarp's epistle and the Vulgate. The Oxford Committee ranks this allusion as a 'c', saying that 'Polycarp's words sound as though he had purposely adapted the expression of 2 Thessalonians for his own object.'[33] This is unlikely to be Polycarp's own phrase: first, because of similarity to 2 Thessalonians; second, because of the other quote (11.3), which is attributed to Paul; and third, because Polycarp tended to quote constantly. In fact, there is very little debate over the origin of this quote, and it can be regarded as an excellent parallel.[34] It would appear that Polycarp is quoting from memory, as he has a habit of doing, and applying it directly to the subject at hand.[35]

The other possible quote from 2 Thessalonians presents more difficulties. In fact, the whole of 11.3 is difficult to understand.

Polycarp *To the Philippians* 11.3

'But I have neither perceived nor heard any such thing among you, among whom the blessed Paul laboured, who are [praised] in the	*ego autem nihil tale sensi in vobis vel audivi, in quibus laboravit beatus Paulus, qui estis in principio epistulae eius. de vobis etenim*	Εγω δε ουδεν τοιουτο ενοησα εν υμιν ουδε ηκουσα, εν οἷς κεκοπίακεν ὁ μακάριος Παῦλος, οἵτινές ἐστε ἐν ἀρχῇ τῆς

---

[32] The Greek and Latin have been taken from Zahn, *Ignatii et Polycarpi*, pp. 128-29.
[33] Oxford Society, *Apostolic Fathers*, p. 95.
[34] Rigaux, *Thessaloniciens*, p. 117. Michael W. Holmes, 'Polycarp's *Letter to the Philippians* and the Writings that Later Formed the New Testament', in *The Reception of the New Testament in the Apostolic Fathers* (ed. A. F. Gregory and C. M. Tuckett; Oxford: Oxford University Press, 2005), rates this as a 'd'. Holmes comments that this quote seems to be to the Philippians (p.214). Paul Hartog, *Polycarp and the New Testament: The Occasion, Rhetoric, Theme, and Unity of the Epistle to the Philippians and its Allusions to New Testament Literature* (Tübingen: Mohr Siebeck, 2002), p. 195, says it could possibly be a quote from 2 Thess., and Kenneth Berding, *Polycarp and Paul: An Analysis of their Literary and Theological Relationship in Light of Polycarp's Use of Biblical and Extra-Biblical Literature* (VCSup 62; Leiden: Brill, 2002), pp.112-13, says it is probable that it is from 2 Thess.
[35] Oxford Society, *Apostolic Fathers*, p. 84. See also David K. Rensberger, 'As the Apostle Teaches: The Development of the Use of Paul's Letters in Second-Century Christianity' (Ph.D. thesis, Yale University, 1981), p. 148.

| beginning of his Epistle. For concerning you he boasts in all the Churches who then alone had known the Lord, for we had not yet known him.'[36] | *gloriatur in omnibus ecclesiis, quae deum solae tunc cognoverant; nos autem nondum noveramus.* | ἐπιστολῆς αὐτοῦ. περὶ ὑμῶν γὰρ ἐν πάσαις ταῖς ἐκκλησίαις καυχᾶται, αἳ μόναι τότε θεὸν ἐπεγνώκεισαν· ἡμεῖς δὲ οὔπω ἐγνώκειμεν.[37] |

The particular portion of 11.3 which concerns us is the phrase 'he boasts in all the churches' [*etenim gloriatur in omnibus* ecclesiis], which is very similar to 2 Thessalonians 1:4: 'among God's churches we boast' [ὥστε αὐτοὺς ἡμᾶς ἐν ὑμῖν ἐγκαυχᾶσθαι ἐν ταῖς ἐκκλησίαις τοῦ θεοῦ], or in the Vulgate, 'so that we boast in you in the churches of God' [*ita ut et nos ipsi in vobis gloriemur in ecclesiis Dei*]. Two major questions arise concerning this particular phrase: (1) To which epistle of Paul does Polycarp refer? (2) If this is a citation or allusion from 2 Thessalonians, why is the citation directed specifically to the Philippian readers?

The phrase in question in Polycarp's letter is similar to 2 Thessalonians 1:4 with respect to the words used and the word order. In the two key words in this citation in *To the Philippians* 11.3, *glorior* and *ecclesia,* the form of *ecclesia* is identical with the Vulgate, and the present tense of *gloriatur* suggests that Polycarp is quoting. In fact, these two words occur together only in one place in the New Testament: 2 Thessalonians 1:4.[38] The only real difference is the addition of 'all', which does not really change the meaning of the citation but only emphasizes what is being said. The word order is almost identical between the Vulgate of 2 Thessalonians 1:4 (*in vobis gloriemur in ecclesiis*) and *To the Philippians* 11.3 (*de vobis etenim gloriatur in omnibus ecclesiis*). The Oxford Committee rates the citation as a 'b'.[39] The 'a' rating is given to citations about which there can be no reasonable doubt, usually because the source is expressly mentioned, while the 'b' rating is given to statements that have a 'high degree of probability' as being a direct citation.[40] In Polycarp's epistle only two of the many citations and allusions are rated as 'a'; therefore a 'b' rating is very significant, especially since Polycarp's epistle is filled with citations and

---

[36]Pol. *Phil.* 11.3 (Lake, *Apostolic Fathers*, LCL).
[37]The Greek and Latin have been taken from Zahn, *Ignatii et Polycarpi*, pp. 126-29.
[38]Oxford Society, *Apostolic Fathers*, p. 95.
[39]Oxford Society, *Apostolic Fathers*, p. 95.
[40]Oxford Society, *Apostolic Fathers*, p. iii.

possible allusions.[41] As Harrison concludes, the evidence that Polycarp is citing from 2 Thessalonians is 'surely decisive'.[42]

Although the citation given by Polycarp in 11.3 is usually deemed to have originated from 2 Thessalonians 1:4, some have attempted to show that reference is actually being made to Paul's letter to the Philippians. In the passage usually suggested, Philippians 4:15-16, Paul does commend the Philippians for sending aid to him while he was in Thessalonica, but his commendation is not a 'boasting in the churches', as Polycarp cites. There are no real verbal connections with Philippians, and if Polycarp had not said specifically that Paul was speaking this 'concerning you' (that is, the Philippians), no one would ever have made the connection with Paul's letter to Philippi at this point. Rensberger lists Philippians 1:3-5 as a possible source for this citation.[43] However, that passage is a prayer of thanksgiving to God and not a boasting in the churches; again there are no verbal connections, making it unlikely that Polycarp is alluding to Philippians 1:3-5. This leaves us with 2 Thessalonians 1:4 as the only possible New Testament source for Polycarp's citation of Paul.

Since Polycarp is citing from 2 Thessalonians, the question then arises, why did Polycarp state that Paul said this 'concerning you'? A number of possibilities have been presented to explain this reference: (1) Polycarp is mistaken and believes that he is quoting from Paul's letter to the Philippians; (2) 2 Thessalonians was originally a letter to the church at Philippi; (3) Paul's letters to the Thessalonians are applicable to other Macedonian churches as well; or (4) Polycarp would have felt free to apply any of Paul's letters directly to his audience, whoever they might be.

(1) The most common way of dealing with the passage is to say that Polycarp was mistaken. According to the Oxford Committee, 'the context shows that Polycarp supposes himself to be quoting words addressed to the Philippians'.[44] This is a possibility, for Polycarp finishes this sentence by pointing out that the Smyrnaeans had become Christians after the Philippians, 'who then alone had

---

[41] Grant, *Apostolic Fathers*, vol. 1, p. 67, counts over forty times that Polycarp touches upon the Pauline corpus. The Oxford Society, *Apostolic Fathers*, pp. 85-104, lists a possible eighty-one citations or possible allusions.

[42] P. N. Harrison, *Polycarp's Two Epistles to the Philippians* (Cambridge: Cambridge University Press, 1936), p. 293. See also Rigaux, *Thessaloniciens*, p. 117; Henning Paulsen, *Die Briefe des Ignatius von Antiochia und der Brief des Polykarp von Smyrna* (Tübingen: Mohr Siebeck, 1985), p. 124; Lightfoot, *Apostolic Fathers*, part 2, vol. 2, p. 927; Schoedel, *Polycarp*, p. 83. Holmes, 'Polycarp's *Letter*', p. 214, rates this a 'd'.

[43] Rensberger, 'As the Apostle Teaches', p. 115.

[44] Oxford Society, *Apostolic Fathers*, p. 95. See also Vielhauer, *Urchristlichen Literatur*, p. 99, who says Polycarp made an error in the assignment of the citation.

known the Lord, for we had not yet known him'. Polycarp also notes in 11.3 that Paul himself had labored in Philippi. If this is a misquote on the part of Polycarp, then it would tend to support the idea that Polycarp had some kind of Pauline collection of letters from which he drew his material and that 2 Thessalonians was part of that collection. Otherwise it would seem unlikely that he would mistakenly attribute something to Paul specifically, since for him Paul is an authority upon which he depends extensively. Schoedel believes the error is a case of imprecision arising from familiarity with the Pauline phraseology.[45]

(2) Eduard Schweizer has suggested that 2 Thessalonians was originally addressed to the Philippians.[46] In *To the Philippians* 3.2, Polycarp says of Paul that 'when he was absent [he] wrote letters [ἐπιστολὰς] to you'. Schweizer believes that this reference to 'letters' cannot be singular, as some commentators have suggested,[47] and thus it suggests the existence of more than one letter from Paul to the Philippians. He also believes that in 11.3 Polycarp implies that Paul wrote what we call 2 Thessalonians to the church at Philippi. He notes that 2 Thessalonians was not expressly called '2 Thessalonians' until the time of Irenaeus.[48] Schweizer uses this theory to solve the problem of the literary relationship of 2 Thessalonians to 1 Thessalonians: to him it shows that these letters with similar outlines were sent to separate communities rather than to the same community. He also believes his theory explains the use of 'first-fruits' in 2 Thessalonians 2:13, for the Philippians were the 'first-fruits' in Europe. Therefore, according to Schweizer, Polycarp was not in error in attributing this reference to a letter to the Philippians, but rather was just following a good tradition.[49] The major problem with this theory is that 2 Thessalonians is not addressed to the Philippians; to make a feasible explanation for the alteration requires a good imagination. Schweizer has to imagine that the Philippians have sent the original of 2 Thessalonians (or a copy) to Thessalonica, where, without any protest from the Philippians, the Thessalonian church replaced mention of the Philippians with its own name. All subsequent copies must come from this amended manuscript and not from the good one, which has been lost, even though Paul's 'other' letter to the Philippians has come down to us.[50] In addition, if problems exist with a

---

[45] Schoedel, *Polycarp*, p. 14.
[46] Schweizer, 'Philipperbrief', pp. 90-105.
[47] Schoedel, *Polycarp*, p. 14, notes that 'letters' in the plural during the classical period often referred to a single letter (see Eusebius *Hist. eccl.* 6.43.3), but in the literature contemporary with Polycarp they seem to be true plurals. J. B. Lightfoot, *St. Paul's Epistle to the Philippians* (1913; repr., Grand Rapids: Zondervan, 1953), pp. 140-42, gives a number of examples of this practice from a variety of time periods.
[48] Schweizer, 'Philipperbrief', p. 91.
[49] Schweizer, 'Philipperbrief', p. 104.
[50] Rigaux, *Thessaloniciens*, p. 68.

difference of tone between 1Thessalonians and 2 Thessalonians, this is equally true, if not more so, between Philippians and 2 Thessalonians. Schweizer's solution has found little if any support.

(3) Theodor Zahn does not regard the reference as a misquote but would group the three letters to the Macedonian churches together. Consequently Polycarp knows of several letters to the Philippians (i.e., the Macedonians), and therefore when Polycarp says 'to you' he means Paul wrote letters to the Macedonians, which would include 1 and 2 Thessalonians and Philippians.[51] To reach his conclusion, Zahn cites essentially the same evidence as Schweizer, and like Schweizer, his solution has not been widely accepted.

(4) The most satisfying solution can be built upon a suggestion by Lindemann in his remarks on *To the Philippians* 3.2. He suggests that Polycarp viewed Paul's letters in general as relevant for all Christian churches.[52] Therefore, according to Lindemann, all the letters from Paul would be 'to them'. This can be seen throughout the letter in Polycarp's frequent use of Paul's writings, which he applies directly to the Philippians. Lindemann would then say of the expression 'wrote letters to you' in *To the Philippians* 3.2 that the 'you' is an *ekklesiologisch* 'you', meaning simply that Paul had sent letters to the Christians in general. The same principle can be applied to *To the Philippians* 11.3. Polycarp would not be intending to quote from Paul's letter to the Philippians; rather, he would be saying that what Paul said in 2 Thessalonians 1:4 is appropriate to apply to the believers at Philippi. Hartog notes that in Ignatius's letter *To the Ephesians* (12.2), 'Paul "in every Epistle makes mention of you in Christ Jesus."' Thus all of Paul's letters are for the Ephesians.[53] This solution not only removes the difficulty but also best fits the overall pattern of Polycarp's epistle and manner of quoting.[54] Thus, since Polycarp uses citations from 2 Thessalonians two separate times, and one of those is explicitly attributed to Paul, it cannot be questioned that he had this letter in his possession.

3. Polycarp's View of Paul

Polycarp specifically attributes one of his quotes from 2 Thessalonians to Paul; thus, in order to evaluate fully the significance of those quotes for Polycarp we need to evaluate how he views the apostle Paul.

Polycarp mentions Paul by name in three passages: 3.2, 9.1, and 11.2-3. In

---

[51] Zahn, *Introduction to the New Testament*, vol. 1, p. 536.

[52] Andreas Lindemann, *Paulus im ältesten Christentum: Das Bild des Apostels und die Rezeption der paulinischen Theologie in der frühchristlichen Literatur bis Marcion*, (BHT 58; Tübingen: Mohr Siebeck, 1979), p. 88.

[53] Hartog, *Polycarp*, pp. 226-27.

[54] It is also possible that the 'concerning you' actually arose from the original quote in 2 Thess., for both the Greek and Latin texts have 'in you' (ἐν ὑμῖν, *in vobis*).

3.2 Polycarp says, 'For neither am I, nor is any other like me, able to follow the wisdom of the blessed and glorious Paul, who when he was among you in the presence of the men of that time taught accurately and steadfastly the word of truth, and also when he was absent wrote letters to you, from the study of which you will be able to build yourselves up into the faith given to you.'[55] Clearly, Polycarp views Paul's teaching as 'accurate', 'steadfast', and identifiable with 'the word of truth'. This accurate, steadfast, and true teaching is extended to Paul's letters as well (notice the insertion of καί before mentioning his letters), and consequently these letters warrant study, or close examination.[56] Polycarp is not willing to compare his own abilities or those of anyone else of his time with the abilities of Paul.[57] In 9.1 he explicitly names Paul along with 'the other apostles' as being examples of obedience and endurance which are to be emulated. In 11.2-3 Paul is quoted and described as being one who labored among the Philippians. He is referred to as the 'blessed' Paul in 11.3 and the 'blessed and glorious' Paul in 3.2. Polycarp speaks of the apostles as a group in 6.3, describing them as the ones 'who brought us the gospel'. Since the apostles are referred to as 'the other Apostles' in 9.1, Paul would obviously be included in this general description as well. Thus Paul is included among the original apostles and viewed as above all other people in terms of wisdom. His words are identified with truth.

Not only is Paul mentioned by name, but his letters permeate Polycarp's letter. Grant counts forty-one times that Polycarp touches upon the Pauline corpus.[58] It has been suggested that the New Testament letter of Ephesians is

---

[55] Pol. Phil. 3.2 (Lake, Apostolic Fathers, LCL).
[56] W. Arndt and F. W. Gingrich, 'ἐγκύπτω', A Greek-English Lexicon of the New Testament and Other Early Christian Literature (Chicago: University of Chicago Press, 1957), p. 216.
[57] Schoedel, Polycarp, p. 13; Rensberger, 'As the Apostle Teaches', p. 116.
[58] Grant, Apostolic Fathers, vol. 1, p. 67. This figure includes thirteen references from the Pastoral Epistles. It goes beyond the scope of this book to discuss whether or not Polycarp viewed the Pastorals as Pauline or even directly used the Pastorals. There is considerable debate about the relationship of Polycarp's epistle to the Pastorals. Many of the possible allusions to the Pastorals are of a proverbial character (see Robert M. Grant, 'Polycarp of Smyrna', AThR 28 [1946], p. 145). Therefore Walter Bauer, Orthodoxy and Heresy in Earliest Christianity (London: SCM, 1972), p. 224, concludes that this was just a standard way of speaking. Hans von Campenhausen, The Formation of the Christian Bible (London: Black, 1972), p.181, says that the author of the Pastoral Epistles must have at least been 'intimately connected with Polycarp'. Vielhauer, Urchristlichen Literatur, p. 564, describes Pol. Phil. as echoing the Pastorals but having no dependence and instead using the same tradition. Hartog, Polycarp, p. 232, includes 1 Tim.

quoted as 'scripture' in 12.1.[59] However, this quotation also includes an Old Testament passage and it may be only that which is described as 'scripture'.

Whether a formal collection of Pauline letters existed at this time is difficult to determine,[60] but it is clear that Paul's letters at least to some extent were in the hands of Polycarp's readers, for Polycarp directs them 'to study' (3.2) the letters. The citations in Polycarp's epistle show that this 'collection' probably at least included 1 Corinthians, Galatians, Romans, Ephesians, Philippians and 2 Thessalonians. The Philippians requested Polycarp to send them a collection of the letters of Ignatius (see 13.2); therefore the idea of sharing a collection of letters was certainly not foreign to Polycarp or to the Philippians, and most likely not to Ignatius. Although Polycarp views Paul as more important than Ignatius, he also highly commends the letters of Ignatius (13.2), in which Ignatius himself expresses the same view of Paul, naming him with Peter as an apostle and as a letter writer (Ign. *Rom.* 4.3; Ign. *Eph.* 12.2). Polycarp never hints that Paul's letters were questioned; instead, 'he seems to presuppose that Paul is an acknowledged authority, for his readers as well as for himself'.[61] To Polycarp, then, Paul is not only an authority to whom he can appeal, but also an authority which he expects his readers to accept. This view of Paul and his writings, in particular 2 Thessalonians, is not debated or argued by Polycarp; he assumes it to be true.

4. Polycarp's Use of Christian Tradition

It is universally agreed that Polycarp was a 'traditionalist' who was unimaginative and steeped in Christian tradition,[62] 'quick to sense and repel any "modern" heresy creeping in to contaminate the original faith of the Apostolic Church',[63] unoriginal in his thinking and writing,[64] and non-intellectual.[65]

---

[59] Charles Merritt Nielsen, 'Polycarp, Paul and the Scriptures', *AThR* 47 (1965), pp. 199-216.

[60] Rensberger, 'As the Apostle Teaches', p. 119; Jack Finegan, 'The Original Form of the Pauline Collection', *HTR* 49 (1956), pp.85-86; Grant, *Apostolic Fathers*, vol. 1, p. 57; and Harry Y. Gamble, *The New Testament Canon: Its Making and Meaning* (Philadelphia: Fortress, 1985), p. 41, all think that a Pauline collection existed about this time, whereas Bauer, *Orthodoxy and Heresy*, p. 221, doubts Polycarp had such a collection.

[61] Rensberger, 'As the Apostle Teaches', p. 117.

[62] L. W. Barnard, *Studies in the Apostolic Fathers and their Background* (Oxford: Blackwell, 1966), p. 35.

[63] John Lawson, *A Theological and Historical Introduction to the Apostolic Fathers* (New York: Macmillan, 1961), p. 154.

[64] Vielhauer, *Urchristlichen Literatur*, p. 564.

[65] Cecil John Cadoux, *Ancient Smyrna: A History of the City from the Earliest Times to 324 AD* (Oxford: Blackwell, 1938), p. 346.

Polycarp desired to keep to the teaching which had been given from the beginning, that is, the teaching of the apostles (see 7.2),[66] which was the traditional Christian teaching (see 6.3; 7.2).[67] Therefore, 'any deviation from the norm of "the faith once delivered" provoked him to strong language',[68] for his convictions were absolutely fixed.[69] In short, he was a preserver rather than a pioneer.[70] Consequently, by citing from 2 Thessalonians and attributing it to Paul, he shows not only what he believed at the time of writing, but also what he had been originally taught. His thoughts and beliefs must go back to his teachers.

Polycarp's epistle, then, shows that he was familiar with 2 Thessalonians, that he considered it a letter from Paul, and that he believed that everything he taught was only what he himself had received. Therefore Polycarp's epistle *To the Philippians* witnesses not only to the time when Polycarp wrote, but also to the time when Polycarp himself was taught. At that time the authority of Paul was not debated, but assumed, and 2 Thessalonians was presumed to have come from Paul. In order to establish a *terminus ad quem* for 2 Thessalonians, dates must first be established for Polycarp's life, for his training, and for his epistle.

B. The Life of Polycarp

1. Sources for the Life of Polycarp

In order to date Polycarp's letter *To the Philippians* and determine when he was taught, we must first review the life of Polycarp. A number of documents other than Polycarp's own epistle inform us concerning his life. The earliest of these documents are the letters of Ignatius. Ignatius wrote seven letters as he was being taken to Rome to be executed. On this trip from Antioch to Rome, he stopped in Smyrna, where Polycarp was the bishop. From Smyrna, Ignatius wrote letters to Ephesus, Magnesia, Tralles, and Rome. Later on his journey, while in Troas, he wrote three more letters, to the Philadelphians, to the Smyrnaeans, and to Polycarp in Smyrna. From Troas he traveled to Philippi and then to Rome. Eusebius (*Hist. eccl.* 3.22.1) states that Ignatius was famous during the reign of Trajan (AD 98-117), and in *Chronicon* he places the death of Ignatius in the tenth year of Trajan (AD 108).[71]

Another helpful document, *Martyrdom of Polycarp*, claims to be the work of

---

[66]P. Batiffol, 'Polycarp', *Dictionary of the Apostolic Church* (ed. James Hastings; 2 vols; Edinburgh: T & T Clark, 1918), vol. 2, p. 246.
[67]Rensberger, 'As the Apostle Teaches', p. 339.
[68]Cyril Richardson, *Early Christian Fathers* (LCC; London: SCM, 1953), vol. 1, p. 123.
[69]Grant, 'Polycarp', p.138.
[70]Grant, 'Polycarp', p. 147. Hartog, *Polycarp*, pp. 172, 236, sees Polycarp as a creative thinker in the way he makes use of his traditional materials.
[71]Lake, *Apostolic Fathers*, vol. 2, p. 166. See also Eusebius, *Hist.eccl.* 3.36.1-11.

The Authenticity of 2 Thessalonians

an eyewitness of Polycarp's death, and its historical reliability is generally accepted.[72] It claims to be written within a year of the death of Polycarp (*Mart. Pol.* 18.3) as a letter from the church at Smyrna to the church at Philomelium. It is actually the earliest of the acts of the martyrs,[73] and as early as AD 177 the Christians of Lyons, relating the martyrdoms at Lyons and Vienne, depended on it for several editorial details.[74] Lucian (about AD 165) seems to echo it.[75] One other document, a *Life of Polycarp,* was supposedly written by Pionius, who died as a martyr about AD 250, but this document, probably written in the fourth century, is of little historical value.[76]

In addition to these records we receive some valuable information concerning Polycarp from Irenaeus quoted in Eusebius, in addition to which Eusebius himself gives some further information.[77] From these ancient sources we are able to draw some conclusions about the life of Polycarp.

2. The Date of Polycarp's Death

The first date to determine is that of Polycarp's death. Although Eusebius dated Polycarp's death at about AD 167, this date is not accepted today.[78] In 1867, W. H. Waddington did a study on the date of the death of Polycarp and concluded that he died on 23 February 155, whereas C. H. Turner and Eduard Schwartz later came up with the date of 22 February 156.[79] A date of AD 155 or 156 is almost universally accepted.[80]

---

[72]Schoedel, *Polycarp*, p. 48; Batiffol, 'Polycarp', p. 243.
[73]Lawson, *Apostolic Fathers*, p. 165.
[74]Batiffol, 'Polycarp', p. 243.
[75]Lawson, *Apostolic Fathers,* p. 166.
[76]Cadoux, *Ancient Smyrna*, p. 306; Batiffol, 'Polycarp', p. 243; Lightfoot, *Apostolic Fathers*, part 2, vol. 1, p. 565.
[77]See *Hist. eccl.* 3.28.6; 3.36–39; 4.14.1; 5.20.5-7; 5.24.16.
[78]Kirsopp Lake, in Eusebius, *The Ecclesiastical History* (LCL; 2 vols; London: Heinemann, 1926-1932), vol. 1, p. 339.
[79]C. Richardson, *Early Christian Fathers*, vol. 1, p. 144.
[80]Lawson, *Apostolic Fathers*, p. 153. Campenhausen, *Formation ,* p. 178, would date the martyrdom at about the end of the sixth decade of the second century. This late date raises more problems than it solves. It would make Polycarp the bishop in Smyrna at the age of about 20, and it would make the echoes of *Mart. Pol* in other literature concurrent with the actual martyrdom. In addition, the reminiscences of Irenaeus would have to be ignored because he would not be a boy as he says he was when Polycarp was aged. Too much information must be discarded to make this theory plausible. For a full critique see Peter Meinhold, 'Polykarpos', *PW* 21 (ed. Konrat Ziegler; Stuttgart: Druckenmüller, 1952), pp. 1676-78. Joachim Jeremias, *Infant Baptism in the First Four Centuries* (London: SCM, 1960), pp.60-62, accepts AD 167-168 as the date for the death of Polycarp. He believes 155-156 is too early for

External Attestation to 2 Thessalonians

The date of Polycarp's death is important because combined with Polycarp's words at the time of his martyrdom it aids us in establishing his approximate date of birth. When the proconsul tried to persuade Polycarp to recant and revile Christ, Polycarp replied, 'I have served him eighty-six years and in no way has he dealt unjustly with me; so how can I blaspheme my king who saved me?'[81] Some have suggested that this means that Polycarp was eighty-six years old at the time of his death; others believe that he was converted eighty-six years before his death.[82] Either way, he is a very old man. If the eighty-six refers to his entire life, then Polycarp was born about AD 69 or 70, a date which seems to fit well with all the information we have about Polycarp. Consequently, when Ignatius came through Smyrna (in AD 108), Polycarp would have been at least thirty-eight years old.

We do not know exactly when Polycarp became bishop in Smyrna. Irenaeus says that Polycarp was instructed and appointed by the apostles, and Eusebius, who also refers to him as a companion of the apostles, says that he 'flourished in Asia' at about the time Clement died and that the works of Ignatius and Polycarp were well known.[83] Tertullian, in his *Prescription Against Heretics*, says that Polycarp was placed in Smyrna by the Apostle John (*Praescr.* 32.2). If Polycarp was placed in office by any of the apostles, it must have been near the end of the first century. Whether or not Polycarp actually knew John is debated, but most likely he became bishop near the end of the first century or the beginning of the second.

C. *The Integrity of Polycarp's Epistle* To the Philippians

The authenticity of Polycarp's epistle and of the seven genuine epistles of Ignatius is no longer greatly debated. The work of Lightfoot and Zahn, which shows the extensive external evidence and demonstrates the consistency of the

---

a visit to Anicetus (which Irenaeus records, and Jeremias accepts), who according to Eusebius became Bishop of Rome in 157. However, most scholars would have Anicetus begin his episcopacy in Rome about 154. Jeremias also must ignore the echoes of *Mart. Pol.* in other writings, which have already been mentioned. His date also makes Polycarp extremely young to be a bishop in Smyrna when Ignatius passed through, let alone to have been installed by one of the apostles, as claimed by Eusebius. Jeremias excludes 177 as a possible date because it is too close to the time of Irenaeus, when Polycarp's successors are in place. See also Harrison, *Polycarp's Two Epistles*, pp. 261-89, and Batiffol, 'Polycarp', p. 243. Hartog, *Polycarp*, p. 30, suggests a date of 161.

[81] *Mart. Pol.* 9.3, as quoted in Schoedel, *Polycarp*, p. 65.
[82] Schoedel, *Polycarp*, p. 65, discusses this information. Hartog, *Polycarp*, p. 32, mentions the 'Harris fragments' that say Polycarp died at age 104.
[83] *Hist. eccl.* 4.14.3; 3.34.1-36.1; 3.39.1 (Lake, LCL).

contents of the epistles with the state of the church during the reign of Trajan, has generally been accepted.[84] Irenaeus clearly states that an epistle of Polycarp was written to the Philippians,[85] and Eusebius quotes directly from the Greek epistle.[86] Therefore it is almost certain that Eusebius had Polycarp's epistle in the same form as we do today, but in Greek rather than Latin.[87] Because Polycarp requests details about Ignatius (13.2), his letter usually has been dated to the same year as the death of Ignatius, between AD 108 and 110.[88] However, primarily because of the work of P. N. Harrison, not only has this date for the letter been challenged, but the integrity of the letter has been as well.

In 1936, P. N. Harrison published *Polycarp's Two Epistles to the Philippians*, in which he makes a direct challenge to the traditional dating of Polycarp's letter *To the Philippians*. Many today accept his theory.[89] While acknowledging his debt to Lightfoot in proving the authenticity of the epistle, Harrison also says that Lightfoot's work has one fatal flaw: the epistle we now possess is not originally one letter, but two separate letters from Polycarp written twenty or more years apart. These two separate letters, he claims, were fused together at an early date, probably soon after the death of Polycarp, because they were written on the same papyrus.[90] Harrison refers to chs 1-12 of Polycarp's letter as the 'crisis letter' and sees chs 13-14 as a cover letter for the epistles of Ignatius. He would date only the cover letter (also called the 'urgent letter') at the death of Ignatius (he says about AD 115), while the longer epistle (chs 1-12) he dates at about AD 135 because he identifies the arch-heretic of ch. 7 with Marcion before his contact with Cerdo. This theory directly affects the attestation of Polycarp to 2 Thessalonians. Both citations of 2 Thessalonians are found within the 'crisis' letter, which Harrison dates about AD 135. If Harrison's theory is true, Polycarp's use of 2 Thessalonians allows for a late dating of 2 Thessalonians. If his theory is false, however, then Polycarp's attestation makes a late date for 2 Thessalonians much more difficult.

Harrison's argument rests on two important points: a supposed contradiction between chs 9 and 13 (that is, in ch. 9 Polycarp views Ignatius as having been

---

[84] Schoedel, *Polycarp*, p. 4. See also Harrison, *Polycarp's Two Epistles*, pp. 43-53.
[85] *Haer.* 3.3.
[86] *Hist. eccl.* 3.36.13-15.
[87] Harrison, *Polycarp's Two Epistles*, p. 26.
[88] Lake, *Apostolic Fathers*, vol. 1, p. 166, says, 'In his chronicon Eusebius fixes the date of his martyrdom in Rome in the tenth year of Trajan, i.e. 108 AD'
[89] von Campenhausen, *Formation*, p. 178; Johannes Quasten, *Patrology* (Utrecht-Antwerp: Spectrum, 1966), vol 1, p. 80; Vielhauer, *Urchristlichen Literatur*, p. 558, who also lists the independent studies of J. A. Fischer and J. A. Kleist, both of whom slightly modified Harrison's theory; Barnard, *Studies in the Apostolic Fathers*, p. 31, who also lists Burkitt and Streeter.
[90] Harrison, *Polycarp's Two Epistles*, pp. 15, 19.

dead for a very long time, whereas in ch. 13 he leaves open the possibility that Ignatius is not yet dead[91]) and the absolute identification of the arch-heretic with Marcion. In the first he overstates his case, and in the second he is simply wrong. But because he makes a cumulative case,[92] it is necessary to examine each of his arguments. This critique will examine six areas focused on by Harrison: (1) the plausibility of two letters; (2) the contradiction between chs 9 and 13; (3) the general character of the two letters; (4) the status of Polycarp; (5) the use of quotes and sources; and (6) the identification of the arch-heretic.

1. The Plausibility of Two Letters

Harrison first introduces the plausibility of his case by citing other examples of separate documents being fused together. Within the New Testament he lists 2 Corinthians, the Pastoral Epistles, Romans 16, Philippians, and 1 Peter all as examples of possible composite letters. Other examples include *Diognetus,* Tertullian's *Prescription against Heretics,* Ignatius's letter to Polycarp, and a number of examples from papyri. In fact, this fusion of documents is actually known to have occurred with Polycarp's *To the Philippians* and *Barnabas,* for we have no Greek manuscript of Polycarp's entire letter; rather, our Greek manuscripts of Polycarp's letter go only through the end of ch. 9, which is followed immediately by *Barnabas* beginning at 5.7.[93] His examples of fused letters in the New Testament, however, are far from being universally accepted and hardly serve to prove that this type of situation occurred regularly. Certainly his best example is the text of Polycarp's own letter, yet this does not support his case, either, for we know that Polycarp's epistle and *Barnabas* have been merged only because we also have documents of each epistle by itself and they are attested elsewhere as individual documents.

Some have thought that because others have come to conclusions similar to Harrison's, Harrison's case is strengthened. Vielhauer says that J. A. Fischer and J. A. Kleist have both come to a similar conclusion,[94] the only major difference being that they both see ch. 14 as part of the longer letter and ch. 13 alone as the cover letter. But this greatly complicates Harrison's theory that the fusion of the two letters arose out of two documents being written on one piece of papyrus and then naively being dealt with as one letter. If ch. 14 was originally joined to chs 1-12, then someone must have intentionally woven the two documents together. This had to have happened very early because Irenaeus, who as a boy was taught by Polycarp, knew of only one letter to the

---

[91]Harrison, *Polycarp's Two Epistles.* p. 14.
[92]Harrison, *Polycarp's Two Epistles.* p. 75.
[93]Harrison, *Polycarp's Two Epistles*, pp. 20-25. The last three words of Pol. *Phil.* 9.2 are omitted [τοῦ θεοῦ ἀναστάντα] and are replaced with τὸν λαὸν τὸν καινόν from *Barn.* 5.7, followed by the rest of *Barnabas.*
[94]Vielhauer, *Urchristlichen Literatur*, p. 558.

The Authenticity of 2 Thessalonians

Philippians, and Eusebius quotes chs 9 and 13 as from the same letter.[95] If Harrison's reconstruction of the situation which joined the two letters really did occur, then one must ask what happened to the salutation on the urgent letter (ch 13). If two letters were simply fused together, then all the parts of both letters should still be present, but the letter we have appears as one letter. The letter has only one salutation and one conclusion, and the list of topics Polycarp discusses easily move from one to the next with no obvious interruptions.[96] In order for this theory to have happened, more editorial revision would have been required at some later time. Furthermore, if the fusion was intentional, which must certainly be the case if the two letters are woven together, why did it happen so early? What was the motive? We know that Polycarp wrote other letters which have been lost;[97] why not preserve both of his letters to the Philippians? We have a collection of the epistles of Ignatius and even a number of much later epistles attributed to Ignatius; if Polycarp had two authentic epistles, why should someone soon after his death desire to weave them together? These questions must be answered for this theory to be plausible.

2. The Contradiction between Chapters 9 and 13

The most significant argument against the integrity of Polycarp's letter made by Harrison and his supporters concerns the timing of the death of Ignatius. Harrison believes that as the letter presently stands, chs 9 and 13 directly contradict each other concerning the death of Ignatius. Chapter 9.1-2 appears to imply that Ignatius is already dead:

> endure with all the endurance which you also saw before your eyes, not only in the blessed Ignatius, and Zosimus, and Rufus, but also in others among yourselves, and in Paul himself, and in the other Apostles; being persuaded that all of these 'ran not in vain', but in faith and righteousness, and that they are with the Lord in the 'place which is their due' with whom they also suffered.[98]

---

[95]Eusebius, *Hist. eccl.* 4.14.8; 3.36.13-15.
[96]Schoedel's (*Polycarp*, p. 6) brief outline summarizes the letter:
Salutation (Inscription)

I. Grounds for rejoicing (1.1-3)	VIII. The martyrs (9.1-2)
II. Service to God (2.1-3)	IX. The brotherhood (10.1-3)
III. Righteousness according to Paul (3.1-3)	X. Love of money: Valens (11.1-4a)
IV. Table of duties I (4.1-3)	XI. Sobriety 'in this thing' (11.4b—12.1)
V. Table of duties II (5.1–6.3)	XII. The prayer (12.2-3)
VI. Docetism (7.1-2)	XIII. The letters of Ignatius (13.1-2)
VII. The imitation of Christ (8.1-2)	XIV. Conclusion (14.1)

[97]Eusebius, *Hist. eccl.* 5.20.8
[98]Pol. *Phil.* 9.1-2 (Lake, *Apostolic Fathers*, LCL).

The end of ch. 13, however, reads, 'Let us know anything further which you have heard about Ignatius himself and those who are with him.'[99] Certainly at first reading there does appear to be a discrepancy as Harrison suggests.

Harrison considers the possible solutions to this problem by Pearson, Wake, and Lightfoot to be weak. Pearson suggests that although Polycarp knew that Ignatius had died, he did not as yet have the full details. Wake and Lightfoot suggest that Polycarp supposed Ignatius to be dead but did not have this fully confirmed.[100] Harrison, however, believes that Ignatius clearly was alive when Polycarp wrote ch. 13,[101] but that in chs 1-12 (and especially in ch. 9), Polycarp is looking back to a glory period in the history of the Philippian church, back to the death of Ignatius, which had occurred many years before.[102] Harrison applies all that is said about Paul and the other apostles in 9.1 to Ignatius, Zosimus and Rufus because 9.2 says 'all of these "ran not in vain"'. Schoedel, however, lists three reasons why these words should not be pressed too far. (1) Although 9.1 says the readers had seen Ignatius, Zosimus, and Rufus, they almost certainly had not seen Paul and the other apostles. Therefore since not everything said about Ignatius, Zosimus, and Rufus applies to Paul and the other apostles, neither must everything appropriate to Paul and the other apostles have direct reference to Ignatius, Zosimus, and Rufus. In fact, since Polycarp says the Philippians saw Ignatius with their own eyes, ch. 9 would seem to imply that Ignatius had passed through relatively recently. (2) 'The construction "not only . . . but also" almost always puts much greater emphasis on the second member of the sentence (cf. Matt. 21:21; John 5:18; Acts 19:27; 26:29; 27:10; Rom. 1:32), and when it is followed by another clause, as here, the latter usually has reference primarily, if not exclusively, to the second member (cf. *4 Macc.* 2.4-5; John 17:20; Rom. 4:16-17; Phil. 2:27)'.[103] This would mean that the phrase that says 'they are with the Lord' (Pol. *Phil.* 9.2) would apply most directly to 'the others among yourselves' and Paul and 'the other Apostles', and not necessarily to Ignatius, Zosimus, and Rufus. (3) 'The allusion to *1 Clement* 5.4 ("in their due place"), which is about Paul and Peter . . . increases the likelihood that the reference to having gone to "their due place" applies only to those mentioned at the end of verse 1', that is, Paul and the other apostles.[104] Therefore Lightfoot's and Wake's solution fits the information much more naturally than Harrison's.[105]

---

[99] Pol. *Phil.* 13.2 (Lake, *Apostolic Fathers*, LCL).
[100] Harrison, *Polycarp's Two Epistles*, pp.35-37.
[101] Harrison, *Polycarp's Two Epistles*, p. 120.
[102] Harrison, *Polycarp's Two Epistles*, pp.133-61.
[103] Schoedel, *Polycarp*, p. 29.
[104] Schoedel, *Polycarp*, p. 29.
[105] See also Stephen Liberty, 'Review of P. N. Harrison's *Polycarp's Two Epistles to the Philippians*', *CQR* 247 (1937), p. 142; and Batiffol, 'Polycarp', p. 245.

Harrison stresses the idea that not only is Ignatius dead, but he has been dead for a long time. He says that it would be strange for Polycarp to put off until ch. 13 to talk about Ignatius if he had so recently passed through; in fact, it would show Polycarp to be heartless.[106] Harrison asserts that the words in 1.1, which describe how the Philippians 'helped on their way, as opportunity was given you, those who were bound in chains', do not have to be recent.[107] But Harrison's reasoning is so unlikely, for it would seem incredible if this reference in 1.1 is to something that happened more than twenty years before,[108] and further, it certainly shows that Polycarp did have Ignatius in his thoughts right from the beginning of the letter. Two writers who think that Harrison is correct in dividing Polycarp's epistle are C. J. Cadoux and L. W. Barnard, both of whom point out that this reference in ch. 1 most naturally refers to a relatively recent time. Consequently they date Polycarp's 'second' letter within just a couple of years of his 'first' letter.[109]

Harrison emphasizes that Ignatius, Zosimus, and Rufus are referred to as blessed ones and so have been dead for a long time.[110] However, just because Ignatius and his companions are referred to as blessed does not mean they necessarily have been dead a long time. It is true that Polycarp describes Paul as 'blessed' (Pol. *Phil.* 3.2; 11.3), but the word 'blessed' was also used at this time for those Christians who were alive (see *1 Clem.* 40.4; 48.4; 50.5-6; 56.6-16; Ign. *Phld.* 10.2). Polycarp himself certainly expects his readers to apply to themselves the beatitude of Jesus recorded in 2.3. Ignatius addresses Polycarp himself as 'most blessed' (Ign. *Pol.* 7.2). Therefore, although Polycarp desires his readers to follow the example of the blessed Ignatius, it does not necessarily imply that he has been dead a long time.

Chapter 13 clearly was written fairly soon after Ignatius passed through Philippi, for in it Polycarp refers to the letters he received from both the Philippians and from Ignatius himself—letters which he has not yet answered. He closes, 'Let us know anything further which you have heard about Ignatius himself and those who are with him.' The debated phrase 'those who are with him' (*qui cum eo sunt*) seems to imply that Ignatius and his companions are still alive. Lightfoot, however, believes that the Greek original would have been 'concerning the ones with him' [περὶ τῶν σὺν αὐτῷ], containing no verb at all and consequently being temporally neutral. In that case the original of ch. 13

---

[106]Harrison, *Polycarp's Two Epistles*, p. 146.

[107]Harrison, *Polycarp's Two Epistles*, p. 156.

[108]Claude Jenkins, 'Review of P. N. Harrison's *Polycarp's Two Epistles to the Philippians*', *Theology* 35 (1937), p. 370.

[109]C. J. Cadoux, 'Review of P. N. Harrison's *Polycarp's Two Epistles to the Philippians*', *JTS* 38 (1937), pp. 268, 270; Barnard, *Studies in the Apostolic Fathers*, p. 33.

[110]Harrison, *Polycarp's Two Epistles*, pp. 149, 151.

would not contradict ch. 9 at all. Lightfoot goes on to show that this blunder by the Latin translator also occurs in 9.1. Harrison admits that Lightfoot has found an incident parallel to what he conjectures for ch. 13, but he does not concede that because it has happened once it has happened a second time. However, even Harrison thinks that Lightfoot's translation is fairly probable.[111] An examination of the verbs in the parallel Latin and Greek sections shows that wherever the verb 'to be' must be supplied to the Greek because there is no verb present, the Latin translator consistently inserts the present tense of 'to be' in Latin (see 1.1; 5.2, 3; 7.2; and 9.1). This makes the probability of Lightfoot's retranslation even more plausible. If this last phrase in ch. 13 is temporally neutral, as seems most likely, then ch. 13 contains nothing to show conclusively that Ignatius is alive. Polycarp is simply asking for information about the final days of Ignatius, a respected bishop and friend, and the party which was with him.[112]

Barnard believes that Harrison's case concerning a contradiction between chs 9 and 13 can be strengthened by considering the quote of Polycarp's letter found in Eusebius. There Eusebius introduces ch. 9 of Polycarp's letter by saying, 'Polycarp, too, mentions these same things in the letter to the Philippians bearing his name.' Then Eusebius links this to ch. 13 with 'and he continues later', but he omits the debated last phrase from ch. 13.[113] Barnard claims that Eusebius saw the contradiction at the end of ch. 13 and intentionally deleted the last sentence. However, a reading of this portion of Eusebius gives no sense of an unnatural break in the letter of Polycarp, but rather, Eusebius concludes simply and naturally with Polycarp's statement expressing the value of Ignatius's letters: 'for they contain faith, patience, and all the edification which pertains to our Lord'.[114] Eusebius is concerned at this point in his history to tell what he knows about Ignatius, not to tell what Polycarp does not know. Immediately before introducing Polycarp's letter, Eusebius mentions that Irenaeus knew of Ignatius's martyrdom, and immediately following the quote from ch. 13, Eusebius says, 'Such is the story concerning Ignatius'.[115] This, then, is a logical place to end the quotation from Polycarp.

Eusebius is very careful in his handling of the documents he receives, as can be seen in his categorization of the books in the New Testament and in the way he recognizes *1 Clement* but objects to *2 Clement*.[116] To say that Eusebius saw a problem with the authenticity or integrity of a letter but attempted to hide or

---

[111]Harrison, *Polycarp's Two Epistles*, pp. 137-38.
[112]Hartog, *Polycarp*, pp. 167-68, points out that *Mart. Pol.* 20 records just such a request for more information, this time about the death of Polycarp.
[113]Eusebius, *Hist. eccl.* 3.36.14-15 (Lake, LCL).
[114]Eusebius, *Hist. eccl.* 3.36.15 (Lake, LCL).
[115]Eusebius, *Hist. eccl.* 3.36.15 (Lake, LCL).
[116]See Eusebius, *Hist. eccl.* 3.25.1-7; 3.16.1; 3.38.4-5.

overlook the problem is totally inconsistent with the whole manner of Eusebius. The way Eusebius combines chs 9 and 13 actually shows that he viewed Polycarp's epistle as one epistle and almost certainly saw no contradiction between the chapters he was copying. Barnard incorrectly uses this silence on the part of Eusebius to support Harrison's argument for two epistles.

Therefore, all the arguments concerning the so-called contradiction between chs 9 and 13 are focused ultimately on the translation of the last sentence in ch. 13, but it is impossible to state confidently with Harrison that Polycarp certainly *knew* that Ignatius was still alive when he wrote ch. 13. Harrison himself admits that Lightfoot's retranslation is likely. Therefore the only way Harrison can hold his theory is to look beyond the explicit statements in Polycarp's epistle.

3. The General Character of the Two Letters

Harrison contrasts the general character of the two supposed letters. He characterizes chs 1-12 as a 'crisis' letter answering a request for help from the church at Philippi, while chs 13-14 comprise merely a hasty 'urgent' cover letter to accompany the Ignatian epistles.[117] According to Harrison, Polycarp's well-thought-out response in chs 1-12 to the grave problems at Philippi contrasts sharply with ch. 13, the urgent letter, in which he believes the recent coming of internal peace and the problem of the next bishop to be elected is at stake. This situation is urgent because Ignatius's whole life's work is at stake. According to Harrison, this urgency is also seen in that Ignatius is possibly still alive.[118] By computing the time it would take for Ignatius to travel from Philippi to Rome, Harrison attempts to show that Ignatius is possibly still alive when Polycarp writes the urgent letter. He further sees the urgency stressed in the words of Ignatius's letter to Polycarp.

The problem with Harrison's generalizations about the letters is that they just do not fit the contents of the letters. When one reads the so-called crisis letter (chs 1-12), the letter does not seem to be dealing with the worst crisis ever.[119] Rather, it is dealing with two explicit problems. The first is the problem with Valens and his wife and their misuse of money, which seems already to have been dealt with, and Polycarp now recommends they be dealt with in compassion and mercy (Pol. *Phil.* 11; see also 6:1). The other explicit problem concerns those who could bring in docetic teachings (Pol. *Phil.* 7). Having warned about these false teachers, he reminds his readers 'to return to the word that was delivered to us in the beginning' (Pol. *Phil.* 7.2). The rest of this letter (chs 1-12) consists of primarily general exhortations about living in righteousness (Pol. *Phil.* 2.3; 3.1, 3; 4.1, 6; 5.2; 8.1; 9.1). This portion of Polycarp's letter (chs 1-12) gives no sense of such a grave crisis.

---

[117]Harrison, *Polycarp's Two Epistles*, pp. 15-19.
[118]Harrison, *Polycarp's Two Epistles*, p. 14.
[119]Harrison, *Polycarp's Two Epistles*, p. 166.

Harrison spends much more space arguing his case concerning the urgent letter (chs 13-14). He believes that much of the urgency for this cover letter can be seen in Ignatius's letter to Polycarp.[120] Yet when the topics are examined in the eight short chapters written to Polycarp, they give a series of very general exhortations: ch. 1—press on in your office as a bishop; ch. 2—disciple the believers; ch. 3—be diligent and patient opposing false teaching; ch. 4—treat widows and slaves appropriately and meet often with the church; ch. 5—flee from wicked practices and preach against these practices; ch. 6—pay attention to your bishop and be patient and gentle; ch. 7—send a trusted delegate to Antioch; and ch. 8—write to the churches. When these topics are read, this appears to be a general pastoral letter regarding the final priorities that Ignatius wants to stress to Polycarp. These topics are important, but they stress continued faithfulness, not immediacy. When Ignatius finally gets to his request about a letter he simply says, 'You ought, O Polycarp, most blessed of God, to summon a godly council, and elect someone who is very dear to you and is zealous, who can be called God's courier; appoint him to go to Syria to glorify your zealous love to the glory of God'.[121] Polycarp's response to this request likewise lacks a sense of urgency, for he says

Both you and Ignatius wrote to me that if anyone was going to Syria he should also take your letters. I will do this if I have a convenient opportunity, either myself or the man whom I am sending as a representative for you and me. We send you, as you asked, the letters of Ignatius, which were sent to us by him, and others which we had by us. These are subjoined to this letter, and you will be able to benefit greatly from them. For they contain faith, patience, and all the edification which pertains to our Lord. Let us know anything further which you have heard about Ignatius himself and those who are with him.[122]

The only word in this response which refers to time is the word 'convenient' [εὔθετος], and it is defined as: 'well-placed, fit, suitable, usable, convenient,' and when linked with 'opportunity' [καιρός], it means a 'convenient time or opportunity'.[123] Thus Polycarp appears to interpret the letters from the Philippians and Ignatius as making a request, not an urgent demand. In referring to their letters he says, 'if anyone is going to Syria'. This hardly sounds like Polycarp must rush about to complete his task.

Harrison believes that Ignatius's request to Polycarp is being made because the church at Antioch is currently at peace (Ign. Pol. 7.1), and in order to keep this tenuous peace, Ignatius urgently desires help from the other churches. He stresses that the verb 'to keep peace, reconcile' [εἰρηνεύω] always has to do

---

[120]Harrison, *Polycarp's Two Epistles*, p. 93.
[121]Ign. *Pol.* 7.1-2 (Lake, *Apostolic Fathers*, LCL).
[122]Pol. *Phil.* 13.1-2 (Lake, *Apostolic Fathers*, LCL).
[123]Arndt and Gingrich, *Lexicon,* 'εὔθετος', p. 320.

with internal peace. From this one word he draws the conclusion there must have been an internal problem at the church in Antioch. Harrison overstates his position on the definition of this word. It is true that most of the seventeen references to this verb in the Apostolic Fathers refer to internal peace, for the contexts of most of these passages are abundantly clear. For example, in The Shepherd of Hermas, a number of times the author uses the phrase 'at peace among yourselves'.[124] Being 'at peace' is also explicit when it is contrasted to strife and quarrels,[125] but these quarrels are not necessarily all internal (within the church) quarrels, for the goal is 'well-being at all times with all men' (Herm. Mand. 2.3). It would appear that 'all men' here would include not only those in the church, but also those outside the church. In *1 Clement* 56.6-15, Clement quotes at length from Job 5:17-26, twice using the verb 'at peace': 'Thou shalt laugh at the unrighteous and wicked, and thou shalt not be afraid of wild beasts; for wild beasts shall be at peace with thee. Then thou shalt know that thy house shall have peace.'[126] In this passage, the verb 'at peace' clearly does not refer only to internal strife; God promises to deliver the 'blessed man' from all manner of evils, and thus 'at peace' clearly can mean the absence of external trouble. In *4 Maccabees* 18.4, the verb 'to live in peace' [εἰρηνεύειν] is used of peace after war. Thus this verb does not always mean internal peace. The problem with the references in Ignatius's epistles is that they are rather vague. Never do they say 'among yourselves'; rather, they simply describe the present state of affairs in Antioch.[127] Furthermore, when Ignatius writes to the Smyrnaeans and Philadelphians about sending a representative to Antioch, he says it is in order to rejoice with [συγχαίρω] them. This is all the evidence we have of the problem at Antioch. The problem there may have been internal or it may refer to the persecution which led to Ignatius's arrest, but either way the churches are to rejoice with the church at Antioch. There is no sense of urgency.

Harrison uses this so-called urgency to strengthen his argument that, in the urgent letter, Polycarp thinks Ignatius is alive by showing it would have taken a longer time for Ignatius to travel from Philippi to Rome than for the Philippians to send a letter to Polycarp and receive a response. Harrison believes the Philippians would have written immediately to Polycarp because it was such an urgent matter, and because the distance from Philippi to Smyrna (469 miles by land) is significantly less than the distance from Philippi to Rome (830 miles, at least a forty-five-day journey), he concludes that Ignatius could still have been alive when Polycarp wrote the urgent letter. However, this scenario is completely dependent on the urgency which Harrison has postulated; as we

---

[124]Herm. *Vis.* 3.12.3; 3.9.2; 3.9.10; 3.6.3; and Herm. *Sim.* 8.7.2 (Lake, *Apostolic Fathers*, LCL).
[125]Herm. *Man.* 2.3; *Barn.*19.12; *Did.* 4.3.
[126]*1 Clem.* 56.11-13 (Lake, *Apostolic Fathers*, LCL).
[127]Ign. *Pol.* 7.1; Ign. *Smyrn.* 11.2; Ign. *Phld.* 10.1.

have seen, it is not clearly in the text of the letter. All of this travel and letter-writing could have taken longer, and it certainly would have taken at least several months to get word back from Rome that Ignatius had died. Based on what Polycarp actually says, it is most likely that he simply wants more information on Ignatius if the Philippians have it. Thus again Harrison has overstated some of the perceived differences between these two sections of the letter from Polycarp.

4. The Status of Polycarp

Another factor which Harrison believes displays the distinction between chs 1-12 and ch. 13 concerns the status of Polycarp. Harrison believes that in order for the Philippians to seek help from Polycarp in the 'crisis' letter, he must be an elderly, respected bishop at the peak of his reputation (between AD 130 and 140). He claims it is highly unlikely that the Philippians would turn to Polycarp in about AD 115, when he was so young (about 45), especially after the elderly and experienced Ignatius had just been with them.[128] He describes the tone of Ignatius's letter to Polycarp as 'schoolmasterly',[129] implying that Ignatius emphasizes Polycarp's youth. Thus Harrison concludes that the status of Polycarp at the times the two letters were written differs: in the 'crisis' letter he is a respected bishop, but in the 'urgent' letter he is still young and inexperienced.

Whether or not Ignatius is addressing Polycarp as a young or immature bishop is difficult to determine because the only letter written directly to any bishop by Ignatius is his letter to Polycarp. Ignatius did, however, make reference to the other bishops in his letters. In his letter *To the Magnesians* he specifically mentions that their bishop, Damas, is young (Ign. *Magn.* 3.1), but he also places great stress on obeying and following the bishop (chs 3-7). In his letter *To the Smyrnaeans*, to Polycarp's own church, he never refers to Polycarp as young or immature; in fact, all the directives concerning following the bishop are essentially identical to those in his other letters.[130] Ignatius does give many directions to Polycarp in his letter, but this does not mean he did not view Polycarp with a great deal of respect (see Ign. *Smyrn.* 12.2). Because Ignatius was quite elderly by this time, probably having become a bishop in AD 69,[131] it would have been quite appropriate for him to give advice to a younger bishop while at the same time respecting this bishop and encouraging a congregation with a problem to seek his counsel. A bishop about the age of forty who had been bishop for some ten years and knew not only Ignatius but also, possibly,

---

[128]Harrison, *Polycarp's Two Epistles*, p. 171.
[129]Harrison, *Polycarp's Two Epistles*, p. 65.
[130]Compare Ign. *Smyrn.* 8.1–9.1 with his comments on other bishops in Ign. *Eph.* 4.1; Ign. *Magn.* 3.1–7.1; Ign. *Trall.* 2.1; Ign. *Phld.* 3.2; 4.1; 7.1-2.
[131]Lawson, *Apostolic Fathers*, p. 103; Vielhauer, *Urchristlichen Literatur*, p. 543.

the apostle John, would still be young enough to welcome instruction from the elderly Ignatius and yet old enough to advise a congregation on an important matter. Ignatius most likely knew Polycarp better than he knew any of the other bishops in that region because Ignatius had visited in Smyrna. Polycarp is well enough known for Ignatius to include his name at the conclusion of some of his other letters (Ign. *Eph.* 21.1; Ign. *Magn.* 15.1). Consequently, Harrison's conclusion—that the Philippians would not have solicited Polycarp's counsel in the midst of their 'crisis' (which, we have seen, was not much of one) and that chs 1-12 must therefore have been written later in his life—is unfounded.

5. Use of Quotes and Sources

Harrison contrasts the numerous allusions and quotes found in chs 1-12 with ch. 13, where there are no echoes or quotes of the letters of Ignatius or the New Testament.[132] He believes that Polycarp's use of the New Testament in chs 1-12 is too advanced for the year AD 115, but if this portion of the letter were dated around AD 135, this use of the New Testament would be consistent with other literature. Furthermore, he finds the allusions to the Ignatian epistles to be far too numerous in the 'crisis' letter (chs 1-12) to have occurred so soon after those epistles of Ignatius were written.[133] He reasons that these allusions indicate that over the years Polycarp has had time to read and re-read these letters, and they are now part of his way of thinking.[134] The Christians at Philippi would also have read and re-read the letters and would also recognize these allusions. Therefore Harrison sees this as supporting his conclusion that chs 1-12 were written at a later time than chs 13-14.

Again Harrison's case is not as clear as he suggests. While it is true that there is a general absence of quotes in ch. 13 of Polycarp's letter, many commentators have pointed out that the subject matter of this chapter is not appropriate for quotes from either the New Testament or Ignatius.[135] Furthermore, if ch. 13 is considered by itself (without the concluding words of ch. 14), one can find a number of sections within the rest of the letter that are of approximately the same length as ch. 13 but do not contain a clear citation from the New Testament (see Inscription–1.2; 3.1-2; 8.2–9.1; 10.3–11.1). If every section that lacked quotes were considered to be later because of a lack of quotes, there would be little left of the letter. In reference to the quotes from Ignatius, Schoedel says, 'Chapters 13-14, as Harrison also grants, have a number of echoes of Ignatian language, and the echoes in chapters 1-12 are in no case so

---

[132]Harrison, *Polycarp's Two Epistles*, pp. 7, 132.

[133]Harrison, *Polycarp's Two Epistles*, pp. 6, 8.

[134]Harrison, *Polycarp's Two Epistles*, p. 132.

[135]Barnard, *Studies in the Apostolic Fathers*, p. 35; Grant, *Apostolic Fathers*, p. 65; Schoedel, *Polycarp*, p. 39.

clear that we felt constrained to enclose them in quotation marks'.[136] An understanding of Polycarp's letter certainly does not depend upon having already read Ignatius's letters exhaustively.

Since Polycarp himself makes it clear that he regards Paul above Ignatius, it is unlikely that he would have spent the amount of time meditating on the letters of Ignatius that he did on Paul's letters. He most likely echoes the letters of Ignatius because he has just copied them and they are very much in the forefront of his thoughts. Therefore the best explanation for the echoes of Ignatius in chs 1-12 would be a recent exposure to the letters of Ignatius, as would have been required if he had recently recopied them for the Philippians.

6. The Identification of the Arch-Heretic

The last major argument for Harrison's thesis concerns the identification of the arch-heretic ('the first-born of Satan') in ch. 7 of Polycarp's letter. According to Harrison, this heretic is unquestionably Marcion before he was influenced in Rome by the heretic Cerdo. He makes this identification because Irenaeus, in his third book against heresies, which is quoted by Eusebius, says, 'And Polycarp himself when Marcion once met him and said, "Recognize us", answered, "I do, I recognize the first-born of Satan."'[137] Harrison says that Polycarp had never used this phrase about anyone else or even applied it to anyone else.[138] This is the only information Harrison can use in any absolute sense for dating Polycarp's so-called later letter. The problem with this conclusion is that it does not fit Polycarp's actual words, the error Polycarp is correcting, or the external evidence concerning this phrase. Polycarp describes the heresy about which he is concerned in 7.1:

> For everyone 'who does not confess that Jesus Christ has come in the flesh is anti-Christ'; and whoever does not acknowledge the testimony of the cross 'is of the devil': and whoever twists the sayings of the Lord to suit his own sinful desires and claims that there is neither resurrection nor judgment,—well, that person is the first-born of Satan.[139]

The errors presented by Polycarp do not describe Marcion's theology —no dualism, no doctrine of two gods, no rejection of the Old Testament[140]—but rather, the list of errors in ch. 7 could be applied to many docetists. These are

---

[136]Schoedel, *Polycarp*, p. 38.
[137]*Hist. eccl.* 4.24.7 (Lake, LCL).
[138]Harrison, *Polycarp's Two Epistles*, p. 199.
[139]Michael W. Holmes, ed, *The Apostolic Fathers: Greek Texts and English Translations* (Grand Rapids: Baker, 1992), pp. 213-15.
[140]For critiques of Harrison's explanations of the terms, see Barnard, *Studies in the Apostolic Fathers*, pp. 34-35; Rensberger, 'As the Apostle Teaches', pp. 108-11; Schoedel, *Polycarp*, pp. 24-25; Hartog, *Polycarp*, pp. 96-97.

also the same errors with which Ignatius is concerned in his epistles.[141] Harrison tries to get around this by saying that the particular errors we associate so much with Marcion should actually be attributed to Cerdo[142] and that the other described errors are misunderstood by the commentators.[143] However, this functionally ignores what Polycarp says about the errors, and Harrison can only speculate what Marcion believed before his contact with Cerdo.

A second problem with Harrison's theory that these words refer specifically to Marcion is that in 7.1 each of the three titles given to the heretics are explicitly introduced with the statement 'whoever' [ὃς ἄν]. Thus Polycarp intended this to be applied to anyone who fit this description.

A third difficulty with Harrison's statement that 'Satan's first-born' is unique to Polycarp is that this title can be found in other religious literature. Nils Dahl points out that 'Satan's first-born' comes from the Talmud.[144] The phrase is also found in the longer recension of Ignatius's letter *To the Trallians*, chs 10-11. As well, in Acts 13:10, Paul calls the false prophet Elymas 'son of the devil'. From these, Dahl concludes that 'first-born of Satan' is a kind of a superlative. Therefore, Polycarp is using a phrase that was used not only by Christians, but also by Jews of that time, to apply to heretics. Because this phrase is the only part of the description which Harrison can definitely link with Marcion, his one absolute for dating what he calls a 'later' letter is invalidated.

7. Conclusion on Harrison

All objections raised by Harrison to the integrity of Polycarp's letter can be either questioned or refuted entirely. Even those authors who still believe that Polycarp wrote two letters now usually put the date for the second letter within just a few years of the death of Ignatius. This would mean that Polycarp's epistle should still be dated in the second half of the reign of Trajan, who reigned AD 98-117, and certainly no later than AD 120.[145] However, in light of the weakness of Harrison's argument for dividing Polycarp's epistle and of the uniform opinion of the ancient authors that this is one letter, it is the letter itself which requires that it be dated within a few months of the death of Ignatius. Therefore it is best to date Polycarp's epistle *To the Philippians* between AD 108 and 110.

---

[141]Lake, *Apostolic Fathers*, vol. 1, p. 167.

[142]Harrison, *Polycarp's Two Epistles*, pp. 184-91.

[143]Harrison, *Polycarp's Two Epistles*, pp. 175-82.

[144]Nils Dahl, 'Der erstgeborene Satans und der Vater des Teufels', in *Apophoreta: Festschrift für Ernst Haenchen zu seinem 70 Geburtstag am 10 Dezember 1964* (ed. Walther Eltester et al.; BZAW; Berlin: Topelmann, 1964), pp. 70-84.

[145]Rensberger, 'As the Apostle Teaches', p. 111.

External Attestation to 2 Thessalonians

D. Polycarp and the Terminus ad quem *for 2 Thessalonians*

Because Polycarp cited extensively from the Pauline corpus, explicitly attributing 1 Corinthians and 2 Thessalonians to Paul, the *terminus ad quem* for 2 Thessalonians can be no later than the date for Polycarp's letter, between AD 108 and 110. Because Polycarp expected the Philippians to study Paul's letters and to recognize his quotes from Paul, we can assume that the Philippians had the same Pauline letters which Polycarp possessed. Philippi and Thessalonica were only 110 miles apart on one of the most traveled roads in the empire, the Egnatian Way.[146] When Ignatius left Philippi to travel to Rome, he had to pass through Thessalonica. Philippi also had close ecclesiastical ties with Thessalonica, for according to Acts 16–17, Paul went to Thessalonica immediately after his work in Philippi and, in fact, commends the Philippians for the way they aided his work in Thessalonica (Phil. 4:15-16). These close ties make it very likely that what one church possessed in terms of Pauline letters, the other church would possess as well. At the time of Polycarp, for a false letter of Paul addressed to the Thessalonians to be accepted in Thessalonica would be extremely unlikely. Many members in the church there would know if they had received a letter from Paul many years before. Therefore Polycarp's letter to the Philippians not only provides us with an early historical witness to the authenticity of 2 Thessalonians, but it also provides a valuable geographical witness to the early acceptance of 2 Thessalonians in Philippi and, most likely, in Thessalonica.

Polycarp's theology was unoriginal and traditional, as seen both by example in his letter, with its abundant citations, and by his own statements about what he believed and taught.[147] Therefore what he taught in his epistle is what he himself had been taught. This is agreed by nearly all those who study the theology of Polycarp. The study of Polycarp's life indicates that he was born about AD 70 and that he was already a bishop in Smyrna about AD 108 when Ignatius passed through on his way to Rome. Polycarp was not a recent convert before becoming a bishop; rather, he had a life-long commitment to his Lord going back to his earliest years, and it is possible he had a connection with one of the Apostles. Therefore it is reasonable to assume that Polycarp's original training occurred well before he became bishop of Smyrna, probably by the time he was a young adult. Because he had grown up in the church and was already a bishop in his thirties, he certainly would have had his initial training by the time he was about twenty years of age, about AD 90. Since Polycarp, who taught only what he himself had been taught, claimed that 2 Thessalonians was written by Paul, then he must have been taught that Paul's writings included 2 Thessalonians.

---

[146]Harrison, *Polycarp's Two Epistles*, p. 112.
[147]Lawson, *Apostolic Fathers*, p. 154.

Thus a careful study of Polycarp's citations shows that he quoted from 2 Thessalonians and believed that it was Pauline in AD 108-110. Furthermore, not only was this view of Paul's letters accepted where Polycarp lived in Asia Minor (Smyrna), but Polycarp also believed this same attitude was true in Macedonia (Philippi). Because of the close connections between Philippi and Thessalonica, it is likely that what the Philippians possessed, so did the Thessalonians. Finally, the implications of Polycarp's traditional and unoriginal theology and his life-long Christian commitment mean that what he believed and taught was what he himself had been taught. This information from Polycarp's epistle and his life enable us to move the *terminus ad quem* of 2 Thessalonians to about AD 90 or before.

External Attestation and the Authenticity of 2 Thessalonians

From the time of Irenaeus, 2 Thessalonians has been accepted as Pauline. This attestation can be seen throughout the whole ancient Christian world, in Africa (Cyprian, Tertullian), in Egypt and Palestine (Origen, Clement of Alexandria, Justin), in Asia Minor (Irenaeus, Polycarp), and in Europe (Hippolytus, Irenaeus, Muratorian Canon, Marcion). Not only was it widely attested by the end of the second and early third centuries, but it was as well attested in some of the earliest Christian writings outside the New Testament: Justin, *Didache*, and Polycarp. In fact, Polycarp's letter shows that it was accepted and used in Macedonia, a location where it most likely would have been accepted if authentic but rejected if pseudonymous. Furthermore, Polycarp's manner of writing and lack of originality show that he was simply passing on what he himself had been taught. Therefore to postulate a *terminus ad quem* later than AD 90 is to deny the evidence.

Chapter 3
Tradition in 2 Thessalonians: Terminology and Identification

Tradition is of major significance in 2 Thessalonians, for twice in this short forty-seven-verse epistle the writer exhorts the Thessalonians to 'hold to' and 'walk according to' the tradition(s) they have received (2:15; 3:6). Disputers of authenticity see this emphasis on tradition as a later development which arose after the time of Paul[1] in order to exalt apostolic dignity.[2] They conclude this because, to them, the traditions appear to be stereotyped and the language which refers to tradition appears to be 'peculiar' and 'conspicuous'.[3] Holland believes that the goal of 2 Thessalonians is to command the Thessalonians to 'live in peace according to apostolic tradition' and that the writer of 2 Thessalonians teaches that salvation is based upon faithfulness to the tradition.[4] Peter Müller describes the writer's use of tradition in 2 Thessalonians as unpauline because it focuses on the apostle himself and it claims to be normative.[5] The content of the tradition in 2 Thessalonians has also been attacked as being unpauline because it does not focus on the historical events in the life of Jesus[6] and, specifically, because the cross and resurrection are conspicuously absent.[7] Some claim that the references to tradition are based on a rewriting of 1 Thessalonians.[8]

Because of the emphasis in 2 Thessalonians itself on tradition and because so many disputers have interpreted this as evidence of the pseudepigraphical character of 2 Thessalonians, tradition must be considered in detail in order to defend the authenticity of the letter. This examination will show that the use of tradition in 2 Thessalonians displays the peculiarities of Paul himself and that a proper understanding of these peculiarities is essential to properly interpret 2 Thessalonians. This chapter will examine: (I) The Terminology of Tradition, (II) The Identification of Tradition in 2 Thessalonians, (III) Tradition in the Undisputed Pauline Epistles, and (IV) Tradition and the Authenticity of 2 Thessalonians.

---

[1] Littleton, 'The Function of Apocalyptic', pp. 159, 182, 192-93.
[2] Hilgenfeld, 'Die beiden Briefe', pp. 260-62.
[3] Trilling, *Untersuchungen*, pp. 61, 69-75, 95-107; 110-14.
[4] Holland, *Tradition*, p. 90.
[5] Peter Müller, *Anfänge*, pp. 262-64.
[6] Holland, *Tradition*, p. 86.
[7] Peter Müller, *Anfänge*, pp. 262-64.
[8] Caroline Vander Stichele, 'The Concept of Tradition and 1 and 2 Thessalonians', in *The Thessalonian Correspondence* (ed. R. Collins; BETL 67; Leuven: Leuven University Press, 1990), pp. 501, 503.

I. The Terminology of Tradition

The particular terms used to describe the transmission of tradition are generally recognized by scholars as technical terms.[9] A study of the terminology of tradition involves not only simple studies of word frequency, but also the study of the concept of tradition itself. The words found in 2 Thessalonians which refer to tradition and its transmission will be examined first, followed by other words within the Pauline corpus which function in a similar way. This terminology will also be examined in the Apostolic Fathers to see if it is used like the New Testament or shows different characteristics of a later time.

A. *Words Found in 2 Thessalonians*

1. Tradition [παράδοσις]

The word 'tradition', used twice in 2 Thessalonians (2:15; 3:6), is usually translated as 'teaching' or 'tradition'.[10] The same word is used throughout the New Testament to refer to different types of tradition: rabbinic, human, and apostolic.

The rabbinic use of tradition can be seen in Mark 7 and its parallel, Matthew 15, the only passages in the Gospels which use the Greek term 'tradition'. Five times in Mark 7:1-23 the word 'tradition' refers to the teaching of the Pharisees and scribes: 'the tradition of the elders' (7:3, 5), 'your tradition that you have handed down' (7:13), 'your tradition' (7:9), and 'the tradition of men' (7:8). This tradition, viewed in a negative manner, is directly contrasted with keeping 'the commands of God' (7:8).

Paul also seems to be familiar with this usage of the word 'tradition'; when describing what he was like before becoming a Christian, he says, 'I was advancing in Judaism beyond many Jews of my own age and was extremely zealous for the traditions of my ancestors' (Gal. 1:14). This use of 'tradition' by Matthew, Mark, and Paul shows a familiarity with the Jewish terminology of the time referring to the rabbinic elaboration of the law.[11] Throughout the New Testament this rabbinic elaboration is viewed negatively.

A second use of the term 'tradition' is found within the Pauline corpus. In Colossians 2:8 the church is warned against being deceived and taken 'captive through hollow and deceptive philosophy, which depends on human tradition

---

[9] R. Bultmann, *Theology of the New Testament* (London: Scribner's Sons, 1955), vol. 2, p. 119; F. Büchsel, 'παραδίδωμι', *TDNT* 2:169; Oscar Cullmann, *The Early Church* (ed. A. J. B. Higgins; London: SCM, 1956), p. 60.

[10] Arndt and Gingrich, *Lexicon*, p. 621, define it generally as 'handing down or over', but more specifically they give two definitions: 1) betrayal or arrest and 2) tradition. The second definition is the only one found in the New Testament.

[11] R. P. C. Hanson, *Tradition in the Early Church* (London: SCM, 1962), p. 10.

and the basic principles of this world rather than on Christ'. Nothing in the immediate context of the phrase 'human tradition' identifies it with the rabbinic elaboration denounced in the Gospels, although it may refer to a form of syncretistic Judaism.[12] Therefore the 'tradition of men' spoken about in Colossians most likely refers to the false beliefs of the opponents in Colossae.

The third type of tradition in the Pauline corpus, apostolic tradition, is seen clearly in 1 Corinthians. In 11:2 Paul says, 'I praise you for remembering me in everything and for holding to the teachings [traditions], just as I passed them on to you'. Here Paul clearly views tradition in a positive light; in fact, it appears to summarize as a whole the teaching which he had proclaimed to the Corinthians. The question which arises concerns the identity of 'the traditions' (11:2): whether this refers to the section which precedes it (1 Cor. 10:23-33) or to the section which follows (1 Cor. 11:3-16). This problem must be dealt with before the tradition referred to in 1 Corinthians 11:2 can be defined.

In 10:23-33, Paul expounds the implications of a believer's freedom. He exhorts his readers to learn from Israel's failures in the wilderness, and he includes himself with them in the need to take Israel's failures to heart (see vv. 8, 9, 16, 17, 22). In the midst of this exhortation, his focus shifts to his own personal example, presenting himself as one whom they are to imitate. The pronouns and verbs specifically point to him: 'my freedom' (v. 29); 'I partake', 'I am denounced', 'I thank' (v. 30); 'I also try to please', 'my own advantage' (v. 33). In fact, Paul emphasizes this by three times inserting the normally unnecessary first person pronoun. He then says, Follow my example, as I follow the example of Christ', or more literally, 'Be imitators of me, as even I am of Christ' (11:1).

It is at this point that Paul praises the Corinthians for remembering him and holding to his 'traditions' (11:2). Both vv. 2 and 3 use the conjunction 'and' or 'but' [δέ] to connect with what precedes, leading some to conclude that v. 3 is logically connected to v. 2. However, v. 3 introduces a new topic with the words 'But I want you to realize that'. That this is a change in topic is clear from Paul's practice elsewhere in 1 Corinthians. For

---

[12] It has been suggested that this phrase, which is exactly like the phrase found in Mark 7:8, refers to the teaching of the rabbinic schools. See N.T. Wright, *The Epistles of Paul to the Colossians and to Philemon* (Leicester: Inter-Varsity Press, 1986), p. 101. See also F. F. Bruce, *The Epistles to the Colossians, to Philemon and to the Ephesians* (Grand Rapids: Eerdmans, 1984), p. 18. However, the phrase parallels the phrase that follows, 'the basic principles of this world', and should be understood as part of 'the hollow and deceptive philosophy' which precedes it. There appears to be basically one set of opponents at Colossae, and because the other phrases surrounding the 'tradition' phrase are most easily understood as including some pagan deities (Wright, *Colossians*, p. 102), this cannot be a simple denunciation of rabbinic elaboration.

example, in 10:1 he introduces a change in subject in a similar way. In ch. 9 he has been defending his rights as an apostle, but in ch. 10 he changes the subject to that of Old Testament examples of conduct, with 'For I do not want you to be ignorant of the fact, brothers, that . . . .' In 12:1 he again introduces a change of topic with a similar form: 'Now about spiritual gifts, brothers, I do not want you to be ignorant'. Thus the words in 1 Cor. 11:3, 'But I want you to realize that', also indicate a change in topic.

Not only does 11:3 introduce a change in topic, but v. 2, where Paul praises the Corinthians 'for remembering me in everything', arises naturally out of what is said in 10:29 –11:1. Paul emphasizes himself in these verses because they must remember him in order to imitate him. The second part of 11:2 is linked to the first part of the verse by 'and' [καί]. Thus the two parts of 11:2 are roughly parallel to each other, 'remembering everything' in 11:2a being equivalent to 'holding fast the traditions I delivered' in 11:2b. Therefore all of 11:2 goes with what precedes it (10:23-33), and from 11:3 onwards Paul presents a new topic which includes nothing about himself. Although Gordon Fee links v. 2 with what follows and suggests that this verse introduces the whole of chs 11-14, he nevertheless recognizes that the 'opening words [of v. 2] seem to flow easily from what has immediately preceded (10:33–11:1)'. He also draws attention to the fact that 'traditions' is plural in 11:2 while 'custom' [συνήθειαν] is singular in 11:16, thus showing that the traditions in 11:2 are not the same as the custom referred to in 11:16 and that these verses should not be seen as parallel brackets to a section comprising 11:2-16. Fee also argues strongly that the 'but' [δέ] at the beginning of v. 3 is 'almost certainly adversative to v. 2'.[13] All of this points to a stronger link between 11:2 and what precedes it than between 11:2 and what follows.[14] Therefore 11:1-2 concludes the section begun in ch. 10, and the 'traditions' refer back to the examples seen in the Old Testament and in Paul.

The only other two places the word *tradition* is found in the New Testament are both in 2 Thessalonians. In 2 Thessalonians 2:15 the author says, 'So then, brothers, stand firm and hold to the traditions we passed on to you, whether by word of mouth or by letter.' The traditions in 2:15 refer explicitly to what had been previously taught, 'whether by word or letter', and thus would certainly cover the eschatological teaching in 2:1-12, for the writer says in 2:5, 'Don't you remember that when I was with you I used to tell you these things?' As in 1 Corinthians 11, the stress is on the person through whom the tradition has come ('I' in 1 Cor.; 'I' in 2 Thess. 2:5; 'us' in 2:15) and on the tradition being 'held' (κατέχετε in 1 Cor. 11; κρατεῖτε in 2 Thess. 2) by the believers. In 2

---

[13]Gordon D. Fee, *The First Epistle to the Corinthians* (NICNT; Grand Rapids: Eerdmans, 1987), pp. 499-501 (see n. 36, p. 501).

[14]William F. Orr and James Arthur Walther, in *1 Corinthians* (AB 32; Garden City, NY: Doubleday, 1977), p. 259, say about v. 3, 'the relations of this to the traditions is tenuous at best'.

Tradition in 2 Thessalonians: Terminology and Identification

Thessalonians 3:6 the Thessalonians are commanded to 'keep away from every brother who is idle and does not live according to the tradition you received from us'. Here again the 'tradition' refers back to what had been taught on a previous occasion. The difference between the two uses of 'tradition' in 2 Thessalonians is that in 2:15 the term is in the plural and seems primarily to refer back to the doctrinal teaching already mentioned in 2 Thessalonians, whereas in 3:6 the term is singular and refers to imitating the missionaries in the way they worked (3:7-9). This stress on the necessity of remembering Paul's teaching and imitating the missionaries' example (μνημονεύετε -2 Thess. 2:5; τὸ μιμεῖσθαι-2 Thess. 3:7) is very similar to 1 Corinthians 11:1-2, where Paul also calls upon the believers to imitate him [μιμηταί] and remember him [μέμνησθε] in everything. Thus the uses of 'tradition' in both 1 Corinthians and 2 Thessalonians may be grouped together in the category of apostolic tradition.

Outside of the New Testament, the term 'tradition' is found twice in the Apostolic Fathers. In *1 Clement* 7.2, 'Wherefore let us put aside empty and vain cares, and let us come to the glorious and venerable rule of our tradition',[15] the reference seems to be to some known, possibly written, body of material (see *1 Clem.*7.1). The tradition is not said to originate with Clement but is exalted by Clement and so appears to have been firmly established by the time he wrote his letter. The term is also found in *Diognetus* 11.6: 'Then is the fear of the Law sung, and the grace of the Prophets known, the faith of the Gospels is established, and the tradition of the apostles is guarded, and the grace of the Church exults'.[16] Again tradition is placed on a very high and exalted level and is explicitly described as apostolic. This letter, later than the rest of the Apostolic Fathers, is placed with them only on account of custom and should be dated in the second, or possibly third, century. The concluding chapters (11-12) appear to have no connection with preceding ones and may possibly be attributed to Hippolytus.[17] Both references to tradition in the Apostolic Fathers appear to be based on the letters of Paul. The veneration of the traditions in the Apostolic Fathers contrasts with the straightforward use of 'tradition' in 1 Corinthians and 2 Thessalonians, where there are no indications of veneration.[18]

2. To Teach [διδάσκω]

Although 'teach' is a very common verb in the New Testament, it is found only fifteen times in the Pauline corpus, five of these in the Pastorals. By definition 'it denotes "teaching" or "instruction" in the widest possible sense,

---

[15]Lake, *Apostolic Fathers*, LCL. [ἐπὶ τὸν εὐκλεῆ καὶ σεμνὸν τῆς παραδόσεως ἡμῶν κακόνα]

[16]Lake, *Apostolic Fathers*, LCL. [καὶ ἀποστόλων παράδοσις φυλάσσεται]

[17]Lake, *Apostolic Fathers*, LCL.

[18]Green, *Thessalonians*, p. 329, also gives examples of how this terminology was used in other Greek writings.

whether the imparting of information, the passing on of knowledge, or the acquiring of skills'.[19] Paul uses the verb to describe his own teaching as well as the teaching done in the Christian community.[20] In 1 Corinthians 4:16-17 he says, 'Therefore I urge you to imitate me. For this reason I am sending to you Timothy, my son whom I love, who is faithful in the Lord. He will remind you of my way of life in Christ Jesus, which agrees with what I teach everywhere in every church.' Through his own teaching, Timothy is able to pass on Paul's way of life, which is part of Paul's teaching everywhere. Colossians 1:28; 2:6-7, and 1 Corinthians 11:14 also have the general concept of teaching in view.

In Galatians 1:12 Paul defends his apostleship and his direct reception of the gospel: 'I did not receive it from any man, nor was I taught it; rather, I received it by revelation from Jesus Christ.' The term used by Paul for 'receiving' the gospel is generally recognized as a technical term for the receiving of traditional material. In this context 'to be taught' is in parallel to 'receive', and therefore it is possible that the verb 'to teach' is also functioning as a technical term.[21]

All the remaining uses of 'teach' in the Pauline corpus (other than in 2 Thess.) are found in the Pastoral Epistles. Each time, the term is used in reference to a command to teach others (1 Tim. 4:11; 6:2; 2 Tim. 2:2) or to place limitations on the practice of teaching (1 Tim. 2:12; Titus 1:11).[22]

It might seem that 2 Thessalonians 2:15 differs from the usage in the undisputed letters of Paul, for it is the only passage where 'teach' is linked with written correspondence. However, it must be remembered that Paul was very self-conscious about the character of his writings (see 1 Cor. 5:9, 11). He demanded that his letters be read to all (1 Thess. 5:27) and expected obedience to his directions (2 Cor. 2:9). It was just as if he were present when his epistle was present (2 Cor. 10:10-11), and his written words carried the authority of the Lord (1 Cor. 14:37-38). Paul's teaching could also be passed on by one of his associates (1 Cor. 4:17). Paul uses 'teach' in reference to the process of passing on traditions (Gal. 1:12), and consequently the use of 'teach' in 2 Thessalonians 2:15 is entirely consistent with Paul's practice in the undisputed letters.

In the Apostolic Fathers 'teach' is used numerous times, most frequently to warn against false or hypocritical teaching.[23] It is also used in reference to the general teaching that must take place within the bounds of the congregation (whether by leaders or all people),[24] to Jesus's teaching,[25] and to the apostles'

---

[19] K. Rengstorf, 'διδάσκω', *TDNT* 2:135.
[20] See Rom. 2:21; 12:7; Col. 3:16.
[21] Seyoon Kim, *The Origin of Paul's Gospel* (WUNT 2; Tübingen: Mohr Siebeck, 1981), p. 67.
[22] 1 Tim. 4:11; 6:2; 2 Tim. 2:2 and 1 Tim. 2:12; Titus 1:11.
[23] See *Did.* 6.1; 11.2, 10, 11; *Ign. Eph.* 15.1; Herm. *Sim.* 9.19.3; *Mart. Pol.* 4.1; cf. *1 Clem.* 18.13; 22.1; 57.3, which are all OT quotes.
[24] *Did.* 4.9; *Barn.* 19.5; Herm. *Sim.* 5.1.3; Ign. *Rom.* 3.1; Pol. *Phil.* 4.1; *Mart. Pol.* 12.2.

teaching,[26] specifically that of Paul.[27]

3. To Receive [παραλαμβάνω]

'To receive', another technical term used for the receiving of traditional material, is equivalent to the Hebrew קבל.[28] Although in the New Testament it most frequently refers to receiving a person, or taking a person with oneself, as can be seen in thirty-six places throughout the Gospels and Acts, 'to receive' can also refer to the receiving of tradition. This usage is found only one time outside the Pauline corpus, in Mark 7:4, where we have already seen the scribes and Pharisees debating with Jesus. The gospel writer makes the editorial comment of the Pharisees and all the Jews, 'And they observe many other traditions, such as the washing of cups, pitchers and kettles'. Literally, they are accused of 'keeping many other things which they have received'. As was noted in the examination of 'tradition', the language in this section refers to the practice of the elaboration of the Law. This is the only place in the Gospels and Acts in which 'to receive' does not mean receive or take someone along.

'To receive' is used eleven times in the Pauline corpus, nine of which refer to the reception of traditional material. In 1 Corinthians 11:23 Paul introduces his account of the Lord's Supper with the words, 'For I received from the Lord what I also passed on to you'. Paul's language shows that he sees himself as a link between the Lord and the Corinthians. The only question debated is the exact meaning of the preposition 'from' [ἀπό], whether it means Paul immediately and directly received this tradition from Christ, or whether he is simply pointing to the ultimate origin of this tradition.[29] Either way, as F. F. Bruce states, 'What is important is the use of the terminology of tradition,

---

[25]See *1 Clem.* 13.1; *Barn.* 5.8; Pol. *Phil.* 2.3; Herm. *Vis.* 4.1.8; *Diogn.* 12.9 (Jesus is called 'the Word').

[26]See Herm. *Vis.* 3.5.1; Herm. *Sim.* 9.25.2; *Diogn.* 11.2

[27]See *1 Clem.* 5.7; Pol. *Phil.* 3.2; cf. *Mart. Pol.* 10.2

[28]Kim, *Origin*, p. 67; Bultmann, *Theology*, p. 119; Jürgen Roloff, *Apostolat-Verkündigung-Kirche* (Gütersloh: Mohn, 1965), p. 85; G. Delling, 'παραλαμβάνω', *TDNT* 4:12-13; Birger Gerhardsson, *Memory and Manuscript: Oral Tradition and Written Transmission in Rabbinic Judaism and Early Christianity* (Lund: Gleerup, 1961), p. 288; Cullmann, *Early Church*, p. 63; E. Earle Ellis, 'Traditions in 1 Corinthians', *NTS* 32 (1986), p. 481.

[29]George Eldon Ladd, in *A Theology of the New Testament* (Grand Rapids: Eerdmans, 1974), p. 389, comments that *para*, not *apo*, would have been used by Paul if he meant it had been received directly from the Lord. F. F. Bruce, in *Tradition: Old and New* (Exeter: Paternoster, 1970), p. 33, suggests this distinction between the two prepositions is doubtful. Cullmann, *Early Church*, p. 67, notes that *apo* in Col. 1:7 is used of the direct reception of the ministry of Epaphras.

paralambanō and *paradidōmi*'.[30] According to Jeremias, although the text of the tradition was not completely fixed at Paul's time, it is clearly pre-Pauline.[31] In 1 Corinthians 15:1, once again the language of transmitting tradition is clear: 'Now, brothers, I want to remind you of the gospel I preached to you, which you received and on which you have taken your stand.' In v. 3 he continues, 'For what I received I passed on to you as of first importance'. The gospel itself was received by the Corinthians—the gospel Paul himself had received and had now passed on, and Paul is the link between what he received and the believers at Corinth. This same emphasis on the reception of the gospel by the Pauline congregations is seen in Galatians 1:9, where Paul warns, 'If anybody is preaching to you a gospel other than what you accepted [received], let him be eternally condemned!', and in 1 Thessalonians 2:13, 'And we also thank God continually because, when you received the word of God, which you heard from us, you accepted it not as the word of men, but as it actually is, the word of God, which is at work in you who believe'. The gospel, which was accepted by the believers, is called 'the word of God' because of its origin from God. As was noted when 'to teach' was examined in Galatians 1:12, Paul is defending his apostleship and his direct reception of the gospel by revelation. Paul again uses the language of transmitting tradition to convey the reception of the gospel.

In other passages, what is received is not what might be described as the 'core' of the gospel, as in 1 Corinthians 15:3-5, but rather ethical instruction which accompanies the gospel proclamation. In Philippians 4:9 Paul says, 'Whatever you have learned or received or heard from me, or seen in me—put it into practice', and in 1 Thessalonians 4:1, 'Finally, brothers, we instructed you how to live in order to please God, as in fact you are living. Now we ask you and urge you in the Lord Jesus to do this more and more.' In the Philippians passage Paul's total example and teaching is presented as a model similar to that in 1 Corinthians 11:1-2, and in 1 Thessalonians the practical outworking [literally 'to walk'—περιπατεῖν] of his teaching is stressed. The same emphasis on teaching and example is found in 2 Thessalonians 3:6, which warns against association with anyone who 'does not live according to the teaching you received from us'. Similarly to 1 Thessalonians 4:1, the tradition which has been 'received from us' in 2 Thessalonians 3:6 concerns how one lives (literally, 'walks'). Although the forms of the words have changed, the idea is the same, not necessarily because 2 Thessalonians is copying 1 Thessalonians, but simply because this is the language of transmitting practical tradition. With its stress on imitation, 2 Thessalonians 3:6-7 is more like Philippians 4:9 with its command to put into practice whatever they saw in Paul.

The only passages in the Pauline corpus which do not use 'to receive' [παραλαμβάνω] to refer to tradition are found in Colossians. Colossians 2:6

---

[30]Bruce, *Tradition*, p.33.
[31]Joachim Jeremias, *The Eucharistic Words of Jesus* (London: SCM, 1966), p. 104.

says the Colossians 'received Christ Jesus as Lord', and Colossians 4:17 commands Archippus, 'See to it that you complete the work you have received in the Lord'. Thus in Colossians a person is received (Jesus, by faith, in 2:6) and a ministry is received (by Archippus in 4:17), whereas in the rest of the Pauline corpus (1 Cor., Gal., Phil., 1 Thess., 2 Thess.) Paul's teaching and manner of life are 'received'.

In the only other instance of 'to receive' in the NT (Heb. 12:28), the author reminds the readers that they are receiving an unshakable kingdom. This usage is closer to the use in Colossians than to the use in most of the letters of Paul.

The use of 'to receive' is rare in the Apostolic Fathers, but it is used in a manner similar to that of Colossians and Hebrews. In three passages it refers to receiving a person. In *Similitude* 6.3.3, Hermas sees the 'angel of punishment' who 'receives [παραλαμβάνει] those who have wandered away from God, and walked in the lusts and deceits of this world, and punishes them'. In *Similitude* 6.2.6 a 'Great Shepherd' is described as 'receiving [παραλάμβανε] sheep from the young shepherd'.[32] And in *Similitude* 9.25.2 it is explained to Hermas that the kind of believers who are on the eighth mountain, which he has seen in his vision, are 'Apostles and teachers who preached to all the world, and taught reverently and purely the word of the Lord, and kept nothing back for evil desire, but always walked in righteousness and truth, even as they had received [παρέλαβον] the Holy Spirit'.[33] Three passages in the Apostolic Fathers use 'to receive' to mean the transmitting of information. Shepherd of Hermas, *Vision* 1.3.4, speaks of 'the ordinances of God, which they received [παρέλαβον] with great faith'.[34] Both *Barnabas* 19.11 and *Didache* 4.13 quote from Deuteronomy 12:23 and apply this to commands which have been received. In *Barnabas* this quotation is near the conclusion of a long list of commands which are described as 'the way of Light' (*Barn.* 19.1, 12), while in the *Didache* it is in the section called 'the way of life' (*Did.* 1.2; 4.14) and immediately follows a section on household responsibilities. This cataloging of general commands for a wide variety of situations contrasts with the limited commands applied to specific situations found in the undisputed Pauline letters and in 2 Thessalonians.

4. To know [οἶδα]

The verb 'to know' [οἶδα] is used in 2 Thessalonians three times (2 Thess. 1:8; 2:6; 3:7). The first time it refers to the response of unbelievers to God, they 'do not know God', and is parallel to the phrase 'do not obey the gospel'. The other two occurrences are found in the overall context of tradition. C. H. Giblin has attempted to show that the meaning of 'to know' in 2 Thessalonians 2:6 is not 'speculative or conceptual knowledge' but mainly 'experiential' or

---

[32]Lake, *Apostolic Fathers*, LCL.
[33]Lake, *Apostolic Fathers*, LCL.
[34]Lake, *Apostolic Fathers*, LCL.

'personal awareness'.³⁵ This is of major importance to Giblin's thesis, for he believes that Paul is referring to a particular problem which the Thessalonians are experiencing.³⁶ This problem concerns 'the restraining' [τὸ κατέχον], which he defines as a seizing or possessing power of Satan exercised by a pseudo-charismatic.³⁷ What Paul is saying, according to Giblin, is that the Thessalonians have personally experienced this problem. Giblin recognizes a variety of possible definitions for 'to know' from 1 Thessalonians and concludes that if Paul had meant to express information about the *katechon* by the use of 'know' here, he would have said 'and now you know what is the katechon'.³⁸

The problem with Giblin's suggestion is threefold. First, the overwhelming use of 'to know' [οἶδα] in Paul refers to information about Paul's work and example, about general sayings which all would be expected to know, or most frequently, about Paul's core teaching (tradition), which he expected to be known.³⁹ In a few instances the verb is used to refer to relationships,⁴⁰ and in some passages it is used to express personal convictions about particular persons or the future.⁴¹ Yet this verb, which is used over 100 times in the Pauline corpus, almost always carries the idea of knowing information. Second, the context of 2 Thessalonians 2:6 also makes it likely that the writer of 2 Thessalonians is using 'to know' with this meaning. Verse 5 'reminds' them of 'these things' which they are expected already to know, and the following verses continue with information which Best says 'does not read as if it was new information' and should be included in 'these things' of v. 5.⁴² Finally, the use of 'to know' in 3:7 clearly introduces what the author considers to be traditional material. Therefore 'to know' in 2 Thessalonians 2:6 and 3:7 refers to information that the writer of 2 Thessalonians presents as part of the tradition.

The same range of meanings of 'to know' is found within the Apostolic

---

³⁵Charles H. Giblin, *The Threat to Faith: An Exegetical and Theological Re-examination of 2 Thessalonians 2* (AnBib 31; Rome: Pontifical Biblical Institute, 1967), pp. 159-60. This definition is accepted by Best, *Thessalonians*, p. 290.

³⁶Giblin, *Threat*, p. 174.

³⁷Giblin, *Threat*, pp. 230, 240-41.

³⁸Giblin, *Threat*, pp. 161-62, 164. [καὶ νῦν οἴδατε τί (ἐστιν) τὸ κατέχον]

³⁹Paul in his work and as an example: Gal. 4:13; Eph. 6:21; Phil. 1:16; 4:15; Col. 4:12; 1 Thess. 1:5; 2:1, 2, 5, 11; 2 Thess. 3:14; 2 Tim. 1:15. General sayings which all would be expected to know: Rom. 6:16; 1 Cor. 9:24. Paul's traditional teaching: Rom. 2:2; 3:19; 6:9; 7:14; 8:22, 28; 11:2; 14:14; 1 Cor. 2:2; 3:16; 5:6; 6:2, 3, 9, 15, 16, 19; 8:1, 4; 9:13; 11:3; 13:2; 15:58; 2 Cor. 4:14; 5:1, 5, 11; Gal. 2:16; Eph. 6:8, 9; Col. 3:24; 4:1; 1 Thess. 3:3, 4; 4:2; 5:2; 2 Thess. 2:6; 3:7; 1 Tim. 1:8, 9; 2 Tim. 3:15.

⁴⁰See Gal. 4:8; 1 Thess. 4:4, 5; Titus 1:16; 2 Thess. 1:8.

⁴¹See Rom. 14:14; 15:29; Phil. 1:19, 25; Phlm. 21.

⁴²Best, *Thessalonians*, pp. 290-91.

Fathers. However, the use of 'to know' to refer to tradition is much less common than the simple definition 'to know something'.[43]

5. To command [παραγγέλλω]

The writer of 2 Thessalonians uses the verb 'to command' or 'to charge' four times, all in ch. 3. One time the verb is used to refer to obeying his commands in general (2 Thess. 3:4), whereas the other three instances are found in the context where the 'idle' are discussed. The 'idle' are commanded to work (2 Thess. 3:12), and those who are not 'idle' are charged to keep away from those who are (2 Thess. 3:6). These present commands are based upon the tradition which had been commanded: 'If a man will not work, he shall not eat' (2 Thess. 3:10).

This verb is found in only three other books in the Pauline corpus. In 1 Corinthians 7:10 Paul commands the married to remain married, and when he introduces the problem of abuses at the Lord's Supper, he begins, 'In the following directives [παραγγέλλων] I have no praise for you' (1 Cor. 11:17).[44] In both passages the verb is in the present tense. In 1 Thessalonians 4:11 the verb is used in the same context as in 2 Thessalonians, its aorist tense reminding them of their previous instruction. In the only other book in the Pauline corpus which uses this verb, 1 Timothy, three times the verb relates to passing on instruction in the future (1 Tim. 1:3; 4:11; 5:7), and twice the writer of 1 Timothy gives personal commands (1 Tim. 6:13, 17).[45]

In the use of 'to command', 2 Thessalonians follows the patterns found in the undisputed Paulines; in terms of context it follows 1 Thessalonians, whereas in terms of form it is closer to 1 Corinthians. The word is used to command adherence to Paul's paraenetic tradition.

6. Testimony [μαρτύριον]

'Testimony' is used once in 2 Thessalonians, to refer to the message that was believed by the Thessalonians (2 Thess. 1:10). The acceptance of this message differentiates the Thessalonians from those who will be judged when the Lord Jesus is revealed. In this context 'testimony' refers to the initial message proclaimed to the Thessalonians and possibly also to the teaching contained in the verses which immediately precede 'testimony'.

---

[43] The idea of tradition can be seen in Ign. *Smyrn.* 3.1; Herm. *Sim.*1.1; 2.6; *1 Clem.* 45.7; *2 Clem.* 7.1; 10.5; 12.1; *Did.* 3.10; 16.1; *Barn.* 19.6; Pol. *Phil* 1.3; 4.1; 5.1; 6.1.

[44] On the problems of the textual variants of this verse see Fee, *1 Corinthians*, pp. 534-35, n. 15).

[45] The verb is found only three times in the Apostolic Fathers. In *1 Clem.* it refers both to the commands given by the church at Corinth to the women (1.3) and to God's command not to lie (27.2). It is also found in Ign. *Pol.* 5.1 as a solemn command 'in the name of Jesus Christ "to love their wives as the Lord loved the Church"'.

This noun is used similarly in the Pauline corpus. In 1 Corinthians, Paul recounts how the testimony about Christ was confirmed among the Corinthians (1:6) and describes his message as 'the testimony of God' (2:1).[46] In both passages 'testimony' refers to the gospel as Paul initially proclaimed it.[47] In 1 Corinthians 1 he does not make specific mention of himself, probably because the section which immediately follows this thanksgiving concerns divisions in the Corinthian church which are specifically identified with certain leaders, whereas in 1 Corinthians 2:1 the message is explicitly identified with Paul. In 2 Corinthians 1:12 Paul speaks of 'the testimony of our conscience' as he defends his ministry before the Corinthians. In 1 Timothy 2:6, 'testimony' refers back to the immediately preceding statement, 'Christ Jesus who gave himself a ransom for all men'. In 2 Timothy 1:8, Timothy is commanded not to be ashamed of 'the testimony of our Lord'. The context would identify this 'testimony' with the gospel. The use of 'testimony' in 2 Thesslonians to refer to the gospel is clearly in line with the use in the Pauline corpus.

The Apostolic Fathers generally use 'testimony' differently from the New Testament. *Barnabas* uses the term to describe the symbolic aspect of the Old Testament sacrifices (8:3, 4) and to quote from the Old Testament (9:3); Ignatius uses the term to mean a witness against someone (Ign. *Trall.* 12:3; Ign. *Phld.* 6:3); *Diognetus* uses it to speak of a proof of election (4:4); and in *Martyrdom of Polycarp* it has come to mean 'martyrdom' (1.1; 19.1). Among the Apostolic Fathers, only Polycarp, *To the Philippians*, uses it in a fashion somewhat similar to Paul: 'Whosoever does not confess the testimony of the Cross is of the devil' (7:1).[48] The diversity of usage in the Apostolic Fathers shows clearly that 2 Thessalonians is like Paul and unlike the Apostolic Fathers in its use of 'testimony'.

B. Words Not Found in 2 Thessalonians

It is also important to determine whether some key words that Paul could have used in reference to tradition have *not* been used in 2 Thessalonians. Although arguments from silence are of limited value, the absence of certain technical terminology may alert the investigator of authenticity to certain tendencies of a particular writer. Other related terms must also be examined because they may show the same concepts expressed elsewhere in different terminology.

---

[46]There are a number of textual variants in 1 Cor. 2:1. For a full discussion on why 'testimony' is to be preferred, see Fee, *1 Corinthians*, p. 88, n. 1.

[47]Fee, *1 Corinthians*, p. 40.

[48]Lake, *Apostolic Fathers*, LCL.

Tradition in 2 Thessalonians: Terminology and Identification

1. To pass on [παραδίδωμι]

'To pass on', another technical term for the transmission of tradition in line with rabbinic practice, is equivalent to the Hebrew word מסר.[49] However, the verb 'to pass on' can be used in three ways in the New Testament: (1) to betray or arrest; (2) to entrust or deliver; or (3) to pass on tradition. The vast majority of New Testament uses of this verb use the first meaning of delivering over someone in the negative sense of the word, that is, to betray or arrest. It can also be used simply to convey the idea of committing or entrusting something to someone.[50] The third meaning, that of delivering information or passing on tradition, is the meaning least found in the New Testament. The verb 'to pass on' is used in the same way the noun 'tradition' [παράδοσις] is used in reference to Jewish oral tradition and Christian tradition. The Jewish tradition is found in Mark 7:13, where Jesus condemns the Pharisees and scribes: 'Thus you nullify the word of God by your tradition that you have handed down [παραδίδωμι]'. Another reference to Jewish tradition is found in Acts 6:14, which shows clearly that the oral tradition was viewed to have been handed down from Moses and that Jesus would change this tradition. This same belief that the oral tradition originated with Moses is found in the Mishnah.[51]

In contrast to Jewish tradition, seven times this verb [παραδίδωμι] refers to Christian tradition in the New Testament. Luke begins his gospel by stressing that he has included the eyewitness tradition concerning Jesus. In Acts 16:4 this word tells how Paul and his companions 'delivered the decisions reached by the apostles and elders in Jerusalem for the people to obey'. Paul uses it of Christian tradition in two letters. In Romans 6:17 he praises God that the Romans 'wholeheartedly have obeyed the form of teaching to which you were entrusted'. A number of commentators, following Bultmann, believe this phrase

---

[49] Ellis, '1 Corinthians', p. 481; Bultmann, *Theology*, vol. 2, pp. 119-20; Büchsel, 'παραδίδωμι', *TDNT* 2:171; Roloff, *Apostolat-Verkündigung-Kirche*, p. 85; Gerhardsson, *Memory*, p. 288.

[50] Money can be entrusted to servants (Matt. 25:14, 20, 22); authority over kingdoms placed in someone's care (Satan—Luke 4:6; Jesus—Matt. 11:27 and Luke 10:22; God—1 Cor. 15:24); individuals' lives committed to God's care (Paul and Barnabas—Acts 14:26; 15:26, 40; Jesus—1 Pet. 2:23); and physical lives sacrificed (John 19:16; 1 Cor. 13:3). The verb 'to pass on' [παραδίδωμι] may also be used to describe the mature grain being ready for the harvest (Mark 4:29).

[51] R. Travers Herford, ed. and trans., *Pirke Aboth* (New York: Bloch, 1925), pp. 19, 22, 23, 24, 26, 28, 30, 31, records the passing on of tradition in the following series of names: 'Moses received [קִבֵּל] Torah from Sinai and delivered [מְסָרָהּ] it to Joshua, and Joshua to the Elders, and the Elders to the Prophets, and the Prophets to the Men of the Great Synagogue.... Hillel and Shammai received [קִבְּלוּ] from them....' Herford notes that the 'Great Synagogue' refers to the time of Ezra (p. 20), and Hillel and Shammai refer to 30 BC onwards (p. 32).

is an early gloss[52] because 'Paul never speaks of his preaching in this way'.[53] They also stress that the parallel between 17a, 'You used to be slaves to sin', and 18a, 'You have been set free from sin and have become slaves to righteousness', is broken by this phrase at the end of v. 17.[54] In contrast to this view, others see 'no reasonable doubt' concerning the authenticity of the phrase[55] and claim that the 'thought . . . is singularly characteristic of Paul'.[56]

The strict parallel between 17a and 18a clearly is interrupted by 'you wholeheartedly have obeyed the form of teaching to which you were entrusted'. For a number of reasons, however, this phrase should be accepted as Pauline. First, even though this phrase does interrupt the parallel, it clearly does not break the context, for the idea of 'obedience' is already present in v. 16.[57] Secondly, no textual evidence is adduced for emending the text, and consequently those who assert that it is a gloss must resort to calling it 'an early gloss', which they usually attribute to the compiler of the Pauline collection. This compiler hypothesis asserts that all the textual traditions we possess are derivative from a single collection of the letters of Paul. The individual letters of Paul were not only collected by the compiler but also edited to produce a single collection. Therefore the letters we possess today, although originally independent of each other, have all passed through this editorial revision in coming to us. Romans 6:17 with its emphasis on a body of teaching is directly attributed to the compiler, who has created this body of material, the *Corpus Paulinium*. However, this hypothesis is categorically refuted by the actual textual evidence we possess, especially of Romans. Harry Gamble has demonstrated that there existed before the time of Marcion two textual traditions for Romans, a shorter version—which contained only chs 1–14 and which Marcion, Epiphanius, and Tertullian all used—and a longer version.[58] Today we possess both these traditions. If all our texts of Romans depended on a compiler, then we would not have these two major traditions, both firmly

---

[52]K. Wegenast, 'διδασκαλία', *NIDNTT* 3:770.

[53]Franz J. Leenhardt, *The Epistle to the Romans* (London: Lutterworth, 1961), p. 172.

[54]Walter Schmithals, *Der Römerbrief* (Gütersloh: Mohn, 1988), p. 198, offers a good summary of the variety of positions, especially of German scholars. He believes the statement is an insertion by the redactor of the Pauline letter collection (p. 199).

[55]John Murray, *The Epistle to the Romans* (2 vols; Grand Rapids: Eerdmans, 1959), vol. 1, p. 232.

[56]Anders Nygren, *Commentary on Romans* (trans. Carl C. Rasmussen; Philadelphia: Juhlenberg Press, 1949), p. 256.

[57]Ulrich Wilckens, *Der Brief an die Römer* (EKKNT 6; Zurich: Benziger, Neukirchener Verlag, 1980), vol. 2, p. 35. See also C. E. B. Cranfield, *Romans* (2 vols; ICC; Edinburgh: T & T Clark, 1975-1979), vol. 1, p. 325.

[58]Harry Gamble, 'The Redaction of the Pauline Letters and the Formation of the Pauline Corpus', *JBL* 94 (1975), pp. 414-16.

established in antiquity. Romans 6:17 is an indisputable part of both textual traditions and therefore cannot be attributed to a compiler. Finally, Paul, in refuting the idea that one can keep on sinning that 'grace may abound' (6:1), reminds his readers of the ethical implications of their baptism (6:3-22).[59] He rebukes them in v. 3 for not following the implications of what they know to be true (see also vv. 8-9, 16). All of this appears to refer back to a body of teaching received when they were baptized and which Paul expects them already to know.[60] Thus the idea of a set body of teaching having been delivered to the Christians at Rome, as expressed in 6:17, fits the context of Romans 6. Therefore, Bultmann's proposal that Romans 6:17b is a gloss is to be refused, as most exegetes have recognized.[61]

Romans 6:17b, however, remains problematical. The problems surround the exact meaning of the three Greek words at the end of the verse 'form of teaching to which you were entrusted' [παρεδόθητε τύπον διδαχῆς] and the grammatical construction, which Cranfield refers to as 'an example of that overburdening of literary structure into which Paul is sometimes betrayed by the richness and vivacity of his thought'.[62] There have been attempts to rewrite the end of v. 17 in order to make it more grammatically correct and understandable to the modern reader. Blass and Debrunner make the following suggestions.[63]

text	εἰς ὃν παρεδόθητε τύπον διδαχῆς
first suggestion	τῷ τύπῳ εἰς ὃν παρεδόθητε διδαχῆς
second suggestion	εἰς τὸν τύπον ὃν παρεδόθητε διδαχῆς

Each of these suggestions would be translated in approximately the same way, as 'you were delivered to the form of teaching'. They have also suggested that ὃν παρεδόθητε could be the same as ὃς παρεδόθη ἡμῖν,[64] resulting in 'the form of teaching which was delivered to us', certainly a clearer translation. These different possibilities of grammatical equivalents need to be kept in mind as the three words 'form' [τύπος], 'teaching' [διδαχή], and 'to pass on' [παραδίδωμι] are examined.

'Form' [τύπος] has a variety of meanings in the New Testament, including marks (as from nails) in John 20:25; idols in Acts 7:43 (from Amos 5:25-27); a

---

[59]Vincent Taylor, *The Epistle to the Romans* (London: Epworth, 1955), p. 43. See also A. M. Hunter, *The Epistle to the Romans* (London: SCM, 1955), p. 68.
[60]F. F. Bruce, *Romans* (London: Tyndale, 1963), p. 142.
[61]Wilckens, *Der Brief an die Römer*, vol. 2, p. 35.
[62]Cranfield, *Romans*, vol. 1, p. 323.
[63]F. Blass and A. Debrunner, *A Greek Grammar of the New Testament and Other Early Christian Literature* (trans. and rev. Robert W. Funk; Chicago: University of Chicago Press, 1961), p. 154.
[64]Blass and Debrunner, *Greek Grammar*, p. 154.

plan (for the tabernacle) in Acts 7:44 and Hebrews 8:5; and the text of a letter in Acts 23:25. The most common use of 'form' [τύπος] is of a personal example for others.[65] In Romans 5:14 the word is used of Adam as he is an example, or type, of the coming one, that is, Christ. First Corinthians 10:6 describes as 'types' the Israelites, who were under the cloud, passed through the sea, and drank from the rock who is Christ. The only other time this word is used is in Romans 6:17. James Moffatt suggests that it does not mean 'type' or 'form' as we use the words, but rather, 'exemplar', 'norm', or 'authoritative standard'. Therefore the phrase would convey the idea of a 'standard of faith and morals'.[66] G. A. Johnston Ross believes that only a 'body of moral teaching' is in view, which is in contrast to dogma.[67] However, this distinction between dogma and teaching is not found in Paul, who consistently bases his moral exhortations upon theological doctrines. That the 'form of teaching' included moral directives as well as doctrine is not to be doubted. Cranfield identifies 'teaching' in this sentence as an appositive genitive so that the idea being conveyed is 'pattern consisting of teaching'.[68] Whatever way 'form of teaching' is translated into English, it certainly carries the idea of a set body of material which has been taught.

We have already seen in our examination of 'to pass on' that Paul and the other New Testament writers use the word in a variety of ways. Commentators think it is used in one of two ways in Romans 6:17. Some think the verb carries the simple meaning 'to deliver over', but not in the sense of 'tradition'. Cranfield says the word here (17b) means simply 'the transfer of a slave from one master to another': 'the persons addressed have obeyed from the heart (not merely formally but with inward commitment) that teaching (concerning the way of life demanded by the gospel—that teaching which is the mould by which their lives are to be shaped), to which they were delivered up (in their baptism?) as slaves to a new master'.[69] According to Nygren, the idea being conveyed is 'the pattern which must set its stamp on the life of a Christian'.[70] Goppelt suggests that 'teaching can be described as the mould or norm which shapes the whole personal conduct of the one who is delivered up to it and has become obedient thereto'.[71] None of these commentators sees the idea of 'tradition'

---

[65] See Phil. 3:17; 1 Thess. 1:7; 2 Thess. 3:9; 1 Tim. 4:12; Titus 2:7; 1 Pet. 5:3.
[66] James Moffatt, 'The Interpretation of Romans 6:17-18', *JBL* 48 (1929), p. 237.
[67] G. A. Johnston Ross, 'That Form of Doctrine: An Appeal', *Expositor*, 7th series 5 (1908), pp. 469, 471.
[68] Cranfield, *Romans,* vol. 1, p. 324.
[69] Cranfield, *Romans,* vol. 1, p. 324. See also F. W. Beare, 'On the Interpretation of Romans 6:17', *NTS* 5 (1959), pp. 206-10, who says this does not refer to the transmission of tradition.
[70] Nygren, *Romans*, p. 257.
[71] Goppelt, 'τύπος', *TDNT* 8:250.

being connoted by this verb in this context.⁷² Others, however, believe the verb carries the idea of passing along tradition.⁷³

It is difficult to choose between these two interpretations. The form of the verb would seem to support those who would simply translate the verb 'to deliver over', for it never says that information was passed on. On the other hand, Moffatt says that the 'change of the active into the passive form is not unnatural' for 'to pass on',⁷⁴ and the cluster of terms (form, teaching, to pass on) would suggest the idea of passing along tradition. No one can say with certainty which meaning the verb itself carries here. But whatever the meaning, commentators on the whole see a parallel between Romans 6:17 and 16:17 ('the teaching you have learned') and agree that 'the phrase clearly refers to a form or pattern of Christian teaching which in some way had become normative'.⁷⁵

'To pass on' [παραδίδωμι] is also conspicuous in 1 Corinthians, where it describes the transmission of all of Paul's teaching (11:2), Paul's account of the Lord's Supper which was passed on to the Corinthians (11:23), and Paul's gospel (15:3). Therefore it is clear that Paul uses this word to describe a certain body of material or teaching that was passed on either by Paul himself (1 Cor.) or by others who proclaimed the same message (Rom. 6:17; 16:17). This material is to be 'received' (1 Cor. 15:1) and 'obeyed' (Rom. 6:17).

This verb is found in only two more passages in the New Testament, 2 Peter 2:21 and Jude 3. In 2 Peter it refers to those who have turned 'their backs on the sacred commandment that was passed on to them'. Although the word 'commandment' is in the singular, no particular commandment is mentioned in 2 Peter 2. The 'commandment' is parallel to 'the way of righteousness' mentioned earlier in the verse. Both are presented in contrast to the 'destructive heresies' mentioned at the beginning of the chapter. Jude 3 gives the purpose of the letter as contending 'for the faith that God has once for all entrusted to the saints'. Although Jude uses the verb in the same way as Paul, there are three differences in the overall context from Paul: (1) it is the only place where God is the subject of the verb, (2) it is the only place where 'the faith' is what is delivered, and (3) this 'faith' has been delivered 'once for all' time.

The Apostolic Fathers show the same breadth of definition found in the New Testament. In only three places is this verb used to refer to the transfer of tradition. *Diognetus* 7.1-2 says of Christians: 'For it is not, as I said, an earthly

---

⁷²See Beare, 'Rom. 6.17', NTS 5 (1959), pp. 206-10, who says it does not refer to the transmission of tradition. See also C. K. Barrett, *The Epistle to the Romans* (London: Black, 1972), p. 132.

⁷³Wilckens, *Der Brief an die Römer*, vol. 2, p. 35. For a summary of the variety of positions see Schmithals, *Römerbrief,* p. 198.

⁷⁴Moffatt, 'Romans 6:17-18', p. 236.

⁷⁵Vernon H. Neufeld, *The Earliest Christian Confessions* (NTTS 5; Leiden: Brill, 1963), p. 25.

discovery which was given [παραδόθη] to them, nor do they take such pains to guard some mortal invention, nor have they been entrusted [πεπίστευνται] with the dispensation of human mysteries. But in truth the Almighty and all-creating and invisible God himself founded among men the truth from heaven, and the holy and incomprehensible word. . . .'[76] In this passage 'was given' is parallel to the verb 'was entrusted'. In *Diognetus*, as in Jude, it is God who has given this information by sending the one who is the creator; this one is both God and man (*Diogn.* 7.4). In this same epistle the writer claims to be a disciple of the apostles who is becoming a teacher of the heathen (11.1). He then says, 'I administer worthily that which has been handed down [τὰ παραδοθέντα] to those who are becoming disciples of the truth'. Because he is included in this group of disciples, he is saying that he is handing down apostolic tradition.

The only other place in the Apostolic Fathers that this verb is used of the passing on of apostolic tradition is in Polycarp *To the Philippians*: 'Wherefore, leaving the foolishness of the crowd, and their false teaching, let us turn back to the word which was delivered [παραδοθέντα] to us in the beginning .' (7.2).[77] Polycarp then briefly quotes1 Peter 4:7, Matthew 6:13 and 26:41, and Mark 14:38. As we have already noted, Polycarp was greatly influenced by Paul's letters; for him to use the tradition terminology as Paul does is not surprising.

2. Teaching [διδαχή]

Arndt and Gingrich define 'teaching' in an active sense as teaching and instructing, or in a passive sense as 'of what is taught'.[78] Because it carries either an active or passive sense, it can be used as an alternative to 'teach' [διδάσκειν] or to 'be taught' [διδάσκεσθαι].[79] In the Gospels it almost always describes Jesus's teaching of the will of God.[80] The only exception to this in the Gospels is Matthew 16:12, where Jesus warns about the 'teaching of the Pharisees and Sadducees'. Acts carries on this same emphasis, but with respect to the teaching of the apostles (Acts 2:42; 5:28) and Paul (Acts 13:12—with Barnabas; 17:19—by himself).

'Teaching' is used six times in the Pauline corpus. In Romans 6:17 Paul says, 'You have obeyed the form of doctrine which was delivered you', and in Romans 16:17, 'I urge you brothers, to watch out for those who cause divisions and put obstacles in your way, contrary to the teaching you have learned'. In

---

[76]Lake, *Apostolic Fathers*, LCL.
[77]Lake, *Apostolic Fathers*, LCL.
[78]Arndt and Gingrich, 'διδαχή', *Lexicon*, p. 191.
[79]Rengstorf, 'διδαχή', *TDNT* 2:163.
[80]See Matt.7:28; 22:33; Mark 1:22, 27; 4:2; 11:18; 12:38; Luke 4:32; John 7:16, 17; 18:19. Rengstorf, 'διδαχή', *TDNT* 2:164.

Tradition in 2 Thessalonians: Terminology and Identification

both cases the whole of the apostolic message is in view.[81] This teaching would include not only the gospel proclamation but also the ethical imperatives that arise out of the gospel, for the context of each of these passages (Rom. 6:16-17; 16:19) stresses obedience to the ethical norms they have been taught. Clearly Paul has confidence that the message taught to the Christians at Rome was the same message he himself taught. Because the content of the teaching is focused upon, a certain body of material (with a strong ethical content) is in view. In 1 Corinthians 14:6, 26, teaching is seen as a spiritual gift to be used for edifying the church. In Romans it would appear to carry the active sense (activity) in contrast to the passive sense (content). The Pastorals display the same range of meanings found in the rest of the Pauline corpus. Timothy is directed to 'preach the Word . . . with careful instruction' (2 Tim. 4:2), describing the manner of preaching, whereas in Titus 1:9 the content of teaching is in view: an elder must 'hold firmly to the trustworthy message as it has been taught.'

'Teaching' is also found in Hebrews 13:9 and Revelation 2:14, 15, 24, where there are warnings concerning false teaching. Hebrews 6:2 makes a passing reference to 'instruction about baptisms', and 2 John 9-10 gives warnings to adhere to the true teaching that Jesus Christ has come in the flesh.

This term is also found in the Apostolic Fathers. The *Didache* contains a body of formalized teaching, which in fact gives the name to the book (*Did.* 1.3; 2.1; 6.1), and a warning concerning false teaching (11.2). *Barnabas* contrasts the 'Two Ways' of teaching (18.1) as light and darkness. It also speaks of the gift of teaching (9.9) and the commands of teaching (16.9). Hermas warns of the false teaching of the angel of wickedness (Herm. *Mand.* 6.2.7) and of the hypocrites (Herm. *Sim.* 8.6.5). Ignatius uses this noun of both false (Ign. *Eph.* 9.1) and true (Ign. *Mag.* 6.2) teaching.

As we have seen, 'teaching' by itself does not always carry an idea of a fixed tradition, but in connection with certain other words it can refer to such a body of material. This material usually contains a strong ethical orientation based on a theological foundation.

3. Word [λόγος]

Paul frequently uses 'word' [λόγος] in a variety of ways in his letters. It can be used to introduce an Old Testament quote.[82] Quite frequently it is used to refer back to the message which Paul preached, using the phrases 'the word of God', 'the word of the Lord', or simply 'the word'.[83] Only the Pastorals refer to

---

[81]Wegenast, 'διδασκαλία', *NIDNTT* 3:770. He states that both these passages refer 'to the whole of *his* [italics mine] apostolic teaching'. This is clearly impossible in both cases since Paul has not been to Rome.

[82]Rom. 9:9; 13:9; 1 Cor. 15:54; Gal. 5:14.

[83]For 'the word of God' see Rom. 9:6; 1 Cor. 14:36; 2 Cor. 2:17; 4:2; Phil. 1:14; Col. 1:25; 1 Thess. 2:13; 1 Tim. 4:5; 2 Tim. 2:9; Titus 2:5. For 'the word of the Lord' see 1

The Authenticity of 2 Thessalonians

tradition as 'faithful sayings' [λόγος].[84] Very often in the Pauline corpus it can imply simply a 'word', 'words', 'report', 'speech', or 'saying'.[85] Frequently it is used in the singular when used to mean someone else's teaching or a saying.

The same range of meanings is found in the Apostolic Fathers; the only major addition is referring to Jesus as the 'Word' in the same fashion as John's gospel.[86]

In 2 Thessalonians 2:2, 15, 'word' is not linked specifically to tradition but is used similarly, as it is used in the undisputed letters of Paul and elsewhere in the New Testament and Apostolic Fathers, to mean preaching or message. Therefore, by itself it neither helps nor hinders the case for authenticity.

4. Other Terms

A variety of terms which refer to 'teaching' are found in the New Testament. Both 1 and 2 Timothy speak of guarding 'the deposit' [παραθήκη] (1 Tim. 6:20; 2 Tim. 1:12, 14), a use found nowhere else in the New Testament or in the Apostolic Fathers. 'Teaching' [διδασκαλία] is used in a quote from Isaiah 29:13 in Mark 7:7 and Matthew 15:9 to refer to the teaching Jesus condemns. In Romans 12:7 the term is applied to the gift of teaching, and in Romans 15:4, to the Scriptures. Ephesians 4:14 and Colossians 2:22 use it to describe false teaching. In the Pastorals, however, it is the dominant term (used fifteen times) to describe all kinds of teaching.[87]

Thess. 1:8; 2 Thess. 3:1; 1 Thess. 4:15 (has the slightly different phrase 'by the word of the Lord'—ἐν λόγῳ κυρίου); 1 Tim. 6:3 (the 'words of our Lord Jesus Christ') and Col. 3:16 ('the word of Christ'). In other references 'word' refers to Paul's preaching and teaching (1 Cor. 1:18; 2:4; 15:2; 2 Cor. 1:18; 5:19; 6:7; 10:10, 11; Gal. 6:6; Eph. 1:13; 6:19; Phil. 2:16; Col. 1:5; 4:3; 1 Thess. 1:6; 2:13; 2 Thess. 2:15; 3:14; 2 Tim. 1:13; 4:15; Titus 1:3). In 1 Tim. 5:17; 2 Tim. 2:15; 4:2; and Titus 2:8, the writer commands the teaching of the word.

[84] 1 Tim. 1:15; 3:1; 4:9; 2 Tim. 2:11; Titus 3:8.

[85] Rom. 14:12; 15:18; 1 Cor. 1:5, 17; 2:1, 13; 4:19, 20; 12:8; 14:9, 19; 2 Cor. 8:7; 11:6; Eph. 4:29; 5:6; Col. 2:23; 3:17; 4:6; 1 Thess. 1:5; 2:5; 4:18; 2 Thess. 2:2; 2:17; 1 Tim. 4:6, 12; 2 Tim. 2:17. The only other definitions found in the Pauline corpus are divine judgment (Rom. 3:4; 9:28—both OT citations or allusions), 'matter' (Phil. 4:15), or 'account' (Phil. 4:17).

[86] Ign. *Mag.* 8.2; *Diogn.* 11.2, 3. For each phrase see the following references: 'the word of God' (*Barn.* 19.4; *1 Clem.* 42.3; Ign. *Phld.* 11.1; Ign. *Rom.* 2.1; Ign. *Smyrn.* 'Greeting'; 10.1; *Did.* 4.1); 'the word of the Lord' (*Barn.* 9.3; 10.11; 19.9; Herm. *Sim.* 9.25.2); 'the word of Jesus Christ' (*Mart. Pol.* 22.1); 'the word of Jesus' (Ign. *Eph.* 15.2); 'the words of the Lord Jesus' (*1 Clem.* 13.1; 46.7); 'the words of Christ' (*1 Clem.* 2.1).

[87] ἑτεροδιδασκαλέω is also found only in the Pastorals (1 Tim. 1:3; 6:3) and nowhere else in the NT or Apostolic Fathers.

C. Evaluating the Terminology

The terminology referring to tradition in 2 Thessalonians can be evaluated most easily by seeing the contrasts and similarities to the other literature examined.

1. Contrasts

1. The terminology used in 2 Thessalonians to refer to tradition and teaching contrasts with that in the Pastorals (Pastorals-διδασκαλία, παραθήκη, ἑτεροδιδασκαλέω, πιστὸς ὁ λόγος).

2. The time perspective of 2 Thessalonians contrasts with the Pastorals. 2 Thessalonians directs its readers to obey what they had been taught by the author. The Pastorals focus on the next generation. This passing on of the 'tradition' to the next generation is never mentioned in 2 Thessalonians.

3. The terminology of 2 Thessalonians also contrasts with Colossians, for 'tradition' [παράδοσις] in Colossians 2:8 refers to 'human traditions', not Jewish or Christian.[88] Furthermore, 'to receive' [παραλαμβάνω] in Col. 2:6 and 4:17 refers to receiving Christ and a ministry. This idea is not found anywhere else in Paul.

4. The terminology of 2 Thessalonians contrasts with the Gospels and the rest of the New Testament (outside of the undisputed letters of Paul).[89] The writer of 2 Thessalonians speaks of Christian tradition, as do the undisputed Paulines, whereas the Gospels speak only of Jewish tradition, which they view negatively. However, the same cluster of terms (in Mark: 'to hold' [κρατέω], 'tradition' [παράδοσις], 'to receive' [παραλαμβάνω], 'to walk' [περιπατέω], 'to pass on' [παραδίδωμι]) associated in the Gospels with Jewish tradition is used by Paul and the writer of 2 Thessalonians with reference to Christian tradition.

5. In general, the terminology in 2 Thessalonians contrasts with the Apostolic Fathers as well. Although the Apostolic Fathers are familiar with the terminology concerning tradition, they use it infrequently to refer to tradition. When they do use the terminology, they exalt the tradition ('glorious and venerable rule of our tradition', *1 Clem.* 7.2; 'tradition of the apostles', *Diogn.* 11.6) and look back to it as something received by them in the past ('in the beginning', Pol. *Phil.* 7.2). The writer of 2 Thessalonians does not exalt the tradition nor ascribe it to the distant past, but claims to have given it himself to the Thessalonians.

---

[88] It is possible that this is in contrast to an implied Christian tradition; however, this is not explicitly stated.

[89] Hebrews speaks of receiving [παραλαμβάνω] a kingdom (12:28). This use is not found in the undisputed Paulines, nor in 2 Thess.

2. Similarities

1. Second Thessalonians can be compared most closely to 1 Corinthians. In fact, in terms of terminology, 2 Thessalonians is more closely aligned with 1 Corinthians than with 1 Thessalonians.[90]

2. Second Thessalonians uses the same clustering of terms concerning the transmission of tradition as is found within the undisputed Pauline letters (see especially Rom. 6:17; 1 Cor. 1:1-2; 1 Thess. 4:1; Phil. 4:9), yet at the same time it does not use the terms in exactly the same order or form as if they were copied from one of Paul's other letters. The writer of 2 Thessalonians clearly felt the same flexibility with the terms concerning tradition as did Paul himself.

3. It can be seen clearly that 2 Thessalonians refers back to portions of a body of material that had been delivered previously. This idea of a set body of material delivered to other congregations is also seen in the undisputed Pauline letters.[91]

4. Second Thessalonians is like the undisputed Pauline epistles in that the content of the body of material (the 'tradition') includes both doctrine (2 Thess. 2:1-12; 1 Cor. 11:23-26; 15:3-5; Rom. 6:17) and ethical exhortation (especially imitation—2 Thess. 3:6-10; Phil. 4:9; 1 Cor. 11:2).

The way Paul uses the tradition terminology in letters to the congregations he founded (especially 1 Thess., 1 Cor., and Phil.) and to a church he did not found (Rom.—see especially 6:17; 16:17) shows that he was conscious that the 'tradition' he was passing on was not just his own teaching, but the tradition of the whole church. Even though he received the gospel directly from the exalted Jesus (Gal. 1:11-12), he used traditional forms to communicate it. This study of tradition terminology shows that the phrases referring to tradition in 2 Thessalonians (2:15; 3:6) are not at all peculiar, but instead, are the type of phrases one would expect Paul to use (contra Trilling) and are not directly drawn from 1 Thessalonians. These phrases do not display a post-apostolic development, but rather, this emphasis on tradition seems particularly Pauline.

II. The Identification of Tradition in 2 Thessalonians

We have seen that the terminology of tradition in 2 Thessalonians is consistent with Paul's use of the terminology. To determine whether these particular traditions are used as Paul uses tradition in his undisputed writings, we must next identify to what the terminology refers in 2 Thessalonians.

---

[90]Vander Stichele, 'Concept', p. 503, agrees with this assessment and believes this could be used as an argument for authenticity, but she still believes the writer of 2 Thess. is copying from 1 Thess.: particularly, that 2 Thess. 2:15 copies 1 Thess. 2:13 and that 2 Thess. 3:6 copies 1 Thess. 4:1 (p. 501).

[91]See for example: Rom. 6:16; 16:17; 1 Cor. 11:2, 23-26; 15:3-5; 1 Thess. 2:13; Phil. 4:9; Gal. 2:2.

Tradition in 2 Thessalonians: Terminology and Identification

A. Tradition in 2 Thessalonians 2

The first passage to speak explicitly of 'tradition' in 2 Thessalonians is 2 Thessalonians 2:15. The verse begins with 'therefore', which suggests a conclusion to what has preceded.[92] It is unlikely that the author, whether Paul or an imitator, would begin a new section in this manner. In the New Testament, this way of beginning a sentence is found only in the Pauline corpus in the New Testament, and in each passage it is used to draw a conclusion from what precedes.[93] Charles Giblin has shown that there is no contextual break between 2:12 and 2:13; rather, 2:13-15 forms 'a pastoral thanksgiving . . . the salvific counterpart of the process described in vv. 11-12'.[94] Therefore, 2:13-17 brings to a conclusion what has been introduced earlier in the chapter.

Verse 15 is not the only place in ch. 2 which refers to tradition, for 2:5-6 does implicitly as well. The author calls upon the readers to 'remember' what he had told them and says they 'know' the information which he is about to write.[95] These two verses clearly are distinct from the information he is giving in this chapter, for the author makes a direct reference to himself and to his readers in these verses but does not use the first person singular again until the end of the letter. Because this is the only time in 2:3b-12 that the author or readers are directly mentioned, these verses (2:3b-4, 7-12) display a rather impersonal tone. This impersonal tone, however, is immediately broken at 2:13, where the author again uses the personal pronouns 'we' (the writers) and 'you' (the readers, who are 'brothers') to contrast their fate to the fate of 'those who are perishing' (2:10). This switch can best be explained as the author incorporating into his own writing a piece of tradition which he applies to the problem faced by his readers. The language of the tradition is general and rather impersonal; when using his own words (2:1-3a, 5-6, 13-17), the author directly addresses his audience in a much more personal manner. Therefore the author incorporates two sections of tradition, 2:3b-4 and 7-12, right into this chapter.

Most commentators have recognized 2:3b-4 as tradition, yet many have thought 7-12 is the writer's own teaching concerning the return of Christ and the final battle. This is unlikely, however, because the writer introduces this material with the expectation that the readers already 'know' this information (2:6). Furthermore, there are clear grammatical breaks at 2:3b, the beginning of

---

[92]This is the view represented by most commentators. See Marshall, *Thessalonians*, p. 209; Best, *Thessalonians*, p. 317; Frame, *Thessalonians*, p. 283. Trilling, *Thessalonicher*, p. 124, sees this verse as beginning a major section (2:15–3:16).

[93]See Rom. 5:18; 7:3, 25; 8:12; 9:16, 18; 14:12, 19; Gal. 6:10; Eph. 2:19 and 1 Thess. 5:6.

[94]Giblin, *Threat*, p. 42.

[95]This has already been shown earlier in this chapter, in the section on the use of 'to know' [οἶδα].

2:5, before 2:7 and after 2:12. The writer introduces the information which he expects his audience to know with 'for' [ὅτι] in 2:3 and 'for' [γάρ] in 2:7, and at 2:5 and 2:13 the breaks are seen in the change in the personal references. Not only this, but the writer calls this information which he expects them to know 'tradition'. The insertion of traditional material followed by the return to directly addressing the readers explains why a number of interpreters have mistakenly thought 2:13 begins a new section; however, the grammatical break for a new section does not occur until 3:1 with 'finally' [τὸ λοιπόν]. Consequently, in terms of context, 2 Thessalonians 2:15 and 2 Thessalonians 2:5-6 refer to the same traditional material (2:3b-4; 7-12). When the writer of 2 Thessalonians says, 'So then, brothers, stand firm and hold to the traditions we passed on to you, whether by word of mouth or by letter', he is not primarily giving a general command for all the Pauline letters and doctrine, as Trilling attempts to show, but he is talking specifically about the traditions he is repeating in this context.

Therefore a thematic outline of 2 Thessalonians 2 can be drawn up:
1. The writer's concern over the situation (1-2a)
2. The problem: someone says 'the day of the Lord has already come' (2b)
3. The warning (3a)
4. Tradition concerning the rebellion and the lawless one (3b-4)
5. Personal warning to remember the tradition (5-6)
6. Tradition concerning the last battle (7-12)
7. Contrast of the Thessalonian believers with those who are perishing and a command to stand fast (13-15)
8. Prayer for strength for the Thessalonians (16-17)

In examining the overall themes of the pieces of tradition, it is important to see that these themes do not in themselves directly address the problem that is raised. The problem is the false teaching about the arrival or the timing of the day of the Lord, but the traditions focus on defining and characterizing the man of lawlessness (3b-4) and describing the final battle and its outcome (7-12).[96] The writer has purposely taken these more general traditions, which do not directly address the problem in 2:2, and applied them to the particular problem. His reasoning is that because the Thessalonians know these traditions and can be sure that the events described in them have not yet occurred, they can know that the error described in 2:2 is false. The doctrinal traditions used in 2 Thessalonians 2 carry more information than is needed to solve the particular problem: although the tradition was not created for this problem, the author thinks that some of the content of the preformed tradition applies to the problem at hand. As we will see, this is a characteristic of Paul's use of tradition.

---

[96]The exegetical details of the pieces of tradition will be dealt with in ch. 4.

B. Tradition in 2 Thessalonians 3

In 2 Thessalonians 3:6, the author again refers to 'tradition'. This is not the only word in this section that refers to tradition; he also says that his readers 'know' this information (3:7), that they have received it (3:6), and that they were commanded this (3:10). The tradition to which the author refers has to do specifically with imitation of the missionaries' example. He contrasts the way 'we' lived with the idle way some of the brothers are living (3:6). After introducing the topic ('idleness') and mentioning 'tradition', the writer then applies the 'tradition' to the problem at hand. His introductory statement, 'For you yourselves know how', alerts the reader to the coming piece of traditional teaching. He continues, '. . . it is necessary to imitate us'. He then returns to the particular problem again, 'because we were not idle among you'. Following this the writer describes the way the missionaries behaved: 'nor did we eat anyone's food without paying for it, but we worked night and day, laboring and toiling so that we would not be a burden to any one of you' (3:8). In 2 Thessalonians 3:9 the author again refers to 'imitating us', and in v. 10 he once more reminds them of the command they were given 'that if a man will not work, he shall not eat'. In 3:11 he again describes the particular problem at Thessalonica ('idleness'). Therefore the only traditions which the author explicitly mentions are the two statements about imitation in 3:7 and 3:9 and the command at the end of 3:10. These pieces of tradition which are incorporated right into the writer's own sentence structure are not as large as those found in 2 Thessalonians 2; in fact, the statement 'if someone will not work he shall not eat' is proverbial in character.

The author does not present the details of the missionaries' example as preformed tradition; rather, it is presented in a very personal way with a use of multiple pronouns. The author takes the general character of the missionaries' ministry and applies it to the problem of idleness. He then reminds them of what they were taught by repeating the proverb found in 2 Thessalonians 3:10. Therefore the author presents two reasons for a change in behavior: the necessity to follow the pattern of missionary behavior, and the obligation to obey the command of the missionaries. In contrast to the doctrinal traditions found in 2 Thessalonians 2, the traditions in ch. 3 are of a paraenetic nature.

C. Tradition in 2 Thessalonians 1

Although 'tradition' is never mentioned as explicitly in 2 Thessalonians 1 as it is in chs 2 and 3, both Dibelius and Bornemann have identified 2 Thessalonians 1:7-10a as Christian cultic language or an early Christian psalm or hymn. These authors, along with most commentators, have recognized the solemn tone[97] and extensive Old Testament allusions[98] in this part of ch. 1 that set it off from the rest of the chapter.

The clearest sign in the text that the writer of 2 Thessalonians intends his readers to recognize a portion of ch. 1 as tradition is the abrupt break in the middle of v. 10. The clause 'When he comes to be glorified among his holy ones and to be marveled at by all those who have believed' is followed by the awkward insertion 'because our testimony was believed by you'. The verse then concludes with the phrase 'on that day', which belongs with the infinitives in the clause which precedes the insertion.[99] As was shown in the earlier section on the terminology of tradition, in Paul the word 'testimony' is identified with his gospel (see especially 1 Cor. 1:6; 2:2). The writer of 2 Thessalonians is making this same identification, saying that what he has just said about the reversal of situations at the final judgment is part of that original proclamation to the Thessalonians.

The section (1:6-10a) is further set off from its context by the author's use of pronouns. This is seen most clearly in the chart on the next page. From this chart it is apparent that in 1:6-10a almost all of the personal references to the writer(s) or readers are absent, especially beginning from 7b ('at the revelation of the Lord Jesus') until the clear break in thought in 10b ('because our witness to you was believed'). This section is also the longest of the three sections (seventy-six words) and yet has the fewest personal references.[100] The reference to 'our Lord Jesus' (1:8) easily could have been a part of a traditional statement.

---

[97]Bornemann, *Thessalonicherbriefe,* p. 336; Dibelius, *Briefe* (1911), p. 27.
[98]The most extensive treatment of these themes has been done by Roger D. Aus. See his 'The Relevance of Isaiah 66:7 to Revelation 12 and 2 Thessalonians 1', *ZNW* 67 (1976), pp. 252-68; and his dissertation, 'Comfort in Judgment: The Use of Day of the Lord and Theophany Traditions in Second Thessalonians 1' (PhD thesis, Yale University, 1971). Aus, 'Comfort', pp. 35-36, 105, 107, does not identify part of ch. 1 as a preformed piece of tradition, but he does acknowledge the extensive use of OT material in this section. See also Rigaux, *Thessaloniciens,* pp. 94-95, 624.
[99]Frame, *Thessalonians,* p. 236; Rigaux, *Thessaloniciens,* p. 635.
[100]Verses 3-5 have seventy-two words, and vv. 10b-12 have sixty words.

Tradition in 2 Thessalonians: Terminology and Identification

The Use of First and Second Person Pronouns in 2 Thessalonians 1:3-12

verse	1st person	2nd person
1:3	**we** ought to thank	concerning **you**, brothers
		your faith
		love each of **you** for one another
1:4	**we** boast	about **you**
		your endurance and faith
		in all **your** persecutions and tribulations
		you are enduring
1:5		**you** may be counted worthy
		for which **you** are suffering

1:6		the ones afflicting **you**
1:7a		to **you** who are being afflicted
	rest with **us**	
1:7b		
1:8	**our** Lord Jesus	
1:9		
1:10a		

1:10b	**our** witness	by **you**
1:11	**we** pray	concerning **you**
		you may be worthy
		the calling of **our** God
1:12	**our** Lord Jesus	glorified among **you**
		and **you** in him
	grace of **our** God	

Grammatically, vv. 6-10a form a unit within the chapter. This section begins with the combined particle 'since' [εἴπερ], used only six times in the New Testament, three of which are in Romans. Paul first uses this particle in Romans to state categorically that the one true God will justify both the circumcised and uncircumcised who have faith. After asking rhetorically in Romans 3:29, 'Is God the God of Jews only? Is he not the God of Gentiles too?', Paul answers, 'Yes, of the Gentiles, too'. In v. 30 he gives the reason he knows this to be true: 'since there is only one God'. Paul's answer does not simply state some theological principle; rather, he states the traditional creed of Judaism[101]—a piece of tradition introduced with the particle 'since' [εἴπερ]. The particle is again used in Romans 8:9 to introduce the reason Paul knows that his readers are not 'in the flesh' but 'in the Spirit': 'since [εἴπερ] the Spirit of God dwells

---

[101] C. E. B. Cranfield, *Romans: A Shorter Commentary* (Edinburgh: T & T Clark, 1985), p. 80.

in you'. Paul is not calling into question whether or not they possess the Spirit; rather, he is making an 'appeal to an acknowledged fact'.[102] This same sort of argument is again used by Paul in Romans 8:17: 'Now if we are children, then we are heirs—heirs of God and co-heirs with Christ, if indeed [εἴπερ] we share in his sufferings in order that we may also share in his glory'. Again, Paul is not calling into question the legitimacy of their experience, but rather, he is giving them assurance by appealing to a fact which confirms what he has said.[103] In 1 Corinthians 8:5 Paul uses the particle [καὶ γὰρ εἴπερ] concessively, meaning 'however much'[104] or 'even if',[105] and in 1 Corinthians 15:15 he uses the particle [with ἄρα] to express an unreal hypothetical premise.[106]

In 2 Thessalonians 1:6, 'since' [εἴπερ] is used in the same way as in Romans, introducing the reason for accepting the preceding statement as true by referring to what they already knew. Therefore, the section which should be identified as tradition in 2 Thessalonians 1 begins at v. 6. The personal references in vv. 6 and 7 are probably inserted into the tradition by the author of 2 Thessalonians in order to show how the general material having to do with the final resolution of tribulation at the parousia applies to his audience. When the passage is arranged according to parallel phrases (see following page), what becomes immediately apparent is its highly organized structure. Every assertion is modified with two parallel phrases. Furthermore, the pronouns that were removed in 1:6-7 (1:6—'you' [ὑμᾶς]; 1:7—'you' [ὑμῖν] and 'with us'[μεθ' ἡμῶν]) actually break the parallel phrases in those two verses. They appear to be added for pastoral reasons, to emphasize that this tradition applies to the readers. The only other break in the structure is in 10b, 'because our testimony was believed by you'. This highly structured form also indicates that these verses are preformed tradition:

---

[102]Cranfield, *Romans: A Shorter Commentary*, p. 181.
[103]Cranfield, *Romans: A Shorter Commentary*, p. 193.
[104]Blass and Debrunner, *Greek Grammar*, p. 237, sec. 454.
[105]Fee, *1 Corinthians*, p. 372.
[106]Fee, *1 Corinthians*, p. 742.

Tradition in 2 Thessalonians: Terminology and Identification

2 Thessalonians 1:6-10
1:6 The righteous judgment of God [will] repay
δίκαιον παρὰ θεῷ ἀνταποδοῦναι
to those who are afflicting: affliction;
τοῖς θλίβουσιν . . . θλῖψιν
1:7 and to those being afflicted: rest;
καὶ . . . τοῖς θλιβομένοις ἄνεσιν . . .
at the revelation of the Lord Jesus from heaven
ἐν τῇ ἀποκαλύψει τοῦ κυρίου Ἰησοῦ ἀπ' οὐρανοῦ
with his powerful angels
μετ' ἀγγέλων δυνάμεως αὐτοῦ
1:8 in flaming fire;
ἐν πυρὶ φλογός
giving punishment
διδόντες ἐκδίκησιν
to those not knowing God
τοῖς μὴ εἰδόσιν θεὸν
and to those not obeying the gospel of our Lord Jesus
καὶ τοῖς μὴ ὑπακούσιν τῷ εὐαγγελίῳ
τοῦ κυρίου ἡμῶν Ἰησοῦ
1:9 who will be punished with everlasting destruction
οἵτινες δίκην τίσουσιν ὄλεθρον αἰώνιον
from the presence of the Lord
ἀπὸ προσώπου τοῦ κυρίου
and from the glory of his power
καὶ ἀπὸ τῆς δόξης τῆς ἰσχύος αὐτοῦ
1:10 when he comes
ὅταν ἔλθῃ
to be glorified among his holy ones
ἐνδοξασθῆναι ἐν τοῖς ἁγίοις αὐτοῦ
and to be marveled at among those who believe
καὶ θαυμασθῆναι ἐν πᾶσιν τοῖς πιστεύσιν . . .
on that day.
ἐν τῇ ἡμέρᾳ ἐκείνῃ.

Roger Aus has concluded that 7b-10a are not inserted material but are the writer's own words. He gives three reasons: (1) The constellation of terms found throughout this whole chapter is not limited to 7b-10a; this repetition of terms shows Pauline style; (2) 7b-10a does not show a piece of Jewish tradition overburdened with Christian additions (contra Dibelius); and (3) The author's use of 'good purpose' [εὐδοκίαν] in v. 11 shows that he knew the original context of a number of the thoughts in 7b-10a (LXX, Ps. 88:18). According to Aus, if the writer had simply adopted 'foreign material', he would not have known the background of the imagery in 7b-10a and would therefore not have chosen this word in 1:11, a word which is used infrequently in the Pauline corpus.[107]

None of these reasons, however, proves that 6-10a is not tradition. Aus lists ten word groups that he finds repeated throughout this chapter and which he thinks show that only one author wrote the entire chapter.[108] Yet when the word groups are examined, it can be seen that vv. 6-10a have only five of these groups in common with the rest of the chapter.[109] Considering that the author thought this tradition was applicable to the readers' situation, it is not too surprising that he uses in his own prose at least a few words which originate in the piece of tradition. The writer of 2 Thessalonians could very well have chosen the terms he uses in 1:3-5 because those terms were already part of the tradition he was about to introduce (1:6-10a). Aus's second reason rightly reacts against Dibelius's suggestion that the writer of 2 Thessalonians has taken a piece of Jewish tradition and incorporated Christian expressions, making the section overburdened.[110] The section does not give the appearance of a piece of Jewish tradition re-worded awkwardly in order to Christianize it; rather, it reads smoothly, with the 'Christian' phrases as an integral part. This does not, however, rule out the possibility that the writer used Christian tradition. Aus's final comment that the author of 2 Thessalonians would not know the Old Testament background to the Christian tradition and so would not have used 'good purpose' [εὐδοκίαν] in his own writing in 1:11 does not substantiate his claim that 2 Thessalonians 1 does not contain a section of preformed tradition. If modern commentators are able to recognize the Old Testament background to 2 Thessalonians 1:6-10a, then why could not the original author of 2 Thessalonians? Furthermore, the word 'good purpose' is used five other times in the Pauline corpus.[111] It is not impossible that the author of 2 Thessalonians

---

[107] Aus, 'Comfort', pp. 35-36, 105, 107.
[108] Aus, 'Comfort', p. 35. He lists:
 1:1 ἐκκλησίᾳ; 1:4 ἐκκλησίαις
 1:2 χάρις; 1:3 εὐχαριστεῖν; 1:12 χάριν
 *1:3 πάντοτε, πάντων; 1:4 πᾶσιν; 1:10 πᾶσιν; 1:11 πάντοτε, πᾶσαν
 *1:3 πίστις; 1:4 πίστεως; 1:10 πιστεύσασιν, ἐπιστεύθη; 1:11 πίστεως
 1:3 ἄξιόν; 1:5 καταξιωθῆναι; 1:11 ἀξιώσῃ
 *1:4 θλίψεσιν; 1:6 θλίβουσιν, θλῖψιν; 1:7 θλιβομένοις
 *1:5 δικαίας; 1:6 δίκαιον; 1:8 ἐκδίκησιν [1:9 δίκην through assonance]
 1:6 ἀνταποδοῦναι; 1:8 διδόντος
 *1:7 δυνάμεως [1:9 ἰσχύος]; 1:11 δυνάμει
 1:9 δόξης; 1:10 ἐνδοξασθῆναι [1:11 εὐδοκίαν through parechetic assonance].
[109] See the words I have starred (*) in the preceding footnote.
[110] Aus, 'Comfort', p. 104.
[111] Rom. 10:1; Eph. 1:5, 9; Phil. 1:15; 2:13.

chose this word by coincidence or because he was reminded of the background to the tradition. Aus does recognize that 6-10a forms a grammatical unit and that in v. 11 the writer again becomes more personal.[112]

The highly organized structure of these verses, the manner with which these verses are introduced and concluded, the impersonal character of these verses, and the way in which the writer of 2 Thessalonians concludes the first two chapters by referring back to the 'traditions which you were taught' show clearly that the author of 2 Thessalonians incorporated into 2 Thessalonians 1:6-10a a piece of preformed tradition which he expected his readers to recognize.

D. Conclusion on the Identification of Tradition in 2 Thessalonians

The writer of 2 Thessalonians uses a variety of forms of tradition. In 2 Thessalonians 1-2 he uses doctrinal traditions which are stylized, with frequent parallels (see especially 1:6-10; 2:3b-4), and are filled with Old Testament allusions. They can be characterized as catechetical or catechetical-liturgical. In ch. 3 the traditions used by the writer of 2 Thessalonians are of a paraenetic nature. The writer shows a great deal of versatility in the traditions used and in the way those traditions are handled.

The overall topics of the traditions which the author incorporates into 2 Thessalonians are the final judgment (ch. 1), the last battle and final opponent (ch. 2), and imitation (ch. 3). These traditions are applied to particular problems which are not actually the primary focus of each tradition. The final judgment tradition (1:6-10) is given to comfort persecuted believers; the last battle and final opponent traditions are directed against the false teaching that 'the day of the Lord has arrived'; and the imitation tradition is directed against the 'idleness' of some in the congregation. In the first two cases, by including the tradition, the author of the letter is presenting more instruction than is required for the specific problem at hand.

The author incorporates these traditions directly into his letter, but breaks in the context usually indicate that something has been inserted into his own argument. The traditional material is frequently referred to by a cluster of words associated with tradition: ch. 1—'testimony', 'believed'; ch. 2—'tradition', 'remember', 'know'; and ch. 3—'tradition', 'know', 'receive', 'command'. The writer can incorporate the smaller traditions right into his own sentence structure (3:7-8, 10) or introduce the tradition with *for* [εἴπερ, γάρ], *because* [ὅτι], or *how* [πῶς]. The traditions tend to be impersonal and general, yet the writer feels free at times to insert an occasional pronoun into the tradition for pastoral reasons (1:6-7).

What is especially interesting is the extent of tradition that the author uses in

---

[112]Aus, 'Comfort', pp. 56, 61, 106.

The Authenticity of 2 Thessalonians

2 Thessalonians: every major argument makes some use of tradition. The author evidently wants his readers to see that the original message, that is, the tradition, must be applied to new problems as they arise. The traditional material accounts for 27% of the entire letter,[113] thus showing the importance of this topic for establishing the authenticity of 2 Thessalonians.

III. Tradition in the Undisputed Pauline Epistles

A number of the disputers of authenticity point to the prevalence of tradition within 2 Thessalonians as evidence that it cannot be Pauline. As we have seen, a careful examination of the text does show an emphasis on tradition in 2 Thessalonians. However, this does not prove that it is unpauline, for this emphasis is not unique to 2 Thessalonians and it is not a post-Pauline development. In order to show that this use of tradition is in fact characteristic of Paul's writing, it is necessary to make a careful and detailed analysis of the undisputed Pauline epistles to determine the amount and the characteristics—form, topics, and manner of use—of tradition in Paul's letters.

It is important to clarify qualifies as tradition in Paul's letters. As E. E. Ellis has said, '"Tradition" means more than a prior idea or story floating in the memory of the Apostle, of his co-traditioners or of the amanuenses and co-senders of the letters. It is, more concretely, a specific item in a traditioning process that was formed and in oral or written usage before Paul incorporated it into his letter'.[114] Because a complete examination of all the undisputed epistles of Paul would go beyond the scope of this book, the use of tradition in only two of his undisputed epistles—1 Thessalonians and 1 Corinthians—will be examined in detail.

A. *The Identification of Tradition in 1 Thessalonians*

If 2 Thessalonians was written by Paul near to the time when he wrote 1 Thessalonians and in a somewhat similar situation, then one would expect a similar use of tradition in the two epistles. As we have seen, the tradition terminology in 2 Thessalonians corresponds more closely to 1 Corinthians than

---

[113] The number of words of tradition in 2 Thess. is based on the following figures: 1:6-10 (75 words); 2:3b-4 (39 words); 2:7-12 (98 words); 3:7 (3 words); 3:9 (2 words); and 3:10 (7 words). The total number of words of tradition, therefore, is 224 (75 + 39 + 98 + 3 + 2 + 7). The letter as a whole contains 823 words, so the percentage of tradition is 27.22 % (224/823).

[114] Ellis, '1 Corinthians', p. 481. See also A. M. Hunter, *Paul and His Predecessors* (rev.ed.; London: SCM, 1961), p. 9, who defines 'pre-Pauline' material as referring to 'the twilight period' between the rise of the Christian church and the time when Paul wrote his extant letters.

Tradition in 2 Thessalonians: Terminology and Identification

to 1 Thessalonians. However, having noted that this terminology is not absent from 1 Thessalonians, it is therefore necessary to examine the whole of 1 Thessalonians to identify which sections are traditional and to see if tradition plays a role in 1 Thessalonians similar to that in 2 Thessalonians.

1. Tradition in 1 Thessalonians 1-3

The only major section of 1 Thessalonians 1 frequently identified as a piece of tradition is 1:9b-10: 'how you turned to God from idols to serve the living and true God, and to wait for his Son from heaven, whom he raised from the dead—Jesus, who rescues us from the coming wrath'. Best lists the following vocabulary as being used in an unusual way for Paul: '**turned**, **real**, **to serve** in relation to God rather than Jesus, **out of heavens**'. He notes that when Paul uses 'from' [ἐκ] with 'heaven' [οὐρανός], he always uses the singular for 'heaven' instead of the plural (see 1 Cor. 15:47; 2 Cor. 5:2; Gal. 1:8), and that Paul uses a different word for **wait** (ἀναμένειν; elsewhere he uses compounds of δέξεσθαι); in the formula raised from the dead (cf. Gal. 1.1; Rom. 4.24; 10.9; Acts 3.15; 4.10; 1 Pet. 1.21; etc.) he uses the article (the evidence for its omission, A C K *al*, is hardly sufficient) whereas elsewhere he omits it; he never uses the word deliver elsewhere in an eschatological context (he uses σώζειν). . . . Moreover when Paul states the content of the Christian faith he makes the cross central (not in place of the resurrection but alongside it) and defines it as 'for us' (Rom. 5.6, 8; 14.15; 1 Cor. 1.13; 8.11; 2 Cor. 5.14; Ga. 2.20); yet there is no reference here even to the death of Jesus. Taken together we have a pre-Pauline statement of the Church's faith.[115]

Others have questioned this understanding of these verses, saying that all the statements contained in these two verses can be accounted for as Paul preparing his readers for what he will expound more fully in the remainder of his letter[116] or as Paul simply using traditional mission terminology.[117] More recently, Wanamaker has given three arguments against identifying these verses as tradition: (1) a pre-Pauline tradition that refers to a mission to the Gentiles is unlikely since Paul's own missionary activity goes back to the earliest days of the Christian Gentile mission; (2) the verses lack the careful construction and balance expected of a formula and even contain a change of person in the midst

---

[115] Best, *Thessalonians*, pp. 85-86. Ivan Havener, 'The Pre-Pauline Christological Credal Formulae of 1 Thessalonians', *SBL Seminar Papers, 1981* (SBLSP 20; Chico, CA: Scholars Press, 1981), pp. 105-28, uses many of these same reasons.

[116] Johannes Munck, '1 Thess. 1.9-10 and the Missionary Preaching of Paul', *NTS* 9 (1962-63), pp. 95-110.

[117] Traugott Holtz, '"Euer Glaube an Gott": Zu Form und Inhalt von 1 Thess 1,9f', in Rudolf Schnackenburg, Josef Ernst, and Joachim Wanke *(eds), Die Kirche des Anfangs: Festschrift für Heinz Schürmann* (Freiburg: Herder, 1978), pp. 459-88.

The Authenticity of 2 Thessalonians

of the section ('you turned'—v. 9; 'us'—v. 10); and (3) the words 'turned', 'to serve', 'his son', and 'heavens' are not as unusual to Paul as Best claims.[118]

The arguments against identifying 1:9-10 as tradition show a number of weaknesses. First, they do not account for the unusual vocabulary and its use in these verses. Second, the idea that 1 Thessalonians 1:9-10 anticipates what Paul will expound more fully later is not negated at all by his use of tradition; in fact, it may very well explain why Paul has chosen this particular piece of tradition.

Wanamaker's first argument, against a pre-Pauline tradition concerning the Gentile mission, can be answered by Best's postulation that the tradition may go back to a Hebrew or Aramaic original. The name 'Jesus' in Hebrew means 'to deliver' and may be a pun with the unusual verb 'to rescue' (v. 10). Best further points out 'the absence of reference to the pre-existence and exalted conditions of Jesus as in Hellenistic formulae (cf. Phil. 2.6-11; 1 Tim. 3.16)'.[119] Furthermore, if the Acts account is correct, then there was pre-Pauline activity that reached out to non-Jews (see Acts 8). Holtz has shown that 1 Thessalonians 1:9-10 displays an unmistakable nearness to the so-called hellenistic-jewish mission literature.[120] By the time 1 Thessalonians was written, Paul had already been a missionary to the Gentiles for many years. It is very likely that after fifteen years of missionary work he had certain set formulations.

Wanamaker's second objection concerns the structure of the verses and the change of person. However, Best has offered a very plausible structural arrangement of the material in two three-line stanzas:

> You turned to God from idols
> > to serve the living and real God
> > (and) to wait for his Son out of heaven
> Whom he raised from the dead
> > Jesus who delivers us
> > from the approaching anger.[121]

Most likely the person changes from second person to first person ('you turned' in v. 9, 'us' in v. 10) because Paul introduces the tradition and applies it directly to his readers, yet he does not change all the personal references in the tradition.

---

[118] Wanamaker, *Thessalonians*, pp. 85-87. Wanamaker identifies the following words: 'turned' (2 Cor. 3:16, Gal. 4:9); 'to serve' (used in variety of ways in Paul); 'his son' (found in sections where Jesus brings eschatological salvation—Rom. 5:8-11; 8:3, 32; Gal. 2:20; 4:4f, see also 1 Cor. 15:24-28—all similar to 1 Thess. 1:10); and 'heavens' (Paul frequently uses the plural).

[119] Best, *Thessalonians*, p. 86.

[120] Holtz, 'Euer Glaube an Gott', p. 472.

[121] Best, *Thessalonians*, p. 86. The following people give a similar analysis of the structure of the passage: Havener, 'Credal Formulae', pp. 105-28; Gerhard Friedrich (see Havener, 'Credal Formulae', p. 108); Marinus de Jonge, *Christology in Context* (Philadelphia: Westminster, 1988), p. 34; and Rigaux, *Thessaloniciens*, p. 392.

Therefore, as most commentators would argue, 1 Thessalonians 1:9b-10 should be seen as pre-Pauline tradition.[122] The tradition is introduced by 'how' [πῶς], which in this context has the same meaning as 'that' [ὅτι].[123]

Wanamaker's third argument about the vocabulary does not respond to what Best actually says. Best does not say that all the vocabulary Paul uses is unique, but that it is being used in a different fashion from the way Paul normally uses this vocabulary. Simply identifying other places where this vocabulary is used in Paul does not explain the manner in which Paul uses this vocabulary here.

In 1 Thessalonians 2–3 Paul looks back on his own ministry at Thessalonica and recalls his intense desire to find out how the new Christians at Thessalonica were doing, which resulted in Timothy's visit to Thessalonica and his return to Paul (2:17–3:10). The section concludes with a prayer (3:11-13). In the opening part of this section (2:1-12) no pieces of preformed tradition are immediately distinguishable from the context; rather, Paul speaks very personally and passionately about his motives and method of ministry. Yet it is interesting to note that the terminology which he uses to describe his ministry is the same terminology he uses elsewhere to introduce tradition. Four times in these verses Paul speaks of what his readers 'know' (2:1, 2, 5, 11), a term which Paul frequently uses to introduce traditional material. In 2:9 he calls upon them to 'remember', another term used to refer back to tradition. He repeatedly uses the phrase 'the gospel of God' (2:2, 8, 9) which appears elsewhere in Paul (Rom. 1:1; 15:16; 2 Cor. 11:7). This section gives the impression that Paul has had to defend his ministry in the past and is repeating at least portions of his defense. A. J. Malherbe has shown that much of the terminology of this section (2:1-12) is not original to Paul, but that Paul 'consciously makes use of descriptions of the ideal moral philosopher'.[124] This borrowing by Paul includes the use of individual words and images as well as patterns of ministry. Malherbe quotes from Dio Chrysostom, a younger contemporary of Paul who wrote in order to distinguish himself from the irresponsible Cynics. Malherbe notes terms which Paul has in common with Dio: 'frankness' [ἐπαρρησιασάμεθα-2:2; παρρησίαν, παρρησιαζόμενον], 'plain terms' [ἀκαθαρσίας-2:3; καθαρῶς], without 'guile' [δόλῳ-2:3; ἀδόλως], 'flattery' [κολακείας-2:5; κολάκων], and 'reputation' [δόξαν-2:6; δόξης].[125] In addition to the terminology used

---

[122]Bruce, *Thessalonians*, p. 18; Leonhard Goppelt, 'Tradition nach Paulus', *KD* 4 (1958), p. 225; Karl P. Donfried, '1 Thessalonians, Acts and the Early Paul' in *The Thessalonian Correspondence* (ed. R. Collins; Leuven: Leuven University Press, 1990), p. 10.

[123]Arndt and Gingrich, *Lexicon*, 'πῶς', 2.a., p. 740.

[124]Abraham J. Malherbe, *Paul and the Thessalonians: The Philosophic Tradition of Pastoral Care* (Philadelphia: Fortress, 1987), p. 55.

[125]Malherbe, *Paul and the Thessalonians*, pp. 3-4, quotes Dio Chrysostom, *Discourse* 32.11-12. The terms from 1 Thess. 2 are followed by the terms from Dio.

here, Paul shares the images of 'nurse' and 'father' with the philosophers of his day.[126] Throughout this section and the whole letter, Paul presents himself as the ideal and is 'confident in offering himself as a model to be imitated'.[127] Malherbe notes, 'As with serious philosophers, Paul's life could not be distinguished from what he preached: his life verified his gospel'.[128] Therefore, although 2:1-12 does not contain pieces of preformed tradition, it does show that Paul is concerned not only to present the content of his message but also to defend his method, for his person and message are linked together. This section also shows that the terminology and imagery which have been considered characteristic of Paul have actually been borrowed from non-Christian sources.

In 1 Thessalonians 2:13, 'And we also thank God continually because, when you received [παραλαβόντες] the word of God, which you heard from us, you accepted it not as the word of men, but as it actually is, the word of God, which is at work in you who believe', Paul uses the standard term for the reception of tradition [παραλαμβάνω].[129] Verse 13 emphasizes that ultimately the missionaries' preaching is from God himself.[130] Paul encourages the Thessalonians by telling them that their suffering imitates that of the churches in Judea, not in conscious imitation, but rather, unconscious.[131] To support this Paul inserts a piece of tradition into his letter (vv. 15-16). Verse 15 makes a grammatical break with the preceding context by a series of participial phrases:

'who killed the Lord Jesus and the prophets,
and who persecuted us,
and who are not pleasing to God,
   and contrary to all men,
forbidding us to speak to the Gentiles,
   in order that they might be saved'.

Two words in this section stand out as unusual for Paul: 'persecute' and

---

[126]Malherbe, *Paul and the Thessalonians*, pp. 55-56, finds the image of 'nurse' in Plutarch (69 BC) and also says it was common for moral teachers to exhort as a father. For more on the nurse imagery, see A. J. Malherbe, '"Gentle as a Nurse": The Cynic Background to 1 Thess ii', *NovT* 12 (1970), pp. 203-17; and for more on the father imagery see A. J. Malherbe, 'Exhortation in First Thessalonians', *NovT* 25 (1983), pp 238-56.

[127]Malherbe, *Paul and the Thessalonians*, p. 109.

[128]Malherbe, *Paul and the Thessalonians*, p. 54.

[129]Best, *Thessalonians*, p. 110; Ronald A. Ward, *Commentary on 1 & 2 Thessalonians*, (Waco, TX: Word, 1973), p. 71; Wanamaker, *Thessalonians*, p. 110; Bruce, *Thessalonians*, p. 44; Neil, *Thessalonians*, p. 48; Marshall, *Thessalonians*, p. 77.

[130]Morris, *Thessalonians*, p. 87.

[131]Best, *Thessalonians*, p. 113.

'contrary',[132] also hinting that this section is pre-formed tradition. Furthermore, there is a clear break at the beginning of v. 17, in which Paul returns to direct address—'But we, brothers'—and changes topics.

The New Testament contains a number of parallels to the tradition found in 1 Thessalonians 2:15-16. Luke 11:47-51, where Jesus accuses 'this generation' of responsibility for the death of the prophets, parallels 1 Thessalonians 2:15-16. Similarly, in Luke 13:34, Jesus accuses Jerusalem of killing the prophets, and in Acts 7:52, Stephen condemns his audience for persecuting and killing the prophets and murdering Jesus.[133] Numerous parallels are found in the book of Acts which attribute to the Jews of Jerusalem responsibility for killing Jesus.[134] The parallel to 1 Thessalonians 2:15-16 most frequently noted is Matthew 23:31-37. The similarities between these two passages include:

1. killing the prophets: 1 Thessalonians 2:15; Matthew 23:31, 34, 37.
2. persecuting: 1 Thessalonians 2:15; Matthew 23:34.
3. not pleasing God: 1 Thessalonians 2:15; all of Matthew 23 (see the 7 'woes' and the whole theme of divine judgment).
4. filling up sin: 1 Thessalonians 2:16; Matthew 23:32, 35-36.
5. God's wrath and judgment: 1 Thessalonians 2:16; Matthew 23:33, 36, 38.[135]

These parallels make it likely that there was some type of literary dependence between, or a piece of common tradition behind, 1 Thessalonians 2:15-16 and Matthew 23:31-37.[136]

---

[132] 'Persecute' [ἐκδιωξάντων] is found only here in the NT and in a variant of Luke 11:49, and 'contrary' [ἐναντίων] is found only here and in Titus 2:8 in the Pauline corpus.

[133] Wanamaker, *Thessalonians*, p. 114.

[134] See Acts 2: 23, 36; 3:15; 4:10, 27; 5:28, 30; 10:39; 13:27, 29.

[135] C. M. Tuckett, 'Synoptic Tradition in 1 Thessalonians?' in *The Thessalonian Correspondence* (ed. R. Collins; Leuven: Leuven University Press, 1990), pp. 166-67, argues that the parallels to the 'wrath to the end' are weak. In terms of exact parallels, this is true, but the idea of God's judgment is clear in both passages. He also argues that the idea of filling up sin is dependent on Matthew's special source and therefore is post-Pauline. It is of course impossible to prove that Matthew's source was post-Pauline. Nevertheless, Tuckett recognizes that Paul and the gospel writer 'share a common fund of ideas and terminology from the Old Testament and Judaism'.

[136] Non-biblical parallels are also frequently noted. Best, *Thessalonians*, p. 117, quotes from Tacitus concerning the Jews, 'towards every other people they feel only hate and enmity' (*Hist.* 5.5), and Philostratus says, 'The Jews have long been in revolt, not only against the Romans, but against humanity' (*Vit. Apoll.* 5.33). On the final statement in 1 Thess. 2:16 there is also a clear parallel in *T. Levi* 6.11: 'But the wrath of the Lord had come upon them, definitely'. H. W. Hollander and M. de Jonge, *The Testaments of the Twelve Patriarchs: A Commentary* (Leiden: Brill, 1985), p. 147, see this

Some have seen 1 Thessalonians 2:13-16 as a post-Pauline insertion.[137] They emphasize four points: (1) the end of v. 16 concerning the wrath of God having come on the Jews must refer to AD 70; (2) the theology of the section is anti-Jewish in a way never found in Paul; (3) 2:13-16 makes an unnatural break in Paul's argument; and (4) the linguistic form is non-Pauline.[138] All of these objections have been answered.[139] First, any number of events could be referred to in the first century, including 'the death of the Jewish King Agrippa in AD 44, the revolt of Theudas in 44-46, the famine in Judea in 46-47, and the expulsion of the Jews from Rome in 49'. There was also a riot in Jerusalem in AD 49 in which thousands were killed.[140] Therefore, if an historical event is required to make sense of the end of v. 16, the fall of Jerusalem is not the only possibility in the first century. It is also possible this phrase is pointed to the parousia.[141] Second, the complete theology of Paul concerning the Jews should not be seen as exhausted in these few verses. Paul is clearly talking about those Jews who have refused to repent, not all Jews, and specifically he is talking about the Jews of Judea.[142] Third, although 2:13-16 can be called a digression, it can still be seen as part of the argument that Paul is making.[143] Wegenast calls these verses the closing words to the first section,[144] and Marshall refers to 2:13-16 as the climax to the first section of the epistle.[145] Therefore, as Wanamaker has said, whether this section is viewed as unnecessary 'is a matter

---

passage from *T. Levi* as being influenced by 1 Thess. 2:16. Best, *Thessalonians*, p. 122, thinks both 1 Thess. and *T. Levi* took up common tradition. Best notes that in *T. Levi* the statement is applied, not to the Jews, but against their enemies.

[137] Birger Pearson, '1 Thessalonians 2:13-16: A Deutero-Pauline Interpolation', *HTR* 64 (1971), pp. 79-94; Hendrikus Boers, 'The Form Critical Study of Paul's Letters: 1 Thessalonians as a Case Study', *NTS* 22 (1975-76), pp. 140-58; Helmut Koester, '1 Thessalonians—Experiment in Christian Writing' in *Continuity and Discontinuity in Church History: Essays Presented to George Huntston Williams on the Occasion of His 65th Birthday* (ed. F. F. Church and T. George; Studies in History of Christian Thought 19; Leiden: Brill, 1979), pp. 33-44; Daryl Schmidt, '1 Thess 2:13-16: Linguistic Evidence for an Interpolation', *JBL* 102 (1983), pp. 269-79.

[138] The first three arguments are found in Pearson, '1 Thessalonians 2:13-16', pp. 79-94, and the fourth in D. Schmidt, '1 Thess. 2:13-16', pp. 269-79.

[139] See Wanamaker, *Thessalonians*, pp. 29-34; and Jon A. Weatherly, 'The Authenticity of 1 Thessalonians 2.13-16: Additional Evidence', *JSNT* 42 (1991), pp. 79-98.

[140] Wanamaker, *Thessalonians*, p. 30.

[141] Weatherly, '1 Thessalonians 2.13-16', pp. 90-91.

[142] Weatherly, '1 Thessalonians 2.13-16', pp. 86-87.

[143] Wanamaker, *Thessalonians*, p. 32.

[144] Klaus Wegenast, *Das Verständnis der Tradition bei Paulus und in den Deuteropaulinen* (WMANT; Assen, NL: Neukirchen Kreis Moers, 1962), p. 49.

[145] Marshall, *Thessalonians*, p. 76; see also p. 9.

of individual opinion'.[146] The fourth argument, put forward by D. Schmidt, that the sentence structure of 2:13-16 is unpauline, can be answered in two ways. As Jewett has pointed out, in 1 Thessalonians 1:2-7 there is a longer sentence than in 2:13-16.[147] Schmidt's analysis of 1 Thessalonians recognizes this, but he does not see the same number of 'embedded sentences' (dependent clauses) in this section. Yet even if Schmidt's grammatical analysis is correct, the degree of difference between 2:13-16 and other Pauline sentences is insignificant.[148] A much stronger argument can be made if one recognizes that vv. 15-16 are not originally Pauline, but pre-Pauline. There are vocabulary and grammatical peculiarities in these verses, but the digression is not totally unrelated, and the textual evidence unequivocally supports the inclusion of this passage in 1 Thessalonians. Only when it is recognized that this is a piece of tradition that Paul has incorporated into his letter can all the data be understood.[149]

The tradition in 2:15-16 is included to encourage the Thessalonians in their response to the gospel proclamation. They had accepted the truth, they had been mistreated as other believers had been mistreated, and ultimately they would be saved, in contrast to their persecutors, who are under God's wrath. The tradition does include 'extra' information (such as some of the statements found in vv. 15-16), but this serves to substantiate the kind of suffering experienced not only by the Christians in Judea, but also by the prophets and Jesus himself. There had always been a persecuting element in every stage of God's people.[150]

In 1 Thessalonians 3:3b-4 Paul explicitly refers back to the content of his preaching at Thessalonica regarding tribulations: 'You know that we were destined for them. In fact, when we were with you, we kept telling you that we would be persecuted'. Paul twice refers to the certainty of tribulation as something the Thessalonians know. By using the imperfect tense for 'said

---

[146] Wanamaker, *Thessalonians*, p. 32.

[147] Jewett, *Correspondence*, p. 41.

[148] Weatherly, '1 Thessalonians 2.13-16', pp. 93-94, gives an extensive treatment of Schmidt's analysis. He notes that there are really only six levels of embedding in this section, only one more than found in 1 Thess. 1:4-6. He also notes that Rom. 4:16-17 has nine levels of embedding; Rom. 15:15-16 has six levels; Phil. 1:12-15 has seven levels; and Phil. 1:27-30 has eight levels. Therefore this level of embedding is not 'un-Pauline'. On other so-called grammatical peculiarities that link this section to the previous part, see pp. 92-93.

[149] For a fuller discussion on the integrity of 1 Thessalonians and especially 2:13-16, see Raymond F. Collins, *Studies on the First Letter to the Thessalonians* (BETL 66; Leuven: Leuven University Press, 1984), pp. 96-135. He lists M. Dibelius (1925), J. B. Orchard (1938), H. J. Schoeps (1943), C. H. Dodd (1947), K. H. Schelkle (1949), C. Masson (1957), U. Wilckens (1961), R. Schipper (1966), and O. Michel (1967) as all concluding that Paul has made use of pre-synoptic tradition (p. 103).

[150] Weatherly, '1 Thessalonians 2.13-16', p. 88.

before', Paul stresses that this was spoken repeatedly in his preaching at Thessalonica.[151] The expectation of tribulation is repeated throughout the New Testament and is 'fundamental' for Paul's thought.[152] The traditional material is incorporated right into Paul's own sentences and probably includes the phrase 'for this we were destined', which is introduced by 'that' [ὅτι] in 3:3, and the phrase 'we are about to be afflicted' in 3:4, which is also introduced by 'that' [ὅτι]. Thus the tradition in ch. 3 consists of two phrases, 'we were destined for them', and 'we would be persecuted'.

2. Tradition in 1 Thessalonians 4–5

Nearly all commentators recognize a major break between chs 3 and 4 of 1 Thessalonians, and the use of traditional material is found in both major sections of the epistle.

The practical exhortation of the letter begins in 4:1-12, where Paul directs the attention of the Thessalonians back to what they 'received', 'know', and were 'given'. The exhortation focuses on what the missionaries themselves delivered ('from us') and gave ('we'). As we have already seen, this language is the language which introduces tradition. The content of the tradition includes teaching about sexual immorality (vv. 3-8), brotherly love (vv. 9-10), and work (vv. 11-12). Paul uses the traditional term for proper behavior, 'to walk', twice in v. 1. There is a grammatical break in the passage at the beginning of v. 9, with the words 'and concerning' [περὶ δέ]. This does not begin a new section but only a subsection, as can be seen at the end of v. 10 in the exhortation to grow, which is almost identical to the end of v. 1. Following v. 12 there is a clear break where Paul introduces the topic of grieving for Christians who have died, a topic about which they lack knowledge ('we do not want you to be ignorant'). The vocabulary is fairly typically Pauline, with only two words not found elsewhere in the New Testament—'wrong'[ὑπερβαίνειν-6] and 'taught by God' [θεοδίδακτοι-9]—and one not found elsewhere in Paul, 'therefore' [τοιγαροῦν-8].

There are those who link the warning in v. 8, 'he who rejects this instruction does not reject man but God, who gives you his Holy Spirit', to Luke 10:16, where it is recorded that Jesus said to the seventy-two as he sent them out, 'He who listens to you listens to me; he who rejects you rejects me; but he who rejects me rejects him who sent me'.[153] The words could simply be 'due to a

---

[151] Frame, *Thessalonians*, pp. 128-29.

[152] Marshall, *Thessalonians,* p. 92. He notes the following parallels: Matt. 5:11-12, 44; 10:17-23; 23:34; 24:9-13; Acts 9:16; 14:22; 1 Pet. 1:6; 3:13-17; Rev. 2:10; and in the Pauline corpus, Rom. 8:17, 36-39; 2 Tim. 2:11-13.

[153] Hunter, *Paul,* p. 49; Dale C. Allison, Jr., 'The Pauline Epistles and the Synoptic Gospels: The Pattern of the Parallels', *NTS* 28 (1982), p. 20; W. D. Davies, *Paul and Rabbinic Judaism* (London: SPCK, 1948), p. 139.

common milieu of ideas, rather than to any direct literary relationship'[154] since the only exact verbal similarity is the verb 'to reject', which is used two times in identical form. However, both verses contain an emphasis on rejecting God himself, and the flow of the two passages is remarkably similar. Thus it is probable that Paul and Luke are both including a piece of pre-Pauline tradition here.[155] The tradition begins at the beginning of v. 3, is introduced by 'for' [γάρ], and goes through the end of v. 8.

Paul introduces his second subsection of traditional paraenetic material (vv. 9-10) by reminding his readers that he does not need to write to them about 'brotherly love' because they have been 'taught of God'. Davies suggests this may show knowledge of the words and teaching of Jesus,[156] and Bruce comments that being taught by God may be a reference 'both to the teaching of Jesus and to the inward action of the Spirit'.[157] It is impossible to make an absolute identification of this verse only with the Jesus-tradition because the command to love one another is also found in the Old Testament and elsewhere in the New Testament, but there can be no question it was a part of Paul's traditional teaching. Verses 11-12 close off this first portion of paraenesis. That these final exhortations are also traditional can be seen in the way Paul interrupts the command to work and reminds the Thessalonians that this current command is 'just as we commanded you' previously. The actual tradition includes the commands to live quietly, to 'mind your own business', and to 'work with your hands', and v. 12 completes the tradition by giving the reason for living this way. Therefore, in examining this paraenetic passage, it is not so much the form of the passage that identifies it as traditional, but rather, the words which are used to introduce it (vv. 1-2) and the way in which Paul refers to previous teaching of the commands.

In 1 Thessalonians 4:13-18, Paul applies two pieces of pre-Pauline tradition to comfort believers about fellow Christians who have died. The first piece of tradition is the simple credal statement in 4:14: 'We believe that Jesus died and rose again'. A number of features distinguish this phrase as a pre-Pauline confession: (1) the introduction of the passage with 'For we believe that', (2) the infrequent use in Paul of the verb 'to rise' [ἀνέστη], and (3) the absolute use of the name 'Jesus'.[158] The credal statement is introduced by 'that' [ὅτι],

---

[154]Tuckett, 'Synoptic Tradition', p. 164.

[155]Rigaux, *Thessaloniciens*, p. 514.

[156]Davies, *Rabbinic Judaism*, p. 139.

[157]Bruce, *Thessalonians*, p. 90.

[158]Havener, 'Credal Formulae', pp. 111-12. Havener notes that the introductory phrase 'we believe' is found in only three places in Paul (1 Thess. 4:14; Rom. 6:8; 10:9). There can be no question about the credal character of Rom. 10:9. On the credal character of this verse see also de Jonge, *Christology*, p. 36; Traugott Holtz, 'Traditionen im 1 Thessalonicherbrief' in *Die Mitte des Neuen Testaments: Einheit*

and Paul then draws his conclusion from the statement beginning 'and so'. Paul bases his conclusion that 'God will bring with Jesus those who have fallen asleep in him', which is not explicitly taught in the credal statement, on the death and resurrection of Jesus. The believers are to be comforted because those fellow Christians who have died will come back with him [σὺν αὐτῷ].

Paul then introduces his second argument to comfort the believers, also based on tradition, in vv. 15-17. He refers to the information he gives about the Lord's return as 'the word of the Lord' [ἐν λόγῳ κυρίου]. This phrase has been understood in two ways: (1) a prophetic saying of the exalted Jesus[159]; or (2) a dominical saying of the earthly Jesus. Those who regard the phrase as a prophetic saying of the exalted Lord give three reasons why this is more probable: (a) the saying as found in 1 Thessalonians 4 is unattested in the Gospels;[160] (b) it is known that Paul and his associates received 'revelations', and the closest passage in the Pauline epistles to these verses is 1 Corinthians 15:51-52, where Paul speaks of a 'mystery' (a term usually synonymous with 'revelation');[161] and (c) the phrase 'the word of the Lord' is used in the LXX to express prophetic revelation.[162]

Although it is true that this passage is not exactly paralleled in the Gospels, a significant number of parallels (especially to Matt. 24:30-31) at least suggest a common tradition behind both passages (coming from heaven, trumpet, 'to meet' [εἰς ἀπάντησιν]—Matt. 25:6).[163] Also we know that there were other

---

und Vielfalt neutestamentlicher Theologie. Festscrift für E. Schweizer zum siebzigsten Geburtstag (ed. U. Luz and H. Weder; Göttingen: Vandenhoeck & Ruprecht, 1983), p. 60; and Lars Hartman, *Prophecy Interpreted* (Lund: Gleerup, 1966), p. 186.

[159] Allison, 'Pauline Epistles', p. 3; Best, *Thessalonians*, p. 192; Collins, *Studies*, p. 159; Adeney, *Thessalonians*, p. 198; G. G. Findlay, *The Epistles of Paul the Apostle to the Thessalonians* (1904; repr., Grand Rapids: Baker, 1982), p. 98; Milligan, *Thessalonians*, p. 58; F. Neirynck, 'Paul and the Sayings of Jesus', in *L'Apôtre Paul: Personnalitié, style et conception du ministère* (ed. A. Vanhoye; Leuven: Leuven University Press, 1986), p. 311; Victor P. Furnish, 'The Jesus-Paul Debate: From Baur to Bultmann', *BJRL* 47 (1964-65), p. 44; Dobschütz, *Thessalonicher-Brief*, p. 194; Nikolaus Walter, 'Paul and the Early Christian Jesus-Tradition', in *Paul and Jesus: Collected Essays* (JSNTSup 37; Sheffield: Sheffield Academic Press, 1989), p. 66; Wegenast, *Verständnis*, p. 110.

[160] John Gillman, 'Signals of Transformation in 1 Thessalonians 4:13-18', *CBQ* 47 (1985), p. 274.

[161] C. L. Mearns, 'Evidence of 1 and 2 Thessalonians', pp. 140-41.

[162] See 1 Kgs. 13:1, 2, 5, 32; 21:35; 1 Chr. 15:15; *Sir.* 48:3, 5. Peter Stuhlmacher, 'Jesustradition im Römerbrief?', *TBei* 14 (1983), p. 243.

[163] For a complete comparison see David Wenham, 'Paul and the Synoptic Apocalypse', in vol. 2 of *Gospel Perspectives: Studies of History and Tradition in the Four Gospels* (2 vols; ed. R. T. France and D. Wenham; Sheffield: JSOT Press, 1981), pp. 345-75; J.

sayings of Jesus which circulated in the early church but are not found in the Gospels (such as Acts 20:35, 'remembering the words of the Lord Jesus: "It is more blessed to give than to receive"'). Paul elsewhere directly appeals to the teaching of Jesus (Rom. 14:14; 1 Cor. 7:10; 9:14; 11:23).[164] Therefore, that the words in 1 Thessalonians 4:15-17 are unattested in this exact form does not disprove Paul thought the words came from Jesus.

That this phrase refers to a later revelation to Paul is unlikely because when Paul receives a direct revelation from the Lord, he refers to it as a revelation or vision (2 Cor. 12:1; Gal. 1:12). He distinguishes between what he receives from the Spirit and what comes directly from the Lord, as is seen most clearly in 1 Corinthians 7. In 1 Corinthians 7:10 Paul qualifies his statement by saying 'not I, but the Lord', while in 7:12 he says, 'I, not the Lord'. Later on in the same chapter (7:25) he says, 'I have no command from the Lord, but I give a judgment as one who by the Lord's mercy is trustworthy'. Finally he concludes the teaching of this chapter (7:40) by saying, 'I have the Spirit of God'.

The use of 'the word of the Lord' in the LXX to express prophetic revelation does not require this phrase to be used that way in this passage. The New Testament does not follow this practice, and 'word' [λόγος] does not 'appear among the variety of other terms used in other New Testament passages for special revelation to Christian prophets'.[165]

Most likely 'the word of the Lord' refers to a dominical saying of the earthly Jesus. This understanding is further supported by Paul's 'regular use of "Lord" for Jesus and . . . increasing scholarly doubt that sayings of early Christian prophets were easily or often transferred to Jesus as the exalted Lord'.[166] All of these reasons taken together make it very probable that Paul believes he is giving a teaching which comes directly from the earthly Jesus.[167]

Bernard Orchard, 'Thessalonians and the Synoptic Gospels', *Biblica* 19 (1938), pp. 19-42; Hartman, *Prophecy,* pp. 178-205; and A. W. Argyle, 'M and the Pauline Epistles', *ExpTim* 81 (1969-70), pp. 340-42. For a view that sees little connection between the Synoptics and 1 Thess., see Tuckett, 'Synoptic Tradition', pp. 160-82.

[164]Marshall, *Thessalonians,* p. 125.

[165] Robert H. Gundry, 'The Hellenization of Dominical Tradition and Christianization of Jewish Tradition in the Eschatology of 1-2 Thessalonians', *NTS* 33 (1987), p. 164.

[166]Gundry, 'Dominical Tradition', p. 164. Gundry goes on to say that Paul has drawn on the saying of Jesus recorded in John 11:25-26, of which the original form was 'The one who has died will rise, and the one who is alive will never die' (p. 165). Tuckett, 'Synoptic Tradition', p. 181, correctly analyzes Gundry when he comments that the phrase found in John's gospel fits Martha's question so is unlikely to be an 'independent pre-Johannine saying'.

[167]See also de Jonge, *Christology,* p. 36; Holtz, 'Traditionen', p. 61; Frame, *Thessalonians,* p. 171; Bailey and Clarke, 'Thessalonians', p. 303; Neil,

The tradition to which Paul refers as 'the word of the Lord' is introduced with 'for' [ὅτι] at the beginning of v. 16. The end of v. 15 retains the Pauline epistolary style and so is most likely a summary of the teaching about to be introduced in 16-17a.[168] After Paul has repeated the tradition he concludes, 'And so we will be with the Lord forever'. The only additions or changes to the tradition are Paul's emphatic 'the Lord himself', which Jeremias postulates may have originally been 'the son of man', the typical Pauline phrase 'in Christ', the addition of the first person plural pronoun in v. 17,[169] and possibly the word 'first' found at the end of v. 16.[170]

This tradition is very closely related to the question about believers who have died, which Paul is addressing. Paul stresses the temporal order so that the believers in Thessalonica will realize that the dead Christians are at no disadvantage compared to those who are still alive at the return of Christ. He also focuses their attention on the truth of the presence of deceased believers with Christ, for they will be brought with Him (4:14) and will always be with Him (4:17).

Paul begins a new topic in 5:1-11, as can be seen in the way he introduces this topic with 'but concerning' (see also 4:9, 13). This passage breaks into three sections: (1) announcement of topic (1-3); (2) Pauline paraenesis (4-10); and (3) final exhortation (11).[171] Paul refers to his topic with the 'stereotyped' expression 'times and seasons', which is found in apocalyptic and sapiential literature.[172] Paul reminds his readers that they have already been taught the information which he is about to write: 'you have no need to be written to'. The reason given is that 'you yourselves know accurately'. As we have already seen, this is one way Paul introduces traditional material. Paul sets off the tradition, as he frequently does, with 'that' [ὅτι]. The traditional piece goes to the end of v. 3, for at the beginning of v. 4 Paul again directly addresses the Thessalonians, 'but you, brothers'. These verses are widely recognized as

---

Thessalonians, p. 97; Rigaux, *Thessaloniciens*, p. 538; Wanamaker, *Thessalonians*, p. 171; Barnabas Lindars, 'The Sound of the Trumpet: Paul and Eschatology', *BJRL* 67 (1985), p. 772; Masson, *Thessaloniciens*, p. 56; and Morris, *Thessalonians*, pp. 140-41.

[168] Best, *Thessalonians*, p. 193.

[169] J. Jeremias, *Unknown Sayings of Jesus* (trans. R. H. Fuller; London: SPCK, 1957), p. 81.

[170] Holtz, 'Traditionen', p. 62, notes that the words 'the remaining ones' are found only here in the New Testament, and both he and Jeremias note the similarity to *4 Ezra*.

[171] Collins, *Studies*, p. 163.

[172] Tuckett, 'Synoptic Tradition', p. 169; Holtz, 'Traditionen', p. 67; Collins, *Studies*, p. 163; Beda Rigaux, 'Tradition et Rédaction dans 1 Th. 5.1-10', *NTS* 21 (1975), p. 321.

traditional because of the parallels with other New Testament passages,[173] the unusual vocabulary,[174] and the awkward grammar.[175] The only real discussion concerns the relationship of this passage to the synoptic parallels.[176]

In 1 Thessalonians 5:4, Paul again directly addresses the Thessalonian Christians. This verse links the previous tradition concerning the 'thief' with the traditions concerning light and darkness found in 5:5-8. In vv. 4-8 it is unlikely that Paul is quoting any one piece of tradition, for the style is his own. However, throughout these verses he uses many terms which are traditional: light/darkness, night/day, sleeping/watchful, drunk/sober. The light/darkness motif is found in all types of religious literature.[177] The phrases 'sons of the light' and 'sons of the day' seem to be of Semitic origin,[178] and in fact the first of these has been found at Qumran.[179] The use of 'watchfulness' and 'drunkenness' suggests the parables found in the eschatological discourse,

---

[173] The passages usually seen as parallel are Matt. 24:36-39, 42-44 (see especially Orchard, 'Thessalonians', pp. 32-36, 40) and Luke 12: 39-40. Other passages that are noted include 2 Pet. 3:10; Rev. 3:3; 16:15 (Holtz, 'Traditionen', p. 67).

[174] The word 'peace', which Paul frequently uses, here carries the idea of security, which is different from the way Paul normally uses it. 'Sudden' [αἰφνίδιος] is found only here in the Pauline corpus, and only one other time in the whole NT, in the eschatological discourse in Luke 21: 34. 'Come upon' [ἐφίστημι] is found only two other times in the whole Pauline corpus (2 Tim. 4:2, 6) but is frequently found in Luke-Acts. Also 'labor pains' [ὠδίν] and 'pregnant' [γαστήρ] are unusual words for Paul, the first word being a Pauline *hapax,* and the second found only here and in Titus 1:12. Paul uses two impersonal plural active verbs, 'they say' [λέγωσιν] and 'they will not escape' [οὐ μὴ ἐκφύγωσιν]. Orchard, 'Thessalonians', p. 26, states that this is the only certain instance of the impersonal plural active verb in Paul. Collins, *Studies,* p. 165, calls the terms 'remarkably non-Pauline'.

[175] Orchard, 'Thessalonians', p. 24, quotes Plummer, who comments that the style 'is so unlike St Paul's style that it is probably either a quotation or an echo of some writing or saying', and he also quotes Lightfoot, who remarks that 'the dissimilarity which this verse (v. 3) presents to the ordinary style of St Paul is striking.'

[176] See Hartman, *Prophecy,* pp. 190-94; Lars Aejmelaeus, *Wachen vor dem Endem* (SFEG 44; Helsinki: Finnish Exegetical Society, 1985); Wenham, 'Synoptic Apocalypse', pp. 345-75; and Tuckett, 'Synoptic Tradition', especially pp. 168-76.

[177] Collins, *Studies,* p. 166; Rigaux, 'Tradition', p. 327-28. Marshall, *Thessalonians,* p. 135, notes the following references from the Old Testament and Judaism: Ps. 27:1; 112:4; Prov. 4:18-19; Isa. 9:2; 5:20; 1QS 3:13–4:26. Aejmelaeus, *Wachen,* pp. 41-42, sees Isa. 13 and Jer. 6 as the primary Old Testament background for these verses as a whole. He would link the day/night imagery to Amos 5:18-20 (p. 49).

[178] Frame, *Thessalonians,* p. 185; Aejmelaeus, *Wachen,* 53-54. See also Luke 16:8 ('the sons of light'), John 12:36 ('sons of light'), and Eph. 5:8 ('children of light').

[179] Marshall, *Thessalonians,* p. 136, lists 1QS 1:9f; 1QM 1:1.

The Authenticity of 2 Thessalonians

especially in Matthew.[180] In 1 Thessalonians 5:8, Paul applies the traditional triad of Christian virtues (faith, hope, and love) to the armor of God found in Isaiah 59:17. This application also appears to be traditional by this time.[181] Therefore, although these verses are not one preformed piece of tradition, Paul has taken a number of known traditions and molded them together to exhort the Thessalonians.

Paul concludes his paraenesis with one further piece of tradition in 1 Thessalonians 5:9-10.[182] These verses are much more formal in style, using the full title 'Lord Jesus Christ' and incorporating the most basic creed concerning Christ, 'who died for us'. The verb 'to sleep' is used here to refer to a group of people different from those in vv. 6-7, where the ones who are 'sleeping' are those who are also 'drunk' and of the 'night' and 'darkness'. In other words, they are not Christians, yet in vv. 9-10 Paul uses the same verb to describe Christians who have died. These two verses are also set off by the introductory 'because' [ὅτι],[183] and v. 11 uses the second person plural and begins with 'therefore' [διό]. This piece of tradition is not immediately relevant to the topic of 'times and seasons' which Paul introduces at the beginning of 5:1-11, but it gives further reason for the Thessalonians to 'encourage one another'.

3. Conclusion on the Identification of Tradition in 1 Thessalonians

1 Thessalonians is a letter filled with tradition. It contains credal statements (1 Thess. 1:9-10; 4:14; 5:9-10), traditions on suffering and persecution (2:15-16; 3:3-4); eschatological traditions (4:16-17; 5:2-10), paraenetic traditions (4:3-12), and even a 'word of the Lord' (4:16-17). Paul applies these traditions to a variety of problems in such a way that the exact topic of the tradition does not always correspond directly to the problem at hand. The traditions account for over 23% of the entire letter.[184]

---

[180] Orchard, 'Thessalonians', p. 30. See especially Matt. 24:42-43; 25:1-13; Mark 13:33-37; and Luke 12:35-40; 21:34-36.

[181] See also Eph. 6:14. Holtz, 'Traditionen', pp. 68-69; Aejmelaeus, *Wachen*, p. 89; Rigaux, 'Tradition', p. 331.

[182] Collins, *Studies*, p. 170.

[183] Havener, 'Credal Formulae', p. 118, comments that the ὅτι used here by Paul is causal and not recitative. But Paul can introduce traditional material with ὅτι where it is being used to substantiate his argument (see Rom. 10:9). The ὅτι then is causal in terms of meaning, yet also sets off the material like a recitative ὅτι.

[184] My examination identified the following number of words from tradition: 1:9-10 (34 words); 2:15-16 (42 words); 3:3-4 (5 words); 4:3-8 (90 words); 4:9-12 (27 words); 4:14 (4 words); 4:16-17 (35 words); 5:2-3 (29 words); 5:5-8 (48 words); 5:9-10 (30 words). The sum of 34 + 42 + 5 + 90 + 27 + 4 + 35 + 29 + 48 + 30 is 344 words. There are 1482 words in the UBS³ text, including the words in brackets in the text. 344/1482 = .2321, or 23.21 %. This does not necessarily exhaust all the possible

The traditions are frequently referred to by 'tradition' words such as those discussed earlier in the terminology section. The traditions are usually introduced with the words 'how' [πῶς], 'for' [γάρ], and especially 'that' [ὅτι]. The traditions usually break the flow of the argument—and consequently have sometimes been misinterpreted as insertions—but this is so that Paul can draw out from these traditions certain ideas that apply to the particular discussion at hand. The doctrinal traditions tend to be highly structured, possibly because they were more easily memorized in this form. The paraenetic traditions tend to show a higher degree of conformity to Paul's own stylistic peculiarities. Yet it is interesting that Paul will sometimes take a doctrinal tradition and insert it in the paraenetic portion of his letter to draw out a practical implication. Paul does not always quote the traditions verbatim but feels comfortable inserting pronouns and adding particular words which emphasize the point he is stressing.

When the traditions are distinguished from the rest of the letter, it is clear that in essentially every major section of 1 Thessalonians Paul not only uses some piece of tradition, but makes it the basis for his argument. The only section where this is not true is 2:1-12, yet even this section, which is highly personal, draws much of its terminology from others with whom Paul contrasts himself. It is also interesting that Paul describes his own ministry in this section with some of the same terminology which he usually uses to refer to tradition. Karl Donfried has aptly summarized the use of tradition in 1 Thessalonians:

> What is remarkable about 1 Thessalonians is the traditional character of the letter, namely, its close coherence with the theology of the Hellenistic Church. In many of its formulations and in its use of traditional materials it appears to be more pre-Pauline than 'Pauline'. Over and over again Paul simply takes over traditions circulating in the Hellenistic Church and appropriated by that Church from a variety of sources including Hellenistic Judaism and, through it, popular Hellenistic philosophy.[185]

B. *The Identification of Tradition in 1 Corinthians*

It will be helpful to examine 1 Corinthians for its use of tradition because, as has been shown, Paul frequently uses the tradition terminology in this letter and because it contains at least some undisputed pieces of tradition. 1 Corinthians

---

traditions within 1 Thess. Some other possible traditions include the opening and closing of the letter, the blessing in 5:23-24, some of the final paraenetic statements to 'Live in peace with each other' and 'Make sure nobody pays back wrong for wrong' (1 Thess. 3:13, 15; see Allison, 'Pauline Epistles', p. 20, and Davies, *Rabbinic Judaism,* p. 139). These have not been included because they are not referred to as tradition in the text or set off from their context to show clearly that they are materials Paul has taken from other sources.

[185]Donfried, '1 Thessalonians', p. 9.

The Authenticity of 2 Thessalonians

also is an appropriate choice because it is probable that Paul wrote to the Thessalonians from Corinth, and consequently what is considered tradition within 1 Corinthians would correspond to what Paul taught while at Corinth and what he would have most likely written to the Thessalonians. Because of the variety of types of tradition and the length of 1 Corinthians, the examination will be broken into the following sections: (1) 1 Corinthians 15:1-11; (2) 1 Corinthians 11:23-26; (3) Words of the Lord; (4) Known Information; (5) Brief Sayings; and (6) Larger Sections.

1. 1 Corinthians 15:1-11

The form of the tradition. First Corinthians 15:3-5 is universally recognized as containing a portion of pre-Pauline tradition.[186] Dodd refers to it as the *locus classicus* for the *kerygma* in Paul.[187] Chapter 15 is the overall context for this piece of tradition; specifically, vv. 1-11 serve as an introduction to the rest of the chapter.

The first clear sign that Paul is referring to tradition is the language which he uses: 'received' (v. 1) and 'delivered . . . and received' (v. 3). This use of language for Paul shows he identified 'tradition' with the gospel (v. 1), with what he preached and believed (vv. 1, 2, 11), and with what was taught by all the apostles (vv. 6-8, 11).

The point at which the tradition actually begins is clearly recognizable because Paul introduces the tradition with the recitative 'for'[ὅτι] in 3b.[188] The extent and the unity of the traditional material in these verses are debated, however. Some see the initial portion of tradition going only through the end of v. 4;[189] more commonly the tradition is seen to extend through the end of v. 5 because of the syntax of the sentence and the importance of the witness of Peter and the twelve in v. 5.[190] Although some have seen the 'tradition' as running

---

[186] Reginald H. Fuller, *The Formation of the Resurrection Narratives* (Philadelphia: Fortress, 1971), p. 10.

[187] C. H. Dodd, *The Apostolic Preaching and Its Development* (London: Hodder & Stoughton, 1944), p. 13.

[188] de Jonge, *Christology*, p. 25.

[189] Jean Héring, *The First Epistle of Saint Paul to the Corinthians* (trans. A. Heathcote and P. Allcock; London: Epworth, 1962), p. 158; H. W. Bartsch, 'Die Argumentation des Paulus in 1 Cor 15:3-11', *ZNW* 55 (1964), p. 271.

[190] Jeremias, *Eucharistic Words*, p. 101; C. K. Barrett, *A Commentary on the First Epistle to the Corinthians* (2nd ed.; London: Black, 1971), pp. 341-42; Hans Conzelmann, *1 Corinthians* (Hermeneia; Philadelphia: Fortress, 1975), p. 251-58; Roy A. Harrisville, *1 Corinthians* (ACNT; Minneapolis: Augsburg, 1987), p. 251; James Moffatt, *The First Epistle of Paul to the Corinthians* (London: Hodder & Stoughton, 1938), p. 238; Archibald Robertson and Alfred Plummer, *The First Epistle of St. Paul to the Corinthians* (ICC; Edinburgh: T & T Clark, 1911), p. 335.

right through v. 7, very few would contend for this today.¹⁹¹ It is very clear that Paul himself is speaking beginning at v. 8 ('and last of all he appeared to me')¹⁹² and in the second half of v. 6, where he makes mention of the 500, 'most of whom are still living, though some have fallen asleep'.¹⁹³

The following stylized outline makes the parallel features evident:

1 Corinthians 15:3-8
15:3 παρέδωκα γὰρ ὑμῖν ἐν πρώτοις, ὃ καὶ παρέλαβον,
For I delivered to you as of first importance what even I received
    ὅτι Χριστὸς ἀπέθανεν ὑπὲρ τῶν ἁμαρτιῶν ἡμῶν
    that Christ died for our sins
        κατὰ τὰς γραφάς
        according to the scriptures
15:4 καὶ ὅτι ἐτάφη
And that he was buried
    καὶ ὅτι ἐγήγερται τῇ ἡμέρᾳ τῇ τρίτῃ
    and that he was raised on the third day
        κατὰ τὰς γραφάς
        according to the scriptures,
15:5 καὶ ὅτι ὤφθη Κηφᾷ,
And that he appeared to Cephas
    εἶτα τοῖς δώδεκα
    then to the twelve
15:6 ἔπειτα ὤφθη ἐπάνω πεντακοσίοις ἀδελφοῖς ἐφάπαξ,
Then he appeared to more than five hundred brothers at once
    ἐξ ὧν οἱ πλείονες μένουσιν ἕως ἄρτι,
    most of whom are still living
        τινὲς δὲ ἐκοιμήθησαν·
        but some have fallen asleep
15:7 ἔπειτα ὤφθη Ἰακώβῳ,
Then he appeared to James
    εἶτα τοῖς ἀποστόλοις πᾶσιν·
    then to all the apostles
15:8 ἔσχατον δὲ πάντων ὡσπερεὶ τῷ ἐκτρώματι
And last of all to one abnormally born
    ὤφθη κἀμοί.
    he appeared even to me.

---

¹⁹¹John Howard Schütz, *Paul and the Anatomy of Apostolic Authority* (SNTSMS 26; Cambridge: Cambridge University Press, 1975), p. 95.
¹⁹²Jerome Murphy-O'Connor, 'Tradition and Redaction in 1 Cor. 15:3-7', *CBQ* 43 (1981), p. 582.
¹⁹³Bartsch, 'Argumentation', p. 272.

The Authenticity of 2 Thessalonians

The clearest grammatical and stylistic peculiarities of vv. 3-5 are the repeated use of 'for' or 'that' [ὅτι] (four times) and the twice-repeated phrase 'according to the scriptures'. In vv. 5-7 the alternating use of two different forms of 'then' is conspicuous, and the parallel use of 'appeared' which Paul applies to himself in v. 8 is also unusual. The parallel use of 'for' or 'that' [ὅτι] has been understood either as linking four credal statements[194] or providing the structure for one extended creed.[195] Murphy-O'Connor cites Wilckens, who has pointed out that there is no known creed with a series of 'that' [ὅτι] statements.[196] Murphy-O'Connor suggests that the creed was received by Paul as a unit and that the 'and that' [καὶ ὅτι] is for emphasis.[197] But whatever way it is understood, it is clear that the credal statement(s) makes a break with the Pauline syntax and is at least initially introduced by 'that' [ὅτι].

Verses 6-8 have also been understood in a variety of ways. As already noted, some have viewed these verses as part of the original creed, and some understand these 'appearances' as part of the tradition but not necessarily part of the gospel that was received and passed on.[198] Others see a variety of parallel or even competing traditions,[199] and others refer to it as Pauline *gemara*.[200] What is clear is that Paul feels free to add Jesus's appearance to him directly onto the traditional appearances, thereby including himself within the traditional witnesses to the gospel. It is also evident that despite Paul's stress on the unity of message which he had received and passed on, he uses those traditional statements with a degree of flexibility, inserting information (such as in 6b) and leaving the closing of the tradition sufficiently vague as to the exact point at which he concludes quoting the tradition.

Jeremias lists six more unpauline characteristics of this passage: (1) The phrase 'for our sins' is unpauline. 'Sin' is used sixty-four times in the Pauline

---

[194]Murphy-O'Connor, 'Tradition', p. 583; Fuller, *Narratives*, pp. 13-14. Gerhardsson, *Memory*, pp. 299-300, says 1 Cor. 15:3-5 is set out 'as a series of *simanim*: each individual part is a short, heading-like designation for some passage of the tradition about Christ'. Later he says 'each element functions as a *siman* for a passage from the gospel tradition', which he believes originates 'from the college of Apostles in Jerusalem'. Hunter, in *Paul,* p. 15, sees the 'that' [ὅτι] as 'tantamount to quotation marks'.

[195]See Murphy-O'Connor, 'Tradition', p. 583, who gives a list of those who follow this view.

[196]Murphy-O'Connor, 'Tradition', p. 583.

[197]Murphy-O'Connor, 'Tradition', p. 589.

[198]Fee, *1 Corinthians*, p. 722.

[199]Ernst Bammel, 'Herkunft und Funktion der Traditionselemente in 1 Kor. 15:1-11', *TZ* (1955), p. 419. Bammel sees different witnesses or groups of witnesses: Peter (Antioch), James (Jerusalem), and Paul.

[200]Héring, *1 Corinthians*, p. 158.

corpus; three of those uses occur in the Pastorals, and five are found in Old Testament quotes. In the fifty-six remaining instances, fifty are in the singular and refer to sin as a personified power. The other six times all show influence of early Christian linguistic usage and are not specifically Pauline (see 1 Cor. 15:3; 1 Cor. 15:17; Gal. 1:4; Rom 7:5; Eph. 2:1; and Col. 1:14). (2) The phrase 'according to the scriptures' is not found anywhere else in Paul. He usually uses 'it is written' or something similar. (3) The perfect passive form of 'he was raised' is found only in 1 Corinthians 15:4 (and, under the influence of this verse, in vv. 12-14, 16-17, 20) and in the confessional formula in 2 Timothy 2:8. (4) The report of Jesus rising on the third day, with the placing of the ordinal number after the noun, is found only here in Paul. (5) 'He appeared' is found only in 1 Corinthians 15:5-8 and in the confessional formula in 1Timothy 3:16. (6) The expression 'the twelve' is unusual for Paul; he normally says 'the apostles'.[201] In addition, the verb 'he was buried' is found only here in Paul. It is used ten other times in the New Testament (in Matt., Luke and Acts) but is never used anywhere else to refer to Jesus's burial.[202] One other stylistic peculiarity must be noted as well. Paul tends to make very good use of connectives, yet in 1 Corinthians 15:3-7 he never uses 'and' [δέ].[203] He uses it before this section in 15:1 and then again in v. 8. A simple glance through ch. 14 and the rest of ch. 15 makes it clear that Paul frequently uses 'and' [δέ] to connect his sentences.[204]

Therefore the grammar, style, and vocabulary of 1 Corinthians 15:3-7 (with the exception of 6b) all point to Paul's incorporating pre-Pauline traditions into his letter here.[205]

The problem addressed by the tradition. The beliefs of Paul's opponents are explicitly defined in 1 Corinthians 15. In v. 12 Paul contrasts Christ's resurrection, which he had preached and which was part of the tradition he had cited, with the view of certain ones who said 'there is no resurrection from the dead'. Paul wants the Corinthians to realize the implication of this false teaching: if no one is raised from the dead, then neither was Christ raised. Paul then, in vv. 14-19, stresses the implications if Christ has not risen. He does not

---

[201] Jeremias, *Eucharistic Words*, pp. 101-102. See also Hunter, *Paul*, p. 117.

[202] For Jesus's burial, Matt. 27:60, Mark 15:46, and Luke 23:53 have ἔθηκεν; John 19:42 has ἔθηκαν.

[203] Jeremias, *Eucharistic Words*, p. 103, also points out that 'and' [καί] is used adversatively in this passage.

[204] In ch. 14, 'and' [δέ] is used twenty-three times, and in ch. 15, twenty-five times.

[205] The only other major question that arises in reference to the tradition is whether the tradition was originally Semitic or Greek. A good summary of the different positions is found in Berthold Klappert, 'Zur Frage des semitischen oder griechieschen Urtextes von 1 Kor. 15:3-5', *NTS* 13 (1966-67), pp. 168-73. He concludes that there is a higher probability that it goes back to a Semitic origin.

say that any of the members of the Corinthian church had denied the resurrection of Christ; even the opponents are not accused of this.[206] The problem concerns the general resurrection and is exclusively doctrinal, as can be seen in the response required by Paul. The Corinthians need to be 'reminded' of the message (v. 1),[207] they must 'stand' on the gospel (v. 1), they are 'saved' by the gospel if they 'hold firmly' to it; otherwise they have 'believed in vain' (v. 2). This stress on believing and faith is mentioned again in vv. 11, 14, and 17. Chapter 15 concludes with the exhortation to 'stand firm', to 'let nothing move' them, and to 'abound in the work of the Lord' as a result of their right belief (v. 58). In vv. 3-5 Paul refers to the content of what the Corinthians have believed, which he explicitly refers to as the 'gospel' (v. 1).[208] However, the error Paul desires to correct ('that there is no resurrection of the dead', v. 12) does not directly contradict any of the propositions which Paul defines as 'the gospel' (vv. 3-8). Only as Paul draws out the implications of the received tradition can the tradition be applied to the error, that is, the belief that there is no future resurrection of the dead. It is also interesting to note that in this particular instance, Paul states the tradition before he directly addresses the problem.

Having seen that Paul is using tradition and also has inserted information to it, and having identified the problem Paul is addressing in this section of the letter, we can now see how Paul makes use of the tradition to address the problem.

(1) Paul shows that the implications of the resurrection of Christ are undeniable by focusing on the multiplicity of the witnesses (including Paul)[209]

---

[206]Wegenast, *Verständnis*, p. 66.

[207]Arndt and Gingrich, *Lexicon*, p. 162, define γνωρίζω as 1. make known, reveal; 2. know. They note, however, in reference to 1 Cor. 15:1, that 'the discussion deals with something already known'. Therefore the NIV translation 'remind' is appropriate in this context. See also John Calvin, *The First Epistle of Paul the Apostle to the Corinthians* (Edinburgh: Oliver & Boyd, 1960), p. 312.

[208]Concerning the relationship of 'gospel' to 'tradition', see Schütz, *Apostolic Authority*, especially pp. 55-77, where he summarizes the variety of views.

[209]Wegenast, *Verständnis*, p. 64, lists three functions for the Pauline additions. They can be summarized as follows: 1) Paul desires to establish and define a circle of legitimate witnesses to the resurrection; 2) Paul wants to identify his gospel with that of the other witnesses, particularly by reporting Christ's resurrection appearance to him; and 3) Paul wants to emphasize himself as an apostle who with his own preaching instructs but is not bound to some tradition. The problem with Wegenast's understanding of the additions is that it focuses almost exclusively on the apostle himself. It is true that Paul does stress his apostleship in this passage, especially in vv. 8-10, but even after that excursus he returns to the unity of the message which was received. Wegenast stresses apostleship at the expense of tradition. It is true that Paul handles the tradition

to the resurrection. His goal is not to prove to the Corinthians that Jesus had risen—for this they already believed (see vv. 1, 11, 14, 17)—but to show the resurrection of Christ as being absolutely central to the gospel.

(2) The unity of the message among all the witnesses is also emphasized; this is the message originally received by Paul and by the Corinthians (vv. 1, 11).

(3) Not only was Paul one of the witnesses of the resurrection (vv. 8-10), but he himself had preached this message to them (vv. 1, 2).

(4) The addition concerning Christ's appearance to the 500, 'most of whom are still living, though some have fallen asleep', not only functions as proof of the reality of the resurrection of Jesus, but also shows that some of these eyewitnesses have died. This would press home the point that there is a need for a general resurrection, for the Christians at Corinth had not yet fully obtained all the benefits of the work of Christ.

(5) The 'extra' information concerning the work of Christ in vv. 3-4 fills out the core of the gospel that was preached and believed and sets the context for the statements about Christ's resurrection. These statements by themselves are not necessary for Paul's argument, although he does allude back to v. 3 ('Christ died for our sins according to the Scriptures') in v. 17 when he says that if Christ is not raised, 'you are still in your sins'. Although Christ's death is not explicitly mentioned in v. 17, its significance is clear.

One further problem must be addressed before completing our examination of 1 Corinthians 15: Galatians 1 and 1 Corinthians 15 are frequently seen to 'contradict' each other. Specifically, Galatians 1:12 is contrasted with 1 Corinthians 15:1, 3. William Baird has pointed out the similarity of the subject matter by paralleling 1 Corinthians 15:1 and Galatians 1:11:

1 Corinthians 15:1	Galatians 1:11
γνωρίζω δὲ ὑμῖν, ἀδελφοί,	γνωρίζω δὲ ὑμῖν, ἀδελφοί,
and I make known to you, brothers	and I make known to you, brothers
τὸ εὐαγγέλιον	τὸ εὐαγγέλιον
the gospel	the gospel
ὃ εὐηγγελισάμην ὑμῖν	τὸ εὐαγγελισθὲν ὑπ' ἐμοῦ
which I preached to you	that which was preached by me

In both passages Paul says he made the gospel known to them. However, in 1 Corinthians 15:3, Paul uses the technical term for passing on tradition to say

---

with a certain amount of flexibility, but at the same time he stresses it is the same gospel that he received (v. 1). Paul sees no divide between his apostleship and the tradition, as if he must correct it. Wegenast also stresses in his list of reasons (p. 67) that Paul wants to present a complete list of legitimate witnesses. Yet Paul nowhere says he has listed the total number of witnesses; this is simply speculation on the part of Wegenast.

that this is the gospel he received and passed on to the Corinthians, whereas in Galatians 1:12 he uses the same technical term to say he did not receive his gospel from men. Baird sees that Dodd stresses 1 Corinthians 15:3-8 at the expense of Galatians 1:11-17, while Bultmann would reverse the emphasis.[210] Most commentators, however, would stress that the two passages have different purposes.[211] Clearly, the purpose of Galatians 1 is to stress the immediate origin of Paul's gospel, that he first of all received it 'by revelation', while in 1 Corinthians 15, as we have seen, Paul is stressing the unity of the message with that of all the apostles and witnesses. He does not say that this is how he first received the gospel, simply that he did receive it and it was the same message proclaimed by all of them (1 Cor. 15:11). In Galatians 2 it is also clear that the Jerusalem apostles agreed with the gospel Paul proclaimed and added nothing to it, extending him the right hand of fellowship (Gal. 2:2, 6, 9). Therefore, in terms of content Galatians shows no distinction between the gospel Paul proclaimed and the gospel proclaimed by the other apostles. Paul received the gospel directly from the resurrected Jesus; however, he uses the traditional forms to express it.[212]

2. 1 Corinthians 11:23-26

The form of the tradition. In 1 Corinthians 11:17-34, tradition is used to correct another problem in Corinth: abuse of the Lord's Supper. Paul begins by emphatically pointing out to the Corinthians the impropriety of their conduct when they gather together as a church (v. 17). Specifically, he points to divisions within the congregation (v. 18), most likely caused by a distinction being made between the 'haves' and the 'have-nots'.[213]

In the middle of this section Paul quotes a portion of tradition, introducing it with the characteristic words 'I received . . . I delivered'. The debate concerning these words does not focus on whether Paul is reminding the Corinthians of a tradition which he had already taught them, but on how Paul himself 'received' this tradition. The debate frequently concentrates on the exact meaning of the preposition 'from' [ἀπό] in this context. Wegenast lists three ways the meaning has been understood: (1) immediate revelation through a vision or saying directly to Paul; (2) passed-on tradition similar to the rabbinic method of

---

[210] William Baird, 'What is Kerygma? A Study of 1 Cor. 15:3-8 and Gal. 1:11-17', *JBL* 76 (1957), pp. 186-87.

[211] Ladd, *Theology,* p. 393; Herman Ridderbos, *Paul and Jesus* (trans. David H. Freeman; Nutley, NJ: Presbyterian & Reformed, 1957), pp. 47-52.

[212] Roloff, *Apostolat-Verkündigung-Kirche*, p. 88. See also Baird, 'Kerygma', p. 191, and Kim, *Origin,* p. 69, who makes a distinction between the 'essence' and the 'form' of the gospel.

[213] Fee, *1 Corinthians*, p. 534.

handing on tradition; and (3) a saying of the pneumatic Lord.[214]

Those who would see the origin of the tradition in 1 Corinthians 11:23-25 as a direct revelation to Paul have rightly criticized some weaknesses of the argument for the second position. Hyam Maccoby, who defends the idea that the tradition was directly revealed to Paul,[215] points out that the preposition 'from' [ἀπό] does not always denote 'origin' but can be used of the immediate reception of information (see Matt. 11:29; Col. 1:7).[216] He has also argued against Jeremias's claim that 'I received' [παραλαμβάνω] implies a process of tradition. Maccoby points out that the Hebrew verb (קבל) which describes Moses's reception of the tradition at Sinai (in *m. 'Abot*) also describes the reception of the tradition at every later stage. Therefore when Paul uses the Greek equivalent of this verb 'I received', he does not necessarily imply that a process of more than one step has taken place.[217] Therefore, Maccoby believes, Paul received the Lord's Supper tradition directly from Jesus, and the Gospel accounts of the Lord's Supper are ultimately dependent on Paul.

Most commentators follow the second view in recognizing that Paul is using traditional terminology from his Jewish background to pass on a tradition that goes back to Jesus.[218] This tradition goes back to Christ in terms of content, but not necessarily in terms of form.[219] A. M. Hunter represents the position that 'from' [ἀπό] indicates 'ultimate source' in this context.[220] He believes that if Paul had meant direct revelation he would have used the preposition 'from' [παρά]. He supports this view by pointing out that when Paul uses the verb 'to receive' [παραλαμβάνω] with the preposition 'from' [παρά], each time it means the information was directly received (Gal. 1:12; 1 Thess. 2:13; 4:1; 2 Thess. 3:6).[221] Others question whether this much weight should be placed upon

---

[214]Wegenast, *Verständnis*, pp. 95-97.

[215]Hyam Maccoby, 'Paul and the Eucharist', *NTS* 37 (1991), pp. 247-67. Maccoby sees himself in continuity with A. Loisy, *The Birth of the Christian Religion* (London: Allen & Unwin, 1948), pp. 230-35, and H. Lietzmann, *Messe und Herrenmahl* (3rd ed.; Berlin: DeGruyter, 1955), p. 255. See also Leon Morris, *The First Epistle of Paul to the Corinthians* (London: Tyndale, 1958), pp. 159-60.

[216]Maccoby, 'Eucharist', p. 247.

[217]Maccoby, 'Eucharist', p. 248.

[218]Jeremias, *Eucharistic Words*, p. 101; Wegenast, *Verständnis*, p. 95; de Jonge, *Christology*, p. 45; Fee, *1 Corinthians*, p. 545; I. Howard Marshall, *Last Supper and Lord's Supper* (Exeter: Paternoster, 1980), p. 51; Harrisville, *1 Corinthians*, p. 196; Conzelmann, *1 Corinthians*, p. 195.

[219]Harrisville, *1 Corinthians*, p. 196.

[220]Hunter, *Paul*, p. 19. See also Héring, *1 Corinthians*, p. 114; Ladd, *Theology*, p. 389; Gerhardsson, *Memory*, p. 321.

[221]Hunter, *Paul*, p. 19.

the preposition.²²²

The third view does not so much contradict the second view as it sees more than a mere repetition by Paul of some information which originated with the earthly Jesus. The phrase 'from the Lord', should 'be understood as not only pointing to the historical Jesus as the chronological beginning and the first link of the chain of the tradition, but to the exalted Lord as the real author of the whole tradition developing itself within the apostolic church'.²²³ Cullmann wants to stress 'the Christ who is in the tradition of the apostles'.²²⁴

The first view, that the tradition was revealed directly to Paul, makes the words of Paul, 'on the night he was betrayed', meaningless. It also totally ignores the Jewish Passover setting. It can be questioned if 'from' [ἀπό] must mean 'origin'; it certainly is appropriate to use in this context. The third view attempts to pour too much 'theology' into the phrase 'from the Lord'. Semantically it seems highly unlikely that in one phrase Paul would be thinking both of direct revelation from the risen Lord and of a statement made by Jesus while he lived on earth. Therefore the second view, that the tradition originates from the earthly Jesus, is the view that most easily fits the context.

Paul introduces the actual tradition in v. 23 with 'for' [ὅτι] as he did in 1 Corinthians 15:3. The difficulty again arises as to what content Paul has inserted into the tradition and where the tradition ends. There is no debate that Paul draws out the implications of the tradition in v. 27. Verse 26 also breaks the flow of the tradition found in vv. 23-25 and gives the first reason for repeating the tradition.²²⁵ It is possible that the reason given in v. 26 is linked with the rest of the tradition, but the change from the first person ('in remembrance of me' in v. 25) to the third person ('the Lord's death until he comes' in v. 26) shows that in its present form it does not go back to Jesus, but perhaps, to the narrative context.²²⁶

The vocabulary and grammar in this section point to this section being a portion of pre-Pauline tradition. 'I delivered' [παραδίδωμι] changes in meaning from 'delivered' in the first part of v. 23 to 'betrayed' in the second part of the verse.²²⁷ This meaning is unique in Paul yet is the predominant meaning found in the Gospels. "Giving thanks' [εὐχαριστέω], quite common in Paul, is usually used of thanking God (e.g. Rom. 1:8); only here is it used of thanking Jesus, and it carries the idea of 'to bless'.²²⁸ 'Broke' [κλάω] and 'cup'

---

[222] Bruce, *Tradition*, p. 32; Wegenast, *Verständnis*, p. 96.

[223] Cullmann, *Early Church*, p. 62.

[224] Cullmann, *Early Church*, pp. 68, 81. See also Barrett, *1 Corinthians*, pp. 265-66.

[225] Fee, *1 Corinthians*, p. 556.

[226] Fee, *1 Corinthians*, p. 556, n. 58. See also Marshall, *Last Supper*, p. 54, who relates this to the statement about the kingdom found in Luke 22:16.

[227] Jeremias, *Eucharistic Words*, p. 104.

[228] Marshall, *Last Supper*, p. 41.

[ποτηρίον] are both found in Paul only in 1 Corinthians 10 and 11. 'Remembrance' [ἀνάμνησις] is found only in Luke 22:19, 1 Corinthians 11:24, 25 and Hebrews 10:3. Certain grammatical features set off this section from the flow of Paul's argument: Paul shifts from direct address in the present tense to the aorist and imperfect in most of vv. 23-26,[229] and he does not use 'and' [δέ] in these verses.

The problem addressed by the tradition. Paul clearly states that the problem he is dealing with in 1 Corinthians 11:18 concerns 'divisions among you'. This problem is of a practical nature, but Paul first gives a theological basis for his practical directives. The tradition itself comes in the middle of the section, after Paul has stated the problem but before he applies the tradition and states the solution. Paul gives two directives to solve the problem: (1) in vv. 27-32, introduced by 'so then' [ὥστε], he tells them they must 'discern the body', and (2) in vv. 33-34, again introduced by 'so then' [ὥστε], he exhorts them to 'wait for each other'.[230] The first exhortation is clearly dependent on both the bread and the cup being 'of the Lord' (v. 27). This relates directly back to the form of the tradition Paul has used. In v. 24 he states that the Lord Jesus said 'this is my body' in reference to the bread; then in v. 26 he says, 'This cup is . . . in my blood'. The personal relationship of Christ to the Supper is stressed with the phrase 'in remembrance of me' repeated after each of the elements. This repetition is found only in Paul and therefore is likely to be a Pauline insertion. Paul also wants the Supper to be taken seriously each time it is partaken of, so he has inserted the two phrases 'whenever you drink it' and 'whenever you eat this bread and drink this cup' (vv. 25, 26).

The response Paul expects from them is to 'wait for each other' (vv. 21, 33) and 'not despise the church of God' (v. 22). This is further defined as not taking the Supper 'in an unworthy manner' (v. 27). Therefore each member must 'examine himself' (v. 28), 'recognize the body' (v. 29), and 'judge' himself (v. 31). In a very practical manner Paul closes off this section by telling them to eat at home if they are hungry (v. 34).

This tradition includes some bits of extra information upon which Paul does not draw for the particular problem. The complete form of the liturgy is ultimately unnecessary to the argument itself; Paul could have simply stressed that the elements are directly related to Christ. Nor was it necessary for Paul to include the phrase 'on the night he was betrayed': it adds nothing directly to the argument, although it does show the origin of the practice and stresses that the

---

[229]The imperatives, 'do' [ποιεῖτε (24)], 'drink' [πίνητε (25)], 'eat' [ἐσθίτηε (26)], are all in the present tense, as would be most natural in a quotation, and the introduction of the quote is also in the present [λέγων (25)]. In addition, Paul's statement of the purpose for the Lord's Supper at the end of these verses is in the present tense [καταγγέλλετε (26)].

[230]Fee, *1 Corinthians*, pp. 532, 558-69.

The Authenticity of 2 Thessalonians

Lord who is directly related to the cup and bread 'was betrayed' for them. The eschatological note, 'until the Lord comes', is not directly applicable to the argument, but may be included in order more fully to define the 'whenever' of vv. 25 and 26.

The only real parallels to this tradition are in the synoptic Gospels, and it is universally recognized that the Pauline account of the Lord's Supper is very similar to the Lucan account.[231] The manner in which Paul quotes the tradition in 1 Corinthians 11:23-26 shows clearly that he was not ignorant about the earthly life of Jesus, nor did he consider the events and teaching of Jesus as having no further application. Considering the historical introduction to the tradition, it seems very likely that Paul had received an account of the passion of Jesus.[232] Thus 1 Corinthians 11:23-26 is a very clear example of how Paul used traditional material and applied it to a very particular problem.

3. 1 Corinthians 7:10 and 9:14—Words of the Lord

Two more examples of pre-Pauline tradition are the words of the Lord found in 1 Corinthians 7:10 and 9:14. Paul introduces 1 Corinthians 7, 'Now for the matters you wrote about: It is good for a man not to marry'. Following some general directions concerning marriage in vv. 2-7, in v. 8 he begins to speak to specific groups within the congregation: the unmarried and widows (v. 8), the married (v. 10), and 'the rest' (v. 15). Following this he addresses a related topic beginning at v. 25: 'now concerning virgins'. In the section directed toward 'the married', he says (v. 10), 'I give this command (not I, but the Lord)', and following this he gives a general statement against divorce. It is generally recognized that this statement is parallel to the statements found in the Gospels concerning divorce;[233] however, the form of the saying found in the

---

[231] This is if the longer account of the Lucan text is accepted as original. For a full discussion of the text see I. Howard Marshall, *The Gospel of Luke* (NIGTC; Grand Rapids: Eerdmans, 1978), pp. 799-807.

[232] Allison, 'Pauline Epistles', p. 16.

[233] Harald Riesenfeld, *The Gospel Tradition and its Beginnings* (London: Mowbray, 1957), p. 14; Davies, *Rabbinic Judaism,* p. 140; David L. Dungan, *The Sayings of Jesus in the Churches of Paul* (Philadelphia: Fortress, 1971), p. 132; James Moffatt, *1 Corinthians,* p. 78; Barrett, *1 Corinthians,* p. 162; Fee, *1 Corinthians,* p. 292; David Wenham, 'Paul's Use of the Jesus Tradition: Three Samples', in *The Jesus Tradition Outside the Gospels* (vol. 5 in Gospel Perspectives; ed. David Wenham; Sheffield: JSOT Press, 1985), pp. 7-8. Peter Richardson, '"I Say, Not the Lord": Personal Opinion, Apostolic Authority and the Development of Early Christian Halakah', *TynBul* 31 (1989), p. 71, says that 1 Cor. 7:10 comes from the exalted Lord, primarily because 'the term Lord is most naturally used of the ascended Jesus'. Wegenast, *Verständnis,* p. 106, and Conzelmann, *1 Corinthians,* p. 120, both want to stress that the command is still valid because it is the living (Wegenast) and exalted

Gospels is case law, whereas Paul explicitly makes it a command in 1 Corinthians.[234] The verbal similarities between 1 Corinthians 7 and the Gospels are not close; Paul's phrase is much briefer, and he even uses a different word for divorce.[235] Paul's primary concern in this verse is reconciliation (see 1 Cor. 7:11), but Jesus's concern in the Gospels is to return to God's original pattern for marriage and to correct the wrong attitudes of the Pharisees (in Matt. 19 and Mark 10).

If the original form of the saying is found in the Gospels (see Matt. 5:32; 19:9; Mark 10:11; Luke 16:18), then Paul has displayed a great degree of freedom in remolding it into a command and changing the wording.[236] Most of the discussion concerning this passage has to do with Paul's view of the command of the Lord in contrast to when he does not have a command from the Lord (v.12). The piece of Jesus tradition that Paul uses applies to the problem in Corinth directly, but not exhaustively. Paul saw the application of this saying as limited in respect to the problems he faced in Corinth. He does not contradict Jesus's statement; he only says that he does not have a saying of Jesus that directly applies to the marriage of believer and unbeliever.[237] Therefore he must give further applications to their situation. This same idea is found again in v. 25, where Paul says, 'I have no command from the Lord, but I give a judgment as one who by the Lord's mercy is trustworthy'. This does not mean that Paul is downgrading his own authority, only that he is speaking in his capacity as an apostle without a statement from the earthly Lord.[238] The only difference between the command in v. 10 and in v.12 is the manner in which the Lord's authority is exercised: through a command he gave while on earth,[239] or through his apostle. Thus 1 Corinthians 7 shows that Paul did not confuse apostolic revelations with tradition.[240]

The second passage where Paul refers to a word from the Lord is found in 1 Corinthians 9:1-27, where he defends his freedom as an apostle. In the middle of this section he maintains he has a right to be supported by others for his

---

(Conzelmann) Lord who gave this command. According to Conzelmann it is a 'supratemporal command'.

[234] Fee, *1 Corinthians*, pp. 292-93.

[235] 1 Cor. 7:10—χωρίζω (literally, to separate); 1 Cor. 7:11—ἀφίημι; Gospels—ἀπολύω.

[236] Dungan, *Sayings*, p. 134, says it is impossible to say to which Gospel it is closest.

[237] Fee, *1 Corinthians*, p. 291.

[238] Wegenast, *Verständnis*, p. 107, says that Paul makes it clear that his wisdom does not possess the same binding authority as the word of the Lord. But 1 Cor. 7:12 does not show this at all; it only shows that Paul did not have a direct word from the Lord on this topic.

[239] Allison, 'Pauline Epistles', p. 3.

[240] C. H. Dodd, *History and the Gospel* (London: Nisbet, 1938), p. 57.

The Authenticity of 2 Thessalonians

preaching ministry (vv. 6-18). He lists a series of reasons, his final reason being that 'the Lord has commanded that those who preach the gospel should receive their living from the gospel' (v. 14). Paul points out that he has not availed himself of these rights in the way others have (vv. 5-6). As with 1 Corinthians 7:10, most commentators agree that this refers to a saying of the earthly Jesus found in Luke 10:7 and Matthew 10:10.[241] By using the aorist of the verb 'to command', Paul points back to the past origin of this teaching from Jesus,[242] showing that referring to 'the Lord' does not necessarily imply that the information was received by direct revelation of the resurrected Lord.[243] It is possible that vv. 7-11 may go back to Jesus as well.[244] This same tradition is found in 1 Timothy 5:18,[245] where not only is Deuteronomy 25:4 quoted (as in 1 Cor. 9:9), but an exact quote of Luke 10:7 is found as well.

Once again it is clear that Paul is concerned, not with producing an exact quote, but with making clear the point made originally by Jesus. The command from Jesus does not function as the sole basis for his argument, but inserting that this is the Lord's command certainly completes his argument in an authoritative manner.[246] The interesting thing is that Paul is stating this 'right' in order to show that he is not making use of it. This does not mean Paul is ignoring the authority of Jesus, for as Fee says 'the command is not given *to* the missionaries but *for* their benefit'.[247] Paul does not make use of this principle because he does not want anything to hinder his missionary work.[248] Paul

---

[241] A. W. Argyle, 'Parallels between the Pauline Epistles and Q', *ExpTim* 60 (1948-49), p. 318; Barrett, *1 Corinthians*, p. 208; John P. Brown, 'Synoptic Parallels in the Epistles and Form-History', *NTS* 10 (1964), p. 37; Conzelmann, *1 Corinthians*, p. 157; Davies, *Rabbinic Judaism*, p. 140; Dungan, *Sayings*, p. 79; Fee, *1 Corinthians*, p. 412; Moffatt, *1 Corinthians*, p. 120; Neirynck, 'Sayings of Jesus', p. 275; Wegenast, *Verständnis*, p. 107.

[242] G. N. Stanton, *Jesus of Nazareth in New Testament Preaching* (Cambridge: Cambridge University Press, 1974), p. 96; Wegenast, *Verständnis*, p. 108.

[243] Stanton, *Jesus*, p. 96.

[244] Dungan, *Sayings*, pp. 79-80.

[245] Barrett, *1 Corinthians*, p. 208.

[246] Peter Richardson and Peter Gooch, 'Logia of Jesus in 1 Corinthians', in *The Jesus Tradition Outside the Gospels* (vol. 5 in Gospel Perspectives; ed. David Wenham; Sheffield: JSOT Press, 1985), p. 44, say that the Lord's command is 'not a base' or foundation of Paul's argument, but functions as 'a capstone'. Although it cannot be said to be the sole base of Paul's argument, it still functions as part of the foundation of Paul's argument. It is one of the proofs of his right to be supported.

[247] Fee, *1 Corinthians*, p. 413, n. 96.

[248] Dungan, *Sayings*, p. 144.

clearly sees these words from Jesus as having a continuing authority.[249]

4. Previously Known Information

First Corinthians shows Paul's great concern for a number of problems at Corinth. Even though Paul begins the letter with a thanksgiving (1:4-9), he immediately follows that section with a rebuke to the church for its divisions (1:10-17). From the tone of much of the letter, it is clear that Paul considers the church at Corinth to be living inconsistently with what he himself had taught during his lengthy stay, and therefore, as we have already seen, Paul refers back to this teaching. The passages already examined which are introduced either by 'tradition' words or as from the Lord do not exhaust the references Paul makes to the teaching the church had already received from him. Paul explicitly says, 'Do you not know that' in a number of passages throughout 1 Corinthians. The purpose of this introductory phrase is not to comment on the ignorance of the Corinthians, but to rebuke them because they have not been true to what they have been taught[250] It carries the idea of 'Have I not told you already?'[251]

In 1 Corinthians 3:16 Paul rebukes the church as a whole:[252] 'Don't you know that you yourselves are God's temple and that God's Spirit lives in you?' The temple motif is found again in 1 Corinthians 6:19, where instead of being addressed to the church as a whole it is applied to the individual.[253] This temple tradition is also reflected in 1 Peter 2:6.[254] Paul applies the temple tradition to the division already mentioned earlier in this chapter.[255] The believers had to realize that to divide the church was to divide God's holy temple and that God

---

[249]It is difficult to determine the extent of material known by Paul. The casual nature in which he quotes these words from Jesus and expects them to be recognized and obeyed suggests that he knew more words from Jesus. Davies, *Rabbinic Judaism*, p. 140, thinks that Paul would have a collection of sayings; Neirynck, 'Sayings of Jesus', pp. 274-75, thinks whether or not Paul knew 'part, or all, of the so-called Q material must remain questionable'.

[250]Robertson and Plummer, *1 Corinthians*, p. 66, note that this phrase of rebuke is frequently found in 1 Cor. The phrase is also found twice in Rom. (6:16; 11:2) and once in James (4:4).

[251]Moffatt, *1 Corinthians*, p. 30. See also Barrett, *1 Corinthians*, p. 90; Fee, *1 Corinthians*, p. 146.

[252]Barrett, *1 Corinthians*, p. 90.

[253]Conzelmann, *1 Corinthians*, p. 112; Barrett, *1 Corinthians*, p. 151; Robertson and Plummer, *1 Corinthians*, p. 128.

[254]Ellis, '1 Corinthians', p. 482.

[255]The application of temple terminology to persons is found referring to Jesus (John 2:19-21; Matt. 26:61; 27:40; Mark 14:58; 15:29; see also Rev. 21:22) and to the church (2 Cor. 6:16; Eph. 2:21; Rev. 3:12).

would punish anyone who was guilty of this crime.[256]

Another passage in which Paul reminds the Corinthians of what they know is 1 Corinthians 5:6, 'Don't you know that a little yeast works through the whole batch of dough?' This saying was probably proverbial, as it is found in exactly the same form in Galatians 5:9.[257] In 1 Corinthians 5:6, however, Paul is very concerned about the illicit sexual relationships in the church at Corinth, whereas in the Galatian churches he is concerned with false teachers demanding circumcision. The Corinthians should have known that the open sinfulness of one member affected the whole church. Paul goes on in 1 Corinthians 5:7-8 to expound the idea of 'yeast' and how it is compared to what is evil, wicked or impure. This explanation of 'yeast' appears also to be traditional because of its general character and because it is not directly concerned with the problem which Paul addresses in 5:1-5 and then again in 5:9-11.

In 1 Corinthians 6 Paul upbraids the Corinthians for their lawsuits against each other. In vv. 2 and 3 he reminds them that they will be judges over the world (v. 2) and over angels (v. 3) on the day of judgment. Paul introduces both of these statements with 'don't you know that', applying the tradition to judging current problems in the congregation. He is not concerned in this context to correct proper doctrinal ideas about the final judgment, but to apply known truths (concerning the final judgment) to their present situation. They should have been able to judge these minor or trivial cases. Once again Paul draws from his overall doctrinal teaching and applies it to a somewhat unrelated practical problem.

Later in ch. 6 Paul again reminds the Corinthians of something they were taught: 'Don't you know that the wicked will not inherit the kingdom of God?' (1 Cor. 6:9). The phrase 'to inherit the kingdom of God' is used by Paul four times (1 Cor. 6:9, 10; 15:50; Gal. 5:21); in each of these cases it is used in a warning about the kind of people who will not receive the kingdom.[258] This eschatological warning is applied to practical behavior, and in this passage and in Galatians 5 the warning is followed by a list. In 1 Corinthians the list describes types of people, whereas in Galatians the list describes sinful activities. Because the list in 6:9-10 is inserted between the twice-used phrase 'will not inherit the kingdom of God', and because the words in the list are used so infrequently in Paul,[259] the whole list needs to be included as part of the

---

[256]Fee, *1 Corinthians*, p. 149.

[257]Fee, *1 Corinthians*, p. 216.

[258]In 1 Cor. 15:50 Paul says that 'flesh and blood cannot inherit the kingdom of God', pointing to the necessity of a resurrection body.

[259]The words 'adulterer' [μοίχος] and 'effeminate' [μαλακός] are found only here in the Pauline corpus. 'Male homosexual' [ἀρσενοκοίτης] is only found here and in 1 Tim. 1:10, and 'thief' [κλέπτης] is only found here and in 1 Thess. 5:2, 4, where it is used in reference to the return of Christ. In addition 'drunkard' [μέθυσος], 'reviler'

tradition. Most likely the phrase 'do not be deceived' was inserted by Paul, as this phrase is found elsewhere in Paul.[260] In 6:11 Paul directly applies the tradition to the Corinthians. This shows that Paul's traditional teaching often includes practical teaching based on his theology.

The phrase 'don't you know that' is used three more times in ch. 6 to introduce three more statements which are linked together in this context. All three statements are applied to individual members. In the first statement (v. 15), 'your bodies are members of Christ himself', Paul is concerned with 'uniting with a prostitute' in contrast to being 'united to the Lord' (v. 17). The second statement (v. 16) reminds them that 'he who unites himself with a prostitute is one with her in body. For it is said, "The two will become one flesh." But he who unites himself with the Lord is one with him in spirit'. The piece of traditional teaching in this case is clear because Paul quotes from Genesis 2:24, 'The two will become one flesh'. The Corinthians knew this teaching and should have realized that it is wrong for a Christian to unite with a prostitute. The third statement (v. 19) gives a reason to flee sexual immorality: 'your body is a temple of the Holy Spirit'. It is clear that Paul expects his audience to understand his applying of a tradition about the Holy Spirit to how they are to live.[261] It is possible that in 1 Corinthians 6:15-19, Paul has linked together two separate traditions, one about chastity and the other about the Christian's relationship to the Lord.

When Paul introduces the topic of meat sacrificed to idols (1 Cor. 8:1), he again stresses what 'we know' concerning knowledge and love in relation to one another and to God (1b-3). Following this Paul again returns to the topic of eating sacrificed meat (8:4-13). Therefore 1b-3 is set apart from its context by its content, for these verses are very general and break the flow in the argument. These verses are also set apart grammatically because they are introduced by 'we know that', and following the verses Paul reintroduces the topic with 'concerning' just as he did at the beginning of v. 1. Therefore once more we see Paul introducing tradition which he knows is 'known' and which he sees can be applied to a somewhat unrelated matter.

When Paul defends his rights as an apostle in 1 Corinthians 9, he concludes his argument with a statement in v. 13 about a practice he expects his audience to know: 'Don't you know that those who work in the temple get their food from the temple, and those who serve at the altar share in what is offered on the altar?' Fee suggests that it is not possible to distinguish whether Paul is

---

[λοίδορος], and 'robber' [ἅρπαξ] are unusual for Paul, found only in this list and the similar list in 1 Cor. 5:10-11. 'Covetous person' [πλεονέκτης] is found only in 1 Cor. 5:10-11; 6:10; and Eph. 5:5.

[260] 1 Cor. 6:9; 15:33; Gal. 6:7.

[261] Dungan, 'Sayings of Jesus', p. 132.

referring to pagan temple rites or Old Testament practices.²⁶² Dungan, on the other hand, insists on the Jewish background.²⁶³ It seems more likely that Paul is referring to the Old Testament practices for a number of reasons: (1) Paul is clearly recommending the practice for which the example is given. Considering Paul's argument against idolatry in 1 Corinthians, it would be difficult to see how he would suggest a pagan practice for imitation. (2) The practice is clearly found in the Old Testament,²⁶⁴ and in this same passage Paul refers his readers to the law of Moses (v. 9). (3) As we have seen, the phrase 'don't you know that' is not just a phrase for common knowledge but implies that Paul had taught these things and that they should have remembered them. Here we have an instance of Old Testament practice being applied by Paul as an example.

Finally, 'don't you know that' is used in 1 Corinthians 9:24: 'Do you not know that in a race all the runners run, but only one gets the prize?' Paul is concerned that all the believers exert self-control as they strive for 'the prize'. The prize is for each of them and not just for one (v. 25b). Paul is using the imagery of athletic contests of his day, and in this instance it could be surmised that he is referring to general information known to all people of that time and culture. For two reasons this information can be seen as arising out of Paul's previous teaching to the Corinthians. First, Paul does not ask them to think about the races or games, but he introduces the imagery in the form of a rebuke, 'do you not know'. When Paul wants to inform without rebuke, he begins in a different manner. For example, in 1 Corinthians 12:2 he says, 'You know when you were pagans, somehow or other you were influenced and led astray to dumb idols',²⁶⁵ and in 1 Corinthians 16:15 he says, 'You know that the household of Stephanas were the first converts in Achaia'. In these cases Paul is either informing them of new information or reminding them of something they know to be true. However, in 1 Corinthians 9, Paul is defending his apostolic rights. It seems unlikely that Paul would rebuke them by introducing information which he had neither given nor used in reference to this issue or something similar. Secondly, the language which Paul uses to speak of his work as 'running' in this passage is used in this same figurative way elsewhere in his letters,²⁶⁶ as is the word for the prize he seeks [$\beta\rho\alpha\beta\epsilon\hat{\iota}ον$—Phil. 3:14]. Therefore this passage also most likely should be understood as part of Paul's previous teaching.

---

²⁶²Fee, *1 Corinthians*, p. 412.

²⁶³Dungan, *Sayings*, pp. 16-17.

²⁶⁴Fee, *1 Corinthians*, p. 412, refers the reader to Lev. 6:16-18, 26-28; 7:6, 8-10, 28-36; Num. 18:8-19.

²⁶⁵Harrisville, *1 Corinthians*, p. 61, also points out 1 Cor. 10:1 as an example of a 'softer' and 'more didactic' tone.

²⁶⁶See Gal. 2:2; Phil. 2:16; also 2 Thess. 3:1.

5. Brief Sayings

A number of other brief phrases and sayings should be seen as 'traditional'.

a. 1 Corinthians 4:11-13: 'To this very hour we go hungry and thirsty, we are in rags, we are brutally treated, we are homeless. We work hard with our own hands. When we are cursed, we bless; when we are persecuted, we endure it; when we are slandered, we answer kindly. Up to this moment we have become the scum of the earth, the refuse of the world'. This cluster of sayings is parallel to Matthew 5:6, 11-12, 44; 10:9-10; 11:19 and Luke 6:21-23, 27-28.[267]

b. 1 Corinthians 7:39: 'A woman is bound to her husband as long as he lives. But if her husband dies, she is free to marry anyone she wishes' (parallel to Rom. 7:2-3, where Paul uses this saying in reference to the authority of the law).[268] Although this verse is not usually cited as 'traditional', nevertheless the close parallel in Romans, where this teaching is used as a well-known example applied to something else, makes it very likely that it is tradition.

c. 1 Corinthians 8:4: 'God [is] one'. This Old Testament quote (Deut. 6:4) appears throughout the New Testament: Mark 12:29; Luke 18:19; Romans 3:30; Galatians 3:20; Ephesians 4:6; 1 Timothy 2:5; James 2:19.

d. 1 Corinthians 8:6: 'Yet for us there is but one God, the Father, from whom all things came and for whom we live; and there is but one Lord, Jesus Christ, through whom all things came and through whom we live'.[269]

e. 1 Corinthians 10:16: 'Is not the cup of thanksgiving for which we give thanks a participation in the blood of Christ? And is not the bread that we break a participation in the body of Christ?'[270]

f. 1 Corinthians 12:3: 'Jesus is Lord'.[271]

g. 1 Corinthians 12:13: 'For we were all baptized by one Spirit into one body—whether Jews or Greeks, slave or free—and we were all given the one Spirit to drink'.[272]

---

[267] Walter, 'Jesus-Tradition', p. 56. Walter begins with a 'minimal hypothesis' regarding the information Paul had of Jesus (p. 53). Furnish, 'Debate', p. 44.

[268] Fee, *1 Corinthians*, p. 355.

[269] George E. Cannon, *The Use of Traditional Materials in Colossians* (Macon, GA: Mercer University Press, 1983), p. 26; Ellis, '1 Corinthians', p. 494; Goppelt, 'Tradition', p. 225; Neufeld, *Confessions*, p. 44; Conzelmann, *1 Corinthians*, p. 144; Barrett, *1 Corinthians*, p. 100.

[270] Fee, *1 Corinthians*, pp. 465-69; Goppelt, 'Tradition', p. 225; Conzelmann, *1 Corinthians*, p. 171.

[271] Goppelt, 'Tradition', p. 225; Conzelmann, *1 Corinthians*, p. 206.

[272] See similar statements in Gal. 3:27-29 and Eph. 4:4-6. Notice also the change to the first person plural and the topic of baptism which is not discussed further in ch. 12.

h. 1 Corinthians 13:2: '... if I have faith that can move mountains' (parallel to Mark 11:23, Matt. 21:21).[273]

i. 1 Corinthians 16:22: 'Marana tha'[274]

6. Longer Sections

A number of longer sections of 1 Corinthians give the distinct appearance of being formed before being used by Paul in 1 Corinthians. It is not really possible to tell if Paul himself formed these at some previous time or if he is incorporating the work of someone else into his letter. Either way the material is considered authoritative and forms part of the Pauline argument in each place.

a. 1 Corinthians 1:18-25. A. W. Argyle has suggested that the general thought of 1 Corinthians 1:18-29 is similar to Luke 10:21-22 and Matthew 11:25-27.[275] When the passage is examined within 1 Corinthians, however, the passage as a whole does not appear to be traditional, but only vv.18-25. In 1 Corinthians 1, Paul speaks very personally in his thanksgiving (1:4-9) and in his initial discussion about divisions within the church (1:10-17). He refers by name to Chloe, Apollos, Cephas, Crispus, Gaius, Stephanas, and himself. Verse 18 makes a grammatical break with this section and up through v. 25 this section is very impersonal. The only references that are at all personal are the very general 'us' (1:18) which refers to all who are being saved, and the 'we preach' (1:23) which can include all who proclaim Christ. The content of vv. 18-25 also seems to be slightly out of context. These verses focus on the response of Jews and Greeks to the gospel, yet this does not seem to be a problem at Corinth as it was in Galatia or Rome. In v. 26 Paul again directly addresses his readers (referring to them as 'brothers' and again using the second person plural verb) picking up on only two thoughts from 18-25, wisdom and calling. This direct personal address continues right through 2:5. In addition to this there are a number of words which are unusual for Paul within 1:18-25.[276]

---

[273]Fee, *1 Corinthians*, p. 632; Hunter, *Paul,* p. 50; Neirynck (who cites C. M. Tuckett), 'Sayings of Jesus', p. 274. Robertson and Plummer, *1 Corinthians*, p. 290, suggest this may be proverbial, but if both Jesus and Paul used this proverb, it still would be pre-Pauline tradition. The same general idea is also found in Barrett, *1 Corinthians,* p. 301, and Conzelmann, *1 Corinthians,* p. 222, who cites Str-B 1:759.

[274]Conzelmann, *1 Corinthians,* p. 300; Fee, *1 Corinthians*, p. 838; de Jonge, *Christology,* p. 48; Hunter, *Paul,* pp. 50, 148.

[275]Argyle, 'Parallels', p. 318. The only close verbal parallel he notes between Paul and Q are 'God was pleased' [εὐδόκησεν ὁ θεός] (1 Cor. 1:21) and 'Yes, Father, for this was your good pleasure' [ναί, ὁ πατήρ, ὅτι οὕτως εὐδοκία ἐγένετο ἔμπροσθέν σου] (Luke 10:21 = Matt. 11:26).

[276]The word 'foolishness' [μωρία] is found only in 1 Cor. It is used three times within this section (1:18, 21, 23), once in 2:14, which has already been identified as tradition, and once in 3:19, which closes off this first major section of the epistle (chs 1-3) and

Tradition in 2 Thessalonians: Terminology and Identification

Therefore the change in person addressed, the unique vocabulary, and the topic of the tradition which is not particularly appropriate to the overall topic show that Paul has incorporated another traditional piece here in order to draw out certain themes which he is discussing.

b. 1 Corinthians 2:6-16. Ellis lists 1 Corinthians 2:6-16 as preformed midrash.[277] Conzelmann states that it 'stands out from its context both in style and content'.[278] Ellis notes that (1) there is a clear break between 2:5 and 2:6 and between 2:16 and 3:1, so that the passage is a self-contained pericope; (2) there is a shift to the first person plural (from the first person singular) and a shift to the present tense from the aorist; and (3) there are a number of peculiar idioms.[279] Fee attributes the uncommon language to Paul's use of his opponents' language;[280] however, this does not take into account the change of person or tense and the self-contained nature of the pericope. Immediately following this passage, Paul again directly addresses his readers, and therefore, as Ellis suggests, 2:6-16 is most likely a preformed piece.

c. 1 Corinthians 7:17-24. 1 Corinthians 7:17-24 is clearly distinct from its context and is usually described as a 'generalizing conclusion'.[281] The overall topic of 1 Corinthians 7 is marriage. This is true with respect to the first part of the chapter (vv. 1-16) and the later portion (vv. 25-40); in fact, it is quite easy to go from v. 16 directly to v. 25.[282] Fee states it well when he says, 'What is of interest is that neither of the specifics in that section (circumcision and slavery) is related to the *subject* matter of chap. 7'.[283] What does link this section with

---

probably draws the word from these traditions. The word 'intelligent' [συνετός] is found only here in the Pauline corpus, and 'disputer' [συζητής] is a New Testament *hapax*. One word that stands out is the Pauline *hapax* 'scribe' [γραμματεύς].

[277] Ellis, '1 Corinthians', p. 490.

[278] Conzelmann, *1 Corinthians*, p. 57.

[279] Ellis, '1 Corinthians', p. 490. Ellis (p. 499, nn. 68-70) mentions the following peculiarities: the word 'taught' [διδακτός](1 Cor. 2:13) is a Pauline *hapax*. He further notes that 1 Cor. 2:6-16 contains a number of phrases 'not found elsewhere in the New Testament: "Rulers of this age" (6), "before the ages" (7), "the spirit of man" (11), "the spirit of the world" (12), "natural man" (14; cf. "old man": Rom. 6.6; Eph. 4.22; Col. 3.9) and the "mind of Christ" (16). Not found elsewhere in Paul: "the Lord of glory" (8; cf. Jas 2.1)'. He as well notes the unusual 'the spirit that is from God' [τὸ πνεῦμα τὸ ἐκ τοῦ θεοῦ] (2:12). In addition to this the word 'spiritually' [πνευματικῶς] is found only here (2:14) in Paul.

[280] Fee, *1 Corinthians*, p. 100.

[281] John C. Hurd, *The Origin of 1 Corinthians* (London: SPCK, 1965), p. 66; Barrett, *1 Corinthians*, p. 167.

[282] S. Scott Bartchy, *ΜΑΛΛΟΝ ΧΡΗΣΑΙ: First-Century Slavery and the Interpretation of 1 Corinthians 7:21* (SBLDS 11; Missoula, MT: SBL, 1973), p. 161.

[283] Fee, *1 Corinthians*, p. 268.

the rest of ch. 7 is the concept which is repeated three times:

v. 17: 'Each one should retain the place in life that the Lord assigned to him and to which God has called him'.
v. 20: 'Each one should remain in the situation which he was in when God called him'.
v. 24: 'Each man, as responsible to God, should remain in the situation God called him to'.

Paul's 'refrain' gives the structure to vv. 17-24 and also links vv. 17-24 with their context:

vv. 1-7 —to the married: stay married with full conjugal rights
vv. 8-9 —to the unmarried and widows: it is good to remain unmarried
vv. 10-11 —to the married (both partners believers): remain married
vv. 12-16 —to those with an unbelieving spouse: remain married
vv. 25-38 —to virgins: it is good to remain unmarried
vv. 39-40 —to married women (and widows): the married are bound to the marriage; when widowed it is good to remain that way.[284]

Thus Paul uses the traditional statements about circumcision and slavery and applies them to the subject of marriage.

Paul's own statement at the end of v. 17, 'This is the rule I lay down in all the churches', shows 1 Corinthians 7:17-24 to be tradition, for Paul is presenting rules he teaches everywhere. In addition there are clear parallels within Paul to at least some of each half of this section. In v. 19 Paul says, 'Circumcision is nothing and uncircumcision is nothing', and in Galatians 5:6 he says, 'for in Christ Jesus neither circumcision nor uncircumcision has any value'.[285] Although the phrase is in a different form, it is obviously an important point of Pauline theology. In the section on slaves (1 Cor. 7:23), he says, 'You were bought with a price', and he says the same thing in 6:20, yet in a context discussing sexual immorality.[286] Although it is difficult to say exactly which words might have formed Paul's tradition about circumcision, slavery, and remaining in one's situation, certainly the topics are part of the content of Paul's traditional teaching. The topics of circumcision and slavery are extra to the overall argument; they function merely as examples of his teaching, illustrating the principle of remaining in the situation in which one is called.

d. 1 Corinthians 10:1-13. Ellis also describes as preformed midrash is 1 Corinthians 10:1-13.[287] He bases this idea on the work of Wayne Meeks,[288] who

---

[284]Fee, *1 Corinthians*, p. 268.
[285]Robertson and Plummer, *1 Corinthians*, p. 146.
[286]Bartchy, *ΜΑΛΛΟΝ ΧΡΗΣΑΙ*, p. 165, links the topics of circumcision, slavery, and male/female relationships together. He sees this illustrated in Gal. 3:28 and suggests that Paul used slavery and circumcision in 1 Cor. 7 as examples because of these links.
[287]Ellis, '1 Corinthians', p. 490.

notes that the passage is carefully structured: (1) the passage divides naturally in two parts by a contrast between 'all' in vv. 1-4 and 'some of them' in vv. 6-10; (2) in vv. 1-4 five parallel clauses all use the word 'all' [πάντες], while vv. 6-10 contain five corresponding statements about 'some of them'; (3) 'The five positive and the five negative *exempla* are both punctuated and linked with the paraenetic conclusion in vv.12-13 by means of an *inclusio,* vv. 6 and 11'; (4) the warning in v. 12 is a generalized third person imperative: 'He who thinks he stands, let him look lest he falls'. This imperative is in contrast to the first and second person plural in the rest of the section.[289] In v. 13, Paul again directly addresses his readers to encourage them in their obedience. Therefore the tradition begins after 'that' [ὅτι] in v. 1 and runs through the end of v. 12.[290] Meeks thinks that the homily is probably of Christian origin,[291] drawing most likely on Deuteronomy 32.[292] In addition to these perceptions by Meeks, the manner in which this section is introduced, 'For I do not want you to be ignorant', suggests that Paul is going to present to them some portion of teaching,[293] probably which they had not received before, or that he is going to put a new slant on previous teaching.[294] Fee makes the comment that Paul may well have composed this section, since the 'seams' are not obvious and Paul also had a rabbinic background.[295] This could be true, but the strong structural arguments presented by Meeks would tend to show that this section was preformed, whether by Paul or someone else.

e. 1 Corinthians 11:3-16. Another passage which most commentators recognize as forming a distinct unit is 1 Corinthians 11:3-16.[296] As was shown earlier, 11:2 more naturally goes with the preceding section as a closing verse, while 11:3, in contrast to v. 2, introduces a new section. Verse 3 begins in a manner very similar to 10:1, where Paul begins: 'For I do not desire you to be ignorant, brothers'. He begins 11:3 in a more positive way: 'But I desire you to know that'. Paul is again imparting information to them, but this does not appear to be totally new information, for the passage ends in v. 16, 'If anyone

---

[288]Wayne Meeks, 'And Rose up to Play": Midrash and Paraenesis in 1 Corinthians 10:1-22', *JSNT* 16 (1982), pp. 64-78.

[289]Meeks, '"Rose up to Play', p. 65.

[290]Meeks, 'Rose up to Play', p. 65, thinks that the phrase 'and the rock was Christ' is possibly a Pauline addition, and the idea of being 'baptized into Moses' has probably been added to the original as well.

[291]Meeks, 'Rose up to Play', p. 66.

[292]Meeks, 'Rose up to Play', p. 72.

[293]Conzelmann, *1 Corinthians,* p. 165.

[294]Fee, *1 Corinthians*, p. 442.

[295]Fee, *1 Corinthians,* p. 442, n. 5.

[296]For bibliographical information see Fee, *1 Corinthians,* p. 491-93, and Conzelmann, *1 Corinthians,* pp. 181-91.

The Authenticity of 2 Thessalonians

wants to be contentious about this, we have no other practice—nor do the churches of God'. Whatever is the exact meaning of this difficult section, Paul is explicitly presenting this information as teaching the churches' traditional practice. The vocabulary is somewhat unusual.[297] The passage also is quite impersonal, a trait that has already been seen in other portions of tradition.[298] At the beginning of v. 3, Paul expresses his desire to inform his readers and then does not use a pronoun directed towards his readers or a verb in the second person again until 'judge' [κρινάτε] in v. 13, where he interrupts the tradition to confront the readers directly with what has been said. In v.14 he continues directly addressing his readers, and thus vv. 13-14 appear as Paul's commentary to the Corinthians on the tradition he has just written. Verse 16 clearly closes off the section. The tradition begins after 'that' [ὅτι] in v. 3 and continues up through the end of v. 12. Therefore, 1 Corinthians 11:3-16 contains a preformed piece of material which Paul has inserted.[299]

f. 1 Corinthians 13. One of the most obvious sections which breaks the flow of Paul's argument is 1 Corinthians 13. In the past, the seams at the end of ch. 12 and the beginning of ch. 14 have suggested to some that 1 Corinthians 13 is not in its original place in the epistle[300] because the argument concerning spiritual gifts would appear to move rather smoothly from 12:31a to 14:1b.[301] More commonly the chapter is viewed as a digression or excursus.[302] Yet at the same time, most commentators see a progression of thought from ch. 12 through ch. 13 to ch. 14.[303] Although nearly all commentators recognize the self-contained unity of this chapter,[304] the following points set this chapter off from its context: (1) It makes sense as a unity by itself;[305] (2) The seams with what

---

[297]'Uncovered' [ἀκατακάλυπτος](vv. 5, 13), 'to cover' [κατακαλύπτω] (vv. 6, 7), 'to wear long hair' [κομάω] (vv. 14, 15), 'hair' [κόμη] (v.15), and 'argumentative' [φιλόνεικος] (v.16) are found only in this passage in the New Testament. 'To shave' [ξυράω] (vv. 5, 6), 'to cut off' [κείρω] (v. 6), and 'covering' [περιβόλαιον] (v. 15) are found only in this passage in the Pauline corpus. 'Disgraceful' [αἰσχρος] (1 Cor. 11:6; 14:35; Eph. 5:12; Titus 1:11) and 'practice' [συνήθεια] (John 18:39; 1 Cor. 8:7; 11:16) are also very rare in the New Testament.

[298]Hurd, *Origin,* p. 183, says of 1 Cor. 11:3-16 that it 'sounds more like one side of an argument'.

[299]On the question of whether 1 Cor. 11:3-16 was a later insertion into 1 Corinthians, see Ellis, '1 Corinthians', p. 493-94.

[300]Héring, *1 Corinthians,* p. 134.

[301]Héring, *1 Corinthians,* p. 134.

[302]Robertson and Plummer, *1 Corinthians,* p. 285.

[303]Hurd, *Origin,* pp. 192-93. See also Harrisville, *1 Corinthians,* p. 216.

[304]Barrett, *1 Corinthians,* p. 297; Fee, *1 Corinthians,* pp. 625-26.

[305]Conzelmann, *1 Corinthians,* p. 217; Barrett, *1 Corinthians,* p. 297.

goes before (12:31) and after (14:1) are 'ragged';[306] (3) the style is different, displaying a certain rhythmical yet irregular structure;[307] and (4) 'the balance of the sentences and the point and power of vocabulary are seldom equaled in Paul, or indeed in Greek literature generally'.[308] All of this points to Paul incorporating a portion of preformed material in order to teach the Corinthians the proper perspective on spiritual gifts.

g. 1 Corinthians 14:34-38. First Corinthians 14:34-38 is often discussed in relation to 1 Corinthians 11. In v. 37 Paul says, 'If anybody thinks he is a prophet or spiritually gifted, let him acknowledge that what I am writing to you is the Lord's command'. The phrase 'the Lord's command' is much more vague than the corresponding commands found in 7:10, where Paul contrasts what he commands with what the Lord commands, and in 9:14, where he seeks to strengthen his argument by appeal to the Lord's command. According to Davies, this verse supports the idea that Paul had a collection of sayings of the Lord;[309] Furnish thinks it is a 'prophetic' word;[310] and Conzelmann suggests 'that everything that is generally valid in the church is a command of the Lord' but then prefers to see the section as a later insertion.[311] Ellis, however, points out that the passage is found in all manuscripts and that it can be understood in the context.[312] Verse 36 explicitly looks back to what precedes it as being part of Paul's authoritative teaching and, therefore, part of his tradition.[313] In v. 33b the statement 'As in all the congregations of the saints' appears to be introducing tradition similar to the closing of the section of tradition found in 11:16. In this context it refers directly to vv. 34-35. Clearly Paul expects his readers to understand. Again, Paul is stressing his established teaching, and the teaching that is found 'in all the churches'.

h. 1 Corinthians 15:50-57. In 1 Corinthians 15:50-57, Paul concludes his argument about the resurrection of the dead. He begins solemnly: 'I declare to you, brothers, that flesh and blood cannot inherit the kingdom of God, nor does the perishable inherit the imperishable'. The phrase 'will not inherit the kingdom of God' appears a number of times in Paul (1 Cor. 6:9, 10; Gal. 5:21; cf. Eph. 5:5). In v. 51 Paul again personally addresses his readers, 'Behold, I tell you'. He then abruptly changes from the first person singular to the third person plural and does not again directly address his audience until v. 58: 'So

---

[306] Conzelmann, *1 Corinthians*, p. 217; Héring, *1 Corinthians*, p. 134.

[307] Conzelmann, *1 Corinthians*, p. 218; Barrett, *1 Corinthians*, p. 299.

[308] Barrett, *1 Corinthians*, p. 299.

[309] Davies, *Rabbinic Judaism*, p. 140.

[310] Furnish, 'Debate', p. 44.

[311] Conzelmann, *1 Corinthians*, p. 246; Fee, *1 Corinthians*, pp. 699-703, thinks only vv. 34 and 35 are later insertions.

[312] Ellis, '1 Corinthians', p. 492.

[313] Fee, *1 Corinthians*, p. 709, does regard this verse as original.

that, my beloved brothers '. Paul refers to what he is about to say as a 'mystery', referring to something that was not known but has now been made known, such as Paul's gospel message as a whole[314] or some particular teaching such as the destiny of Israel (Rom. 11:25) or, in this case, what will happen to the dead at the return of Christ. This passage is similar to 1 Thessalonians 4:16-17 and Matthew 24:31. The vocabulary also displays a number of peculiarities.[315] Therefore, the change of person, the peculiarities of vocabulary, the similarity to 1 Thessalonians 4:16-17, and Paul's reference to this information as a 'mystery' all point to 1 Corinthians 15:51-57 as preformed tradition.[316]

7. Conclusion on the Identification of Tradition in 1 Corinthians

In 1 Corinthians, Paul employs a variety of forms of tradition: liturgical, confessional, catechetical, and proverbial. These various forms come from a number of different sources, such as the Lord, the apostles, the Old Testament, and Paul himself. Paul uses these traditions with a great deal of flexibility: he feels free to insert his own editorial comments into the midst of the tradition and to draw out implications from the tradition which are not explicitly mentioned. Sometimes he introduces the tradition with traditioning words; other times he refers back to what he has taught; and other times the tradition is worked right into his prose. Despite this flexibility and variety, a number of conclusions can be drawn from Paul's use of tradition in 1 Corinthians.

(1) Most pieces of tradition are conspicuous. They can be identified by their introductory words ('received', 'delivered', 'tradition', 'you know', 'we believe', 'for' [ὅτι]), by a definite grammatical break (seams, unusual vocabulary, change of style and structure, different persons addressed), and by their content (a digression with only some portion of the tradition directly applicable or a general teaching that can be applied to a variety of situations).

(2) The traditions Paul uses pervade his letters. In almost every section of 1 Corinthians some form of tradition is included. Based on my examination, I calculate that 22% of 1 Corinthians is tradition.[317] Furthermore, 1 Corinthians

---

[314]See Rom. 16:25; 1 Cor. 4:1; cf. Eph. 1:9; 3:3, 4, 9; 6:19; Col. 1:26, 27; 2:2; 4:3. See also Bornkamm, 'μυστήριον', *TDNT* 4.823.

[315]Two words are found only here in the New Testament: 'moment' [ἄτομος (15:52)] and 'twinkling' [ῥιπή (15:52)]. A few others are unusual for Paul: 'sound the trumpet' [σαλπίζω (15:52)], 'incorruption' [ἀφθαρσία (15:53, 54; and 1 Tim. 6:16 where it is used of God)], and 'victory' [νῖκος (15:53, 54, 57)].

[316]See Argyle, 'M and the Pauline Epistles', p. 341.

[317]This calculation is made by counting the words of the individual portions of tradition and dividing that number by the total number of words (6820) found in the UBS³ text of 1 Corinthians. The following figures were used to compute this total: 126 (1:18-25) + 211 (2:6-16) + 11 (3:16) + 35 (4:11-13) + 42 (5:6-8) + 5 (6:2) + 2 (6:3) + 28 (6:9-10) + 6 (6:15) + 23 (6:16-17) + 10 (6:19) + 2 (6:20) + 5 (7:10) + 92 (7:17-24) + 19

also contains at least sixteen Old Testament quotes which are recognized by the UBS text,[318] they too should be considered part of Paul's 'traditional' teaching. This would raise the percentage of tradition to over 23%.[319] Therefore Paul the letter-writer, when writing to a congregation which he had founded, constantly referred back to the 'tradition' which he taught when he was among them.

(3) The tradition is considered absolutely authoritative. This is true whether it be the gospel proclamation (1 Cor. 15:3-5), the word of the Lord (1 Cor. 7:10; 9:14), the communion liturgy (1 Cor. 11:23-26), or Paul's own example (1 Cor. 11:1-2) and teaching (1 Cor. 3:16).

IV. Tradition and the Authenticity of 2 Thessalonians

The examination of the terminology of tradition and the identification of the traditions in the undisputed letters of 1 Thessalonians and 1 Corinthians have shown that Paul intentionally incorporated tradition into his letters and that this is not some post-Pauline development. These traditions cover a variety of topics and are found incorporated into almost every section of the undisputed letters. In fact, over 23% of both 1 Thessalonians and 1 Corinthians are traditional material. Furthermore, tradition is used throughout the Pauline corpus.[320]

(7:39) + 30 (8:1-3) + 2 (8:4) + 25 (8:6) + 16 (9:13) + 8 (9:14) + 12 (9:24) + 160 (10:1-13) + 24 (10:16) + 153 (11:3-16) + 76 (11:23-26) + 2 (12:3) + 23 (12:13) + 196 (13:1-13) + 36 (14:34-35) + 42 (15:3-7) + 101 (15:51-57) + 2 (16:22) = 1525. 1525/6820 = 22.36%.

[318] On the use of Scripture, see C. H. Dodd, *According to the Scriptures* (London: Nisbet, 1952), pp. 126-27.

[319] The following figures were used to compute this total: 11 (1:19) + 5 (1:31) + 21 (2:9) + 7 (2:16) + 8 (3:19) + 9 (3:20) + 6 (5:13) + 6 (6:16) + 4 (9:9) + 10 (10:7) + 8 (10:26) + 15 (14:21) + 6 (15:27) + 6 (15:32) + 8 (15:45) + 5 (15:54) + 10 (15:55) = 145. However, a number of these OT quotes are part of the traditional sections already counted above (1:19; 2:9, 16; 6:16; 10:7; 15:54-55); therefore, the total number of words that should be added to get a total figure for tradition in 1 Cor. is only 75, not 145. 1525 + 75 = 1600. 1600/6820 = 23.46%.

[320] Neumann, *Authenticity*, p. 131, n. 52, notes that Romans contains 19.1% quotations and salutations. On other possible traditions in Romans, see Paul Beasley-Murray, 'An Early Confession of Faith in the Lordship of Jesus', *TynBul* 31 (1980), pp. 147-54; J. P. Brown, 'Synoptic Parallels', pp. 27-48; Kendrick Grobel, 'A Chiastic Retribution-Formula in Romans 2', in *Zeit und Geschichte: Dankesgabe an Rudolf Bultmann zum 80 Geburtstag* (ed. Erich Dinkler; Tübingen: Mohr Siebeck, 1964), pp. 255-61; Hunter, *Paul*, especially pp. 24-30, 47-48, 53, 63, 101; Neirynck, 'Sayings of Jesus', pp. 265-321; Vern Poythress, 'Is Romans 1:3-4 a Pauline Confession After All?', *ExpTim* 87 (1975-76), pp. 180-83; Stuhlmacher, 'Jesustradition?', pp. 240-50;

Consequently, the terminology of tradition and the volume of tradition found in 2 Thessalonians (over 27%) are entirely consistent with Paul. Indeed, if 2 Thessalonians did *not* contain a significant portion of traditional material, it would be more likely to be non-Pauline.

The traditions in 2 Thessalonians appear in three larger blocks of material (1:6-10a; 2:3b-4, 7-12) and three smaller pieces (3:7, 9, 10), the same kind of mixture of smaller and larger pieces of tradition seen in 1 Thessalonians and 1 Corinthians. The traditions are introduced in a similar fashion to those in the undisputed Paul, yet their form shows no signs of having been copied from 1 Thessalonians or any other undisputed letter. The first piece of tradition follows the word 'for' [εἴπερ], a word used only in Romans to introduce tradition (3:30). Twice the traditions are introduced by 'that' [ὅτι—2:3; 3:10], once by 'for' [γάρ—2:7], and once by 'how' [πῶς—3:7]. These words are frequently used by Paul to introduce the traditions in 1 Thessalonians and 1 Corinthians. The writer of 2 Thessalonians shows the same flexibility in introducing tradition that Paul shows. The writer of 2 Thessalonians shows 'seams' when doctrinal traditions are incorporated into his letter, yet when paraenetic traditions are used they are incorporated right into his own writing (see 3:6-10). Both traits are seen in Paul.

The writer of 2 Thessalonians also feels free to insert his own emphases into the tradition (see the discussion of 2 Thess. 1:6-10). This is especially important for a discussion of the authenticity of 2 Thessalonians because nearly all of the disputers since the time of Wrede have stressed that 2 Thessalonians is literarily dependent on 1 Thessalonians. Yet, as has been shown, although tradition pervades both 2 Thessalonians and the undisputed Paul, the form of the traditions shows no signs of literary dependence. This suggests two possibilities: (1) the writer of 2 Thessalonians had a very extensive collection of Pauline letters (not just 1 Thessalonians) from which he freely drew; or (2) the writer of 2 Thessalonians was Paul himself, and consequently his writing shows the same flexibility as do the other writings of Paul. The problem with the first suggestion is that it requires a collection of Pauline letters at a very early date that does not include 2 Thessalonians, and the highly unlikely scenario that immediately after being written, 2 Thessalonians was accepted universally into this collection as authentic. This leaves the second possibility, that Paul wrote 2 Thessalonians, as the logical conclusion.

The overall contents of the traditions in 2 Thessalonians include teaching on judgment (1:6-10), the final opponent and the last battle (2:3b-4, 7-12), and imitation and work (3:6-10).[321] These traditions in 2 Thessalonians have been

---

Michael Thompson, *Clothed with Christ: The Example and Teaching of Jesus in Romans 12.1–15.13* (JSNTSup 59; Sheffield: JSOT Press, 1991), pp. 29-34, 60.

[321] A more detailed examination of the contents of these traditions can be found in the next chapter.

characterized as unpauline because they do not focus on the crucifixion and resurrection of Christ.[322] Yet if all the traditions in 1 Thessalonians and 1 Corinthians are examined, it is clearly seen that many of the traditions are not explicitly related to the 'Christ-event'.[323] Furthermore, these traditions in 2 Thessalonians contain numerous Old Testament allusions, as do a number of the traditional sections identified in 1 Corinthians. Paul himself does not explicitly mention the death and resurrection of Christ in tradition or in his teaching on certain subjects; therefore, this cannot be used as a criterion against the authenticity of 2 Thessalonians.

The traditions Paul uses in 1 Corinthians and 1 Thessalonians are of abiding authority, and they function to remind the Christians of what they have been taught. The recalling of these traditions impresses upon the readers the necessity to apply these doctrinal and paraenetic traditions to new situations that arise, for these traditions show them that what Paul taught when the church was founded is still to be applied. The same function is seen in 2 Thessalonians, where the recipients are to hold to the traditions but also to apply them when faced with a new situation, such as false teaching.

Paul can even use the same proverbial tradition and apply it to two very different situations. In 1 Corinthians 5:6 he says, 'Don't you know that a little yeast works through the whole batch of dough?' and applies this proverb to expelling the immoral brother from the church. In Galatians 5:9, however, he applies the same proverb to those who are preaching circumcision. Similarly, Paul can apply proverbial terminology (toil and hardship, night and day) to his relationship to the Thessalonians in 1 Thessalonians 2:9, and the writer of 2 Thessalonians can use the same terminology and apply it as an example to be followed (2 Thess. 3:8-9). This shows, not a simple copying of the tradition from one letter to the other, but the same kind of versatility seen in the undisputed Paul.

The identification of tradition within 2 Thessalonians also shows something about the relationship of the two Thessalonian epistles. Only one of the topics covered in the traditions of 2 Thessalonians (imitation, in 3:6-10) can be directly identified with the teaching in 1 Thessalonians. The writer of 2 Thessalonians has used traditions different from those in 1 Thessalonians to support his teaching in 2 Thessalonians 1–2. Consequently 2 Thessalonians is not explicitly a commentary on 1 Thessalonians, for if it were, the traditions would have to be the same and be reinterpreted by the author. Instead, the author of 2 Thessalonians presents further teaching, making the major teaching in 2 Thessalonians supplementary to 1 Thessalonians. Whether 2 Thessalonians is seen as authentic or not, it is not simply a rewriting of 1 Thessalonians.

2 Thessalonians has been criticized for presenting the traditions as

---

[322]See Müller, *Anfänge*, p. 261.

[323]See 1 Thess. 3:3-4; 5:2-10; 1 Cor. 3:16; 4:11-13; 5:6-8; 6:2-3, 9-10; 7:10, 17-24, 39; 10:1-12; 11:3-12; 13:1-13; 14:34-35.

'normative', that is, as standardized teaching applicable to all Christians. There is no question that the traditions in 2 Thessalonians *are* presented as normative. Yet the traditions found within 1 Thessalonians and 1 Corinthians are equally presented as normative, as can be seen in the introduction to the tradition found in 1 Corinthians 15:3-7: 'Now, brothers, I want to remind you of the gospel I preached to you, which you received and on which you have taken your stand. By this gospel you are saved, if you hold firmly to the word I preached to you. Otherwise, you have believed in vain'. The same is true of Paul's comments about the 'word of the Lord' (see 1 Cor. 7:10; 9:14; 1 Thess. 4:16-17), his own authority (1 Cor. 7:25, 40), and the practice in all the churches (1 Cor. 11:16; 14:33). Paul, in his undisputed letters, does not regularly reflect on the source or ultimate origin of particular traditions. He views some of these traditions as originating from the Lord (1 Cor. 7:10; 9:14; 11:23; 1 Thess. 4:16-17) or, in at least one case, as having a connection with the apostles of Jerusalem (1 Cor. 15:11).[324] He also speaks about the general practice of the churches (1 Cor. 11:16; 14:33). Yet generally Paul simply incorporates the tradition right into his writing, expecting his readers to respond to the authority of these teachings. This is what has been shown in 1 Thessalonians and 1 Corinthians and is seen as well in 2 Thessalonians.

Nor does the use of tradition within 2 Thessalonians put a greater stress on apostolic dignity. There is no veneration of Paul or any of the apostles as is seen in the Apostolic Fathers. In fact, most of the pieces of tradition found in 2 Thessalonians (1:6-10; 2:3-4, 7-12) make no direct mention of the apostle at all. The writer of 2 Thessalonians does not issue any commands on the basis of 'apostleship'; rather, like Paul he simply refers back to teaching that was 'delivered' in the past and to the missionary example (see 1 Cor. 11:2; Phil. 4:9

---

[324]For different theories on the origin of tradition see: Allison, 'Pauline Epistles', pp. 1-32; Baird, 'Kerygma', pp. 181-91; Bultmann, *Theology,* vol. 2, pp. 119-31; Cullmann, *Early Church,* pp. 59-104; Davies, *Rabbinic Judaism,* esp. pp. 128-45; and W. D. Davies, 'Reflections on a Scandinavian Approach to the Gospel Tradition', in *Neotestamentica et Patristica*: *Eine Freundesgabe Herrn Professor Dr. Oscar Cullmann zu seinem 60 Geburtstag Überreicht* (NovTSup 6 ; Leiden: Brill, 1962), pp. 14-34; Dodd, *History,* pp. 57-65; C. H. Dodd, *New Testament Studies* (Manchester: Manchester University Press, 1953), pp. 53-66; Dodd, *Apostolic Preaching,* pp. 16, 37; Dungan, *Sayings* , pp. 145-50; Gerhardsson, *Memory,* pp. 273, 300, 321; Leonhard Goppelt, *Theology of the New Testament* (ed. Jürgen Roloff; trans. J. E. Alsup;), vol. 2, esp. pp. 40-46; Goppelt, 'Tradition', pp. 213-33; Riesenfeld, *Gospel Tradition,* pp. 83-104; Schütz, *Apostolic Authority,* pp. 55-56; Morton Smith, 'A Comparison of Early Christian and Early Rabbinic Tradition', *JBL* 82 (1963), pp. 169-76; Stanton, *Jesus,* esp. pp. 94-97; Wegenast, *Verständnis,* esp. pp. 9-23 for a summary of various positions; Klaus Wengst, 'Der Apostel und die Tradition', *ZTK* 69 (1972), pp. 145-62.

Tradition in 2 Thessalonians: Terminology and Identification

and 1 Thess. 1:6).

Not only have some disputers thought that the apostle was being exalted in 2 Thessalonians, but Holland has suggested that tradition itself has become exalted so that it has become the basis for salvation. The doctrines and ethics covered by tradition do teach what one must believe and how one must act, but this is no more than is found in the doctrinal, confessional, and paraenetic traditions in the undisputed letters of Paul (see 1 Cor. 11:2; 1 Thess. 4:1-2). Therefore, Holland's contention that in 2 Thessalonians tradition is the basis for salvation is completely unfounded. Rather, in 2 Thessalonians, 1 Thessalonians, 1 Corinthians or the rest of the undisputed letters of Paul, Paul is the theologian of tradition.[325]

The use and identification of tradition within 2 Thessalonians also begins to solve the problem raised by disputers concerning the mood or tone of the letter. Disputers of authenticity have commented that 2 Thessalonians exhibits a solemn and formal tone or mood, while a defender of authenticity claims that 'the personal concern of the author for the readers shines through the letter'.[326] With such differing views of the letter one wonders if defenders and disputers are reading the same document. By identifying the traditions within 2 Thessalonians, however, the tone or mood of the letter can be explained. When 2 Thessalonians 1:6-10 and 2:3b-4, 7-12 are read, they are seen to be impersonal, formal and solemn. Yet when one reads 2 Thessalonians 1:3-5, 11-12; 2:1-3a, 13-17; 3:1-15, the writer addresses the readers directly ('brothers' in 1:3; 2:1, 13, 15; 3:1, 6, 13, 15), he refers to his past ministry and his goals for the future (2:5-6; 3:1-5), he shows genuine appreciation for their spiritual progress (1:3-5) and concern for theological and practical dangers which they face (2:1-3a; 3:6-10), and he prays for them (1:11-12; 2:16-17). When traditions were identified in 1 Thessalonians and 1 Corinthians, in nearly every case the traditions exhibited a change of person and a certain formality or solemnity. Furthermore, in 1 Thessalonians we have seen that a number of the warm or personal images ('nurse', 'father'—see 1 Thess. 2:1-12) are not characteristically Pauline but were taken by Paul from other contemporary authors. Therefore the disputers, by concentrating on the eschatological portions of 2 Thessalonians (the core of which are pieces of tradition) and then comparing these to a portion of 1 Thessalonians which is not characteristically Pauline, have deduced that compared to Paul the writer of 2 Thessalonians writes in a solemn and formal manner. But if one were to take some of the larger pieces of tradition from 1 Corinthians as typical of that letter and compare them to this same section of 1 Thessalonians, then the conclusion would have to be the same, that Paul could not have written 1 Corinthians. A proper understanding of the particular traditions in 2 Thessalonians and in

---

[325] Rigaux, *Thessaloniciens*, p. 656; Schütz, *Apostolic Authority*, p. 54.
[326] Marshall, *Thessalonians*, p. 34.

Paul's undisputed epistles aids us in understanding the tone of different sections of the letters and the letters as a whole, and again we see that the writer of 2 Thessalonians writes like Paul.

Trilling, in his section entitled 'Formgeschichtliche Untersuchung', notes that Bornemann and Dibelius thought 2 Thessalonians 1 contained an early Christian hymn or psalm. Trilling considers such a possibility to be unlikely because of the close relationship of the content of this section with 2 Thessalonians 2:8-10.[327] His view, however, is unfounded because the traditions found in 1:6-10a and 2:7-12, although both concerned with the return of Christ, have a very different focus from each other. The tradition in ch. 1 concerns the reversal of situations when the final judgment is executed, and the tradition in 2:7-12 concerns the defeat of the great opponent and those who follow him. Furthermore, the grammatical, stylistic, and contextual examination of these chapters shows that both include tradition. Because Trilling assumes that stereotyped tradition did not develop strongly until the second generation, he therefore does not fully examine the undisputed letters of Paul for evidence of Paul's use of tradition. By ignoring the abundant use of 'stereotyped' or preformed materials in the undisputed letters of Paul, Trilling has presented a caricature of Paul which is not consistent with the evidence. The dependence of the writer of 2 Thessalonians on tradition does not give the impression of looking back from a later time, as Trilling suggests,[328] any more than the dependence of 1 Corinthians on tradition looks back from a later time. Paul, in his letter to the Corinthians, says that what he taught when he was with them still applies (1 Cor. 15:1-2), and the writer of 2 Thessalonians claims this as well. Therefore the use of tradition in 2 Thessalonians does not show the characteristics of the generations after the time of Paul, but rather, of Paul himself.

The argument from tradition—the forms of those traditions, the terminology referring to tradition, the overall topics of the traditions, the function of tradition, the volume of tradition, the comparison in detail to Paul's use of tradition in his undisputed letters—presents a powerful reason for accepting the authenticity of 2 Thessalonians. This identification of the traditions within 2 Thessalonians will also greatly affect the interpretation of the doctrine and the literary characteristics in the discussion of authenticity.

---

[327] Trilling, *Untersuchungen*, pp. 72-73.
[328] Trilling, *Untersuchungen*, pp. 72-73, 98-99.

Chapter 4

Doctrinal Content of 2 Thessalonians

The previous chapter has shown that use of tradition is not a post-Pauline development, but rather, an integral part of Paul's letter writing. However, the doctrinal content of the traditions identified within 2 Thessalonians has frequently been used by the disputers of authenticity to show that Paul could not have written the letter. This chapter will show that the doctrinal teaching in 2 Thessalonians concerning eschatology (the last battle and final judgment), imitation, Christology, and soteriology is consistent with the teaching of the undisputed letters of Paul, and yet, not a mere copying of those doctrines from 1 Thessalonians or any of Paul's other letters.

I. Eschatology

The two largest pieces of tradition identified in 2 Thessalonians concern the last battle (2:3-4, 7-12) and the final judgment (1:6-10). Because these two topics are so closely related, it is necessary to examine both sections before drawing conclusions as to whether the eschatological teaching within these sections shows 2 Thessalonians could not have been written by Paul.

It was the eschatology of 2 Thessalonians (particularly of 2:1-12) which caused J. E. C. Schmidt, the first disputer, to question the letter's authenticity. This stress on the non-Pauline character of the eschatology of 2 Thessalonians is found in virtually every disputation of authenticity, as seen, for example, in Bailey's comparison of the eschatologies of 1 and 2 Thessalonians:

> These two eschatologies are contradictory. Either the end will come suddenly and without warning like a thief in the night (1 Thessalonians) or it will be preceded by a series of apocalyptic events which warn of its coming (2 Thessalonians). Paul might have said both things—in differing situations to one church, or to different churches—but he can hardly have said both things to the same church at the same time, i.e. to the Thessalonian church when he founded it. Moreover, corresponding to Paul's different messages to them, the situations in the two churches are quite different. In the church to which 1 Thessalonians was addressed, it was believed that the end had not yet come, and the delay in it was causing concern about Christians who had died (iv. 13-18); perhaps it was also causing some to doubt that the end would come at all (v. 1-12). In the church to which 2 Thessalonians was addressed, it was widely believed that the end had come (ii.2, iii. 6-12).[1]

Although the eschatological differences discerned between the two Thessalonian epistles do not necessarily present to the disputers an absolute reason for disputing the authenticity of the second letter, they nevertheless do

---

[1] J. A. Bailey, 'Who Wrote 2 Thessalonians?', pp. 136-37.

believe it at least confirms or adds to the case for classifying 2 Thessalonians as pseudepigraphy. Trilling describes his own discussion on the theology of 2 Thessalonians as a 'cross-check' (*Gegenprobe*) on the question of authenticity.[2]

The primary difference stressed by disputers between the eschatology of 2 Thessalonians and that of the undisputed Paulines concerns the expectation of the parousia. They suggest that Paul speaks with joy about the imminent and unexpected return of Christ, whereas the author of 2 Thessalonians writes with solemnity and desires to cool enthusiasm because the parousia will be delayed and a whole series of preliminary signs must first take place, thus enabling one to approximately calculate the time of the return of Christ. In addition, the disputers believe the writer of 2 Thessalonians creates the unpauline idea of a 'restrainer'. They also say the eschatological and apocalyptic perspective of 2 Thessalonians differs from Paul in that it focuses on the future, not on the present, it is not based on the Christ event, and it shows a non-Pauline stress on retributive justice.

Progress has been made in the understanding of the eschatology of 2 Thessalonians since the beginning of the dispute of the authenticity of the letter. Due to the work of Charles and Bousset, disputers no longer attempt to identify 'the man of lawlessness' with Nero.[3] The disputers also have come generally to accept that the eschatologies of 1 and 2 Thessalonians are not absolutely contradictory. Most defenders have stressed that 'signs' and 'imminence' are found side-by-side in apocalyptic literature in general and specifically in the eschatological discourse of the Synoptics. Most of the disputers, however, put a late date on the eschatological discourse in the Synoptics. The following reexamination of the eschatology of 2 Thessalonians will show that the writer of 2 Thessalonians does not present a series of signs which warn of the end or enable one to calculate the time of the end, but rather, he sets forth the events which are an integral part of the day of the Lord—a day which may occur at any time in the immediate future and which is entirely consistent with Paul's teaching.

A. *2 Thessalonians 2:1-12*

1. The Error at Thessalonica

Because most studies of the eschatology of 2 Thessalonians focus on ch. 2 of the epistle, this section will be examined first, and the teaching found in ch. 1 will be studied within this examination. The theological problem addressed by the writer of 2 Thessalonians concerns false teaching that 'the day of the Lord has already come' (2:2). He begins the chapter by introducing the general topic 'the coming of our Lord Jesus Christ and our being gathered to him'. The 'coming' Day of Christ and 'gathering' are linked together as one event, both

---

[2]Trilling, *Untersuchungen*, p. 109.
[3]The last major disputer to do so was Hollmann, 'Unechtheit', pp. 28-38.

being governed by one preposition and one article.[4] After expressing his concern for the Thessalonians, he states that the missionaries are not the source of the erroneous teaching. By combining the parousia and 'our being gathered' in his introduction to the topic (2:1), in contrast to those who say the day of the Lord has already happened, the writer makes it clear that he sees the parousia of Christ and 'our being gathered' as two aspects of the day of the Lord.[5]

The most significant question arising from the eschatology in the first two verses is the meaning of the verb in v. 2, 'to have come' [ἐνίστημι]: in this context, does it mean 'is imminent' or 'has come'? This verb, found in the New Testament in only seven passages, is used in the perfect tense in all but one place, and because the meaning 'has come' for the perfect tense is undeniable, the overwhelming number of commentators now accept this definition.[6] This is seen in Romans 8:38 and 1 Corinthians 3:22, where Paul contrasts 'present things' with 'future things'.[7] In Galatians 1:4, Paul says Christ's death delivers us 'from this present evil age'.[8] Hebrews 9:9 describes the first tabernacle as 'a parable for the present time'.[9] Because the situation addressed by Paul in 1 Corinthians 7:26 is unclear, it is best not to place much emphasis on 'the

---

[4]Best, *Thessalonians*, p. 274.

[5]D. J. Stephens, 'Eschatological Themes in 2 Thessalonians 2:1-12' (Ph.D thesis, St. Andrew's University, 1976), p. 93, notes that it is clear from 1 and 2 Thess. that Paul understood the parousia and the day of the Lord as referring to the same event, one emphasizing expectancy and the other judgment. Trilling, *Thessalonicher*, p. 73, also identifies the parousia with the day of the Lord in 2 Thess.

[6]Best, *Thessalonians*, p. 276; Findlay, *Thessalonians*, p. 166; Frame, *Thessalonians*, p. 248; Marshall, *Thessalonians*, p. 186; Milligan, *Thessalonians*, p. 97; Morris, *Thessalonians*, p. 216; Wanamaker, *Thessalonians*, p. 240. Trilling, *Thessalonicher*, p. 78, says the sense is unequivocal: it is 'da sein' ['is there'] and not 'nahe sein' ['is near']. Trilling, *Untersuchungen*, p. 124, is more emphatic in his disputation of the authenticity of 2 Thessalonians when he says, 'Daß (ὡς ὅτι) ἐνέστηκεν ἡ ἡμέρα τοῦ κυρίου übersetzt werden muß als "der Tag des Herrn is da", und nicht "ist im Anbrechen" oder "steht unmittelbar bevor", ist grammatisch an sich sicher' ['That the day of the Lord has come must be interpreted as "the day of the Lord is here", and not "it is breaking in", or "it stands immediately before us", is grammatically certain.']. Those in the past who have defended 'is imminent' include Dibelius, *Thessalonicher* (1937), p. 44; von Dobschütz, *Thessalonicher-Briefe*, p. 267; and B. B. Warfield, 'The Prophecies of St. Paul', *Expositor* 3rd series, 4 (1886), p. 37, n. 1. More recently, A. M. G. Stephenson, 'On the Meaning of ἐνέστηκεν ἡ ἡμέρα τοῦ κυρίου in 2 Thessalonians 2.2', *SE* 4 (1968), pp. 442-51, has defended 'is just at hand'. He believes there is some lexical ambiguity and that the meaning 'has come' is logically impossible.

[7]'Present things' is ἐνεστῶτα, and 'future things' is μέλλοντα.

[8]ἐκ τοῦ αἰῶνος τοῦ ἐνεστῶτος πονηροῦ

[9]ἥτις παραβολὴ εἰς τὸν ἐνεστηκότα

present necessity'.[10] However, it does seem most probable that whatever this 'necessity' was, it required the people to act at that time, and not just in the future.[11] Other than 2 Thessalonians 2:2, the only other use of this verb is found in 2 Timothy 3:1: 'in the last days perilous times shall come'.[12] This use of the verb does clearly point to the future, but that is because of the tense (future), not of the lexical meaning of the verb. The lexical meaning 'present' is also confirmed in the Apostolic Fathers[13] and the papyri and inscriptions.[14] As Frame says, 'ἐνέστηκεν means not "is coming" (ἔρχεται 1 Thess. 5:2), not "is at hand" (ἤγγικεν Rom. 13:12), not "is near" (ἐγγύς ἐστιν Phil. 4:5), but "has come," "is on hand," "is present"'.[15] The word ὁ ἐνεστὼς χρόνος was even

---

[10] τὴν ἐνεστῶσαν ἀνάγκην

[11] Most commentators interpret the 'present necessity' as related to the general eschatological perspective in which Christians always live. For example, Calvin, *1 Corinthians*, p. 156, says, 'In view of the "difficulties" (*propter necessitatem*) which always press hard upon the saints in this life, I think that the best solution is for all to enjoy the freedom and independence of celibacy, for it would be a real benefit to them'. Fee, *1 Corinthians*, pp. 328-30, says the idea of 'impending' is against Paul's use elsewhere and that, as Paul taught elsewhere, the present distress is the common lot of all Christians (1 Thess. 3:3-4). Robertson and Plummer, *1 Corinthians*, p. 152, follow Lightfoot (on Gal. 1:4) that the meaning is 'present' and not 'imminent'. See also Barrett, *1 Corinthians*, p. 174. Others who would stress 'imminent' include Héring, *1 Corinthians*, pp. 56-58; Moffatt, *1 Corinthians*, p. 91; and Conzelmann, *1 Corinthians*, pp. 130-32. Conzelmann uses 2 Thess. 2:2 as a parallel for this meaning. Another possibility which also requires the meaning 'present' is the suggestion made by Bruce W. Winter, 'Secular and Christian Responses to Corinthian Famines', *TynBul* 40 (1989), pp. 86-106. He thinks the 'present necessity' refers to the particular problem of famine within Corinth at the time the letter was written; this would explain the unusual directions given by Paul in this special circumstance.

[12] ἐν ἐσχάτος ἡμέραις ἐνστήσονται καιροὶ χαλεποί

[13] The verb is used only six times in the Apostolic Fathers. In *1 Clem.* 55.1, Clement speaks of 'when a time of pestilence has set in' [ἐνστάντος καιροῦ]. The context makes it clear that he is referring to examples of this behavior in the past. Ignatius (Ign. *Eph.* 11.1) contrasts fear 'for the wrath to come' [μέλλουσαν ὀργὴν] with 'present grace' [ἐνεστῶσαν χάριν]. The verb is found four times in *Barnabas*. In *Barn.* 1:7 and 5:3, the writer compares three periods of time which the Lord has made known, 'things past and things present and . . . things to come' [τὰ παρεληλυθότα καὶ τὰ ἐνστῶτα, καὶ τῶν μελλόντων]. In 4:1 he speaks of inquiring 'into the things that now are' [ἐνεστώτων]. These are the things which are able to save and are in opposition to the present works of the law. In 17:2, he again explicitly compares 'things present' with 'things to come' [τῶν ἐνστώτων ἢ μελλότων].

[14] See Milligan, *Thessalonians*, p. 97.

[15] Frame, *Thessalonians*, p. 248.

used to identify the name of the present tense in Greek.[16] Consequently, the problem explicitly being addressed by the writer of 2 Thessalonians is not the delay of the parousia, but its supposed presence.[17]

2. The Answer to the False Teaching

The writer of 2 Thessalonians refutes the false teaching that the day of the Lord has arrived by incorporating two pieces of tradition (3b-4; 7-12) into his teaching. In order to understand his argument, three items in these verses must be identified and their relationship to each other explained: the opponent, the apostasy, and the *katechon*.[18]

a. The opponent. The focus of the two pieces of tradition in ch. 2 is on the opponent described in 3b-4 and 8-9 as 'the man of lawlessness', 'the son of perdition', and 'the lawless one'.[19] This opponent will claim divinity and present himself as the sole object of worship (2:4). In terms of his work, he will perform false miracles according to the working of Satan (2:9) and will deceive those who do not believe the truth (2:10). In this chapter the writer twice mentions when the opponent will come. In 2:3b he states 'except the apostasy come first and the man of lawlessness'. The sentence as it is found in 2 Thessalonians is incomplete—not an unusual occurrence in Paul's letters[20]— and commentators or translators usually insert 'that day will not come' before the piece of tradition in order to clarify the meaning.[21]

Giblin has challenged this insertion, saying Paul is focusing on the 'qualitative', not the chronological, aspects of the parousia. He believes that what should be inserted is 'the judgment of God will not have been executed against the powers of deception once and for all', or 'the Lord will not have come in judgment to end definitely the deception that is the work of Satan'.[22] There are a number of problems with Giblin's proposal. First, the readers of the letter are obviously expected to understand the sentence, but the more complicated the required unwritten assertion is, the less likely it is to be

---

[16]Stephenson, 'ἐνέστηκεν', p. 444.

[17]W. H. Burkeen, 'The Parousia of Christ in the Thessalonian Correspondence' (Ph.D. thesis, University of Aberdeen, 1979), p. 318.

[18]The term *katechon* will be used to refer to the general concept being described by both τὸ κατέχον ['the restraining'] and ὁ κατέχων ['the restrainer'] from 2:6-7.

[19]'The man of lawlessness' translates as ὁ ἄνθρωπος τῆς ἀνομίας; 'the son of perdition' translates as ὁ υἱὸς τῆς ἀπωλείας; and 'the lawless one' translates as ὁ ἄνομος.

[20]Best, *Thessalonians*, p. 280, also lists 1 Thess. 2:11-12, 19; Gal. 1:20; 2:4; 2 Cor. 8:13; Rom. 4:16; 5:12, etc., showing this same characteristic.

[21]Best, *Thessalonians*, p. 280; Milligan, *Thessalonians*, p. 98; Wanamaker, *Thessalonians*, p. 244; von Dobschütz, *Thessalonicher-Briefe*, p. 268; Marshall, *Thessalonians*, p. 118.

[22]Giblin, *Threat*, p. 135.

understood. Giblin's suggested insertion is much more complicated than the simple 'that day will not come'. Second, the information that Giblin wants to include in the unwritten assertion which the readers must supply does not arise from the preceding context but from information that comes later in the letter, thus making it difficult for the original readers to understand.[23] And third, there is a temporal emphasis throughout the passage. The false teaching described in 2:2 concerns the time of the arrival of the day of the Lord.[24] The writer of 2 Thessalonians stresses in 2:6 that the revelation of the man of lawlessness will occur 'in his own time'.[25] This same temporal aspect is seen in 2:8, where the revelation of the opponent is said to follow ('and then'[26]) the removal of the *katechon*. The temporal aspect is also seen in this passage because the return of Jesus is viewed as a temporal event which will bring about the downfall of the opponent. Therefore, the unfinished sentence is better understood with the insertion of 'that day will not come'. Even better is the contrast proposed by Frame between the understood part of the sentence and the false teaching: 'the day of the Lord will not be present'[27] 'except the apostasy come first and the man of lawlessness'.

The tradition in 2:3-4 links together the apostasy and the revelation of the man of lawlessness. Both are described by use of the aorist tense in the subjunctive mood, they are linked only by 'and', and there is no temporal word inserted between their descriptions.[28] Therefore the writer is saying that the apostasy and revelation of the man of lawlessness (and all that goes with that revelation) would have occurred if the day of the Lord had arrived.

The opponent is given three explicit titles: the man of lawlessness, the son of perdition, and the lawless one. Most commentators identify the opponent as 'the antichrist', that is, as some agent acting in Satan's behalf yet distinguished from Satan himself. Frequently in the past this opponent has been identified with some historical figure, yet in such cases the historical individual has neither displayed the fullness of evil described in this passage nor been defeated by the return of Christ. Therefore it is best to see the opponent being described in these verses as the ultimate apocalyptic opponent who must finally be defeated by Jesus Christ at his return. This opponent is Satan.

The description of the opponent is based upon descriptions of the king of

---

[23] Marshall, *Thessalonians*, p. 188.

[24] The use of the word 'first' [πρῶτον] can be understood temporally (i.e. this is the first thing(s) that must occur) or logically (i.e. this is the first reason you can know the day has not occurred). The sentence does not include any other temporal elements that occur 'second' or 'then', which suggest 'first' is used logically. The NIV leaves the word untranslated.

[25] ἐν τῷ ἑαυτοῦ καιρῷ

[26] καὶ τότε

[27] Frame, *Thessalonians*, p. 250.

[28] ἔλθῃ ἡ ἀποστασία πρῶτον καὶ ἀποκαλυφθῇ ὁ ἄνθρωπος τῆς ἀνομίας

Babylon (Isa. 14:3-23), the king of Tyre (Ezek. 28:2), and an unnamed king in Daniel (Dan. 11:36).[29] The similarity of description can be seen if the three Old Testament passages are read side by side.

Isaiah 14:13-14	Ezekiel 28:2	Daniel 11:36-37
You said in your heart, 'I will ascend to heaven; I will raise my throne above the stars of God; I will sit enthroned on the mount of assembly, on the utmost heights of the sacred mountain. [14] I will ascend above the tops of the clouds; I will make myself like the Most High.'	In the pride of your heart you say, 'I am a god; I sit on the throne of a god in the heart of the seas.'	The king will do as he pleases. He will exalt and magnify himself above every god and will say unheard-of things against the God of gods. He will be successful until the time of wrath is completed, for what has been determined must take place. [37] He will show no regard for the gods of his fathers or for the one desired by women, nor will he regard any god, but will exalt himself above them all.

In each case the individual involved claims some form of divinity, in some way exalts himself, and, in Isaiah and Ezekiel, claims to sit where only God sits. There are very few exact verbal parallels between 2 Thessalonians 2:4 and any one of the three Old Testament passages listed above. The picture in 2 Thessalonians 2:3b-4 is a composite picture, choosing the most extreme claims and combining them to describe the opponent here. He demands all worship for

---

[29]Two other sources are suggested by commentators for the background of the description of the opponent. Roger D. Aus, 'God's Plan and God's Power: Isaiah 66 and the Restraining Factors of 2 Thess 2:6-7', *JBL* 96 (1977), pp. 537-53, suggests that Ps. 88:23 (LXX) forms the background to the two phrases 'the man of lawlessness' and 'the son of perdition' because it uses the phrase 'son of lawlessness' [υἱὸς ἀνομίας]. This, however, seems very unlikely because (1) the phrase is not the same as either phrase in 2 Thess. 2:3, and (2) the phrase in Ps. 88 is without any articles and is intended to apply to any wicked person, as the surrounding context makes clear. This is in contrast to the emphasis on a particular individual to be revealed, who deceives and works miracles in 2 Thess. 2. Wanamaker, *Thessalonians*, pp. 245-46, suggests the background is *Pss. Sol.* 17:11-22, which shows some similarities, such as calling the opposing leader 'the lawless one' [ὁ ἄνομος]. However, the rest of the passage does not focus on him as an individual (as does 2 Thess. 2) but on the desolation of God's people afterwards. It is these people who suffer 'destruction' (*Pss. Sol.* 17:22) [ἀπωλεία], not the lawless one. The focus is on Jerusalem and the land, which receive no emphasis in 2 Thess. 2. Therefore this suggestion appears weak as well.

himself and does not willingly see himself under some other authority; rather, he presents himself as the ultimate being to be worshiped in opposition to the one true God, just as the devil did when he desired even Jesus to worship him.[30] The verb 'to oppose' [ἀντίκειμαι] found in 2 Thessalonians 2:4 is used of a variety of opponents in both the LXX and the New Testament, but the devil is explicitly called 'the opposer' or 'the accuser' in Zechariah 3:1.[31] He is the great opponent to be defeated at the return of Christ. These ultimate claims make it unlikely that the opponent described in these verses is merely a satanic agent; the opponent described here seeks the ultimate position, not a secondary or subordinate rank. He claims to be God. Furthermore, the picture of judgment is ultimate: there are no further opponents.

According to 2:4, the opponent 'sits in the temple of God'.[32] Commentators have identified the temple as a reference to the church, the papal office, the temple in Jerusalem, or the temple in heaven.[33] Frequently this 'sitting in the temple' is linked with the 'abomination of desolation' which is prophesied by Jesus to stand in the temple, yet none of the references to the abomination is really very similar to what is said in 2 Thessalonians 2:4 (see Dan. 9:27; 11:31; 12:11; Matt. 24:15; Mark 13:14). None of the passages in Daniel speaks about an individual sitting in the temple or even uses the same word for temple.[34] On the other hand, both Ezekiel 28:2 and Isaiah 14:13 describe individuals who claim deity because they sit where only God can sit. These passages are not meant to be taken literally, for these individuals did not actually sit where only God can sit; it was merely a way of expressing their divine claims.[35] The prophet Isaiah, however, actually sees 'the Lord seated [καθήμενον] on a throne . . . [in] the temple [οἶκος]' (Isa. 6:1), being worshipped in the position of highest exaltation. The description of the opponent in 2 Thessalonians 2:3b-4 is a composite picture based upon Isaiah, Ezekiel, Zechariah, and Daniel. Therefore if Isaiah 6:1 is added to the passages that form the background to 2 Thessalonians 2:3b-4, then the most exalted place for the opponent to sit is not just in the seas (Ezek. 28:2), nor above the stars, nor on the sacred mountain (Isa. 14:13-14), but in the temple. Since the temple is not mentioned again in 2 Thessalonians, and since 'sitting' is a figurative way for claiming deity in the background passages, then all that can be said for certain from 2 Thessalonians 2:4 is that this is a figurative description of the opponent's claim to deity.[36]

---

[30]Matt. 4:9; Luke 4:7.

[31]ὁ διάβολος . . . τοῦ ἀντικεῖσθαι

[32]αὐτὸν εἰς τὸν ναὸν τοῦ θεοῦ καθίσαι

[33]R. J. McKelvey, *The New Temple: The Church in the New Testament* (London: Oxford University Press, 1968), pp. 135-36.

[34]τὸν ναόν

[35]Stephens, 'Eschatological Themes', p. 248.

[36]See also Herman Ridderbos, *Paul: An Outline of this Theology* (Grand Rapids: Eerdmans, 1977), pp. 520-21. All the other references in the Pauline corpus that use

The opponent is greater than the Old Testament human types by being able to work 'miracles, signs and wonders' (2:9). These miraculous deeds are described as 'false', not because they do not occur, but because they are designed to deceive and they originate from Satan, who is a liar.[37] These lying miracles are linked to his deception of those who are perishing (2:10). This ultimate, final, and worldwide deception is the work of Satan.[38]

The superhuman character of the opponent is also seen in the way he comes to earth, for he is 'revealed' (2:3, 6, 8).[39] This stress on the lawless one being 'revealed' and even having a 'parousia' (2:9) is a mocking of Christ's 'revelation' (1:7) and 'parousia' (2:1, 8). It is the antithesis of Christ's coming, for it will occur with lying wonders and all deceit of unrighteousness (2:9-10). The fact that 'the mystery of lawlessness is already working' (2:7) and the idea that the opponent will be 'revealed' in a manner similar to Christ's revelation suggest both his present existence and his superhuman character. That this lawlessness is associated with the opponent is clear, for he is 'the man of lawlessness' and 'the lawless one'. The fact that the opponent is going to be 'revealed' suggests that he will appear visibly in a human-like form. Therefore, because this opponent was already working at the time the letter was written and yet was going to be revealed just before Jesus's return, he must be superhuman.

The tradition in 2:3-4 presents the opponent as the final opponent whose revelation is directly linked with 'the apostasy' (2:3) and whose defeat will come at the return of Jesus (2:8). There is no further opponent to be vanquished,

---

this word 'temple' [ναός] refer to Christians or to the church (1 Cor. 3:16, 17; 6:19; 2 Cor. 6:16; Eph. 2:21). It seems very unlikely that this is the meaning in 2 Thess. 2:4, for the church is 'in God the Father and the Lord Jesus Christ' (1:1). The whole point of ch. 1 is the ultimate division between the church itself and those persecuting the church, and even the deception which the opponent uses is only over 'those who are perishing' (2:10). Therefore the context and the book as a whole speak against this identification.

[37] Frame, *Thessalonians*, p. 269; Marshall, *Thessalonians*, p. 202; Morris, *Thessalonians*, p. 232; Trilling, *Thessalonicher*, p. 105; Wanamaker, *Thessalonians*, p. 259.

[38] See also Rev. 12:9; 20:3, 8, 10.

[39] On 2:6, Best, *Thessalonians*, pp. 291-92, comments, 'Who is to *be revealed*? Within the context it could be Christ (in his Parousia, v. 2), the man of rebellion (vv. 3f) or the *katechon* (v. 6). The first is improbable because of its remoteness. The third is unlikely because *him* would not then be normally expressed in Greek as it is here and because it is masculine whereas *katechon* is neuter; it is possible that since in v. 7 the *katechon* does become masculine the masculine *him* might be intended to prepare for this and deliberately expressed because of the change of gender. However since vv. 3, 8 also refer to the revelation of "the man of rebellion" the reference is most probably to him here also'. See also Marshall, *Thessalonians*, pp. 194-95; Milligan, *Thessalonians*, p. 101; Wanamaker, *Thessalonians*, p. 254.

no greater power of evil to be defeated. If he were only a satanic agent, then Satan would remain undefeated. Yet the description of the day of the Lord in this passage and in 2 Thessalonians 1 does not allow for that possibility, for that day is the day of Jesus's glorious coming when he personally destroys the opponent (2:8) and judges all who follow this opponent (2:12). It is the final defeat of all enemies, the final battle. This opponent who is linked to the final apostasy, who is the last personal opponent against Christ, who goes beyond all Old Testament types of evil, who demands ultimate worship for himself and subordinates himself to no other, who works lying miracles and is the ultimate deceiver, who was already working when 2 Thessalonians was written yet would not be revealed until just before Christ returned, must be Satan himself.

There are two possible objections from 2 Thessalonians 2 to this identification of the opponent with Satan: (1) the opponent must be human because he is referred to as 'the *man* of lawlessness' and 'the *son* of perdition', and (2) the opponent cannot be Satan because in 2:9 he is said to do his lying miracles 'in accordance with the work of Satan'.

It is generally recognized that the two epithets 'the man of lawlessness' and 'the son of perdition' are Semitisms.[40] This means each phrase focuses not on the 'man' or the 'son', but on the quality—perdition or lawlessness—expressed in the genitive case, and thus the individual is seen as a 'supreme example of the quality spoken of'.[41] Therefore the opponent is being characterized as one who is both doomed and lawless. His total opposition to God as the 'arch-opponent of God' means that he is 'doomed to destruction'.[42] When the use of this type of Semitic phrase is examined throughout the Old Testament and other Semitic literature, it becomes clear that the referent need not be human. Genesis 6:2 describes the improper relationships between 'the sons of God' and 'the daughters of men', and the book of *Jubilees* identifies these 'sons of God' with 'angels'.[43] In Genesis 18–19, Abraham entertains three heavenly visitors, referred to both as men and as angels, two of which go on to destroy Sodom and Gomorrah.[44] In Genesis 32:25, the individual with whom Jacob wrestles is referred to as a man,[45] yet Jacob claims to have seen God (32:30). In the MT of

---

[40] James H. Moulton and Wilbert F. Howard, *Accidence and Word Formation*, vol. 2 of *A Grammar of New Testament Greek*, (Edinburgh: T & T Clark, 1929), p. 441. See also Best, *Thessalonians*, p. 283; Frame, pp. 252-53; Marshall, *Thessalonians*, p. 189; Morris, *Thessalonians*, p. 222; Geerhardus Vos, *The Pauline Eschatology* (1930; repr. Grand Rapids: Baker, 1979), p. 112; Wanamaker, *Thessalonians*, p. 245.

[41] Vos, *Eschatology*, p. 112. For example, in Psalm 8:4 'man' is parallel to 'son of man', showing that the focus of such a phrase is on the final word.

[42] Marshall, *Thessalonians*, pp. 189-90.

[43] *Jub.* 5.1.

[44] As 'men' [ἄνδρες] in 18:2, 3, 22; 19:5, 8, 10, 12, and as 'angels' [ἄγγελλοι] in 19:1, 15 in the LXX.

[45] ἄνθρωπος

Exodus 15:3, the song of Moses speaks of the LORD as 'a man [אִישׁ] of war'. The individual who appears and announces the birth of Samson in Judges 13 is referred to both as an angel and as a man.[46] In Job 1–2, in two scenes which take place in the presence of God, the angels and Satan (who appears to be included among the angels) present themselves before God. In the MT the angels are called 'the sons of God', while in the LXX they are called 'the angels of God'.[47] All these examples show that the Semitic description of the opponent as 'the man of lawlessness' and 'the son of perdition' does not in any way support the case that the opponent must be human. Furthermore, not only is Satan included among the angelic beings in Job 1–2, but in the Talmud Satan is also identified as the 'angel of death',[48] and Paul says that 'Satan himself masquerades as an angel of light'.[49] Therefore, because the phrases 'son of' and 'man of' frequently denote angelic beings among which Satan is included, then the description of the opponent as 'the man of lawlessness' and 'the son of perdition' gives an excellent characterization of the individual who stands absolutely against the will of God and so is doomed to destruction: Satan himself.[50]

The writer's use of the term 'lawless' to describe the opponent also gives a clue to his identity. Very likely the term 'lawlessness' is a translation of the Hebrew 'belial' [בְּלִיַּעַל].[51] According to Geerhardus Vos, in the Old Testament 'beliar' or 'belial' is not a name for a person but is used to describe '"sons," "daughters," "men," even "brooks" of Belial'.[52] The term seems to be a general term used for one who causes trouble; for example, the sons of Eli are called 'sons of belial' (1 Sam. 2:12).[53] In 2 Samuel 22:5 and Psalm 17:5 (MT—Ps. 18:5), the LXX translates 'belial' as 'lawlessness'.[54] Frequently the word 'belial' in the phrase 'son(s) of belial' is translated by the LXX with 'lawless' [παράνομος],[55] showing the likelihood that 'the lawless one' (2 Thess. 2:8) who is 'the man of lawlessness' (2:4) is to be identified as 'belial'. But as has been shown by Vos in his critique of Bousset's work, in the canonical

---

[46]'Angel' [ἄγγελος] in 13:3, 6, 9, 11, 13-21, and as a 'man' [ἄνθρωπος, ἀνήρ] in 13: 6, 8, 10, 11.

[47]בְּנֵי אֱלֹהִים in 1:6; 2:1 of the MT, and οἱ ἄγγελλοι τοῦ Θεοῦ in LXX

[48]B. Bat. 16a; Ber. 4b.

[49]2 Cor. 11:14.

[50]Vos, *Eschatology*, p. 112, recognizes that these phrases do not exclude the possibility of referring to Satan.

[51]W. Bousset, *The Antichrist Legend* (London: Hutchinson, 1896), pp. 137, 153.

[52]Vos, *Eschatology*, pp. 96-97, gives the following references: Deut. 13:3; Judg. 19:22; 20:13; 1 Sam. 1:16; 2:12; 10:27; 25:17, 25; 30:22; 2 Sam. 16:7; 23:6; 1 Kgs. 21:10, 13; 2 Chr. 13:7.

[53]בְּנֵי בְלִיַּעַל

[54]בְּלִיַּעַל (MT); ἀνομίας (LXX)

[55]Deut. 13:14; Judg. 19:22; 2 Sam. 16:7; 20:1; 2 Chr. 13:7.

The Authenticity of 2 Thessalonians

Scriptures and even in the *Testaments of the Twelve Patriarchs*, Belial cannot be seen as 'an Antichrist figure differentiated from Satan'.[56] In the same way, the Apostle Paul shows his familiarity with the name 'Belial' in 2 Corinthians 6:15—'What harmony is there between Christ and Belial?'—where he uses it synonymously with Satan.[57] Therefore, 'the lawless one' or 'the man of lawlessness', derived from 'belial', is another title for Satan himself.

The second reason most commentators say that the opponent cannot be Satan is that the opponent does counterfeit miracles 'in accordance with the work of Satan',[58] and thus with this single phrase the opponent 'is distinguished from Satan as his tool'.[59] For most commentators this is the only textual reason for not identifying the opponent as Satan. This understanding of the prepositional phrase 'in accordance with the work of Satan' is based on the assumption that a writer would be unlikely to describe the work of Satan himself in such a manner. However, a careful examination of New Testament usage shows this assumption to be false.

The noun 'working' is used eight times in the New Testament, all within the Pauline corpus. In six of these occurrences it is used with the preposition 'according to' as in 2 Thessalonians 2:9. In two of these instances, the one doing the 'working' is clearly distinct from the one being worked in. Colossians 1:29 says, 'I labor, struggling according to the working of him which is operating in me in power',[60] and Ephesians 3:7 says, 'I became a minister according to the gift of the grace of God given to me according to the working of his power'. In both these cases Paul is distinguished from the one working in him.

The situation is somewhat different in Ephesians 4:16: 'From him the whole body, joined and held together by every supporting ligament, grows and builds itself up in love, as each part does its work' (literally, 'according to the working of each part').[61] In this sentence, each part that 'does its work' is not distinguished from 'the whole body'. The phrase 'each part' in the second half of the sentence is used to focus attention on each individual's responsibility but does not distinguish each individual from being part of 'the whole body'. Therefore this sentence shows that 'according to the working of' can refer to both subject and object.

---

[56] Vos, *Eschatology*, p. 100. *T. 12 Patr.* uses the terms 'Beliar' (28 times), 'Satan' (45 times) and the 'devil' (5 times) interchangeably. *Jub.* uses the terms 'Mastema', 'Satan' and 'Beliar' interchangeably. *Mart. Ascen. Isa.* also adds the name 'Sammael' to refer to Satan or Beliar.

[57] Vos, *Eschatology*, p. 96.

[58] κατ' ἐνέργειαν τοῦ Σατανᾶ

[59] Best, *Thessalonians*, p. 283; Weima, *Thessalonians*, p. 513.

[60] Col. 1:29 has κατὰ τὴν ἐνέργειαν αὐτοῦ, and Eph. 3:7 has κατὰ τὴν ἐνέργειαν τῆς δυνάμεως

[61] κατ' ἐνέργειαν ἐν μέρῳ ἑνὸς ἑκάστου μέρους

In the only other two places in the New Testament which use both the preposition 'according to' and the noun 'working', the one doing the working is identical with the subject of the sentence. Ephesians 1:15-19 is an extended complex sentence. The first major part of the sentence, vv. 15-16, focuses upon giving thanks for the believers' faith and love. The beginning of v. 17 divides the sentence with the subordinating conjunction 'that' [ἵνα] and the introduction of a new subject, God. This dependent clause concludes with the phrase 'according to the working of the might of his strength'; thus it is God who works according to the power of his own strength.[62] In Philippians 3:20-21, Paul says, 'and we eagerly await a Savior from there, the Lord Jesus Christ, who, by the power that enables him to bring everything under his control, will transform our lowly bodies so that they will be like his glorious body'.[63] Jesus Christ is the one who transforms, and he does it by his own power.[64]

Therefore, using the form 'according to the working of' does not necessarily make a distinction between the person doing the work and the individual by whose power it is accomplished. Because the evidence in the Pauline corpus is equally divided, the only way to determine whether the person himself is working, or someone else is working through him, is to identify in each case the individual(s) being talked about. Thus the phrase 'in accordance with the work of Satan' found in 2 Thessalonians 2:9 in no way prohibits the identification of the opponent with Satan. The author cannot use a pronoun to describe the opponent's working, for then 2:9 would read 'whose parousia is according to his power', making it very unclear whose parousia is being discussed. It is necessary to identify the opponent explicitly at this point in order to distinguish his 'parousia' from Christ's parousia (2:8) and his 'working' from God's 'working' (2:11). It is also appropriate that the title 'Satan' be introduced at this point in the tradition because of the nature of his evil acts. Satan is the one who is scheming and deceitful, who even 'masquerades as an angel of light' (2 Cor. 2:11; 11:14). He is the preeminent liar (John 8:44) and 'the deceiver of the whole earth' (Rev. 12:9; 20:10). These activities which are particularly associated with Satan elsewhere are the activities of the opponent, whose lying and deceitful acts at his parousia (2:9-10) affect all who do not believe (2:10, 12). These are his own acts, for he is the one who sets himself above all others (2:4), and he is the final evil opponent of Jesus Christ (2:8).

The primary focus of the traditions found in 2 Thessalonians 2 is on the final eschatological opponent, Satan. As has already been seen, the opponent—who is characterized by lawlessness and doomed to perdition, who exalts himself

---

[62] κατὰ τὴν ἐνέργειαν τοῦ κράτους τῆς ἰσχύος αὐτοῦ

[63] κατὰ τὴν ἐνέργειαν τοῦ δύνασθαι αὐτὸν καὶ ὑποτάξαι αὐτῷ τὰ πάντα

[64] Gerald F. Hawthorne, *Philippians* (WBC 43; Waco: Word, 1983), pp. 172-73; Marvin R. Vincent, *The Epistles to the Philippians and to Philemon* (ICC; Edinburgh: T & T Clark, 1897), p. 122; J. B. Lightfoot, *Philippians,* p. 157; Joachim Gnilka, *Der Philipperbrief* (Freiburg: Herder, 1969), p. 208.

The Authenticity of 2 Thessalonians

above all others and willingly subordinates himself to no one, who even claims to be God, who will be revealed yet is already working, who is the arch deceiver through unrighteousness and lying miracles, and who is the final great opponent to be defeated at the return of Jesus—can be none other than Satan. If this opponent is not Satan, then the coming of Jesus is not the end, and there is no hope or ultimate joy and comfort at the work of Christ because the ultimate opponent is yet to be defeated.

b. The apostasy [ἡ ἀποστασία]. According to the author of 2 Thessalonians, the 'apostasy' must have already happened if the day of the Lord has arrived. Because it has not occurred, then the Thessalonians can know that the day of the Lord has not yet arrived (2:3). As was noted above, the 'apostasy' is linked to the revelation of the man of lawlessness: both are described by use of the aorist tense in the subjunctive mood, they are linked only by the coordinating conjunction 'and', and there is no temporal word inserted between their descriptions.[65] Therefore it is best to see the apostasy and the revelation of the man of lawlessness as essentially connected and contemporaneous with each other.

The word translated as 'apostasy' or 'rebellion' can refer to a rebellion, abandonment, or apostasy.[66] It can be used of political revolt[67] or of religious apostasy.[68] The meaning found throughout Scripture is of religious rebellion, the idea generally recognized in this passage. Three ideas have been suggested for identifying the apostasy in 2 Thessalonians 2:3: (1) the apostasy of the Jews,[69] (2) the apostasy of the church in the last days,[70] and (3) the final great rebellion of unregenerate humanity against God.[71]

---

[65] ἐὰν μὴ ἔλθῃ ἡ ἀποστασία πρῶτον καὶ ἀποκαλυφθῇ ὁ ἄνθρωπος τῆς ἀνομίας

[66] Arndt and Gingrich, *Lexicon*, p. 97.

[67] Josephus (*Life* 43) speaks of a revolt [ἀποστασίαν] against Rome.

[68] In the LXX see Josh. 22:22; 2 Chr. 29:19; Jer. 2:19; and 1 Macc. 2:15. The only place the word is used in the New Testament (other than 2 Thess. 2:3) is in Acts 21:21, when Paul is accused of 'teaching apostasy from Moses' [ἀποστοσίαν διδάσκεις ἀπὸ Μωυσέως].

[69] Denney, *Thessalonians*, p. 309.

[70] J. W. Bailey and Clarke, 'Thessalonians', p. 327; Hendriksen, *Thessalonians*, pp. 169-70; John F. Walvoord, *The Thessalonian Epistles* (Grand Rapids: Zondervan, 1967), p.74.

[71] Best, *Thessalonians*, pp. 281-83; Bruce, *Thessalonians*, pp. 166-67; Frame, *Thessalonians*, p. 251; Marshall, *Thessalonians*, p. 189; Morris, *Thessalonians*, p. 218; Neil, *Thessalonians*, p. 160; Rigaux, *Thessaloniciens*, p. 654; and Trilling, *Thessalonicher*, p. 82. Giblin, *Threat*, pp. 81-88, suggests the apostasy includes not only a rejection of the gospel, but also an ultimate division between believer and unbeliever. Although a final rebellion by those who reject the gospel would divide between believer and unbeliever, that is not the focus of the word (see Marshall, *Thessalonians*, p. 189).

The apostasy in 2:3 is difficult to identify because the only information explicitly given about it is that it 'comes', that it is linked with the revelation of the man of lawlessness, and that one can be sure the day of the Lord has not yet arrived because the apostasy has not yet come. The word 'apostasy' is not mentioned again in the passage, and apostasy is never defined, as it is in such places as Acts 21:21 (away from Moses), 1 Maccabees 2:15 (away from Moses) and Jeremiah 2:19 (forsaking the Lord). It is simply referred to as 'the apostasy'. Therefore, within this passage, the only clear exegetical clue to understanding what the apostasy refers to is its link to the revelation of the man of lawlessness. This 'revelation' is explicitly mentioned again in vv. 8 and 9. Associated with that revelation of the opponent is his deceiving with miraculous works and evil (2:9-10) those 'who are perishing', 'who did not receive the love of the truth', 'who believed the lie', 'who did not believe the truth', and 'who had pleasure in unrighteousness' (2:10-12). These are the ones who will be judged with the opponent and defeated by the return of the Lord. All of this is directly associated with the revelation of the opponent, just as the apostasy in 2:3 is directly associated with the revelation of the opponent. Therefore the apostasy is not some large-scale turning from the church, nor a Jewish revolt or rejection of Christianity, but rather, it is the final great rebellion under Satan against the returning Lord Jesus Christ. This final rebellion occurs with the revelation of the opponent and is then vanquished by the breath of the mouth of the Lord Jesus at his glorious coming (2:8).

c. **The *katechon* [τὸ κατέχον, ὁ κατέχων]**. The most difficult element to identify in 2 Thessalonians 2 is the *katechon*.[72] The only information given in the passage is: (1) the readers already know about the *katechon* (2:5-6), (2) the *katechon* can be referred to by a neuter or masculine participle (2:6-7), (3) the *katechon* will be removed before the revelation of the lawless one (2:7), and (4) the *katechon* is contemporaneous with the mystery of lawlessness (2:7). Because the information is limited, any identification of the *katechon* must be made cautiously, a situation which has tended to focus attention on defining the two participles.[73] Yet the variety of definitions has allowed the commentator to choose almost any meaning because the context is inconclusive. Before identifying the *katechon*, therefore, it is important to examine the use of the word elsewhere.

This word is used ten times in the Pauline corpus; in each case it refers to

---

[72] In this section the word *katechon* will be used instead of 'the restraining' or the 'the restrainer'.

[73] Arndt and Gingrich, *Lexicon*, pp. 423-24, list the following definitions: 1. transitive use: a. hold back, hold up: α. hold back, hinder, prevent from going away; β. hold down, suppress; γ. restrain, check; δ. hold back something; b. hold fast: α. keep in one's memory; β. hold fast, retain; γ. keep, possess; δ. keep, confine; c. take into one's possession, occupy; d. in the passive—be bound; α. by the law; β. by disease; 2. intransitive, nautical technical term—make for, head for, steer toward.

holding, keeping, or possessing someone or something. In Romans it is used in a negative sense for those who are under the judgment of God, who 'hold to the truth in unrighteousness' (1:18), and of Christians, who were formerly 'held by the law' (7:6). Paul also uses the verb to command Christians to 'hold fast' to good things: 'the traditions' (1 Cor. 11:2), 'the word I preached' (1 Cor. 15:2), and 'that which is good' (1 Thess. 5:21). The verb is used in reference to 'possessing' things (1 Cor. 7:30; 2 Cor. 6:10) and to 'retaining' Onesimus for service (Phlm. 13). In the rest of the New Testament the word is used only eight times. In Hebrews 3:6, 14; 10:23; and Luke 8:15, it means to 'hold fast'. Luke 4:42 speaks of crowds 'detaining' Jesus, while Luke 14:9 uses the verb simply to express the position a person 'takes' at a banquet table. In the poorly attested John 5:4, the verb describes one who 'possesses a disease', and in Acts 27:40 it reports how a ship is 'steered' for shore. Therefore the predominant definition in the New Testament, and especially in the Pauline corpus, is of possessing or holding to something.

The definition usually chosen for 2 Thessalonians 2:6-7 is 'to restrain' because the *katechon* must be removed before the revelation of the lawless one. It is reasoned that whatever the *katechon* refers to, it restrains or delays the revelation of the lawless one. This idea is stressed by Trilling, who believes the author of 2 Thessalonians desires to explain the lengthened period of delay.[74] In fact, he defines the *katechon* as 'the delaying power'.[75] However, this conclusion is not strictly based on what the passage says. Verses 7 and 8 speak of the 'removal' of the *katechon,* which is followed by the revelation of the lawless one. Verse 6 also links the presence of the *katechon* to the revelation of the lawless one. The use of εἰς with the articular infinitive expresses purpose or result.[76] Literally the sentence would then say, 'and now the *katechon* you know so that he may be revealed in his own time'. The 'he' cannot refer to the *katechon* here because it is a masculine pronoun and the participle in v. 6 is neuter, so it is best understood as a reference to the opponent,[77] who will be revealed at a set time. The problem with v. 6 centers around the relationship between the first part of the sentence, 'and now the *katechon* you know', and the second part of the sentence, 'so that the lawless one will be revealed in his own time'.[78] In particular, the problem concerns whether the articular infinitive ('to be revealed') is governed by the neuter participle ('the *katechon*') or by the main verb ('you know'). Best attempts to show that where the verb 'to know' is followed by a direct object and a dependent clause, the dependent clause

---

[74] *'weiteres retardierendes Moment'* [another retarding factor]
[75] Trilling, *Thessalonicher*, p. 102, 'aufhaltenden Macht'.
[76] Blass and Debrunner, *Greek Grammar*, p. 207.
[77] Neil, *Thessalonians*, p. 165.
[78] 2:6 – καὶ νῦν τὸ κατέχον οἴδατε, εἰς τὸ ἀποκαλυφθῆναι αὐτὸν ἐν τῷ ἑαυτοῦ καιρῷ.

'relates to, amplifying or explaining, the idea contained in the noun'.[79] Yet when his examples are examined, none seems to be similar to 2 Thessalonians 2:6. The problem with 2 Thessalonians 2:6 is that the pronoun 'he' does not directly refer to something in the first part of the sentence, but rather to the lawless one mentioned earlier. In each of Best's examples the idea being referred to in the dependent clause is in some way mentioned in the first part of the sentence. Therefore he believes there must be some kind of ellipsis in the sentence as it presently occurs. One way of dealing with this problem is to say the author meant to say 'and now you know about the restraining *of him,* so that he may be revealed in his own time'. This is possible but is not required of the text. It depends on defining *katechon* as 'restraining', inserting the words 'of him', and ignoring that the articular infinitive immediately follows the main verb ('you know') and not the object ('the *katechon*') which is placed before the main verb.

Giblin has argued persuasively from the word order that the articular infinitive in 2:6 should be governed by the main verb and not the participle:

One never finds εἰς τό + inf. (or any other preposition with articular infinitive) unless that on which the articular infinitive construction depends precedes almost immediately. The link between the articular infinitive construction and that on which it depends is never interrupted by a main verb (e.g., a verb which would precede the articular infinitive but not govern it). In short, there is absolutely no parallel in the NT for taking εἰς τό + infinitive in 2 Thes 2,6b as dependent on the participle τὸ κατέχον; for, in 2 Thes 2,6b, a main verb (οἴδατε) intervenes.

Furthermore, we never find anything of the following sort: a phrase in which the direct object (e.g., a participle) and the subject of a verb are different entities and are placed in the order object-subject so that the preposition + articular infinitive follows this combination and yet depends on the object.[80]

This means that the dependent clause is part of what the readers were expected to know and does not function to explain the direct object, 'the *katechon*'. Thus v. 6 should be translated, 'and now the *katechon* you know about, so that (you know) the lawless one will be revealed in his own time'. This interpretation of the grammar of 2:6 shows that a variety of definitions for *katechon* are possible.

The terminology in 2 Thessalonians 2:7-8 is the same as in 2:6 and is also difficult grammatically. The first part of the verse is clear: 'For the mystery of lawlessness is already working'. The only question concerns whether the verb 'working' is in the middle or passive voice. It is simplest to take it in the middle and to say that the hidden evil activity was occurring already as the epistle was

---

[79]Best, *Thessalonians,* p. 291, gives the following verses as examples: Rom. 13:11; 1 Cor. 2:2; 16:15; 2 Cor. 9:2; 12:3; 1 Thess. 1:4f; 2:1; cf. 4:2f.
[80]Giblin, *Threat,* pp. 206-207.

The Authenticity of 2 Thessalonians

being written.[81] This is not greatly different from the passive voice if Satan is seen as working behind the scene in this hidden evil activity.[82]

The second part of the sentence is more difficult. The commentator must explain not only the use and meaning of the masculine participle of *katechon*, but also the meaning of the phrase 'out of the midst', the unusual word order, and the subject of the verb 'to be, become' [γένηται].

In 2 Thessalonians 2:7, the *katechon* is 'removed' or 'out of the midst'.[83] In Scripture, the phrase 'out of the midst' consistently means to be taken out of some place or removed. In Judges 3:19, Eglon commands everyone in his presence to leave so that he can receive a secret message.[84] Job 29:17 talks about removing prey 'from the midst of their teeth'.[85] Ezekiel 11:23 describes the vision of the glory of the Lord leaving from the midst of Jerusalem.[86] The phrase is used only seven times in the New Testament: the angels will remove the evil ones from the righteous at the end of the age (Matt. 13:49); Paul leaves a meeting (Acts 17:33); Paul is removed from a crowd for his own safety (Acts 23:10); the Corinthians are commanded to remove the unrepentant sinner (1 Cor. 5:2); the people are required to separate from sinfulness (2 Cor. 6:17, quoting Isa. 52:11); and the commandments held 'against us' have been removed by nailing them to the cross (Col. 2:14). In addition, Bruce gives other examples from Greek literature: 'Plutarch, *Timoleon* 5.3, "he decided to live by himself, having moved away (ἐκ μέσου γενόμενος) out of public view"; Achilles Tatius, *Leucippe and Clitophon* 2.27, "when Clio has been removed (τῆς Κλειοῦς ἐκ μέσου γενομένης)"; Ps.-Aeschines, *Ep.* 12.6, "what they formerly covered up is clearly revealed, now that they have been removed (ἐκ μέσου γενομένων)"—i.e. by death or exile'.[87] In each case the main idea is removal and separation, a change of location.[88] Based on all of these examples, it is clear that 2 Thessalonians 2:7 is simply saying that the *katechon* will be removed, and after this has occurred, the lawless one will be revealed.

---

[81] Marshall, *Thessalonians*, p. 195.

[82] Bruce, *Thessalonians*, p. 170; Frame, *Thessalonians*, p. 263; Milligan, *Thessalonians*, pp. 28, 102; Morris, *Thessalonians*, p. 229; Rigaux, *Thessaloniciens*, pp. 669-70; Wanamaker, *Thessalonians*, p. 255. Burkeen, 'Parousia', p. 353, also takes it as a passive but sees the passive referring to God's ultimate control.

[83] ἐκ μέσου γένηται

[84] ἐκ μέσου

[85] ἐκ δὲ μέσου τῶν ὀδόντων

[86] ἐκ μέσης τῆς πόλεως

[87] Bruce, *Thessalonians*, p. 170.

[88] This is against the views of Aus, 'God's Plan', pp. 537-53, and M. Barnouin, 'Les Problèmes de Traduction Concernant 2 Thess. II. 6-7', *NTS* 23 (1977), pp. 482-98. Aus, p. 551, says 'the mystery of lawlessness' is the subject of the verb γένηται: 'The mystery of lawlessness is to be active until its mysterious aspect is removed or disappears'.

Numerous suggestions have been given as to the identification of the *katechon;* it is simplest to categorize the suggestions under three headings: (1) those who view the *katechon* as neutral, (2) those who view the *katechon* as evil, and (3) those who view the *katechon* as good.

Those who view the *katechon* as neutral define the *katechon* as a person or force that limits the effects of the lawless one but is not directly identified with either God's power or with the power of the opponent. This position is represented by Tertullian and many others who have identified τὸ κατεχον with the Roman Empire, and ὁ κατέχων with the Roman emperor. Some see it as a reference to one of the emperors restraining the appearance of Nero, who is the lawless one, while others see the masculine participle referring to any of a number of emperors. This view, modernized by Lightfoot, has most recently been suggested by Leon Morris, who believes that the principle of order restrains the working of evil; when this system of law is removed, the lawless one will rule.[89]

This neutral view presents a number of problems. First, it introduces someone or some force which has not been explicitly mentioned elsewhere in the passage.[90] Furthermore, it is unlikely that the *katechon* refers to a particular emperor because the reference is so vague. There would be no reason for the author to be vague in speaking about an emperor who restrains evil. Although the more generalizing approach of Morris and Lightfoot removes the objection about the Roman Empire having come and gone without the return of Christ, it does not give a satisfactory answer to the use of the masculine participle in 2:7. It is possible that the neuter participle could refer to a principle of law and order, but the masculine participle would most naturally refer to a person(s). Paul does present a rather favorable impression of civil government in Romans 13:1-7, but only with difficulty does it fit the picture in this passage. The problem addressed in 2 Thessalonians 2 is not how to view the present government, but how to be certain that that final day of the Lord has not arrived. The picture in 2 Thessalonians is apocalyptic: there is a final division of humanity, a battle of two kingdoms, and a war between two leaders, the lawless one and the Lord Jesus. This passage explicitly states that 'those who do not believe the truth' (2:12) actually side with the lawless one; they do not simply limit him. It is difficult to see how at any time in the first two centuries of the church a Roman emperor and his empire could be defined as 'believing'; rather, they do not believe, and therefore in this passage they would be included with 'all . . . who have not believed the truth' (2:12).[91] Clearly, they are not neutral.

---

[89] Morris, *Thessalonians*, p. 227.

[90] Wanamaker, *Thessalonians*, p. 252.

[91] For further criticism of this view see Burkeen, 'Parousia', pp. 340-42; Wanamaker, *Thessalonians*, p. 250; and Marshall, *Thessalonians*, pp. 196-97. Otto Betz, 'Der Katechon', *NTS* 9 (1963), pp. 276-91, has sought to support this view by finding

Two other suggestions have been made that can be grouped within the 'neutral' category. B. B. Warfield suggests that the restraining power was the Jewish state, and the restrainer was James of Jerusalem.[92] This view suggests that Christianity was able to develop under the protection of the Jewish state. Once that was removed, Christianity was open to far more severe persecution. This idea is weak because James is not presented as having such an important role in the New Testament that his removal is what stops the man of lawlessness.[93] Nor is James directly linked to the Jewish state, yet the very choice of using neuter and masculine participles in 2:6-7 requires a very close association of 'the restrainer' and 'that which restrains'. Furthermore, the accounts of the missionary work of Paul hardly support the idea of the Jews restraining evil, for at Thessalonica he was so persecuted by the Jews that he had to flee not only from Thessalonica but also from Berea (Acts 17:5-14). In 1 Thessalonians 2:14-16 Paul also mentions the persecuting activity of the Jews in Judea. Therefore Warfield's suggestion is implausible.

J. B. Orchard has identified the *katechon* with 'all these things' in Matthew 24:34. Because 'all these things' refers to the destruction of Jerusalem, and since Jerusalem has not yet been destroyed, then the lawless one is being held back. Michael, the defender of Jewish liberties (Dan. 10:21) is 'the restrainer' who is removed at that time.[94] Although it is true that there are some obvious parallels between the synoptic apocalypses and 2 Thessalonians, this particular identification by Orchard does not seem very close. In Orchard's scheme, the 'all these things' of Matthew 24 includes the abomination of desolation which stands in the holy place (Matt. 24:15), and the temple at Jerusalem is 'the one great obstacle to the Second Coming of Christ'.[95] But this position is impossible to hold in 2 Thessalonians 2, for in v. 7 the *katechon,* which Orchard identifies with 'all these things' (including the destruction of the temple) in Matthew 24, is removed *before* the revelation of the lawless one. Yet in 2 Thessalonians 2:3-4 this same lawless one is revealed and sits in the temple. Consequently, according to Orchard's scheme, the lawless one is revealed *before* the temple is destroyed (2:3-4), yet *after* it is removed (2:7-8).

Therefore the neutral view, that some power other than the power of God or the power of Satan is in view, can be held only with great difficulty. The picture of the passage as a whole is of the final conflict of the forces of good versus the

---

parallels at Qumran, but as both Giblin, *Threat,* pp. 168-76, and Burkeen, 'Parousia', p. 342, point out, the parallels he proposes are never very close.

[92] Warfield, 'Prophecies', pp. 41-42.

[93] Warfield sees 'the man of sin' as a near contemporary to Paul, probably a Roman emperor.

[94] Orchard, 'Thessalonians', pp. 19-42 (esp. pp. 40-41).

[95] Orchard, 'Thessalonians', pp. 41-42.

forces of evil; to insert some historically neutral figure does not fit the context.[96]

A number of commentators, including Frame, Giblin, Best, and Wanamaker, have viewed the *katechon* as evil. Giblin's view is unique among those who see the *katechon* as something evil, for he defines the verb κατέχω as 'to be seized or possessed'. According to Giblin, the *katechon* is a present known threat to the community who will be ousted, and then the man of lawlessness will be revealed. The individual is seized or possessed by the power of Satan.[97]

The view of Giblin has been criticized, not only by those who would see a neutral or good view of the *katechon*, but also by those who see the *katechon* as evil. Wanamaker correctly analyzes Giblin's weak position:

> In the first place, the verb κατέχειν normally refers to seizure in a religious sense only in the passive, not in the active. Secondly, Giblin's very localized interpretation of the κατέχον seems to make the coming of Christ dependent upon the happenings in one small Christian community, whereas the event is actually to be cosmic. That Paul believed the coming of Christ would or could be held up until some local false prophet was out of the way seems highly unlikely.[98]

Wanamaker presents the *katechon* as evil by defining κατέχω as 'to hold sway, rule, prevail', identifying the principle of prevailing, which is referred to by the neuter participle τὸ κατέχον, with the mystery of lawlessness in 2:7.[99] According to him, the 'for' [γάρ] at the beginning of 2:7 shows that what follows more fully explains what was already said in the previous verse. Wanamaker then suggests that the individual 'who prevails' is some historical figure such as the emperor Gaius, whom Paul expected to be removed. Wanamaker believes Paul had a negative view of present political figures, citing for example 1 Corinthians 2:8: 'None of the rulers of this age understood it, for if they had, they would not have crucified the Lord of glory'. Wanamaker also suggests that the appointed time for this hostile evil activity is under the control of Satan, not God.[100]

The most powerful reason for accepting the conclusion that some evil force is behind the *katechon* is that, because the forces of evil are so prevalent throughout this passage, it does not require the introduction of some other element or force. Furthermore, the linking of the neuter participle with the neuter phrase 'the mystery of lawlessness' also seems at first very plausible. However, there are a number of weaknesses with the proposal that the *katechon*

---

[96] For a further critique of this view, see Burkeen's critique of what he defines as the 'historical' view ('Parousia', pp. 340-50).

[97] Giblin, *Threat,* pp. 206, 216, 234.

[98] Wanamaker, *Thessalonians,* p. 252.

[99] τὸ μυστήριον ἤδη τῆς ἀνομίας

[100] Wanamaker, *Thessalonians,* pp. 250-57. Best, *Thessalonians,* pp. 295-301, and Frame, *Thessalonians,* pp. 259-62, are sympathetic to the idea that the *katechon* represents an evil force but are more hesitant in their conclusions.

is evil: (1) It seems unlikely that an evil force will be removed so that an evil lawless one will be revealed (2:6-7). (2) In nearly all apocalyptic literature, God, not Satan, is in charge of time and continues to rule. This is a particular weakness in Wanamaker, who suggests that 'the "appointed time" of the person of rebellion is under the dominion of Satan rather than God'.[101] (3) The fact that the author uses the masculine participle in the same sentence with the phrase 'the mystery of lawlessness' makes the identification of the neuter participle with the 'the mystery of lawlessness' unlikely. This identification would be more likely if the author spoke of the mystery of lawlessness first and then referred back to it with the neuter participle. (4) As Best acknowledges,[102] the interpretation of the *katechon* depends on the meaning of the verb, yet the meaning of 'to prevail, hold sway, or to restrain' could just as easily refer to God's activity as to Satan's or some evil force. (5) The suggestion by Frame that 'out of the way' refers to Satan's expulsion from heaven seems totally arbitrary in the context. (6) Wanamaker's suggestion that 'he who prevails' refers to a particular historical personage like Gaius makes his argument open to all the criticisms of the historical or neutral approach. If Paul, as Wanamaker believes, wrote that the lawless one would be revealed following the reign of Gaius, then all sorts of speculation would arise in Thessalonica. In addition, this would be the only place in Paul's letters that he would so explicitly identify Caesar in such an eschatological setting. Therefore the linking of the *katechon* with the forces of evil seems improbable.

The idea that the *katechon* is something good seems likely from 2:6-7 because only when the *katechon* is removed is the lawless one revealed, thus implying that the *katechon* is opposed to the lawless one in some way. At the present time the mystery of lawlessness is at work, and also at the present time the *katechon* exists, just as good and evil coexist in this world and will continue to do so until the return of Christ. Among those who see the *katechon* as good, however, there is a difference of opinion as to how to interpret it.

According to Calvin, 2 Thessalonians 2:6-7 teaches that the gospel must first be spread and that consequently there will be a delay until the career of the gospel is completed.[103] Oscar Cullmann and Johannes Munck have made similar suggestions but have particularly identified 'he who restrains' with the Apostle Paul and his ministry.[104] Marshall raises two objections to the view of Cullmann and Munck: (1) Paul at least reckoned with the possibility of his own survival

---

[101] Wanamaker, *Thessalonians*, p. 254.

[102] Best, *Thessalonians*, p. 296.

[103] John Calvin, *Commentaries on the Epistles of Paul the Apostle to the Philippians, Colossians, and Thessalonians* (trans. John Pringle; Edinburgh: Calvin Translation Society, 1851), pp. 332-33.

[104] Oscar Cullmann, 'Le caractère eschatologique du devoir missionaire et de la conscience apostolique de S. Paul', *RHPR* 16 (1936), pp. 210-45; Johannes Munck, *Paul and the Salvation of Mankind* (Richmond: John Knox, 1959), pp. 36-42.

until the parousia, and (2) it is questionable that Paul 'saw himself as the essential factor in God's saving plan for mankind'.[105] Marshall presents a variation of the views of Cullmann and Calvin. He too thinks the preaching of the gospel is what restrains but suggests that an angelic figure may be in view for 'he who restrains'.[106] The figure then is withdrawn at God's command just before the final battle.[107] Nothing in this view explicitly contradicts the grammar or context of the passage, but neither does the passage make any mention of the preaching of the gospel or the restraining angel. This view also depends on defining κατέχω as 'to restrain'.

More recently, Colin Nicholl has sought to strengthen the identification of the *katechon* with angelic activity, in particular that of Michael.[108] His primary argument is that: 1) only an angel can fulfill the positive role of the *katechon* because the *katechon* opposes the lawless one until the end, is contemporary with the mystery of lawlessness, and yet is removable; 2) the description of the lawless one is based on Daniel 11, and so the identification of the *katechon* should arise from that context; 3) Michael is explicitly referred to as the *katechon* in a later writing,[109] and his removal is also referred to in another later writing.[110]

Nicholl is correct that an angelic being could both be contemporaneous with the first century and also last until the end. Also, by attempting to base his argument on Daniel, he is certainly making use of what is arguably the most important Old Testament apocalyptic book. However, his explanations of the two terms are not only stretched historically, but also require such a complexity of arguments that they are extremely unlikely.

Nicholl believes the writer of 2 Thessalonians 2 is primarily focused on Daniel 11–12. However, as was already shown, not all of the terminology concerning the opponent in 2:3-12 appears in Daniel 11:36-37, but instead, some of it is drawn from Isaiah 14, Ezekiel 28 and Zechariah 3. Thus it is a composite picture, and linking the opponent only to Michael in Daniel 11–12 is overstating the situation.

Nicholl also notes a citation from the Greek Magical Papyri which refers to Michael as the *katechon*: 'both Orion and Michael who sits on high: you hold the seven waters and the earth, keeping in check [κατέχω]

---

[105]Marshall, *Thessalonians*, pp. 198-99.
[106]See Mark 13:10; 2 Pet. 3:9; Rev. 14:6.
[107]Marshall, *Thessalonians*, pp. 199-200.
[108]Nicholl, Colin, 'Michael, the Restrainer Removed (2 Thess. 2:6-7)', *JTS* 51 (2000), pp. 27-53. Also see Nicholl, *Hope to Despair* (SNTSMS 126; Cambridge: Cambridge University Press, 2004). The masculine participle refers directly to Michael, while the neuter participle refers to Michael's restraining activity.
[109]Nicholl, 'Michael', p. 38.
[110]Nicholl, 'Michael', p. 46

the one they call the great serpent'.[111] Although Nicholl acknowledges that this reference is only from the third or fourth century AD, he thinks it reflects earlier traditions based on Daniel 10–12.[112] Yet this is very speculative, for the statement links Michael with Orion, and the whole section, entitled 'Another love spell of attraction,' consists of a spell focused on and spoken to Hecate, the goddess of magic.[113] Furthermore, there is no reference in Daniel to any serpent being slain. Thus, this identification of Michael with the *katechon* in 2 Thessalonians is very weak.

Nicholl believes the phrase in 2 Thessalonians 2:7 referring to the *katechon*, 'until he is removed' [ἄρτι ἕως ἐκ μέσου γένηται], is based on Daniel 12:1, which says 'Michael . . . will arise'.[114] He states that the Hebrew verb 'to arise' [עמד] can have a number of meanings and that the meaning here is like that of the Greek verb used in the Septuagint [παρελεύσεται], which normally means to 'pass by'.[115] Thus Michael passes by, or is temporarily removed. Nicholl finds one instance in which a later Rabbi, reflecting on the meaning of Michael 'arising' in Daniel 12:1, says that 'to arise' means 'he remains silent'.[116] This silence is defined as 'not defend[ing] my children'.[117] Since Michael is referred to as the protector of God's people (Dan. 12:1) and he has, with another unnamed angelic being, been fighting against the (demonic) princes of the nations, then Nicholl identifies him as 'the restrainer', who for a short time stops this activity of restraint, and so 'is removed'. Nicholl's interpretation is very tenuous: it basically has to bypass the Hebrew text, put an unusual meaning on the Septuagint, and use a very obscure third century rabbinic interpretation.[118]

Thus Nicholl's specific identification of the *katechon* with Michael has no literary proof before the time of 2 Thessalonians and depends, at best, on a much later syncretistic text. It further requires the introduction into the text of 2 Thessalonians of an important personage—the angel Michael—who plays no other role in the text and is unnamed. The only time angels are explicitly mentioned in 2 Thessalonians is in 1:7 when Jesus returns with his powerful angels.

---

[111] *PGM* IV :2768–72 (H. D. Betz).

[112] Nicholl, 'Michael', p. 38.

[113] See *PGM* IV .2714, 2724, 2727, 2730, 2745 (H. D. Betz).

[114] Nicholl, 'Michael', pp. 41-46.

[115] Arndt and Gingrich, *Lexicon*, p. 631, 'παρέχομαι'.

[116] Cited in Jacob Neusner, *The Components of the Rabbinic Documents, from the Whole to the Parts, III. Ruth Rabbah*, Number 80 (Atlanta: Scholars Press, 1997), p. 4.

[117] Neusner, *Components*, p. 4.

[118] Nicholl, 'Michael', p. 47.

Doctrinal Content of 2 Thessalonians

A second way of seeing the *katechon* as good is by linking it to God and his plan. Burkeen states that, as restrainer, God withdraws his influence.[119] Stephens has argued this position thoroughly. He would define 'the restraining' as God's fixed plan, and God himself as 'he who restrains'. He believes that the theocentric view is the only one that fits.[120] Stephens is aware of the difficulty of saying that God must be taken 'out of the midst' (2:7), but he asserts that in apocalyptic literature one cannot ask where God withdraws to. It is true that the word *katechon* refers to God in the LXX (Isa. 40:22);[121] however, the definition of the word in this context does not carry the meaning 'to restrain', but 'to possess or inhabit'.

This position has two major weaknesses: (1) this terminology is a very vague way to refer to God and, particularly, to his plan, and (2) it strains the natural meaning of the phrase 'out of the midst', which is one of the major pieces of information given us about the *katechon*.[122]

Others would identify 'the restrainer' with the Holy Spirit, who is then withdrawn from earth at the time of the 'rapture'.[123] This view is weak because it also introduces an individual not mentioned elsewhere in the passage, and furthermore, nowhere else is the Holy Spirit called the 'restrainer'. Walvoord refers to Genesis 6:3, 'My Spirit will not contend with man forever', to support the idea of the Spirit as a restrainer. However, the verb in the MT [יָדוֹן] is a *hapax*, the meaning of which is uncertain,[124] while the verb in the LXX [καταμείνῃ], 'to stay or live', does not make the link any more likely.

Any identification of the *katechon* must address a number of factors:

(1) Because of the scarcity of information, the definition of the verb κατέχω is critical. This definition should not be a highly unusual definition.[125]

(2) Both the neuter and masculine participles of the *katechon* must be explained.

---

[119] Burkeen, 'Parousia', p. 355.

[120] Stephens, 'Eschatological Themes', pp. 343-61. A number of others would also follow this basic line of thinking, each with his own peculiarities of detail. See A. Strobel, *Untersuchungen zum eschatologischen Verzögerungsproblem auf Grund der spätjudisch-urchristlichen Geschichte von Habakkuk 2,2ff* (NovTSup 2; Leiden: Brill, 1961); J. Ernst, *Die eschatologischen Gegenspieler in den Schriften des Neuen Testaments* (Biblische Untersuchungen 3; Regensburg: Pustet, 1967); Aus, 'God's Plan', pp. 537-53; Robert L. Thomas, '1-2 Thessalonians' (*Expositor's Bible Commentary* 11; ed. Frank E. Gaebelein; Grand Rapids: Zondervan, 1978); Trilling, *Thessalonicher*, pp. 90-102; Burkeen, 'Parousia', pp. 348-65.

[121] ὁ κατέχων τὸν γῦρον τῆς γῆς

[122] Best, *Thessalonians*, p. 297.

[123] Walvoord, *Thessalonian Epistles*, pp. 77-78.

[124] Francis Brown, S. R. Driver, and Charles A. Briggs, *A Hebrew and English Lexicon of the Old Testament* (Oxford: Clarendon, 1975), p. 189.

[125] Best, *Thessalonians*, p. 295.

(3) Because the passage implies a contrast between the evil one and his power and the *katechon*, the *katechon* should be understood as something or someone good.

(4) The *katechon* must be 'removable'.[126] To try to change the meaning of this important phrase removes one of the major pieces of information from the context.

(5) The *katechon*, which is contemporary with 'the mystery of lawlessness', must be already present when the author is writing yet must be removable as part of the events surrounding the day of the Lord.

(6) If possible, the *katechon* should refer to something in the context of 2:1-12; only as a last resort should some other individual or force be introduced.

(7) The *katechon* should refer to something or someone found elsewhere in the New Testament, and especially in Paul, because the author claims this teaching was part of the original missionary proclamation (2:5).

With all the above qualifications taken into account, in particular the likely background for the passage, the immediate context, and the most common definition for κατέχω, one other view must be considered: that the *katechon* refers to all Christians and their possessing of the kingdom of God. Thus 2 Thessalonians 2:6-8a would be translated, 'And now the possessing [of the kingdom] you know about, so that [you know] he [the lawless one] will be revealed in his own time. For the mystery of lawlessness is already working, [but] only until whoever possesses [the kingdom] is removed. And then the lawless one will be revealed'. As we shall see, this identification of the *katechon* with Christians fits all the above considerations.

(1) Definition of κατέχω. The most common way of defining κατέχω in this passage is 'to restrain', yet as has already been shown, nothing is said to be 'restrained' in this passage. In fact, the only relationship between the *katechon* and the lawless one is temporal: the *katechon* will be removed 'and then' the lawless one will be revealed (2:7-8). The statement in 2:6 is simply not clear enough to require *katechon* to be defined as 'to restrain'. As Vos has said, 'Perhaps more attention ought to have been given by exegetes to the not uncommon alternate significance of *katechein*, viz. "to occupy," "hold in possession." It is not unthinkable that through its over-ready acceptance of the meaning "to keep back" or "to restrain" the exposition may have been thrown

---

[126]Robert H. Gundry, *The Church and the Tribulation* (Grand Rapids: Zondervan, 1973), p. 123, n. 18, lists the following passages which clearly show that the phrase 'out of the midst' must mean an exit from the scene: Exod. 31:14; Deut. 4:34; Isa. 52:11; 57:2—all in the LXX; Matt. 13:49; Acts 17:33; 23:10; 1 Cor. 5:2; 2 Cor. 6:17; Col. 2:14; *1 Clem.* 29.3. F. F. Bruce, '2 Thessalonians', in *The New Bible Commentary: Revised* (ed. D. Guthrie and J. A. Motyer; Grand Rapids: Eerdmans, 1970), p.1164, refers to this as an idiom meaning 'to take out of the way'.

upon a wrong track'.[127] Best has also suggested that other meanings of the word should be considered.[128] Certainly 'to restrain' is not the most common definition in Paul or the rest of the New Testament. With so little context in 2 Thessalonians 2:6-7 to draw upon, one might conclude that it is impossible to establish a definition with any certainty. However, a definition is not so impossible as it might appear.

All commentators recognize that the phrases concerning the man of lawlessness were originally derived from the Old Testament, primarily from Isaiah, Ezekiel and Daniel. Throughout the New Testament, the primary Old Testament source for apocalyptic or eschatological background is Daniel. Therefore the logical place to seek a definition for κατέχω is in Isaiah, Ezekiel, and especially Daniel. The verb κατέχω is used only four times in these three books. As was already mentioned, God is called 'the *katechon*' [ὁ κατέχων τὸν γῦρον τῆς γῆς] in Isaiah 40:22, not as one who 'restrains' but as the one who 'possesses' or 'inhabits' the circle of the earth. Because the *katechon* in 2 Thessalonians 2:7 is removed, and because of the vagueness of reference, it is unlikely that in this passage God is the *katechon*. However, it must be considered whether the definition of 'to possess' might be applied to someone or something else.

The verb is also used only once in Ezekiel: 'Son of man, the ones dwelling in the barren land of Israel are saying, "Abraham was only one, yet he possessed [κατέσχεν] the land, and we are many, the land has been given to us for a possession [κατάσχεσιν]"' (33:24). This passage is one of many in the Old Testament that refers to the promised kingdom of Israel as a possession. In fact, one of the most common definitions in the Old Testament for κατέχω is 'to possess'.[129]

Because the picture for the lawless one is drawn from the imagery found in Daniel, the definition and use in Daniel should be foundational for explaining the terminology of 2 Thessalonians. The verb κατέχω is used two times in Daniel, both in ch. 7, which contains the first of Daniel's visions of the future. This particular vision speaks of four successive beasts which represent four human kingdoms that will rise and fall and finally be succeeded by one 'like a son of man' who is given authority and whose kingdom is 'one that will never be destroyed' (7:13-15). When the vision is explained to Daniel, he is told that 'the saints of the most high will receive the kingdom and they will possess [καθέξουσι] the kingdom forever and ever and ever' (7:18). This same idea is again expressed in 7:22, when the Ancient of Days defeats the evil horn: 'he

---

[127]Vos, *Eschatology*, p. 133, n. 20.
[128]Best, *Thessalonians*, p. 301.
[129]To possess the land: see Exod. 32:13; Josh. 1:11; Ps. 68:37; 2 Chr. 15:8; Ezek. 33:24; Job 27:17; Jdt. 5:19; Sir. 46:9. One can possess riches (Ps. 72:12), a sword (Song. 3:8), or a sickle (Jer. 27:16). Darkness possesses Saul as he is about to die (2 Sam. 1:9).

The Authenticity of 2 Thessalonians

gave judgment to the saints of the most high and the time was given and the saints possessed [κατέσχον] the kingdom'. In Daniel, as well as in Isaiah and Ezekiel, the definition of κατέχω is 'to possess', and Daniel 7 says that those who will possess the kingdom are the saints of the Most High. In the New Testament, that terminology would refer to Christians, for they are the ones who will receive the kingdom of God (2 Thess. 1:5). Therefore, from the most probable background for 2 Thessalonians 2, the definition for κατέχω is 'to possess', and according to its Old Testament background, it refers to the saints' possession of God's kingdom.

(2) Neuter and masculine participles. The immediate question raised against this identification is whether the author could refer to Christians first by a neuter participle [τὸ κατέχον] and then by a masculine singular participle [ὁ κατέχων]. Most commentators believe that the neuter participle refers to the task, the topic, or the principle which is being carried out by the person referred to by the masculine participle. Therefore, if the verb κατέχω is translated as 'possess', then the author of 2 Thessalonians would be saying in 2:6, 'And now the possessing [of the kingdom] you know about, so that [you know] he (the lawless one) will be revealed in his own time'. The use of a neuter participle to refer to a topic which is known about by the readers (see 2:5) does not do any violence to the grammar. The more difficult problem concerns the masculine singular participle.

The masculine singular participle of κατέχω found in 2 Thessalonians 2:7 is usually read today as referring to an individual; thus the question concerns the identity of that individual. However, the masculine singular participle can also be used as a generic substantive[130] and consequently can also be translated 'he who' or 'whoever'. This usage is found throughout the New Testament.[131] In

---

[130] Blass and Debrunner, *Greek Grammar,* pp. 212-13.

[131] For example, in Matt. 24:13—'but he who endures to the end will be saved' [ὁ δὲ ὑπομείνας εἰς τέλος οὗτος σωθήσεται]—the sense is not that only one person will be saved but that every individual who endures will be saved. Paul frequently uses the attributive participle in this generic sense. In Romans alone Paul speaks about 'he who judges' [ὁ κρίνων] (2:3), 'he who teaches' [ὁ διδάσκων] (2:21), 'he who proclaims' [ὁ κηρύσσων] (2:21), 'he who says' [ὁ λέγων] (2:22), 'he who detests' [ὁ βδελυσσόμενος] (2:22), 'he who replies against' [ὁ ἀνταποκρινόμενος] (9:20), 'he who believes' [ὁ πιστεύων] (9:33), 'he who does' [ὁ ποιήσας] (10:5), 'he who teaches ... exhorts ... shares ...takes leadership ... does mercy ... '. [ὁ διδάσκων ... ὁ παρακαλῶν ... ὁ μεταδιδοὺς ... ὁ προϊστάμενος ... ὁ ἐλεῶν] (12:7-8), 'he who resists authority' [ὁ ἀντιτασσόμενος] (13:2), 'him who does evil' [τῷ τὸ κακὸν πράσσοντι] (13:4), 'he who loves' [ὁ ἀγαπῶν] (13:8), 'he who is weak' [ὁ ἀσθενῶν] (14:1-2), 'he who eats' [ὁ ἐσθίων] (14:3), he who judges' [ὁ κρίνων] (14:4), 'he who regards the day' [ὁ φρονῶν τὴν ἡμέραν] (14:6), 'to him who reckons' [τῷ λογιζομένῳ] (14:14), 'he who serves' [ὁ δουλεύων] (14:18), 'one who

each case the focus is not on one individual doing something, but rather, on anyone who does the particular action. Because the generic use of the attributive participle is so frequent, especially in Paul, then this use must be considered a possibility in 2 Thessalonians 2:7 for the *katechon*.

The masculine singular participle [ὁ κατέχων] in 2:7 is often read as referring to an individual, probably because in 2:4 there are masculine attributive participles referring to an individual. In the case of 2:3-4, however, it is clear that an individual is envisioned, for he is called 'the man of' and 'the son of', and he is repeatedly referred to with masculine singular pronouns (see 2:4, 6). Because no pronouns or descriptive phrases are used with respect to the *katechon* in 2:7, the generic sense is grammatically as likely as the specific sense.

(3) Contrast between the opponent and the *katechon*. We have noted that the *katechon* seems to be someone or something good in contrast to the opponent, who is clearly evil. If the *katechon* is translated as 'he who possesses', then it would be the Christians who are promised possession of the kingdom of God. This translation fits the contrast between good and evil very well. In 2 Thessalonians 1:5 the author specifically refers to the Thessalonians as those who will be 'counted worthy of the kingdom of God' when Christ returns, and in 1:6-10 he explicitly explains how their situation will be reversed at that time. Since the author is writing to Christians who are concerned that the day of the Lord has already arrived, it seems likely that in the apocalyptic scenario in 2:2-12 he would continue to refer to them in some way. If, as in traditional interpretations, the *katechon* does not refer to the Christians, however, then this passage is silent about them. One must wonder where the Christians are. Some commentators remark on this silence,[132] while others simply refer back to the parallel idea in 1 Thessalonians 4:13-18 and the eschatological gathering of God's people promised in the Old Testament.[133] However, because the idea of those 'possessing the kingdom' at the eschaton is not something new to the overall context, this interpretation best explains the identity of the *katechon*.

(4) Removal of the *katechon*. According to 2:7-8, the *katechon* will be removed, and then the lawless one, who will be destroyed by the Lord Jesus, will be revealed. If the *katechon* refers to whoever possesses the kingdom, then the writer is saying that the Christians will be removed just before the final battle and will be gathered to the Lord (2:1) and return with him. This interpretation parallels Paul's teaching in 1 Thessalonians 4:17 that Christians who have died or are still living are caught up to meet the Lord in the air. The next event mentioned in 1 Thessalonians is destruction (1 Thess. 5:2), just as

---

does not judge himself' [ὁ μὴ κρίνων ἑαυτόν] (14:22), and 'one who doubts' [ὁ διακρινόμενος] (14:23).

[132]Best, *Thessalonians*, p. 274.

[133]Weima, *Thessalonians*, p. 500; Green, *Thessalonians*, p. 302.

the next event mentioned after the *katechon* is removed is the destruction of the opponent and all who follow him. This also parallels 1 Corinthians 15:23-24, where Paul says the raising of Christians when Christ comes will be followed by the end, when Christ has destroyed all his enemies. Therefore, it can be seen that in Paul's undisputed letters, the one event that must occur before the final destruction of Christ's enemies is the meeting in the air of all Christians with the Lord. This is the removal of the *katechon*.

(5) **Presence of the *katechon*.** The *katechon* is contemporaneous with 'the mystery of lawlessness', and both are present at the time of writing the letter. Again, the contrast between Christians and the forces of evil fits the picture extremely well. In fact, this distinction of groups is exactly what is mentioned in ch. 1, where the troublers, who do not know God and do not obey the gospel (1:6, 8), are punished with everlasting destruction and are separated from the presence of the Lord and the glory of his power (1:9). Those who are afflicted—who believe and who are called 'the saints' (1:6, 10)—receive rest and glorify and marvel at their Lord. The relief for the afflicted and the punishment for the afflicters both come at the time described as 'the revelation of Jesus Christ from heaven' (1:7) or 'that day' when he comes (1:10). This is the same picture as in ch. 2, where Christ comes to rescue the Christians (*katechon*) and to judge the evil opponent, who is revealed at that time, and those who follow him.

(6) **Contextual reference to the *katechon*.** One of the criticisms of a variety of positions in identifying the *katechon* is that someone must be added to the apocalyptic scenario who is not mentioned elsewhere in the passage. Since only four individuals/groups are mentioned in the passage—the opponent, the opponent's followers, the Lord Jesus, and the *katechon*—to avoid adding someone to the context, commentators frequently identify either God or some hostile individual with the *katechon*. However, if the *katechon* is understood as referring to the Christians, no new individual or group must be inserted into the context because the *katechon* refers to a group that has already been introduced in v. 1. The writer of 2 Thessalonians introduces the subject as 'concerning the parousia of our Lord Jesus Christ and our gathering together to him' (2:1). This idea of God's people being 'gathered' is a regular part of both Jewish and Christian apocalyptic expectation.[134] If, as most commentators think, the writer never refers to this gathering again in this passage,[135] why has he stated this as his topic? The most likely answer is that he *does* refer to it again with the removal of the *katechon*. The original audience, remembering the teaching they had received based on Daniel, would immediately understand the reference. Thus the picture of the day of the Lord shows the Lord Jesus gathering his followers ('whoever possesses [the kingdom] is removed') and then defeating the opponent and his followers. All four individuals/groups mentioned in the

---

[134] Burkeen, 'Parousia', pp. 307-308.
[135] Burkeen, 'Parousia', p. 309.

passage are accounted for, and no one else must be added to the passage.

(7) Other references to the *katechon*. The *katechon* is not some later development nor some obscure teaching, but rather, a regular part of the original teaching of the whole church. The gathering to Christ of the Christians is found both in Paul (1 Thess. 4:17) and in other New Testament eschatological passages (see Matt. 24:31; Mark 13:27; John 14:3).

3. Summary of Eschatology of 2 Thessalonians

The problem which gave rise to 2 Thessalonians 2:1-12 was the erroneous idea that the day of the Lord had already arrived. The writer counters this false teaching by directing the readers back to what they had previously been taught. Although evil was present in the world ('the mystery of lawlessness is already working', 2:7), this did not mean the day of the Lord had arrived. On that day, Christ would come back and remove the Christians, Satan would be revealed and deceive all of his followers, and Christ would then destroy Satan and his followers. The passage says nothing about a delay of the parousia; nor does it mention any preliminary signs which would enable someone to calculate the date of the day of the Lord. The Christians could know the day had not yet arrived because they had not yet experienced the events of that great day.

This same basic eschatological picture is also found in 2 Thessalonians 1, where the specific problem concerns current suffering by the Christians. The hope of the believers is in the return of Christ, when all will be set right and the present situation will be reversed. No expectation of delay is expressed in this chapter either: the readers themselves are expected to get relief at the return of Christ (see 1:6, 7, 10). The enemies of Christ will be punished. Nothing in either passage postpones or suggests that the parousia could not occur very soon, even in the lifetime of the original readers or of Paul himself.

B. *The Eschatological Parallels to 2 Thessalonians*

A number of commentators have stressed the relationship between 2 Thessalonians 2 and the eschatological discourses found in the Gospels, concluding that the eschatology of the Gospels informs the identifications in the difficult portions of 2 Thessalonians 2. H. A. A. Kennedy, for example, says, 'It is no exaggeration to say that Matt. xxiv is the most instructive commentary on the chapter before us'.[136] Others who have stressed the relationship between these include G. R. Beasley-Murray, J. Bernard Orchard, Desmond Ford, and David Wenham.[137] Therefore it is important to determine the degree of

---

[136] Quoted in Richard N. Longenecker, 'The Nature of Paul's Early Eschatology', *NTS* 31 (1985), p. 92.

[137] G. R. Beasley-Murray, *Jesus and the Future* (London: Macmillan, 1954), pp. 232-34; Orchard, 'Thessalonians', pp. 19-42; Desmond Ford, *The Abomination of Desolation*

similarity between the eschatological discourses in the Gospels and 2 Thessalonians 2 in order to interpret the eschatology in 2 Thessalonians as it sheds light on the question of Pauline authorship. Beasley-Murray has presented the most extensive list of parallels between 2 Thessalonians and the eschatological discourse in the synoptic Gospels:

Beasley-Murray's Parallels between 2 Thessalonians and the Synoptics

2 Thess. 1.3-5	=	Mark 13.9-13
2 Thess. 1.6-10	=	Mark 13.26-27
2 Thess. 1.11-12	=	Luke 21.36
2 Thess. 2.1-2	=	Mark 13.26-27
2 Thess. 2.3	=	Mark 13.5, Matthew 24.12
2 Thess. 2.4-6	=	Mark 13.14
2 Thess. 2.7	=	Matthew 24.12
2 Thess. 2.8-12	=	Mark 13.22 (cf. Luke 24.11, Mark 1.36)
2 Thess. 2.13	=	Mark 13.27 (cf. Luke 21.8)
2 Thess. 2.15	=	Mark 13.23 (cf. v. 31)[138]

Beasley-Murray concludes that 'the entire eschatological passages of 1 and 2 Thessalonians reflect the spirit of the eschatological discourse'.[139] However, when Beasley-Murray's parallels are examined carefully, it becomes evident that many of them do not exist at all,[140] and therefore it is best to list the parallels from his chart that really do exist:

Verbal Parallels Referring to the Second Coming

	2 Thessalonians	Synoptics
power	δυνάμεως –1:7	δυνάμεως – Mark 13:26; Matt. 24:30
glory	δόξης –1:9	δόξης – Mark 13:26; δόξη – Matt. 25:31
angels	ἀγγέλων –1:7	ἀγγέλους – Mark 13:27; ἄγγελοι – Matt. 25:31

---

in Biblical Eschatology (Washington, DC: University Press of America, 1979), pp. 194-225; Wenham, 'Synoptic Apocalypse', pp. 345-75.

[138] Beasley-Murray, *Jesus and the Future*, pp. 232-33.

[139] Beasley-Murray, *Jesus and the Future*, p. 233.

[140] The following so-called parallels do not have a single verbal parallel, and even the general idea is not very similar: 2 Thess. 1:3-5 paralleled to Mark 13:9-13; 2 Thess. 1:11-12 paralleled to Luke 21:36; and 2 Thess. 2:15 paralleled to Mark 13:23. Furthermore, in 2 Thess. 1:3-5, the writer praises his readers for their love and faith and for enduring suffering, whereas Mark 13:9-13 is concerned about betrayal and being delivered up to courts. Only in the broadest possible way can these be conceived as parallel. Though they both generally have to do with suffering, the origin and character of these sufferings are very different.

Doctrinal Content of 2 Thessalonians

coming	ἔλθη –1:10	ἐρχόμενον – Mark 13:26; Matt. 24:30
that day	ἡμέρα ἐκείνη –1:10	ἡμέρας ἐκείνης – Matt. 24:36
heaven	οὐρανοῦ –1:7	οὐρανοῦ – Matt. 24:30
gathering	ἐπισυναγωγῆς –2:1	ἐπισυνάξει – Mark 13:27
		ἐπισυνάξουσιν – Matt. 24:31
not disturbed	μηδὲ θροεῖσθαι –2:2	μὴ θροεῖσθε – Mark 13:7; Matt. 24:6
appearing	ἐπιφανείᾳ –2:8	φαίνεται – Matt. 24:27
parousia	παρουσίας –2:8	παρουσία – Matt. 24:27

These parallels are all true parallels, for the words are all used to refer to the return of Christ.[141] In addition, one more verbal parallel occurs in this same section. In 2 Thessalonians 2:7 the mystery of lawlessness is 'already' [ἤδη] working, and Matthew 24:12 speaks about the increase of lawlessness that will characterize the time up until the end while the gospel is being preached.[142]

A number of other words are mentioned by commentators who stress the parallels. These include the reference to the temple, the mention of signs and wonders, and the words 'love' and 'saved'.[143] When the contexts for these so-called parallels are examined, however, there are significant differences between the Synoptics and 2 Thessalonians; thus they are not true parallels, as we shall see.

Most commentators note that the major emphasis in both Mark 13 and Matthew 24 is on the destruction of the temple. In the Synoptics, observations about the temple are used to introduce the discourse. Jesus then responds to the disciples' observation about the temple buildings by prophesying that these buildings will be completely destroyed.[144] The first question that arises from this prophetic proclamation concerns 'when' [πότε] these things will happen. Mark's account focuses almost exclusively on the question of the temple, as can be seen by the way the questions from the disciples are addressed, while Matthew's account also includes explicit reference to the parousia and the end of the age (Matt. 24:3). This emphasis on the temple is very important to see in examining the so-called temple parallels. First, there are *no* verbal parallels between 2 Thessalonians 2:4 and the synoptic accounts in Mark 13:14 and Matthew 24:15. The particular location in the Synoptics is called 'the holy

---

[141] The phrase 'do not be disturbed' in both passages appears to refer to being disturbed that the end has come (see 2 Thess. 2:2; Matt. 24:6; Mark 13:7), yet in each case the end has not yet come. The idea of not being deceived is also similar, but different words are used (2 Thess. 2:3–ἐξαπατήση; Mark 13:5, Matt. 24:4–πλανήση).

[142] τὸ πληθυνθῆναι τὴν ἀνομίαν

[143] Orchard, 'Thessalonians', p. 34, and Wenham, 'Synoptic Apocalypse', p. 350, mention the temple (2 Thess. 2:4; Mark 13:14; Matt. 24:15), signs and wonders (2 Thess. 2:9; Mark 13:22; Matt. 24:24), and the words 'love' and 'saved' (2 Thess. 2:10; Mark 13;13; Matt. 24:12-13).

[144] Matt. 24:1-2; Mark 13:1-2.

The Authenticity of 2 Thessalonians

place' or 'where it does not belong', whereas in 2 Thessalonians 2:4 it is called the 'temple' or 'sanctuary'.[145] The evil involved in the synoptic accounts is called 'the abomination of desolation',[146] whereas in 2 Thessalonians 2 it is an individual, 'the man of lawlessness'. In the Synoptics, the action of the evil thing is to 'stand',[147] whereas in 2 Thessalonians 2 the evil individual 'sits'. Secondly, the desired response of the readers is also very different. In Mark 13:14 and Matthew 24:16 the command is to 'flee'. There is obviously some time left and it is advantageous to leave the distressful situation. This response, however, is impossible in 2 Thessalonians 2 because it is the day of the Lord. Therefore, although many have seen a parallel between the two accounts at this point, the differences far outweigh the similarities. Matthew 24 cannot be used as a commentary on 2 Thessalonians 2 here.[148]

Some see another parallel between 2 Thessalonians 2:9, 'The coming of the lawless one is . . . with all power and signs and lying wonders' and Matthew 24:24, 'For false Christs and false prophets will appear and perform great signs and miracles to deceive even the elect—if that were possible'.[149] There are a number of problems with this parallel. First, these miracles are said to be performed by many individuals (Matt. and Mark), whereas in 2 Thessalonians they are performed by the lawless one. Second, the purpose mentioned in Matthew is to deceive, if it were possible, the elect, whereas in 2 Thessalonians the deception is directed only toward 'those who are perishing' (2:10). Third, this warning is part of the same section as the 'abomination of desolation'' which allows for time to 'flee' from the dangers; in 2 Thessalonians it is part of the day of the Lord and the final deception before the judgment. Again the differences outweigh the similarities.

The third suggested parallel also shows individual words in parallel, but they are not in parallel contexts. The words 'love' and 'saved' in the synoptic eschatological discourses are used to describe people who are different from those described in 2 Thessalonians. Matthew 24:12, 'the love of many will grow

---

[145] Matt. 24:15 has ἐν τόπῳ ἁγίῳ and Mark 13:14 has ὅπου οὐ δεῖ, whereas in 2 Thess. 2:4 it is called τὸν ναὸν του θεοῦ.

[146] Τὸ βδέλυγμα τῆς ἐρημώσεως

[147] Matt. 24:15 –ἑστός; Mark 13:14 –ἑστηκότα.

[148] This is contrary to Ford, *Abomination*, pp. 200-201, who identifies the abomination of desolation with the man of lawlessness.

[149] Orchard, 'Synoptic Gospels', p. 34. Matt. 24:24 reads, 'for false Christs and false prophets will arise and will give great signs and wonders in order to deceive if possible the elect' [ἐγερθήσονται γὰρ ψευδόχριστοι καὶ ψευδοπροφῆται καὶ δώσουσιν σημεῖα μεγάλα καὶ τέρατα ὥστε πλανῆσαι εἰ δυνατόν καὶ τοὺς ἐκλεκτούς], and Mark 13:22 reads, 'for false Christs and false prophets will arise and will give signs and wonders in order to deceive if possible the elect' [ἐγερθήσονται γὰρ ψευδόχριστοι καὶ ψευδοπροφῆται καὶ δώσουσιν σημεῖα καὶ τέρατα πρὸς ἀποπλανᾶν, εἰ δυνατόν, καὶ τοὺς ἐκλεκτούς].

cold', appears to describe those whose affections change, whereas in 2 Thessalonians 2:10, those who follow the lawless one do not 'love the truth'. This does not express a change of affections but is a general description of a negative response to the gospel. Matthew 24:13 promises that 'he who stands firm to the end will be saved', whereas 2 Thessalonians 2:10 describes those who will not be saved because of their refusal to love the truth. It is true that the individual words are the same, with common definitions, but the groups referred to by these words are distinct.

Therefore in terms of true parallels, the greatest similarity is in the description of the return of Christ—a glorious, powerful coming from heaven with his angels to gather his people. Thus it is not the entire synoptic eschatological discourse which is parallel to 2 Thessalonians 2, but primarily just two verses—Mark 13:26-27 (parallel to Matt. 24:30-31)—and consequently, the eschatological discourses cannot be used as a commentary on 2 Thessalonians 2 in order to explain the difficult portions of 2 Thessalonians 2.

C. 2 Thessalonians and Apocalyptic Literature

Many view 2 Thessalonians as more apocalyptic than 1 Thessalonians,[150] while others simply view that the apocalyptic perspective of the second letter is quite different from the first letter.[151] Either way, it is necessary to compare 2 Thessalonians to other apocalyptic literature to determine if it is dependent on other apocalyptic literature or is typical of Paul's writing.

An apocalypse is an historical or cosmological narrative which is 'presented as supernatural revelations, mediated by an angel or some heavenly being, and they invariably focus on the final end of life and history. This final end usually entails the transformation of this world (the new creation of the book of Revelation) but it also involves the judgment of the individual dead and their assignment to eternal bliss or damnation.'[152] The following characteristics are frequently associated with apocalyptic literature: divine transcendence, angelology, fantastic symbolism, cosmic imagery, foreign mythology, reinterpretation of prophecy, visionary form of inspiration, distinct literary form, cataclysm and judgment, day of the Lord, destruction of Gentiles, promise of a golden age, messianic deliverer, resurrection, pseudonymity, and the use of symbolic numbers (especially 3,

---

[150]Linda McKinnish-Bridges, 1 and 2 *Thessalonians* (Smith and Helwys Bible Commentary; Macon, GA: Smith and Helwys, 2008), p.194.

[151]Littleton, 'Function of Apocalyptic', especially pp. 3, 148-50, 161, 181, 197-99.

[152]Frederick J. Murphy, *Apocalypticism in the Bible and Its World: A Comprehensive Introduction* (Grand Rapids: Baker Academic, 2012), p. 8, quoting John Joseph Collins.

4, 7, 10, 12 and multiples).[153] Furthermore, this literature often fills in the silences, especially of the Old Testament, with regard to particular names of angels[154] and historical persons.[155]

A distinction is usually made between prophecy—God's triumph seen in present world order—and apocalyptic—God's triumph seen in a new world order with a despair in the present situation. However, this line has often been drawn too absolutely, and it seems more realistic to speak of a continuum between these forms of literature.[156] There is debate about whether apocalyptic is a true distinct genre or just a theological mindset.

When the usual characteristics of apocalyptic literature are taken into consideration, it is clear that as far as genre goes, 2 Thessalonians is not an apocalypse, but rather, is a typical Greco-Roman epistle.[157] Furthermore, 2 Thessalonians is also quite different in content from these extra-biblical apocalypses. The specifics in the eschatological sections of 2 Thessalonians do not easily tie themselves to specific historical events as do many items in the Jewish apocalyptic literature. In contrast to apocalyptic pseudepigraphy, which claims to be written by ancient figures, Paul is not an ancient figure. The writer of 2 Thessalonians does not depend on mediation by an angel for his information; he presents it as coming from himself. He shows none of the despair of the Jewish apocalyptic literature

---

[153]D. S. Russell, *The Method and Message of Jewish Apocalyptic* (Philadelphia: Westminster, 1964), pp. 91, 127.

[154]See for example the *Greek Apocalypse of Ezra* 6:1-2 'Then God said to me, "Ezra, do you know the names of the angels who are over the consummation: Michael, Gariel, Uriel, Raphael, Gabuthelon, Aker, Arphugitonos, Beburos, Zebuleon?"' qtd. in James H. Charlesworth, *Old Testament Pseudepigrapha* (2 vols.; Garden City, NY: Doubleday, 1983), vol. 1, p. 577.

[155]For example, in *Sib. Or.* 5.14-25, the identities of the people referred to (which I have inserted in brackets) can be identified by the readers based on hints in the text: 'He shall have his first initial of ten: and after him shall reign one who has the first of letters [referring to Augustus]. Before him Thrace shall cower, and Sicily, and, later, Memphis . . . After a long time he shall hand over the empire to another, who shall have his first letter of the number of three hundred, and a river's own name [referring to Tiberius], who shall also reign over the Persians and Babylon . . . . Then one shall reign who has the letter of the number three [referring to Gaios Caligula]. The next king who shall reign shall have twice ten for his number [referring to Klaudios]'. The list continues through Marcus Aurelius. The above quote is taken from R. H. Charles, ed., *The Apocrypha and Pseudipigrapha of the Old Testament in English* (2 vols; Oxford: Clarendon, 1913), vol 2, p. 397. The identifications in brackets were taken from Charlesworth, *OTP*, vol. 1, p. 393.

[156] Russell, *Jewish Apocalyptic,* pp. 96-100.

[157]See ch. 5 on the epistolary structure of 2 Thess.

as it waits for God to act, for he sees the gospel going forth (2 Thess. 3:1-3). Yet he still sees the coming of a final day of judgment with a reversal of situation (2 Thess. 1:6-10; 2:8). The writer of 2 Thessalonians does not focus on the details of judgment as do many of the Jewish apocalyptic writers, but rather, he simply presents that on the day of the Lord there will be a removal of the *katechon* (2:7, which is the same as 'our being gathered to him' in 2:1) followed by a revelation of the lawless one, the final rebellion (2:3, 9-10), and an immediate judgment by Jesus (2:8). There is no hint of a time period of delay which has caused despair.

The two items in 2 Thessalonians, other than the final judgment itself, that are somewhat similar to apocalyptic literature are the varied names for Satan and the fact that angels have a part in these final events.

Apocalyptic literature uses a variety of names for Satan, as does 2 Thessalonians. *The Testaments of the Twelve Patriarchs* interchangeably uses the terms 'Beliar' (twenty-eight times), 'Satan' (forty-five times) and the 'Devil' (five times). The book of *Jubilees* uses the terms 'Mastema' (twelve times), 'Satan' (five times) and 'Beliar' (two times) interchangeably. In ch. 2 we saw that one of the earliest external witnesses to 2 Thessalonians is the eschatological section of the *Martyrdom and Ascension of Isaiah* (*Mart. Isa.* 3.13 – 4.22).[158] The opponent in this section of this book is explicitly Beliar, who at the end comes down in the form of a man and is referred to as 'the great angel, the king of this world, which he has ruled ever since it existed' (4.2).[159] Furthermore, he alone claims to be God (4.7) and works miracles (4.11). *Martyrdom and Ascension of Isaiah* adds the name 'Sammael' (three times) and also refers to 'Satan' (two times). That these terms, used in a variety of sources, all refer to Satan can be seen clearly in the way in which they overlap. Mastema is called chief of the spirits (*Jub.* 10:8) and the spirits are referred to as belonging to Satan (*T. Dan* 6.1). Sammael dwells in Manasseh (*Mart. Isa.* 2:1) and Beliar dwells in Manasseh (*Mart. Isa.* 3:11). Both Beliar and Satan are directly associated with lawlessness (*Mart. Isa.* 2:4, 7; *T. Dan* 3:6).

This variety of names is consistent with 2 Thessalonians, in which 'he who opposes', 'the lawless one', and 'Satan' all refer to the same individual.[160] It has already been shown that the term 'Beliar' (with its variant Belial) is derived from the term for 'lawlessness' in the Old Testament. This same terminological variation is seen in Paul, who explicitly contrasts 'Belial' and Christ: 'For what do righteousness and

---

[158] Usually dated about the end of the first century. See Charlesworth, *OTP*, vol. 2, p. 149.

[159] Charlesworth, *OTP*, vol. 2, p. 149.

[160] It is also likely there is another title for Satan in 2 Thess. 3:3, 'the evil one' [τοῦ πονηροῦ]. See Best, *Thessalonians*, p. 328.

wickedness [lawlessness; ἀνομίᾳ] have in common? Or what fellowship can light have with darkness? What harmony is there between Christ and Belial?' (2 Cor. 6:14-15). Most commentators see Belial, who is associated in this passage with lawlessness, as referring to Satan.[161] Thus 2 Thessalonians uses these names in a manner similar to Paul.

Angels function not only as revelatory intermediaries in Jewish apocalyptic literature, but are explicitly named and designated with particular tasks. In contrast to this, the only explicit mention of angels in 2 Thessalonians is when they are associated with Christ's return (1:7). This use in 2 Thessalonians is very similar to the traditions found in the Gospels which identify the angels participating in the gathering of the saints at the end of the age.[162]

Thus it can be seen that 2 Thessalonians, though similar in terminology for Satan, is much less detailed than the Jewish apocalyptic literature. It simply presents a brief series of events associated with the end: the removal of the *katechon*, the final battle and the revelation of the evil opponent, and the return of Christ.

D. *Eschatology and the Problem of Authenticity*

According to the disputers of authenticity, Paul speaks of the return of Christ with joy, urgency, and immediacy but without mentioning any preliminary signs. This contrasts with their understanding of the picture found in 2 Thessalonians, which they believe describes the return of Christ as a solemn, delayed event preceded by a series of signs. A careful examination of 2 Thessalonians, however, shows that the problem is not the delay of the parousia, but the teaching that it has *already* arrived (2:2). The writer's response to this false teaching does not mention a series of preliminary signs at all, but instead, presents the day of the Lord as a complex event which includes the gathering [removal] of the Christians, the final rebellion, and the revelation and defeat of

---

[161] R. V. G. Tasker, *2 Corinthians* (TNTC; Grand Rapids: Eerdmans, 1963), pp. 98-99; M. E. Thrall, *2 Corinthians 1-7* (ICC; New York: T & T Clark, 1994), pp. 474-75; Philip E. Hughes, *Paul's Second Epistle to the Corinthians* (NICNT; Grand Rapids: Eerdmans, 1962), p. 248; George H. Guthrie, *2 Corinthians* (Baker Exegetical Commentary on the New Testament; Grand Rapids: Baker Academic, 2015), p. 352.

[162] See Matt. 13:39 ('The harvest is the end of the age, and the harvesters are angels.'), 41, ('his angels . . . will weed out of his kingdom everything that causes sin and all who do evil'), 49 ('the angels will come and separate the wicked from the righteous'); 16:27 ('For the Son of Man is going to come in his Father's glory with his angels'—parallel Mark 8:38 and Luke 9:26); Matt. 24:31 ('And he will send his angels with a loud trumpet call, and they will gather his elect from the four winds'—parallel Mark 13:27); Matt. 25:31('When the Son of Man comes in his glory, and all the angels with him').

Satan and his followers. This is really nothing more than is found elsewhere in Paul.[163] In fact, it is similar to Paul's sharp criticism of the Corinthians for expressing an over-realized eschatology: 'Already you have all you want! Already you have become rich! You have become kings—and that without us! How I wish you really had become kings so that we might be kings with you!' (1 Cor. 4:8).

The author of 2 Thessalonians teaches the same eschatology as Paul, with no theology of delay. He gives no time scale which would enable one to calculate even approximately the time of the end. Furthermore, the way in which he inserts the pronouns 'you' and 'us' into the tradition in 1:6-7 shows that he believes Christ could return in the immediate future. He presents the day of the Lord as coming suddenly and dramatically.

The final day comes as a day of joy and relief for Christians in 2 Thessalonians as well as in 1 Thessalonians. The believers in 2 Thessalonians will receive rest from their suffering (1:7) and will glorify and marvel at their returning Lord (1:10). Certainly to glorify and marvel at Jesus upon his return, having received the promised rest, is the most joyful experience possible for the believer. It is true that the day will be a solemn day of judgment upon all who do not believe and do not repent, but this is no different from what Paul says in Romans 2:5-10 when he speaks of God's righteous judgment being revealed. Furthermore, the picture of unrepentant sinners who are deluded and who believe the lie (2 Thess. 2:10-12) is essentially what Paul himself argues in Romans 1:18-32.[164] The great promise for Christians is that they will be saved from God's wrath (Rom. 5:9; 1 Thess. 1:10). Those who suffer will share in the glory (Rom. 8:17-18) and will be revealed as sons (Rom. 8:23), while those who do not repent will be judged by Christ (1 Cor. 4:5-6; 2 Cor. 5:10) and will not inherit the kingdom of God (Gal. 5:21) but will 'reap what they sow' (Gal. 6:7-8). Paul tells the Philippians not to be 'frightened in any way by those who oppose you' because those who oppose them 'will be destroyed, but . . . you will be saved—and that by God' (Phil. 1:28). The picture of divine retribution is clear in 2 Thessalonians, but it does not contain anything not found elsewhere in the undisputed letters of Paul. The picture of judgment in 2 Thessalonians is one of both solemnity and joy—the same worldview held by Paul, who expected final relief only at the parousia.

The writer of 2 Thessalonians also uses tradition about eschatology in a manner similar to Paul. When Paul refers back to eschatological tradition in 1 Corinthians 15 and 1 Thessalonians 4-5, he focuses, not on when the day of the Lord will occur, but on the person of Jesus and what he will do, thus showing the same perspective found in 2 Thessalonians.

Some commentators have suggested that the eschatology of 2 Thessalonians is simply a commentary on or adjustment of—or even a replacement of—the

---

[163]See for example Rom. 16:20; 1 Thess. 4:13–5:11; 1 Cor. 15:23-28, 50-57.

[164]Marshall, *Thessalonians,* p. 204.

eschatology in 1 Thessalonians.[165] However, there is no discrepancy between the eschatology presented in the two letters. Both letters focus on the Christ who returns for his people and judges the unrepentant. Although 2 Thessalonians does contain information which is not found in the first epistle, particularly concerning the opponent, the idea that Satan will finally be defeated is certainly a Pauline thought: 'The God of peace will soon crush Satan under your feet' (Rom. 16:20).[166] That the teaching in 2 Thessalonians is only a commentary is also implausible because the writer refers to what was taught when the church was founded, not to the teaching of 1 Thessalonians.

The interpretation of the phrase 'sitting in the temple' (2:4) as a figurative way of expressing divine claims based on the Old Testament background could be used by either defenders or disputers of authenticity. However, it seems unlikely that an author writing after the fall of Jerusalem, an event that would be known to all Christians, would use this imagery, for it could create the impression of exactly what he was combatting: the idea that because the temple has been destroyed, the day of the Lord has arrived. For the same reason, it is equally unlikely that the author, who in vs. 2 carefully defines the error he that he is opposing, would carelessly leave this piece of tradition untouched, as some disputers claim. Thus the use of this imagery, even in a figurative way, fits much better before the fall of Jerusalem than after.

Therefore the eschatology of 2 Thessalonians does not present a theology of delay or a list of preliminary signs or an apocalyptic timetable which enables one to calculate the time of end. Rather, it presents the day of the Lord as the final great day when Christ comes to gather his people and give them rest and to judge Satan and his followers. The writer is not anti-enthusiastic; he is against an over-realized eschatology. That final day could come immediately. This is the same eschatology found in the undisputed letters of Paul.

II. Imitation

The major paraenetic theme in 2 Thessalonians applies the tradition of imitating the missionaries to the problem of the *ataktoi* (the disorderly or idle).[167] A number of disputers view this application as evidence of the unpauline character of the letter. Four reasons have been given to support this view: (1) This section of 2 Thessalonians excessively stresses apostolic dignity. The apostle's manner of life has become the standard criterion of obedience; his life alone has become normative. This is in contrast to Paul, who does call for

---

[165]Holland, *Tradition*, pp. 4, 60, 152, thinks it is a commentary. Lindemann, 'Zum Abfassungszweck', pp. 35-36, and Hughes, *Early Christian Rhetoric*, pp. 83-84, say it is a replacement.

[166]Cranfield, *Romans,* vol. 2, p. 803.

[167]Because of the difference of opinion concerning how to translate this word group, this term will hereafter be used to describe those who are being admonished in 2 Thess. 3.

imitation of himself, but only as he imitates Christ. In addition, Paul's usual paraenetic practice is to base his exhortations upon Christology, which is conspicuously absent from 2 Thessalonians.[168] (2) Although Paul speaks of his missionary practice of not burdening his hearers financially (1 Cor. 9:6; 1 Thess. 2:9), he never gives it as an example for all other Christians to imitate (as does the author of 2 Thess. 3:7-9). Furthermore, the Thessalonians would know that he had received financial aid from Philippi, making it unlikely that he would ask them to imitate him in this (Phil. 4:15).[169] (3) It is unlikely that Paul would have called for imitation so soon after founding the church at Thessalonica; most likely this is a later development.[170] (4) The instruction to imitate the missionaries (3:6-10) was necessary to order the daily lives of the people because of the delay of the parousia.[171] From these points, the disputers conclude that although the writer of 2 Thessalonians knew of Pauline terminology, he used it in an unpauline manner. To answer these disputations, we must first determine what 2 Thessalonians actually teaches about imitation and then characterize the view of Paul presented in 2 Thessalonians.

A. *The Concept of Imitation*

1. Imitation in 2 Thessalonians

In 2 Thessalonians, the need to imitate the missionaries is identified as part of the original teaching, or tradition, given by Paul when he founded the church at Thessalonica (3:6-12). The particular tradition is found in the brief statement 'it is necessary to imitate us' (3:7).[172] The writer then focuses his attention on the missionary practice of Paul (3:7b-9). Finally, he states a proverb which he expects his readers to know because they were taught it when the church was founded: 'If a man will not work, he shall not eat' (3:10). Therefore the tradition is not doctrinal, as in 2 Thessalonians 1–2, but is practical in nature.

The writer focuses on the hard work of the missionaries, who 'worked night and day, laboring and toiling' so that they would 'not be a burden to any of you'. In fact, the writer claims they even paid for all of their own food (3:8). The writer presents not only Paul but also all the missionaries as examples, in contrast to two places where the writer focuses on Paul himself (2:5; 3:17). He focuses on the need for his readers not to work unpaid but to work hard and not be a burden on others.

---

[168]Hilgenfeld, 'Die beiden Breife', pp. 243, 260-62; Trilling, *Untersuchungen,* pp. 95-101, 118-21; Marxsen, *Der zweite Thessalonicherbrief,* p. 32; Laub, 'Paulinische Autorität', pp. 411-14; and P. Müller, *Anfänge,* pp. 209, 215, 225-27, 234-37.

[169]Hilgenfeld, 'Die beiden Breife', pp. 261-62; Laub, 'Paulinische Autorität', pp. 415-17; J. A. Bailey, 'Who Wrote 2Thessalonians?', pp. 137-39.

[170]J. A. Bailey, 'Who Wrote 2 Thessalonians?', pp. 137-39.

[171]Trilling, *Untersuchungen,* pp. 95-101.

[172]δεῖ μιμεῖσθαι ἡμᾶς

The Authenticity of 2 Thessalonians

The first difficulty in interpreting this passage concerns the meaning of the word group *ataktoi*. Within the Bible this word group is found only in 1 and 2 Thessalonians. In 1Thessalonians 5:14, Paul uses the adjectival form, exhorting the Thessalonians to 'admonish the idle'.[173] Commentators usually link this exhortation with the commands he gives earlier in the epistle concerning working with one's hands and leading a quiet life (1 Thess. 4:11-12). In 2 Thessalonians the writer uses the adverbial form of the word [ἀτάκτως] to describe those who are not 'walking' according to the tradition (3:6, 11) and the verb form [ἠτακτήσαμεν] to emphasize that the missionaries did not act improperly (3:7). The question concerns whether the word group should be translated 'be idle' or 'idly' or whether it should be 'disorderly' or 'unruly'. The context seems to suggest the idea of idleness whereas the actual definition of the word implies the idea of disorderliness.

Commentators are divided over which definition is most appropriate.[174] Spicq's extensive article concludes that the word must mean 'disorderly' because the most frequent extra-biblical uses describe insurgents who disobey or soldiers who break rank rather than people who exhibit a lack of activity.[175] Similarly, Jewett refers to the *ataktoi* as 'rebellious' or 'insubordinate'.[176] In contrast, Arndt and Gingrich say 'the context [in 2 Thessalonians] demands the meaning "be idle, lazy"'.[177] One of the best discussions is still that found in an appendix in Milligan's commentary. Like Spicq, he notes that the word did not normally convey the idea of lack of activity. He then makes the insightful comment that 'the only question that remains is whether [those being addressed] are to be understood positively of actual wrong-doing, or in a more negative sense of a certain remissness in the conduct of life'.[178] He shows that this word is used in the Oxyrhynchus Papyri (275 and 725) in contracts for apprenticeship to describe a boy who as an apprentice may 'fail to attend' or 'play the truant' and to warn that an apprentice must not exceed a certain number of holidays because of idleness. From this information he draws a conclusion that fits both the context in 2 Thessalonians and the actual meaning of the word: the *ataktoi* were 'those members of the Thessalonian Church who . . . were neglecting their

---

[173] νουθετεῖτε τοὺς ἀτάκτους

[174] For the older commentaries, see the list in C. Spicq, 'Les Thessaloniciens "inquiets" étaient-ils des paresseux?', *ST* 10 (1957), p. 1, nn. 2, 3. More recently Best, *Thessalonians*, p. 335; Marshall, *Thessalonians*, pp. 150, 224; Morris, *Thessalonians*, p. 253; and Wanamaker, *Thessalonians*, p. 286, have stressed the idea of idleness (or 'loafer') from the context, while Bruce, *Thessalonians*, p. 205, uses the word 'disorderly'.

[175] Spicq, 'Thessaloniciens', pp. 1-13.

[176] Jewett, *Correspondence*, p. 105.

[177] Arndt and Gingrich, *Lexicon*, p. 119.

[178] Milligan, *Thessalonians*, p. 153.

daily duties, and falling into idle and careless habits'.[179] Therefore the disorderly conduct is not a general disorderliness or insubordination, but a neglect of the command to work and to follow the example of the missionaries' work. The *ataktoi* have become 'busybodies'.

The second difficulty in interpreting this passage concerns the reason the Thessalonians were neglecting these commands. The most common idea is that this was a result of eschatological enthusiasm. Milligan says they were neglecting their duties 'because of their expectation of the immediate parousia of the Lord';[180] Jewett, following Marxsen, suggests this same link between enthusiasm and disorderliness.[181] Trilling says this idleness resulted from an emphasis on the nearness of the end.[182] This link between the expectation of the parousia and the problem with the *ataktoi* has been challenged, and sociological interpretations have been offered. R. Russell has reviewed these different sociological models which include: (1) that 'idleness should be understood against the background of the disdain the Greeks and Romans had for manual labour'; (2) that the Thessalonians were in danger of 'embracing social attitudes similar to the Epicureans, who retired from public life, lived off others'; and (3) that the writer of 2 Thessalonians is following a general moral appeal (as in Dio Chrysostom or Lucian) recommending a proper occupation for the idle or for a free man.[183] To this list Russell adds the idea that 'these disorderly ones through lack of work have become poor and depend on support from members of the congregation who are becoming weary in well-doing (2 Thess. 3.13, cf. 3.7-8)'.[184] According to him, the church would have consisted primarily of workers or artisans who may have sought benefactors.[185]

This sociological emphasis is sustained by a careful reading of 2 Thessalonians. First, there are no verbal links between the problem addressed in 3:6-12 and the problems addressed in 2 Thessalonians 1–2. Nothing in 2 Thessalonians 3:6-12 suggests that the reason for the problem was an improper eschatological expectation. Second, the tradition which is referred to in 2 Thessalonians 3 is of a paraenetic character. It includes the practical idea of imitation and a proverb which probably comes from Jewish sources:[186] 'If a man will not work, he shall not eat'. Again, nothing in either of these traditions suggests an eschatological background to the problem. Third, the writer says the missionary example was given as an example to be followed, implying that the

---

[179] Milligan, *Thessalonians*, p. 154.
[180] Milligan, *Thessalonians*, p. 154.
[181] Jewett, *Correspondence*, pp. 104-105.
[182] Trilling, *Thessalonicher*, p. 150.
[183] Ronald Russell, 'The Idle in 2 Thess 3.6-12: An Eschatological or a Social Problem?', *NTS* 34 (1988), pp. 105-19.
[184] R. Russell, 'Idle', p. 108.
[185] R. Russell, 'Idle', pp. 111, 113.
[186] Marshall, *Thessalonians*, p. 223.

missionaries intentionally presented themselves from the beginning as examples of hard work to be emulated, and so, anticipated the problem in the church. Consequently, the problem did not arise from recent eschatological speculation or misunderstanding at Thessalonica. Fourth, as Russell points out, the oral instruction was repeated at the founding of the church, as is implied by the use of the imperfect tense in 3:10.[187] Therefore the problem was not a problem that arose as a result of eschatological enthusiasm, nor because of the delay of the parousia, but was a problem that was anticipated by the missionaries and had its roots in the sociological environment of the first-century Greek city.

The Thessalonians are given a solemn command 'in the name of the Lord Jesus Christ' to 'keep away' from the *ataktoi*. Despite this warning, the *ataktoi* are still referred to as 'brothers' in v. 6. This same emphasis is found in v. 15, where the church as a whole is to admonish the erring individuals, regarding them not as enemies but as brothers. Trilling has commented that vv. 14-15 are actually a general exhortation, forming a separate section from vv. 6-13.[188] This, however, is very unlikely, for (1) there is no strong break in the context between 3:6-13 and 3:14-15; (2) the erring individuals involved are in both cases referred to as 'brothers' (3:6, 15); (3) the general manner of dealing with these people is the same, for they are to be 'avoided' [στέλλεσθαι] (3:6) and 'not associated with' [συναναμίγνυσθαι] (3:14);[189] and (4) the definite article before 'letter' is in this case equivalent to the demonstrative pronoun 'this', showing that the writer is referring to the immediately preceding command found in 2 Thessalonians.[190] It is likely that the 'association' which is forbidden concerns, at the least, the common church meal, which may have been the occasion for the abuse.[191] However, there is not a total breaking off of relationships because the individuals can still be admonished as brothers. The *ataktoi* are to be disciplined to cause them 'shame' [ἐντραπῇ] and to bring them to repent of their wrong actions.[192]

Two other passages in 2 Thessalonians imply the idea of imitation without explicitly using the terminology. In 2 Thessalonians 1:3-10, the writer addresses the problem of suffering or affliction. He introduces a piece of tradition in 1:6-10 and, as was noted previously, has inserted into the tradition the pronouns found in 1:6b and 7a. Originally the tradition would have said, 'God is just, he will render to those troubling, trouble; to those being troubled, rest'. The author applies this general doctrinal tradition directly to the readers ('to you') as the ones being troubled and includes the missionaries with the readers by inserting 'with us'. The phrase 'with us' indicates that the Thessalonians are included

---

[187]R. Russell, 'Idle', p. 108. [παρηγγέλλομεν]
[188]Trilling, *Thessalonicher*, pp. 153-54.
[189]Findlay, *Thessalonians*, p. 205.
[190]Morris, *Thessalonians*, p. 259.
[191]Greeven, 'συναναμείγνυμι', *TDNT* 3:852-55.
[192]Marshall, *Thessalonians*, p. 228.

with the missionaries not only in the promise of rest but also in the condition of being troubled. The missionaries themselves were also facing trouble, as the exhortation to pray for them in 3:1-2 shows. The writer therefore explicitly links the problems faced by the missionaries and the promise given to the missionaries with the problems faced by the Thessalonians and the promise given to the Thessalonians. In this way the missionaries are an example for the Thessalonians.

The second passage that implies the need for imitation is found in 3:5: 'May the Lord direct your hearts into God's love and Christ's perseverance'. The question in this verse is how the final two prepositional phrases should be understood; in particular, whether the genitives are objective (love toward God, perseverance toward Christ), subjective (God's love, Christ's perseverance), or genitives of quality (God-like love, Christ-like perseverance). Trilling has argued for objective genitives. Looking back to 2:16 ('God our Father, who loved us'), he states that the writer wanted to direct the readers to love God. This position has been well refuted by Wanamaker who gives three reasons for preferring the subjective genitive in this context:

(1) The idea that the Lord should direct people to love for God seems somewhat unusual; love for God should be the response of individuals to God's prior love. Such a response should hardly require the direction of the Lord. (2) If the author, whoever he was, had wished to call his readers to love God, then it would have been much more natural and decisive to have employed the infinitive τὸ ἀγαπᾶν with the object τὸν θεόν. (3) The context necessitates that v. 5 encourage obedience in areas of Christian behavior. Reflection on the character of God's love and commitment to the followers of Christ would appear to be a stronger motivational force for Christian behavior than a call for Christians to love God without at the same time offering a precise reason for doing so. Trilling's reference to 2:16 is unconvincing as it is too distant to serve this purpose.[193]

In addition, Best has pointed out that 'Paul rarely writes of men loving God; when he uses our phrase in other passages it means that God loves men (subjective genitive; Rom. 5.5; 8.39; 2 Cor. 13.13); when he does speak of men loving God he uses a verbal form (Rom. 8.28; 1 Cor. 2.9; 8.3)'.[194]

Wanamaker mentions the interpretations by von Dobschütz and Trilling, who think the second phrase should be taken objectively. They interpret the phrase to mean 'the Thessalonians [are] to have a patient expectation for the coming of Christ' (von Dobschütz), or they are to be steadfast 'toward Christ in the face of "distress and disturbance"' (Trilling).[195] Wanamaker gives two reasons for why it is best to interpret the second prepositional phrase as a subjective genitive:

(1) The two prepositional phrases should be grammatically parallel as they

---

[193] Wanamaker, *Thessalonians*, pp. 278-79.

[194] Best, *Thessalonians*, p. 330.

[195] Wanamaker, *Thessalonians*, p. 279.

are linked by a coordinating conjunction. If the first genitive is subjective, then we should also expect τοῦ Χριστοῦ to be subjective. (2) Both von Dobschütz's and Trilling's interpretations necessitate amplifying the text with ideas not contained in the immediate context.[196]
In addition, the only other use of 'endurance' in 2 Thessalonians is in 1:4, where the author uses a genitive pronoun to define who is enduring. There the endurance is clearly the endurance displayed by the Thessalonians in the midst of persecution. This is a very close grammatical parallel using the same word; the noun in the genitive also defines who is 'enduring'.[197]

A third possibility is that both phrases are to be understood as genitives of quality.[198] Therefore the writer's prayer would be that the Lord would enable the readers to have love like God's and endurance like Christ's. This fits the context very well and makes both parallel prepositional phrases meaningful.

Whether the parallel prepositional phrases are understood as subjective genitives or genitives of quality, the concern of the prayer must be understood in the same way. Wanamaker, who understands the phrase as a subjective genitive, says it most likely means 'taking Christ's perseverance as an example (cf. Jas. 5:11; Pol. 8:2) ',[199] while Marshall, who by defining the genitive as a genitive of quality means we ought to show this quality, says the phrase means 'the kind of steadfastness shown supremely by Christ'.[200] Therefore, whether the phrase is a subjective genitive or a genitive of quality, the writer is presenting Christ in his suffering as an example of perseverance for the Thessalonians, who are also suffering.

To summarize, the picture of imitation in 2 Thessalonians is three-fold: (1) the Thessalonians are to imitate the missionaries in working for their food (3:6-12); (2) the Thessalonians have been suffering persecution as had the missionaries and so also are given the promise of rest with the missionaries at the return of Christ; and (3) the Thessalonians are to imitate Christ in his perseverance (3:5).

2. Imitation in the Undisputed Pauline Epistles

Having examined the theme of imitation in 2 Thessalonians, we can now address the question of whether the stress on imitation in 2 Thessalonians is post-Pauline or is characteristic of the undisputed Paul. The initial problem is to determine Paul's concept of imitation, a question which has provoked diverse interpretations among scholars.

---

[196]Wanamaker, *Thessalonians*, p. 279.
[197]1:4 – ὑπὲρ τῆς ὑπομονῆς ὑμῶν; 3:5 – εἰς τὴν ὑπομονὴν τοῦ Χριστοῦ.
[198]Marshall, *Thessalonians*, pp. 217-18.
[199]Wanamaker, *Thessalonians*, p. 279. See also Best, *Thessalonians*, p. 330; Bruce, *Thessalonians*, pp. 201-202; Frame, *Thessalonians*, p. 296; and Neil, *Thessalonians*, p. 190.
[200]Marshall, *Thessalonians*, pp. 217-18.

According to Hans Dieter Betz, Paul calls upon Christians to imitate the Christ myth, not the historical Jesus; in fact, Paul knows nothing of the idea of 'following Jesus' as found in the Gospels (2 Cor. 5:16).[201] Betz attributes such passages as 1 Corinthians 4:17, which speaks about Paul's own way of life, to later catholic insertions.[202] He believes the call to imitation is not to any ethical or moral example of the historical Jesus or a pre-existent Christ figure or Paul, but to the Christ myth itself.[203]

A second position is that of W. Michaelis, who says that while there is plainly an 'ethical thrust' in the language of imitation in Paul,[204] it must be understood in terms of authority and obedience. Therefore the imitation of Paul does not focus on Paul himself but on the authority with which he is invested. To imitate Paul as he imitated Christ is to obey Paul as he obeyed Christ.[205]

A third position is that of David M. Stanley, who draws three conclusions about Paul's understanding of imitation: (1) Paul urges imitation only on those congregations he actually founded himself (Thessalonica, Corinth, Philippi, Galatia); (2) Paul's 'preaching and way of life have their own characteristic modalities, determined chiefly by his conviction that he carries on the role of Christ as the Suffering Servant of God'; and (3) Paul presents a mediated *imitatio Christi* which springs from both his apostolic authority and the need to have a concrete norm (*Vorbild*).[206]

Such variety of understandings makes it necessary, before drawing any conclusions concerning the Pauline view of imitation, to examine each of the texts in the undisputed letters of Paul which speak about imitation.

The terminology concerning 'imitation' is found most frequently in the Pauline corpus, the only exceptions being Hebrews 6:12 and 13:7 and 3 John 11. The terminology is found in five places in the undisputed letters, once in Ephesians, and twice in 2 Thessalonians.

In 1 Corinthians, Paul speaks of imitation in two passages. In the first, 1 Corinthians 4:14-15, he reminds the Corinthians that he has been a father to them through the gospel, and then he says, 'Therefore I urge you to imitate me' (v. 16). Paul is sending Timothy to remind them 'of my way of life in Christ Jesus, just as I teach everywhere in every church' (v. 17). What he means by

---

[201] Hans Dieter Betz, *Nachfolge und Nachahmung Jesu Christi im Neuen Testament*, (BHT; Tubingen: Mohr Siebeck, 1967), pp. 138, 186.
[202] H. D. Betz, *Nachfolge und Nachahmung*, p. 153.
[203] H. D. Betz, *Nachfolge und Nachahmung*, p. 168.
[204] Michaelis, 'μιμέομαι, μιμητής, συμμιμητής', *TDNT* 4:659-74.
[205] Michaelis, 'μιμέομαι', *TDNT* 4:668-69.
[206] David M. Stanley, '"Become Imitators of Me": The Pauline Conception of Apostolic Tradition', *Bib* 40 (1959), pp. 859-77. See also David M. Stanley, 'Imitation in Paul's Letters: Its Significance for His Relationship to Jesus and to His Own Christian Foundations', in *From Jesus to Paul* (ed. Peter Richardson and John C. Hurd; Waterloo, Ont: Wilfrid Laurier University Press, 1984), pp. 127-41.

The Authenticity of 2 Thessalonians

'my way of life in Christ' is evident in vv. 9-13, where he contrasts the Corinthians' view of their own present position as rich kings (4:8) with the fact that God has made a spectacle of the apostles, who are condemned, weak, dishonored, hungry, and thirsty, and who have to work hard with their own hands (1 Cor. 4:9-13). This way of life, which he teaches 'everywhere in every church', includes working hard with his own hands.

The second passage in 1 Corinthians which speaks of imitation is 11:1: 'Be imitators of me, just as I am of Christ'. As has already been shown in ch. 3, this section actually concludes at the end of 11:2. In the immediately preceding context Paul has stressed doing all to God's glory (10:31) and not causing others to stumble but seeking their good (10:32-33). He has given them an example of this in his own behavior, just as Christ did in his behavior. In fact, this teaching is part of his tradition which they must remember (11:2). They are called upon to remember him in 'all things'. Therefore part of Paul's regular teaching included his example. In this case he links his example to that of Christ, but there is a focus on himself as the concrete example (11:2).

In 1 Thessalonians, Paul speaks of imitation in two passages. In 1:6, he says, 'You became imitators of us and of the Lord, welcoming the word in much affliction with joy of the Holy Spirit'. They imitated the missionaries and the Lord in the way they welcomed the gospel in affliction.[207] The next verse shows that the Thessalonians' reception of the gospel became an example [τύπον] to others (1:8), not only in accepting the gospel with suffering but also in repenting of idolatry (1:9). The second passage in 1 Thessalonians to mention imitation speaks of how the Christians at Thessalonica imitated the churches in Judea by being willing to suffer from their own countrymen (2:14). Therefore, the idea of imitation in 1 Thessalonians includes both imitation of the missionaries and the Lord and also imitation of the action of other churches. Furthermore, the Thessalonians have themselves become examples to be imitated.

The concept of imitation is also seen in Philippians 3:17, where Paul says, 'Join with others in imitating my example, brothers, and take note of those who live according to the pattern we gave you'. Paul again stresses his own example as the norm or standard to be followed.[208] In addition, in Philippians 4:9 he says, 'Whatever you have learned or received or heard from me, or seen in me—put it into practice'. Although the language of imitation is not explicitly used here, the idea is the same. The norm for Paul's converts is not only his teaching, but his practical example as well.

Therefore the concept of imitation as found in the undisputed letters of Paul can be summarized in three points. (1) Paul presents his own life as a concrete

---

[207]Wanamaker, *Thessalonians*, p. 80.
[208]Συμμιμηταί μου γίνεσθε, ἀδελφοί, καὶ σκοπεῖτε τοὺς οὕτω περιπατοῦντας καθὼς ἔχετε τύπον ἡμᾶς.

Doctrinal Content of 2 Thessalonians

example for all those converted under his ministry to follow.[209] It is part of his foundational teaching and the tradition delivered to all the churches.[210] This exemplary behavior is seen both in his own actions and in his converts' response to the gospel.[211] (2) This concept of imitation is sometimes linked to Paul's own imitation of Christ,[212] but equally as often, Paul presents only himself.[213] (3) His example includes suffering[214] and the willingness to forgo privileges for the sake of others,[215] and it explicitly includes his hard work.[216]

When 2 Thessalonians is compared to this picture, it is seen that the writer does not go beyond Paul's own use of the concept of imitation. The writer puts no more emphasis on Paul or on imitating him than Paul himself does in his undisputed letters. In 2 Thessalonians 3:6-10, the writer calls upon his readers to imitate Paul's manner of working. Some have suggested that since Paul worked only so that he would not be a burden to those hearing his message (1 Thess. 2:9; 1 Cor. 9), this call to imitation cannot be Pauline. However, Paul also says in 1 Thessalonians that he worked to demonstrate to his hearers the holy, righteous, and blameless character of the preachers (2:10), who shared not only the gospel but their very lives with the Thessalonians (2:8). Furthermore, 1 Corinthians 9 presents yet another perspective on the work of Paul. Throughout 1 Corinthians 9, Paul points out that even though as an apostle he has the right to receive financial help from the Corinthians, he works for a living so that he can present the gospel freely. Therefore, Paul himself gives different reasons for his work: he does not want to be a burden to his hearers, he wants to set an example of character, and he wants to present the gospel freely. In 2 Thessalonians 3:8 the idea of working rather than being a financial burden is also included (as in 1 Thess. 2:9), but in this context Paul works to model the way the believers should work. If Paul's practice of working for a living rather than receiving financial support must be explained in the same manner every time he writes, then either 1 Thessalonians or 1 Corinthians is out of character and could be considered pseudepigraphy as well.

The problem which faced the writer of 2 Thessalonians and caused him to refer to the necessity to imitate the missionaries' work was not eschatological, but sociological. This sociological understanding is substantiated in that there are no verbal links between this section of the letter and the eschatological sections; the traditions mentioned are of a paraenetic character; and the author explicitly says this teaching occurred when the mission took place—that is, the

---

[209] Phil. 4:9; 1 Cor. 11:2.
[210] 1 Cor. 4:17; 11:2.
[211] 1 Thess. 1:7.
[212] 1 Cor. 11:1; 1 Thess. 1:6.
[213] 1 Cor. 4:16-17; Phil. 3:17; 4:9.
[214] 1 Thess. 1:6; 1 Cor. 4:9-13.
[215] 1 Cor. 10:32-33.
[216] 1 Cor. 4:12.

teaching was not brought in because of a later eschatological confusion. The Christians who are admonished in this section are not some false teachers, nor those who display a general disorderliness, but instead, those who are 'neglecting their daily duties, and falling into idle and careless habits'.[217] Thus the problem arose out of the sociological environment of the first-century Greek city and was anticipated by the missionaries. Nothing in 2 Thessalonians suggests that the problem arose because of a delay of the parousia.

The Christians addressed in 2 Thessalonians are called to imitate the missionaries not only in working for their food, but also, it is implied, in enduring suffering and waiting for the promised rest (1:6-7). In doing so, they are also imitating Christ (3:5).

When the undisputed letters of Paul are examined, it is seen that Paul presents his whole life, including his work with his own hands, as an example to be imitated (1 Cor. 4:9-17; 11:2; Phil. 3:17; 4:9). He speaks of not being a burden to his hearers in two different contexts: his righteous motives (1 Thess. 2:9) and his desire to present the gospel freely (1 Cor. 9). The writer of 2 Thessalonians does not copy either of these contexts but focuses on the apostle not being a burden in order to present his life as an example of work. This is entirely in accord with the pattern found in the undisputed letters of Paul. The writer of 2 Thessalonians shows no sign of being a slavish imitator of Paul's letters, but rather is as original as Paul in applying the tradition of imitation to the problem in view.

B. *The Character of Paul Presented in 2 Thessalonians*

The second claim disputers make about the language of imitation in 2 Thessalonians is that Paul is focused upon in a way that is more exalted than in the undisputed epistles. To examine all aspects of Paul in all his letters is beyond the scope of this work, but it is possible to see if the characteristics of Paul emphasized in 2 Thessalonians are also found within the undisputed letters.

1. Letter Writer

In 2 Thessalonians Paul is presented as a self-conscious letter writer who speaks authoritatively. The epistle begins with his name (1:1), and in the closing words the author says, 'I, Paul, write this greeting in my own hand, which is the distinguishing mark in all my letters. This is how I write' (3:17). Though 2 Thessalonians clearly presents Paul as the primary writer (see 2:5; 3:17), he is not presented alone, for three individuals—Paul, Silas, and Timothy (1:1)—are named as authors of the epistle, and the epistle is written in first person plural. Paul is not singled out from the other missionaries as the one to be imitated; he tells the Thessalonians to imitate 'us'.

---

[217]Milligan, *Thessalonians*, p. 164.

In four places, the writer of 2 Thessalonians mentions the word 'epistle' (2:2, 15; 3:14, 17). First, in 2:2, the writer claims that the doctrinal error he is correcting has come 'neither through spirit, nor through speech, nor through an epistle as from us'. Commentators generally agree that 'spirit' in this passage must refer to some kind of prophetic utterance and that 'report' must mean oral teaching.[218] The difficulties with this passage include: (1) to what 'epistle' the author is referring; (2) whether the phrase 'as from us' applies only to epistle, to epistle and speech, or to epistle, speech and spirit; and (3) whether the phrase 'as from us' implies a forgery in circulation, a misunderstanding of Paul's previous epistle, or a general denial that the false doctrine originated with the authors. Lindemann, following Hilgenfeld and Holtzmann, believes that the epistle in question is 1 Thessalonians and that the author wants to replace it with his own letter (2 Thess.).[219] Hughes believes this verse implies a 'refutation' of 1 Thessalonians.[220] Trilling, on the other hand, believes the verse (along with 3:17) implies the presence of a forgery (not 1 Thess.) but considers the existence of such a forgery to be likely only after Paul's lifetime.[221] These suggestions, however, all infer much more than the passage actually says.

The word 'epistle' in 2:2 is anarthrous, as are 'report' and 'spirit', and thus all three possible sources are left general, not specific. Another difficulty is to determine whether the phrase 'as from us' in 2:2 is meant to apply to epistle, to epistle and report, or to epistle, report, and spirit. In 2:15, the author commands the readers to hold to the traditions 'we passed on to you whether by report or our epistle. Because 2:15 is found within the same overall context as 2:2, and because both report and letter in 2:15 are linked to the missionaries, then it is probable that the phrase 'as from us' in 2:2 should be applied at least to 'report or epistle in 2:2. Because spirit, report, and epistle are all found in parallel in 2:2, it is very unlikely that the phrase 'as from us' would only apply to the last two items in the list.[222] Thus, because the phrase 'as from us' applies to spirit, report, and epistle, and because all three are anarthrous, then all the author is saying is that it is impossible to link the erroneous teaching to the missionaries. He does not express an opinion on the source of the error; he simply asserts that it could not possibly have come from the missionaries.

This manner of condemning every source of false information is consistent with the undisputed Paul: 'But even if we or an angel from heaven should preach a gospel other than the one we preached to you, let him be eternally condemned!' (Gal. 1:8). Paul is not suggesting that he or an angel from heaven had preached another gospel; he is simply condemning any source of false

---

[218] Morris, *Thessalonians*, p. 215; Bruce, *Thessalonians*, pp. 163, 164; Trilling, *Thessalonicher*, p. 75.

[219] Lindemann, 'Zum Abfassungszweck', pp. 36-39.

[220] F. W. Hughes, *Early Christian Rhetoric*, pp. 83-84.

[221] Trilling, *Thessalonicher*, pp. 76-77.

[222] Best, *Thessalonians*, p. 278.

information. Thus the statement in 2:2 does not mean the writer of 2 Thessalonians knew of any pseudonymous Pauline epistles, reports, or revelations 'as from us', nor is he condemning a particular letter of Paul such as 1 Thessalonians; rather, he is declaring that the false teaching did not originate with the missionaries.

The second passage to use the word 'epistle' is 2:15: 'hold to the traditions you were taught whether by word of mouth or by our epistle'. This verse is similar to 2:2 with the mention of 'report' and 'epistle', yet the authors explicitly link the two forms of communication to themselves [εἴτε διὰ λόγου εἴτε δι' ἐπιστολῆς ἡμῶν]. As was shown earlier, 2:13-17 is more closely associated with 2:1-12 than with 3:1-5. This is seen in the repeated form of thanksgiving found in 1:3 and 2:13, in the clear grammatical break at 3:1 ('Finally' [τὸ λοιπόν]), and in the comparison of the Thessalonian Christians in 2:13-14 with those being condemned in 2:10-12. As we have already seen, the specific traditions referred to in 2:15 are those found in 2 Thessalonians 1–2 or in a previous letter or preaching. Therefore, Trilling goes far beyond this statement when he identifies the traditions as referring to the whole Pauline corpus.[223] Lindemann interprets 'epistle' in this verse as referring to 2 Thessalonians itself.[224] But as Best has shown, the absence of the definite article in this context in contrast to the presence of the definite article in 3:14, clearly referring to 2 Thessalonians, shows that some other letter(s) by the authors is in view.[225] Therefore the writer of 2 Thessalonians seems to imply that he has written to the Thessalonians previously, and that his epistle must be accepted, along with his oral teaching, as authoritative.

Only in the third passage, 2 Thessalonians 3:14, does the author use the definite article with the word 'epistle': 'If anyone does not obey our instruction in this epistle, take special note of him'. Most commentators recognize that the author must be commanding obedience to the teaching found in 2 Thessalonians.[226] Trilling believes the instruction refers to the whole letter and that this is part of the canonizing process.[227] However, the context suggests that the author intends the warning particularly for the problem of 'the idle' addressed in 3:6-12. This is the only section of the letter in which disciplinary action is explicitly mentioned: they are 'to keep away from every brother who is idle' (3:6), a command almost identical to the command in 3:14 'not to associate with him'. Therefore the command is specific to 2 Thessalonians and in particular to the exhortation in 3:6-12.

---

[223]Trilling, *Thessalonicher*, pp. 154-55.

[224]Lindemann, 'Zum Abfassungszweck', p. 37; see also Wanamaker, *Thessalonians*, p. 269.

[225]Best, *Thessalonians*, p. 318; see also Rom. 16:22; Col. 4:16; and 1 Thess. 5:27.

[226]Best, *Thessalonians*, p. 342; Bruce, *Thessalonians*, p. 206; Milligan, *Thessalonians*, p. 116; Wanamaker, *Thessalonians*, p. 289.

[227]Trilling, *Thessalonicher*, pp. 154-55.

Doctrinal Content of 2 Thessalonians

The last verse in 2 Thessalonians to use the word 'epistle' is 3:17. The author writes, 'I, Paul, write this greeting in my own hand, which is the distinguishing mark in all my epistles. This is how I write.' The disputers claim that this verse demonstrates an exaltation of Paul which could occur only in a post-Pauline time period and also that it contradicts some of Paul's other letters because Paul does not sign all his letters.

However, an examination of Paul's letters as a whole shows that this verse does not exalt Paul any more than the undisputed letters do. Paul frequently refers to himself by name throughout his letters.[228] He references his own 'epistles or 'writing' often in his undisputed letters.[229] In fact, he views them as an extension of his ministry, as he says in 2 Corinthians 13:10: 'This is why I write these things when I am absent, that when I come I may not have to be harsh in my use of authority—the authority the Lord gave me for building you up, not for tearing you down.' He also frequently focuses attention on himself, his ministry and his example.[230] He stresses his ministry in Romans 11:13 when he says, 'I am talking to you Gentiles. Inasmuch as I am the apostle to the Gentiles, I make much of my ministry'; in 1 Corinthians 9:1-2, 'Am I not free? Am I not an apostle? Have I not seen Jesus our Lord? Are you not the result of my work in the Lord? Even though I may not be an apostle to others, surely I am to you! For you are the seal of my apostleship in the Lord'; and in Galatians 2:8, 'For God, who was at work in the ministry of Peter as an apostle to the Jews, was also at work in my ministry as an apostle to the Gentiles.' In these passages Paul does not hesitate to emphasize his ministry, even stating that it is apostolic. Furthermore, Paul sees his life as an example to the lives of the believers to whom he writes. In 1 Corinthians 4:16-17, Paul says, 'Therefore I urge you to imitate me. For this reason I am sending to you Timothy, my son whom I love, who is faithful in the Lord. He will remind you of my way of life in Christ Jesus, which agrees with what I teach everywhere in every church.' Thus Paul's manner of life is set as an example in all the churches, and the writer of 2 Thessalonians clearly does not exalt Paul beyond what is found in the undisputed epistles. In fact, in 3:17 there are actually no words exalting Paul.

Trilling describes 2 Thessalonians 3:17 as 'fatal' to the case for authenticity, for he believes the 'distinguishing mark' is Paul's signature, and this clearly is *not* in all of Paul's letters. However, similar passages occur three times in the undisputed letters of Paul: 1 Corinthians 16:21, 'I, Paul, write this greeting in my own hand'; Galatians 6:11, 'See what large letters I use as I write to you with my own hand'; and Philemon 19, 'I, Paul, am writing this with my own hand. I will pay it back—not to mention that you owe me your very self.' In

---

[228] 1 Cor. 1:12-13; 3:4-5, 22; 16:21; 2 Cor. 10:1; Gal. 5:2; 1 Thess. 2:18; Phlm. 9, 19.

[229] Paul explicitly refers to 'writing' in Rom. 15:15; 1 Cor. 4:14; 5:9, 11; 9:15; 14:37; 2 Cor. 1:13; 2:3, 4, 9; 7:12; 9:1; 13:10; Gal. 1:20; 6:11; Phil. 3:1; 1 Thess. 4:9; 5:1; Phlm. 19.

[230] See especially Rom. 7:9-25; 11:1, 13, 19; 1 Cor. 2:1-4; 4:1-21; 5:3; 7:10, 12, 28; 9:1-27; 15:9-11; 2 Cor. 10–12; Gal. 1–2; 5:2, 11; 6:17.

each of these passages Paul takes pen in hand to highlight the truth of what immediately follows the statement. These verses, along with Romans 16:22, in which the amanuensis for Paul's letter is explicitly named, demonstrate that Paul regularly used an amanuensis but could insert his own writing in the midst of a letter (Phlm.) or at the end of the letter (1 Cor., Gal.). The distinguishing mark in 2 Thessalonians 3:17, then, is not the signature, but the writing itself: 'in my own hand' and 'this is how I write'. Thus the writer of 2 Thessalonians is displaying the common practice of his time to conclude his letter in his own handwriting,[231] which would only be visible in the autographa.[232]

Furthermore, Trilling's belief that the distinguishing mark is the signature actually presents difficulty for the disputers. This is not simply because the signature claims Pauline authorship, but because this would mean that the author of 2 Thessalonians believes any letter that does not have the final signature of Paul is non-Pauline. Of the undisputed letters this would include Romans, 2 Corinthians, Philippians, and 1 Thessalonians. Thus Trilling's interpretation of 3:17 would exclude from the canon all of Paul's other letters except Galatians and 1 Corinthians. At the same time, Trilling believes that the writer of 2 Thessalonians had a collection of Paul's letters and that 2 Thessalonians (especially in 3:14) is his attempt to recognize Paul's letters as canon.[233] Consequently, Trilling's interpretation of 3:17 contradicts what he thinks is happening in 3:14. Therefore the most consistent approach to the Pauline letters as a whole sees this verse near the close of 2 Thessalonians as merely showing a change in handwriting that would only be visible to those reading the original document.

Lindemann and Hughes suggest that in 3:17, the writer claims 2 Thessalonians is the only 'authentic' epistle from Paul to the Thessalonians.[234] They suggest that the writer uses 1 Thessalonians, knowing it is from Paul, to compose 2 Thessalonians and to exalt the apostle. If this is true, then the writer is denying the truthfulness and authority of Paul's letter while at the same time exalting Paul's authority in his own pseudonymous letter, an impossible position for any writer of integrity to hold. Holland, another disputer, has rightfully said that if it is the goal of 3:17 to replace or refute 1 Thessalonians,

---

[231] Marshall, *Thessalonians*, p. 232; Morris, *Thessalonians*, p. 264.

[232] Bruce, *Thessalonians*, p. 216, notes that when Cicero used an amanuensis, he finished the letter in his own writing (*Att.* 13.28), and Cicero mentions that Pompey did this as well (*Att.* 8.1). Milligan, *Thessalonians*, p. 125, mentions the different handwriting found at the end of Egyptian papyri (P.Oxy. 45) and many of the Egyptian papyrus-letters (p. 130). Neil, *Thessalonians*, p. 199, refers to the letter of Mystarion, which shows a different handwriting at the end and yet makes no mention of this change of hand.

[233] Trilling, *Thessalonicher*, p. 155.

[234] Lindemann, 'Zum Abfassungszweck', pp. 35-36; Hughes, *Early Christian Rhetoric*, pp. 83-84.

then history has shown the author was a 'manifest failure'.[235]

As we have seen, the author of 2 Thessalonians presents Paul as a self-conscious letter writer (2:15), just as Paul presents himself in his undisputed letters. The epistle is not directed against pseudepigraphy (2:2) but simply against linking the false teaching, in any fashion, with the missionaries. The writer does not exhibit a later stage of the canonizing process (3:14), as Trilling suggests, but simply directs that his particular commands in this letter are to be obeyed. Finally, the writer closes the letter with his own handwriting (3:17), as is the practice of Paul (Gal. 6:11). Therefore the verses in 2 Thessalonians which speak about an epistle are not indicative of a post-Pauline time, nor do they present a fatal objection to the case for authenticity; rather, they are most easily understood as part of an authentic letter of Paul. He does not exalt Paul above the other missionaries in 2 Thessalonians; he simply reminds them to hold on to the original teaching, as Paul does in his other letters (see 1 Cor. 4:1; Gal. 1:6-9).

2. Preacher-Missionary

Paul is presented in 2 Thessalonians not only as a writer of epistles, but also as a preacher-missionary. In this capacity he is singled out from his co-senders only in 2:5: 'Don't you remember that when I was with you I used to tell you these things?' Throughout the rest of the letter, the picture of the preacher-missionary is applied to the three senders together. As missionaries they had contact with a variety of churches (1:4), their testimony was believed when they founded the church (1:10), and the content of their message was their gospel (2:14). As has been shown previously, their teaching at the time the church was established included tradition (2:15; 3:6), and they were very self-conscious not only about their doctrinal teaching (2:2; 3:5) but also about their own personal examples of working hard (3:7-9). The ministry of the missionaries takes a variety of forms within the epistle, not only in terms of doctrinal and paraenetic material, but also as they encourage (1:3-4, 6-7; 2:13-14), pray for (1:3, 11-12; 2:13, 16-17; 3:5), correct and remind (2:3,5; 3:6,11), command (2:15; 3:4, 6, 10, 12-15), directly discipline (3:12-15), and bless (3:16, 18). In this manner the missionaries show a full range of emotions, activities, and pastoral concerns. All of these activities apply equally to all the missionaries.

It has already been shown that, as a preacher-missionary, Paul made use of preformed materials and frequently referred back to what he had originally taught. A variety of forms of ministry such as encouragement, prayer, correction, and blessing is found in virtually every one of his letters. The aspect of ministry in 2 Thessalonians which disputers usually identify as unpauline is the command to work and the discipline for disobeying that command, found in ch. 3. Trilling states that this command is general, not concrete as in 1

---

[235]Holland, *Tradition*, p. 155.

Thessalonians.[236] However, the command is no less concrete than the traditional commands found in 1 Thessalonians 4:1-12 and, in fact, appears to be directed to a very particular situation in 3:6-15. The discipline he recommends is given with authority 'in the name of the Lord Jesus Christ' (3:6) and 'in the Lord Jesus Christ' (3:12), yet at the same time there is a gentleness concerning those who may refuse to obey (3:15). This discipline sounds very like that given by Paul in 1 Corinthians 5, where the sinner is to be 'handed over to Satan' when they are assembled 'in the name of the Lord Jesus' (1 Cor. 5:4). They are not 'to associate' with the sinner in question, nor even to eat with him (1 Cor. 5:11). And whether or not 2 Corinthians 2:5-11 concerns the same individual as found in 1 Corinthians, it is clear that Paul's goal in discipline is restoration, as it is in 2 Thessalonians. Discipline was a regular feature of Paul's ministry. Not only does he command congregations to exercise discipline, as in 1 Corinthians 5 and 2 Corinthians 2, but he also warns them of the discipline he can personally administer: 'What do you prefer? Shall I come to you with punishment, or in love and with a gentle spirit?' (1 Cor. 4:21). Nothing in 2 Thessalonians is contrary to the discipline found in Paul's undisputed epistles; if anything, it tends to show 'a very early stage of development'[237] like that of 1 Corinthians.

Some disputers believe the writer of 2 Thessalonians displays a non-Pauline stress on apostolic dignity, but this is difficult to sustain for two reasons: (1) Paul, when the occasion requires, stresses his own position as an apostle and is very self-conscious in defending his ministry;[238] and (2) the writer of 2 Thessalonians does not put any stress on the 'apostleship' of Paul: he does not defend it, exalt it, or even explicitly mention it. The writer simply exercises the authority which Paul exercises in his undisputed letters. There is no special 'dignity' afforded to Paul in 2 Thessalonians; rather, in almost every instance, he is just one of the missionaries, for the writer of 2 Thessalonians refers to Paul with his co-workers in the plural. As in 1 Thessalonians, his apostleship is not stressed because it is not a matter of dispute.

3. Fellow Christian

In 2 Thessalonians Paul is presented not only as a letter writer and as one of the missionaries, but also as a fellow Christian. The readers are addressed repeatedly as brothers, which would imply the missionaries view themselves as on at least somewhat the same level as their readers.[239] Those who are being afflicted and are promised rest include not only the readers, but also the

---

[236] Trilling, *Untersuchungen*, pp. 95-101, 118-21; see also Peter Müller, *Anfänge*, pp. 160, 168.

[237] Best, *Thessalonians*, p. 345.

[238] On Paul's apostleship see 2 Cor. 2:17; 3:1; 4:1; 5:11; 6:3-13; 10:8; 11:4–12:14; Gal. 1:1, 8; 2:14; 4:14; on his self-conscious ministerial defense see Rom. 1:8-16; 11:13; 15:15-32; 1 Cor. 1:10-17; 2:1-4; 3:4-12; 4:8-21.

[239] 2 Thess. 1:3; 2:1, 13, 15; 3:1, 6, 13, 15.

missionaries (1:6-7), and the missionaries need the help of their readers to pray for them in their difficult work (3:1-2). This is similar to Paul in his undisputed letters: he sees himself as a fellow Christian, most commonly referring to his fellow Christians as brothers. In Philippians 1:29-30 his fellow believers suffer as he suffers and will be saved as he will be saved, similarly to 2 Thessalonians 1:3-10, where suffering and future promised salvation are also linked together as a 'sign' of God's work.[240] In Philippians 1:19, Paul also expresses his need for his readers to pray for him.[241] Therefore the picture of Paul as a fellow Christian in 2 Thessalonians is very similar to that found throughout his undisputed epistles.

C. *Conclusion on Imitation*

The disputers have presented four reasons to view the teaching about imitation in 2 Thessalonians as post-Pauline. Yet when 2 Thessalonians and the undisputed letters of Paul are examined carefully, it is evident that each of these reasons is incorrect, either because 2 Thessalonians has been interpreted incorrectly or because the teaching within the undisputed letters of Paul has not been fully understood.

First, they claim that the stress on apostolic dignity shows a later time in which the life of the apostle has become normative. However, the writer of 2 Thessalonians places no more stress on apostolic dignity than is found in the undisputed letters of Paul. In fact, 2 Thessalonians is most like the undisputed Pauline epistles in which Paul did not need to defend his apostolic commission because it was accepted by the readers. Furthermore, the example to be imitated in 2 Thessalonians is not focused on Paul himself, but on all three missionaries. As in the undisputed epistles, Paul presents his working with his own hands and his whole life as a pattern to be imitated and as a part of the tradition he taught.[242] The character of Paul in 2 Thessalonians as letter writer, preacher-missionary, and fellow Christian is also consistent with the undisputed letters of Paul. Even the response to the gospel by Paul's converts is a model to be imitated.[243]

Second, the disputers often argue that in 2 Thessalonians the missionary practice of working with their hands has changed in purpose, from the desire not to be a burden to their hearers (1 Cor. 9:6; 1 Thess. 2:9) to setting an example for them to imitate. However, Paul does say in 1 Corinthians 4:12 that 'we work hard with our own hands' and then concludes this section by saying that he is to be imitated (4:16) and that the Corinthians are to follow his 'way of life' which he taught in every church (4:17). Thus Paul does present his hard

---

[240] Phil. 1:28 [ἔνδειξις]; 2 Thess. 1:5 [ἔνδειγμα].
[241] 2 Cor. 1:11; Phil. 1:19; 1 Thess. 5:25.
[242] 1 Cor. 4:12-17; 11:1-2; Phil. 3:17; 4:9.
[243] 1 Thess. 1:6-7.

work while a missionary as an example to be imitated.

Third, some think the command to imitate the apostle's life must be post-Pauline because such a command would be unlikely so soon after establishment of the church. This does not take into account that Paul does use the language of imitation in his undisputed letters, but only in those epistles directed to congregations he actually founded (Thessalonica, Corinth, Philippi, and Galatia), for imitation requires a close personal contact of the apostle with the recipients. Therefore imitation is not a later development after the time of Paul, but is part of Paul's own missionary teaching.

Finally, the disputers say that it is the delay of the parousia that has made it necessary to order daily life according to apostolic example. It is true that the writer tells the Thessalonians to order their lives, but not because of the delay of the parousia. This teaching was given right from the beginning of the church because of the socioeconomic background of the community, and it was not a later development. Nothing in the section on imitation in any way links it to the eschatological confusion mentioned in 2 Thessalonians 2.

Therefore the teaching about imitation found in 2 Thessalonians is consistent with that found in the undisputed letters of Paul and actually enhances the case for the authenticity of the letter.

III. Christology

A third area of theology which is often discussed with reference to authenticity is the doctrine of Christ. The overall teaching about Jesus Christ in 2 Thessalonians fits well within the bounds of Pauline theology. Jesus Christ is the source (with God the Father) of grace and peace in the church;[244] he will return to rescue his people and defeat all his enemies;[245] he is active among his people and is to be imitated by them;[246] and he speaks authoritatively through his apostle.[247] Yet despite this overall agreement, the disputers of authenticity have focused attention on three areas of Christology in 2 Thessalonians which they claim distinguish it from the undisputed letters of Paul: (A) the transfer to Jesus Christ of attributes traditionally ascribed to Yahweh;[248] (B) the absence of the cross and resurrection from the Christology of 2 Thessalonians;[249] and

---

[244] 2 Thess. 1:1-2, 12; 3:16, 18; cf. Rom. 1:7; 1 Cor. 1:3; 16:25; 2 Cor. 1:2.

[245] 2 Thess. 1:6-10; 2:1, 8-12; cf. 1 Cor. 5:5; 15:24-27; Phil. 1:28; 3:20-21; 1 Thess. 1:10; 4:17; 5:1-11.

[246] 2 Thess. 2:17; 3:3-5; cf. Rom. 8:10; 1 Cor. 11:1; 1 Thess. 1:6; 3:12-13.

[247] 2 Thess. 3:6, 12; cf. Rom. 15:30; 1 Cor. 5:4; 7:10, 12; 9:14; 14:37; 2 Cor. 13:10; 1 Thess. 5:27.

[248] Those who note this include Hilgenfeld, Wrede, Braun, Trilling, Krodel, J. A. Bailey, Holland, and P. Müller.

[249] Those who note this include Trilling, Laub, and P. Müller.

(C) the predominance of the title 'Lord' used to describe Jesus Christ.[250]

A. *Transfer to Jesus Christ of Attributes Traditionally Ascribed to Yahweh*

The disputers of authenticity believe that the writer of 2 Thessalonians shows post-Pauline characteristics by moving from a Pauline theocentric theology to a Christocentric theology, which Holland describes as Christ eclipsing the Father.[251] The problem with this argument is three-fold: first, it fails fully to account for what is taught about God the Father in 2 Thessalonians; second, it fails to take note of the fact that Christ is central in the undisputed letters of Paul; and third, it does not appreciate that the transfer of attributes traditionally ascribed to Yahweh is found not only in 2 Thessalonians but also in the undisputed epistles of Paul.

(1) There is no question that the person of Christ is emphasized in 2 Thessalonians, yet this does not mean that God is ignored or irrelevant within the letter. In fact, the references to God and his activity are nearly as frequent as the references to Jesus Christ and his activity. The church is not only in the Lord Jesus Christ, but also in God our Father (1:1); grace and peace, encouragement and strength come from both the Father and the Son (1:2, 12; 2:16-17). God is thanked (1:3; 2:13) as the just judge who gives relief and punishment (1:4-7). The kingdom and the church are preeminently his (1:4, 5). He is the one who elects (2:13), calls (2:14), loves (2:16; 3:5), encourages, and gives hope (2:16). It is primarily God's position that the opponent attempts to usurp (2:4). Therefore to say that the author of 2 Thessalonians puts God into the back ground is not accurate.

(2) This balance is seen throughout Paul's undisputed letters as well. Paul refers to the work of the Father and the Son approximately the same number of times throughout his letters. Often when he makes reference to 'the Lord' in his letters, he does it repeatedly in one section, as in 2 Thessalonians 3:1-5, 16.[252] Therefore in terms of emphasis on God or Jesus Christ, the writer of 2 Thessalonians shows the same approximate priorities as the undisputed Paul.

(3) L. Joseph Kreitzer has shown that not only does the writer of 2 Thessalonians transfer attributes from Yahweh to Jesus Christ, but Paul also has the same tendency, especially when teaching about reconciliation, Christology, or eschatology.[253] He shows how Paul does this in Romans, Philippians, and 1 Thessalonians, and also in 2 Thessalonians:

---

[250]Raymond F. Collins, *Letters That Paul Did Not Write: The Epistle to the Hebrews and the Pauline Pseudepigrapha* (GNS 28; Wilmington: Glazier, 1988), pp. 226-27.
[251]Holland, *Tradition*, p. 90.
[252]Rom. 14:4-8; 16:2-22; 1 Cor. 16:19-24; 2 Cor. 3:16-18; Phil. 4:1-5; 1 Thess. 4:15-17.
[253]L. Joseph Kreitzer, *Jesus and God in Paul's Eschatology* (JSNTSup 19; Sheffield: JSOT Press, 1987), pp. 21-22.

NT Lord = Jesus	OT Background Lord = God
Romans 10:13	Joel 2:32
Romans 10:11	Isaiah 28:16
Philippians 2:10-11	Isaiah 45:23
1 Thessalonians 3:13	Zechariah 14:5
1 Thessalonians 4:14	Zechariah 14:5
1 Thessalonians 4:15-18	Zechariah 9:14
Romans 9:33	Isaiah 28:16
Romans 11:26	Isaiah 59:20
1 Thessalonians 5:8	Isaiah 59:17
2 Thessalonians 1:7, 10	Zechariah 14:5
2 Thessalonians 1:9	Isaiah 2:10
2 Thessalonians 1:6-12	Isaiah 66:4-6, 15
2 Thessalonians 2:8	Isaiah 11:4

Kreitzer categorizes these shifts in three ways: (1) a referential shift of 'Lord' from God to Christ; (2) a referential shift of pronouns from God to Christ; and (3) a referential shift of description of the day of the Lord from God to Christ.[254]

The transfer of attributes from God to Christ in an eschatological context actually shows that the writer of 2 Thessalonians is totally consistent with Pauline practice. It also helps to explain why this letter, with its emphasis on eschatology, and 1 Thessalonians, with its similar emphasis, use the title 'Lord' so frequently. Therefore the transfer of attributes from God to Christ in an eschatological context actually enhances the case for authenticity.

B. *Absence of the Cross and Resurrection from the Christology of 2 Thessalonians*

There are no explicit references in 2 Thessalonians to the cross or resurrection of Jesus Christ. The only passage that even implies this work is 2 Thessalonians 3:5, which speaks about 'Christ's perseverance'. Whether this is understood as a subjective genitive or a genitive of quality, it is clear that the author wants his readers to follow Christ's example of perseverance as seen in the way he endured suffering. This is certain because of the similar phrase in 2 Thessalonians 1:4 which describes how the Thessalonians have endured in their trials. Because the only period of time when Jesus Christ is explicitly said in the New Testament to suffer is during his passion, the author of 2 Thessalonians obviously does know of the death of Jesus and refers to it in his teaching.

The manner in which a particular writer addresses a problem is determined by the nature of that problem, and this explains why the cross and resurrection are absent from 2 Thessalonians. The particular eschatological problem addressed in 2 Thessalonians is that some are saying that 'the day of the Lord

---

[254]Kreitzer, *Jesus and God*, pp. 113-26, 168.

has already arrived', and it is difficult to see how the death and resurrection of Jesus Christ could be directly applied to correcting this problem. In 1 Thessalonians, however, the eschatological problem being addressed is the confusion of Christians about fellow believers who have died (4:13, 18), and thus Christ's conquering of death has direct relevance. When dealing with a topic not directly related to death and resurrection, such as the problem of the idle [*ataktoi*] in 1 Thessalonians (4:11-12; 5:14), Paul does not apply the death and resurrection of Jesus to the problem. In the same way the author of 2 Thessalonians need not make explicit reference to the death and resurrection of Jesus Christ when addressing the particular problems associated with 2 Thessalonians.

Likewise, there are large sections in Paul's undisputed letters in which he does not make explicit reference to Christ's sacrificial work even though it is clearly foundational for his gospel. For example, in 1 Corinthians 7:1-40, Paul deals with some of the problems associated with marriage in Corinth. This passage consists of 687 words, yet it contains no explicit reference to the death and resurrection of Jesus Christ and only one brief allusion: 'you were bought with a price' (7:23). In 1 Corinthians 12–14 Paul deals with the problem of the use and abuse of spiritual gifts, and the only possible reference to Christ's work is the brief statement of being 'baptized into one body' (1 Cor. 12:13). This section is 1275 words long, about 50 % longer than all of 2 Thessalonians. Thus Paul does not deal with every problem by focusing his attention on the death and resurrection of Jesus any more than the author of 2 Thessalonians does: it all depends on the topic at hand.

Therefore the argument that 2 Thessalonians is non-Pauline because of an absence of reference to the cross and resurrection is seen to be false; first, because Christ's suffering is referred to indirectly in 3:5; second, because the problems dealt with in 2 Thessalonians cannot be solved by direct reference to the death and resurrection of Jesus Christ; and third, because Paul himself does discuss some major topics with little or no reference to the death and resurrection of Jesus Christ.

C. *The Titles for Christ in 2 Thessalonians*

Jesus Christ is explicitly referred to by name twenty-three times in 2 Thessalonians, twenty-two of which include the title 'Lord'. The predominance of the title 'Lord' is not characteristic of the undisputed letters of Paul, and according to the disputers this means that Paul's theocentric emphasis is missing. Furthermore, they point out, in 2 Thessalonians the Christology is focused on the future. The disputers also note that the author, unlike Paul, avoids the independent use of the name of Jesus and the title 'Christ'.[255]

However, though the author of 2 Thessalonians never uses the name of Jesus

---

[255] Collins, *Letters*, pp. 226-32.

independently, nor the title 'Christ' very frequently, this does not prove the letter is not Pauline. In fact, Paul does not use the terminology for Jesus Christ in a numerically consistent pattern throughout his undisputed letters, as can be seen in the following chart. Instead, he chooses his titles for Jesus Christ by the topic or context he is addressing. An examination of all the explicit titles for Jesus Christ found in the Pauline corpus will help us to determine if the writer of 2 Thessalonians follows the Pauline pattern.

The Names of Jesus in the Pauline Corpus

	Paul	Rm	1C	2C	Gl	Ep	Pp	Cl	1Th	2Th	1T	2T	Tit	Pm
Ἰησοῦς simplex	16	2	1	7	1	1	1		3					
Χριστός simplex	206	33	45	37	21	27	17	18	3	1	1			3
Κύριος simplex	155*	17*	44*	18*	2	16	9	10	13	9	2	14*		1
Ἰησοῦς Χριστός	26	8	2	3	5	1	3				1	3		
Χριστός Ἰησοῦς	82	12	8	1	8	10	13	3	2		10	11	1	3
Κύριος Ἰησοῦς	25	3	5	3		1	1	1	6	4				1
Ἰησοῦς Κύριος	2	1	1											
Κύριος Χριστός	2	1						1						
Κύριος Ἰησοῦς Χριστός	49	5	8	4	3	6	4	1	5	9	2			2
Ἰησοῦς Χριστός Κύριος	5	3	1	1										
Χριστός Ἰησοῦς Χριστός	7	2				1		1			2	1		
total Ἰησοῦς	212	36	26	19	17	20	22	6	16	13	14	13	4	6
total Χριστός	377	64	64	46	37	45	37	24	10	10	15	13	4	8
total Κύριος	245	32	59	26	5	24	14	14	24	22	6	15		4
Total titles	575	87	115	74	40	63	48	35	32	23	17	27	4	10

Doctrinal Content of 2 Thessalonians

A close examination of this chart reveals an emphasis on 'Lord' in 2 Thessalonians (twenty-two out of twenty-three titles include 'Lord') that is not found in any of the other letters attributed to Paul.[256] However, it is also clear that there are no numerical norms found in the undisputed letters of Paul. If abnormal distribution of titles is used as a criterion for authenticity, then 2 Corinthians and 1 Thessalonians should be excluded because of the excessive use of Jesus ['Ἰησοῦς] simplex, while 1 Corinthians and 1 Thessalonians should be excluded for the excessive use of Lord [κύριος] simplex. In fact, every letter shows some kind of numeric peculiarity. Like 2 Thessalonians, 1 Thessalonians shows a strong emphasis on the use of the title 'Lord': twenty-four of the thirty-two times Jesus Christ is mentioned, his title includes the word 'Lord'. This similarity can be explained either as the writer of 2 Thessalonians imitating 1 Thessalonians or as Paul writing to a similar situation, in a similar manner, about the same topics. In fact, if 2 Thessalonians were to show a use of titles for Jesus that was very different from 1 Thessalonians, this could be used to show it was pseudonymous, for the letter presents itself as written soon after 1 Thessalonians, to a very similar situation. The only way to see if the terminology used by the writer of 2 Thessalonians is Pauline is to examine each title used in 2 Thessalonians and compare it to Paul's use of that same title in his undisputed letters.

1. 'Lord'

As can be seen in the chart, the title 'Lord' is the second most frequent way in which Paul refers to Jesus. Although this use is almost completely absent from Galatians and infrequent in Romans, 2 Thessalonians uses the title nine times; 1 Thessalonians, thirteen times; and 1 Corinthians, forty-four times. In 2 Thessalonians, the title 'Lord' refers to Jesus Christ as both the eschatological Lord and the sovereign saving Lord.

Jesus Christ is presented as the eschatological Lord in 1:9 and 2:2. In 1:9 the disobedient are punished by being 'shut out from the presence of the Lord', while in 2 Thessalonians 2:2, the great day is called 'the day of the Lord'. Likewise, in the undisputed epistles of Paul, the Lord will judge,[257] and Paul can refer to the final day as 'the day of the Lord', 'the day of the Lord Jesus', 'the day of our Lord Jesus Christ', 'the day of Christ', and 'the day of Christ

---

[256]This information is based on NA[26] and UBS[3]. The column labeled 'Paul' refers to the total from the whole Pauline corpus. The numbers which are starred (*) indicate that the word 'Lord' [κύριος] in that epistle is also used a number of times in OT quotations; these uses of 'Lord' have not been included in the numbers. (See Rom. 4:8; 9:28, 29; 10:13, 16; 11:3, 34; 12:19; 14:11; 15:11; 1 Cor. 1:31; 2:16; 3:20; 10:26; 14:21; 2 Cor. 6:17, 18; 10:17; 2 Tim. 2:19).

[257]Rom. 14:4; 1 Cor. 4:4-5; 1 Thess. 4:6.

Jesus'.[258] Therefore the presentation of Jesus Christ in 2 Thessalonians as the eschatological 'Lord' who will judge is the same as Paul presents.

The second way the author of 2 Thessalonians employs the title 'Lord' is in reference to the present sovereign saving activity of Jesus Christ in sending forth his word (3:1), guarding and strengthening (3:3) and loving (2:17) his people. The writer has 'confidence in the Lord' about the believers' obedience (3:4). It is the Lord who is sought to influence hearts and bring peace (3:5, 16). These same types of activities are attributed to the Lord in the undisputed letters of Paul. The 'word of the Lord' is the gospel message (1 Thess. 1:8), and the Lord strengthens his people (1 Thess. 3:12-13). It is the Lord whom Paul sees as sovereign over events (1 Cor. 4:19; 16:7). Paul is 'confident in the Lord' about the believers' obedience (Gal. 5:10). It is the Lord whom Paul seeks when he makes a personal request (2 Cor. 12:8). It is the Lord who is served and who commands his people (Rom. 12:11; 14:4-8; 1 Cor. 3:5; 6:13; 7:32, 34). When the sovereign power of Jesus Christ is stressed, it is not the name 'Jesus' or 'Christ' that is used by Paul or the writer of 2 Thessalonians, but the name 'Lord'.

Three verses in 2 Thessalonians use 'Lord' in a way that is not closely paralleled in the undisputed letters of Paul. In 2 Thessalonians 2:13, the writer refers to the 'brothers loved by the Lord'. This phrase is very similar to 1 Thessalonians 1:4, where Paul calls them 'brothers loved by God'. Disputers believe this is an excellent example of the writer of 2 Thessalonians copying from Paul and then inserting this emphasis on 'Lord'. However, Paul himself speaks often about the love of Jesus Christ,[259] almost as frequently as he does about the love of God.[260] Furthermore, the writer of 2 Thessalonians does speak of the love of God two times (2:16; 3:5). Since the writer of 2 Thessalonians expressly writes of the love of God, then there must be some contextual reason in 2:13 to specifically mention being 'loved by the Lord'. This is found in the writer's contrast of the believers' status with God and Christ with that of those who follow the opponent and are deluded by God (2:10-12). The author uses the title 'Lord' here because he has just focused on the eschatological Lord (1:9; 2:2), and the believers need to be reminded that the returning Lord loves them. Therefore within this context 'Lord' is perfectly understandable and does not show any post-Pauline characteristics.

The second passage which uses 'Lord' in a unique manner is 2 Thessalonians 3:3: 'the Lord is faithful'. Although Paul ascribes faithfulness to God in four

---

[258]'The day of the Lord'—1 Cor. 5:5; 1 Thess. 5:2; 'the day of the Lord Jesus'—2 Cor. 1:14; 'the day of our Lord Jesus Christ'—1 Cor. 1:8; 'the day of Christ'—Phil. 1:10; 2:16; and 'the day of Christ Jesus'—Phil. 1:6.

[259]Rom. 8:35, 37; Gal. 2:20; 2 Cor. 5:14; possibly also Phil. 2:1.

[260]Rom. 5:5, 8; 8:39; 9:25; 2 Cor. 9:7; 13:11, 13; 1 Thess. 1:4.

passages,[261] he more often uses 'faithfulness' [πιστός] to refer to particular individuals[262] or in a general sense.[263] Therefore since 'faithfulness' is attributed to both God and humans, it certainly would be appropriate for Paul to attribute it also to Jesus Christ. Most likely the title 'Lord' is used here because the author has already used 'Lord' throughout this section (3:1, 3, 4, 5). As was shown previously, this same clustering of the title 'Lord' is found in Paul's undisputed epistles.

The final passage in 2 Thessalonians that uses the title 'Lord' in a somewhat unusual way is 3:16: 'Now may the Lord of peace himself give you peace at all times and in every way. The Lord be with all of you.' The usual Pauline pattern calls God the Father the 'God of Peace'.[264] Peace is also said to come from both God the Father and the Lord Jesus Christ.[265] Colossians 3:15 speaks of the 'peace of Christ', while Ephesians 2:14-17 describes how Christ is our peace and has made peace. Although peace is associated throughout the whole Pauline corpus with both the Father and the Son, the phrase 'the Lord of peace' (2 Thess. 3:16) is unique. It is also rather awkward, for 'the Lord' is emphasized with the additional pronoun 'himself'. 'Peace' is also stressed by repetition, for the Lord of peace gives peace to his people. The Lord's presence is also promised. The emphasis on 'Lord' in this verse is clearly not accidental; nor can it possibly be construed as an attempt by the writer to imitate Paul, for it is unique. The author's stress on the Lord giving peace is understandable in the context of 2 Thessalonians as a whole. The Thessalonians needed peace: external peace from suffering, which would be brought by the coming of the Lord Jesus (1:3-6); peace concerning the arrival of the day of the Lord (2:1-12); and peace within the congregation because some members were not fully recognizing the authority of the Lord Jesus Christ (3:6-13). They needed this peace 'at all times and in every way' (3:16). Therefore this passage neither enhances nor detracts from the case for authenticity; rather it simply reiterates the author's concerns throughout his letter.

2. 'The Lord Jesus Christ'

The title 'the Lord Jesus Christ' is the most common triplex title found in the Pauline corpus. It is most frequently found in letter openings and closings and

---

[261] 1 Cor. 1:9; 10:13; 2 Cor. 1:18; 1 Thess. 5:24.

[262] Timothy—1 Cor. 4:17; Paul—1 Cor. 7:25; Abraham—Gal. 3:9; see also Tychicus—Eph. 6:21 and Col. 4:7; Epaphras—Col. 1:7; Onesimus—Col. 4:9.

[263] 1 Cor. 4:2; 2 Cor. 6:15; see also Eph. 1:1; Col. 1:2.

[264] See Rom. 15:33; 16:20; 1 Cor. 14:33; 2 Cor. 13:11; Phil. 4:9; 1 Thess. 5:23.

[265] See Rom. 1:7; 1 Cor. 1:3; 2 Cor. 1:2; Phil. 1:2; see also 2 Thess. 1:2; Eph. 1:2; 1 Tim. 1:2; 2 Tim 1:2; Titus 1:4.

in prayers.²⁶⁶ In most occurrences of this title in 2 Thessalonians, it is used in this same fashion (1:1, 2, 12; 2:16; 3:18). This title also commonly refers to the returning Lord.²⁶⁷ The writer of 2 Thessalonians uses the title in a similar manner (2:1, 14). A third use of this title is to focus on one aspect of salvation from Jesus Christ, such as grace, justification, or reconciliation.²⁶⁸ The title is also used when a strong appeal is made, such as in 1 Corinthians 1:10, where Paul says, 'I appeal to you in the name of the Lord Jesus Christ'. This usage is almost identical to that in 2 Thessalonians 3:6 and 12. Therefore the writer of 2 Thessalonians uses the most common triplex title for Jesus Christ in a manner exactly like Paul.

Second Thessalonians 2:16 is somewhat unusual in that 'our Lord Jesus Christ' is mentioned before 'God our Father'. However, when the verse is examined carefully, this does not put a greater stress on the Lord Jesus Christ over the Father; in fact, just the opposite is true. Both Jesus Christ and the Father encourage and strengthen the believers (2:17), but it is only 'God our Father' who is said to have 'loved us and by his grace gave us eternal encouragement and good hope'. Although the order of the persons mentioned is switched from the usual order found in Paul's undisputed letters and in 2 Thessalonians, nevertheless the focus is still on the work of the Father.

The only real question that arises from the use of this title is whether or not the writer of 2 Thessalonians identifies 'the Lord Jesus Christ' as God himself in 1:12. This identification is grammatically possible because there is no article before 'Lord Jesus Christ' in this verse, and this links the Lord Jesus Christ with God.²⁶⁹ It is not theologically impossible that Paul would make this identification, as Romans 9:5 shows. However, deity is most likely not being directly ascribed to Jesus Christ in this verse because (1) it closely parallels 2 Thessalonians 1:2, where the two persons are distinguished; and (2) the pronoun 'our' separates the two titles.²⁷⁰

3. 'The Lord Jesus'

The title 'Lord Jesus' is used four times in 2 Thessalonians, and in three of those four instances it is used within tradition sections (1:7, 8; 2:8). The title 'Lord Jesus' is also common within the undisputed letters of Paul and is frequently used within tradition such as Romans 10:9, 'If you confess with your mouth the Lord Jesus', and 1 Corinthians 11:23, 'The Lord Jesus on the night

---

²⁶⁶See Rom. 15:30; 1 Cor. 1:2, 3; 15:57; 2 Cor. 1:2, 3; 13:13; Gal. 1:3; 6:18; Phil. 1:2; 4:23; 1 Thess. 1:1, 3; 5:9, 28; Phlm. 3, 25; see also Eph. 1:2, 3; 5:20; 6:23-24; Col. 1:3.
²⁶⁷1 Cor. 1:7, 8; Phil. 3:20; 1 Thess. 5:9; see also 1 Tim. 6:14.
²⁶⁸Rom. 5:1, 11; 1 Cor. 6:11; 8:6; 2 Cor. 8:9; 6:14; Phil. 2:11.
²⁶⁹κατὰ τὴν χάριν τοῦ θεοῦ ἡμῶν καὶ Κυρίου Ἰησοῦ Χριστοῦ
²⁷⁰Collins, *Letters,* pp. 230-31.

passages,[261] he more often uses 'faithfulness' [πιστός] to refer to particular individuals[262] or in a general sense.[263] Therefore since 'faithfulness' is attributed to both God and humans, it certainly would be appropriate for Paul to attribute it also to Jesus Christ. Most likely the title 'Lord' is used here because the author has already used 'Lord' throughout this section (3:1, 3, 4, 5). As was shown previously, this same clustering of the title 'Lord' is found in Paul's undisputed epistles.

The final passage in 2 Thessalonians that uses the title 'Lord' in a somewhat unusual way is 3:16: 'Now may the Lord of peace himself give you peace at all times and in every way. The Lord be with all of you.' The usual Pauline pattern calls God the Father the 'God of Peace'.[264] Peace is also said to come from both God the Father and the Lord Jesus Christ.[265] Colossians 3:15 speaks of the 'peace of Christ', while Ephesians 2:14-17 describes how Christ is our peace and has made peace. Although peace is associated throughout the whole Pauline corpus with both the Father and the Son, the phrase 'the Lord of peace' (2 Thess. 3:16) is unique. It is also rather awkward, for 'the Lord' is emphasized with the additional pronoun 'himself'. 'Peace' is also stressed by repetition, for the Lord of peace gives peace to his people. The Lord's presence is also promised. The emphasis on 'Lord' in this verse is clearly not accidental; nor can it possibly be construed as an attempt by the writer to imitate Paul, for it is unique. The author's stress on the Lord giving peace is understandable in the context of 2 Thessalonians as a whole. The Thessalonians needed peace: external peace from suffering, which would be brought by the coming of the Lord Jesus (1:3-6); peace concerning the arrival of the day of the Lord (2:1-12); and peace within the congregation because some members were not fully recognizing the authority of the Lord Jesus Christ (3:6-13). They needed this peace 'at all times and in every way' (3:16). Therefore this passage neither enhances nor detracts from the case for authenticity; rather it simply reiterates the author's concerns throughout his letter.

2. 'The Lord Jesus Christ'

The title 'the Lord Jesus Christ' is the most common triplex title found in the Pauline corpus. It is most frequently found in letter openings and closings and

---

[261] 1 Cor. 1:9; 10:13; 2 Cor. 1:18; 1 Thess. 5:24.

[262] Timothy—1 Cor. 4:17; Paul—1 Cor. 7:25; Abraham—Gal. 3:9; see also Tychicus—Eph. 6:21 and Col. 4:7; Epaphras—Col. 1:7; Onesimus—Col. 4:9.

[263] 1 Cor. 4:2; 2 Cor. 6:15; see also Eph. 1:1; Col. 1:2.

[264] See Rom. 15:33; 16:20; 1 Cor. 14:33; 2 Cor. 13:11; Phil. 4:9; 1 Thess. 5:23.

[265] See Rom. 1:7; 1 Cor. 1:3; 2 Cor. 1:2; Phil. 1:2; see also 2 Thess. 1:2; Eph. 1:2; 1 Tim. 1:2; 2 Tim 1:2; Titus 1:4.

in prayers.²⁶⁶ In most occurrences of this title in 2 Thessalonians, it is used in this same fashion (1:1, 2, 12; 2:16; 3:18). This title also commonly refers to the returning Lord.²⁶⁷ The writer of 2 Thessalonians uses the title in a similar manner (2:1, 14). A third use of this title is to focus on one aspect of salvation from Jesus Christ, such as grace, justification, or reconciliation.²⁶⁸ The title is also used when a strong appeal is made, such as in 1 Corinthians 1:10, where Paul says, 'I appeal to you in the name of the Lord Jesus Christ'. This usage is almost identical to that in 2 Thessalonians 3:6 and 12. Therefore the writer of 2 Thessalonians uses the most common triplex title for Jesus Christ in a manner exactly like Paul.

Second Thessalonians 2:16 is somewhat unusual in that 'our Lord Jesus Christ' is mentioned before 'God our Father'. However, when the verse is examined carefully, this does not put a greater stress on the Lord Jesus Christ over the Father; in fact, just the opposite is true. Both Jesus Christ and the Father encourage and strengthen the believers (2:17), but it is only 'God our Father' who is said to have 'loved us and by his grace gave us eternal encouragement and good hope'. Although the order of the persons mentioned is switched from the usual order found in Paul's undisputed letters and in 2 Thessalonians, nevertheless the focus is still on the work of the Father.

The only real question that arises from the use of this title is whether or not the writer of 2 Thessalonians identifies 'the Lord Jesus Christ' as God himself in 1:12. This identification is grammatically possible because there is no article before 'Lord Jesus Christ' in this verse, and this links the Lord Jesus Christ with God.²⁶⁹ It is not theologically impossible that Paul would make this identification, as Romans 9:5 shows. However, deity is most likely not being directly ascribed to Jesus Christ in this verse because (1) it closely parallels 2 Thessalonians 1:2, where the two persons are distinguished; and (2) the pronoun 'our' separates the two titles.²⁷⁰

3. 'The Lord Jesus'

The title 'Lord Jesus' is used four times in 2 Thessalonians, and in three of those four instances it is used within tradition sections (1:7, 8; 2:8). The title 'Lord Jesus' is also common within the undisputed letters of Paul and is frequently used within tradition such as Romans 10:9, 'If you confess with your mouth the Lord Jesus', and 1 Corinthians 11:23, 'The Lord Jesus on the night

---

²⁶⁶See Rom. 15:30; 1 Cor. 1:2, 3; 15:57; 2 Cor. 1:2, 3; 13:13; Gal. 1:3; 6:18; Phil. 1:2; 4:23; 1 Thess. 1:1, 3; 5:9, 28; Phlm. 3, 25; see also Eph. 1:2, 3; 5:20; 6:23-24; Col. 1:3.

²⁶⁷1 Cor. 1:7, 8; Phil. 3:20; 1 Thess. 5:9; see also 1 Tim. 6:14.

²⁶⁸Rom. 5:1, 11; 1 Cor. 6:11; 8:6; 2 Cor. 8:9; 6:14; Phil. 2:11.

²⁶⁹κατὰ τὴν χάριν τοῦ θεοῦ ἡμῶν καὶ Κυρίου Ἰησοῦ Χριστοῦ

²⁷⁰Collins, *Letters,* pp. 230-31.

he was betrayed took bread . . . .'[271] This second passage also contains an eschatological emphasis, for it ends in v. 26: 'you proclaim the Lord's death until he comes'. In addition to these instances, the title 'Lord Jesus' is used as a formula in an interchangeable way with the title 'Lord Jesus Christ'.[272] Paul can stress the importance of the Christians coming together when he speaks of them being 'assembled in the name of the Lord Jesus' (1 Cor. 5:4). This usage is much like 2 Thessalonians 1:12, where the author prays that 'the name of our Lord Jesus may be glorified'. Therefore the author of 2 Thessalonians uses the title 'Lord Jesus' in a manner almost identical to Paul.

4. 'Christ'

The title 'Christ' is used only once in 2 Thessalonians, and its meaning has already been discussed. As was shown, this title found in the phrase 'the perseverance of Christ' (2 Thess. 3:5) is either a subjective genitive or a genitive of quality. Either way, it focuses on Christ's example in his suffering, which is to be emulated by the believers. This use of 'Christ' to refer the sacrificial work of Christ is identical to Paul's use of the term.[273]

D. *Conclusion on Christology*

The transfer of attributes from Yahweh to Jesus Christ in an eschatological context is a practice that Paul himself regularly employed in his undisputed letters. The relative absence of the cross and resurrection from 2 Thessalonians is consistent with Paul's approach to certain topics where the death and resurrection of Jesus are not explicitly mentioned. The use of titles for Jesus Christ within the letters of Paul shows that he used the titles, not in a numerically consistent pattern throughout his letters, but rather, according to the topic he was addressing. The use of the titles for Jesus Christ in 2 Thessalonians follows the same patterns for content as do the undisputed letters of Paul. Therefore the Christology of 2 Thessalonians actually strengthens the case for authenticity, for the writer consistently uses the terminology used by Paul himself throughout his letters.

IV. Soteriology

Those who dispute the authenticity of 2 Thessalonians claim that the soteriology of the letter is contrary to Pauline doctrine on the grounds that the gospel of grace which is so central to Pauline theology is missing and that the kingdom of God is viewed as merited.[274] Furthermore, they suggest that the

---

[271] See also Rom. 14:14; 1 Cor. 12:3; 1 Thess. 2:15; 4:1, 2.
[272] Rom. 16:20; 1 Cor. 5:5; 16:23; 2 Cor. 1:14; 4:14; 1 Thess. 3:13.
[273] Collins, *Letters*, p. 227.
[274] As per Hilgenfeld, P. W. Schmidt, Braun, Laub.

author of 2 Thessalonians uses a definition for 'faith' different from that used by Paul, a 'faith' that must be defined as faithfulness to the truth.[275] Because the disputers claim that these differences in the two concepts, grace and faith, show that 2 Thessalonians is a pseudonymous letter, it is necessary to examine whether they truly are different from Paul's usage.

A. *Grace*

The author of 2 Thessalonians uses the word 'grace' four times (1:2, 12; 2:16; 3:18). In 1:2 and 3:18, the author uses 'grace' in the standard opening and closing found in all of Paul's undisputed letters. In 1:12, the author offers a prayer and concludes it with 'according to the grace of our God and the Lord Jesus Christ', thus showing that he views his requests as dependent on the grace of God. These requests include being counted worthy of their calling, accomplishing their good works and good purposes, glorifying the name of Jesus, and being glorified in him; in fact, according to the author, the whole of the Christian life is dependent on the grace of God. In 2:16 the author offers a prayer-wish in which he describes what God has done for the Thessalonian Christians: God 'loved us and by his grace gave us eternal encouragement and good hope'. This prayer, although focused upon the future, is based upon the grace which has already been given [δούς] to the Thessalonian Christians. Their expectation for the future, then, is not a result of their own efforts but is given to them by God's grace.

The passage usually focused upon by disputers as showing a merited salvation is 1:5-10. Most defenders of authenticity have linked this passage with Philippians 1:28b-30, where Paul says, 'This is a sign to them that they will be destroyed, but that you will be saved—and that by God. For it has been granted to you on behalf of Christ not only to believe on him, but also to suffer for him, since you are going through the same struggle you saw I had, and now hear that I still have'. There are many obvious verbal and thematic links between the two passages. Bassler has challenged the understanding that these passages are mutually interpretive and believes this conclusion has been drawn because of a presupposition of the authenticity of 2 Thessalonians.[276] She believes that the 'sign' in Philippians 1:28 is the church's constancy under affliction, while the 'sign' in 2 Thessalonians 1:5 is the suffering and affliction of the Thessalonians.[277] According to Bassler, closer parallels are found in *Psalms of Solomon* 13:9-10, 2 Maccabees 6:12-16, and especially, *2 Baruch* 13:3-16. From these parallels she lists four elements of a theology of suffering (*Leidenstheologie*) which these books have in common with 2 Thessalonians

---

[275] As per Petersen, Littleton, Holland, P. Müller.

[276] Jouette M. Bassler, 'The Enigmatic Sign: 2 Thessalonians 1:5', *CBQ* 46 (1984), pp. 496-510.

[277] Bassler, 'Enigmatic Sign', p. 499.

1:5-10: (1) God's justice is strictly retributive; (2) the present suffering of God's people is a chastisement or atonement in order to make them worthy for their future inheritance; (3) the eschatological future will see an inversion of the present situation for the elect and the godless; and (4) the present afflictions of the elect show that God has accepted them because he is exercising his justice upon them now so that they will not be punished in the future. She believes that this interpretation is contrary to Paul's theology of grace.[278]

There are a number of problems with Bassler's understanding as it applies to 2 Thessalonians 1, particularly with the second and fourth points. First, she does not distinguish between God's chastisement of his people and the idea of people having to atone for their own sins. Paul recognizes that the Lord disciplines his people directly (1 Cor. 11:30-32), possibly involving sickness and even death, but never does Paul speak about atoning for one's own sins. Nor does the author of 2 Thessalonians link the suffering which the readers are enduring to anything they have done wrong. In fact, they are commended for their faith, love, and perseverance (1:3-4). Their tribulation is not due to anything they have done; rather, responsibility for their afflictions is upon those who afflict them (1:6). Therefore their suffering is in no way to be understood to atone for their own wrongdoing.

Second, Bassler fails to show that the verb καταξιόω means 'to make worthy'—an absolutely critical point in order for her interpretation to work in 2 Thessalonians 1:5. Although she acknowledges that this verb [καταξιόω] can mean either *deem* worthy or *make* worthy, she bases her interpretation on 'to make worthy'.[279] The verb is used only three other times in the New Testament. In Luke 20:35 Jesus, in answer to questions about marriage and the resurrection, speaks about those 'who are considered worthy of taking part in that age' but never explains why they might be considered worthy. In Acts 5:41, after being flogged for the sake of the gospel, the apostles react by 'rejoicing because they had been counted worthy of suffering disgrace for the Name'. In this context it is clear that the word means *deemed* or *counted* worthy, not *made* worthy. This definition is also clearly found in Josephus (*Ant.* 4.281), Diodorus of Sicily (2.60.3) and *2 Maccabees* 18:3.[280] In 2 Thessalonians 1:5, before talking about being deemed or made worthy, the writer introduces the concept of the righteous judgment of God. This righteous judgment refers to the future because the content of vv. 6-10 is the future day of judgment.[281] Immediately following the statement concerning the righteous judgment, the writer states the purpose of this righteous judgment by using the articular infinitive of the verb. Therefore

---

[278] Bassler, 'Enigmatic Sign', p. 505.
[279] Bassler, 'Enigmatic Sign', p. 499, n. 8.
[280] Wanamaker, *Thessalonians*, p. 233, says the verb must mean 'to consider worthy' because with only one possible exception (*Diogn.* 9.1) there are no known examples where the word means 'to make worthy'.
[281] Best, *Thessalonians*, p. 255.

the purpose of the righteous judgment in the future will be to declare the worthiness of the Thessalonian Christians, and God will punish those who afflict them. God's future judgment does not make them worthy but declares that these who have been afflicted are worthy.

Third, Bassler makes too much of the differences between the 'sign' in Philippians 1:28-30, which she identifies as constancy, and the sign in 2 Thessalonians 1:5, which she identifies as suffering. Although the sign in Philippians 1:28 initially seems to arise from the idea of the constancy of the Philippians, the focus of the passage is actually on the fact that they have been granted to suffer for Christ (1:29), and this suffering is like that which Paul himself is going through (1:30). Furthermore, the sign in 2 Thessalonians 1:5 can refer back not only to the word 'afflictions' but also to the entire sentence, which includes the Thessalonians' faith and endurance in persecution and trials. Milligan states that 'it is more in keeping with classical usage to regard such noun phrases as accusatives, in apposition to the whole idea of the foregoing sentence (cf. Rom. viii.3, xii.1, 1 Tim. ii. 6)'.[282] Therefore the sign in 2 Thessalonians 1:5 does not show that the Thessalonian Christians are suffering in order to make them worthy but distinguishes Christians from non-Christians. The Christians who are presently persevering in afflictions will be deemed worthy on that final day.

Finally, Bassler's idea does not take into account the use of 'grace' within 2 Thessalonians. The glorifying of Jesus is according to grace (1:10, 12), as is the whole future expectation (2:16). Nor does she take into account the way in which the Thessalonians came to be part of the group who are afflicted and promised rest. The author of 2 Thessalonians explicitly repeats who will be given relief: those who have 'believed' (1:10).

Bassler's understanding of 2 Thessalonians 1:5, that the suffering of the believers was in order for them to atone for their own sins and as a result not receive any future judgment, cannot be sustained from the text of 2 Thessalonians. She fails to show (1) that καταξιόω means *make* worthy rather than the more probable *deem* worthy; (2) that the believers are suffering for their own sins rather than the afflicters being responsible for the suffering; (3) that Philippians 1:28-30 and 2 Thessalonians 1:5-10 refer to different topics rather than both discussing persevering in suffering; and (4) that the Christians are made worthy by their suffering rather than by 'believing' (1:10) and by the grace of God (1:12; 2:16).

Therefore, 2 Thessalonians does not teach a merited salvation but promises future inheritance of the kingdom of God to all the believers (1:5, 10), as Paul himself taught the inheritance of the kingdom in the future by all who believe.[283]

---

[282]Milligan, *Thessalonians*, p. 88.
[283]See 1 Cor. 6:9-10; 15:50; Gal. 5:21.

B. Faith

The second major area of soteriology which the disputers believe disproves the authenticity of 2 Thessalonians concerns the definition of 'faith'. Holland states that throughout 2 Thessalonians the word πίστις means 'faithfulness' to the tradition,[284] in contrast to Paul's usual definition of 'faith'.[285]

In 2 Thessalonians 1:3-4 the author commends the Thessalonians for their faith [πίστις], which he says is growing, as is their love. The definition of 'faith', rather than of 'faithfulness', fits this context more easily, very much like 2 Corinthians 10:15, where Paul speaks about the Corinthians' faith growing.[286] The author of 2 Thessalonians continues his commendation by boasting about their faith and perseverance. Since πίστις in v. 3 means 'faith', the same meaning is likely to be true in v. 4.[287] There is no reason in this context to interpret πίστις as 'faithfulness', which has a meaning similar to perseverance; rather, it is more likely that the author is commending two virtues, faith and perseverance, and not just one using two different words. In 1:11 the author prays that God may fulfill their 'work of faith in power'.[288] Once again it is probable that πίστις means 'faith', for just previous to this verse the author has used the verb 'to believe' to describe the reaction of the Thessalonians, and thus the phrase would mean 'activity inspired by faith'.[289] In 2:13 he commends the readers for 'belief in the truth'.[290] To translate this instead as 'faithfulness to the truth' would be awkward, and since the author has been correcting doctrinal error in 2:1-12, the concept of believing the truth fits the context. In the final instance of πίστις in the letter (3:2), the author requests prayer for deliverance 'from wicked and evil men, for not everyone has faith'. The definition of πίστις in this context must be faith, not faithfulness, for the writer is contrasting not faithful and unfaithful Christians, but belief and unbelief as the gospel message is spread. Immediately following this, the author remarks, 'but the Lord is faithful' [πιστός]. This might be used to say that the definition of πίστις in the preceding verse should be faithfulness. However, even though there may be a play on words, it does not require the definition of πίστις to be changed.[291] In fact, by using the word πιστός and not πίστις in this context, the author distinguishes between the two. In 2 Thessalonians πιστός is never used to refer to the Thessalonians' response. In addition, the author stresses the

---

[284] Holland, *Tradition*, p. 90.

[285] According to Arndt and Gingrich, *Lexicon*, p. 668, Paul usually uses the definition 'faith', but he can also mean 'faithfulness' (see Rom. 3:3; Gal. 5:22).

[286] Wanamaker, *Thessalonians*, p. 217.

[287] Milligan, *Thessalonians*, pp. 86-87.

[288] ἔργον πίστεως ἐν δυνάμει

[289] Milligan, *Thessalonians*, p. 94.

[290] πίστει ἀληθείας

[291] Marshall, *Thessalonians*, p. 215.

idea of 'believing' when he repeats the verb found in the tradition of 1:6-10 ('all those who have believed') and says this describes the Thessalonian Christians' reaction as well ('because our testimony to you was believed'). Therefore in every context in the letter the idea of 'faith' fits better than 'faithfulness'.

The content of 'faith' in 2 Thessalonians is the 'witness' of the missionaries (1:10) and 'truth' (2:13). As was already shown in the previous chapter, in the section on the terminology of tradition, Paul uses 'witness' in a manner synonymous with 'gospel' (1 Cor. 1:6; 2:1). It is also relevant to note that Paul repeatedly makes mention of 'truth' in reference to one's response to the gospel. Unbelievers 'change the truth' (Rom. 1:25), 'disobey the truth' (Rom. 2:8), and 'hold the truth in unrighteousness' (Rom 1:18), whereas in a positive sense 'the word of God' is equivalent to truth (2 Cor. 4:2), the message is 'the word of truth' (2 Cor. 6:7), Paul holds to 'the truth of the gospel' (Gal. 2:5, 14), and believers are expected to 'obey the truth' (Gal. 5:7). Therefore the linking of 'truth' and 'witness' with 'faith' is entirely consistent with Paul.

Disputers interpret calling and election, two other doctrines in 2 Thessalonians which are closely linked with the response of faith, as exhibiting non-Pauline characteristics. The doctrine of election is seen in 2 Thessalonians 2:13: 'God chose you to be saved through the sanctifying work of the Spirit and through belief in the truth.' Wrede concludes that because the writer of 2 Thessalonians uses a different verb [αἱρέω] for choosing than Paul uses [ἐκλέγομαι], the writer therefore cannot be Paul.[292] It is true that Paul does not use this verb [αἱρέω] elsewhere in his undisputed writings for election to salvation; however, he is familiar with this verb, for he uses it in Philippians 1:22. Furthermore, the verb Paul uses for choosing [ἐκλέγομαι] appears only three times—and in only one passage (1 Cor. 1:27-28)—in the undisputed letters.[293] Thus Paul uses a variety of terms when he refers to God's sovereignty in salvation, and the use of another word cannot be considered a sign that Paul did not write 2 Thessalonians. Certainly the concept of election is a part of Pauline theology.

'Calling' is also a part of the soteriology of 2 Thessalonians (1:11; 2:14). In Paul, it is God who calls, and this appears to be specifically related to the time of conversion.[294] The purpose of this calling is for freedom, fellowship, peace and worthy living.[295] This calling also has a future perspective, for it calls one

---

[292] Wrede, *Echtheit*, p. 75.

[293] The only other time this verb is used in the Pauline corpus is in Ephesians 1:4, which speaks of God's election of Christians before the foundation of the world. Paul uses the noun 'election' [ἐκλογή] in Rom. 9:11; 11:5, 7, 28; 1 Thess. 1:4 and the adjective 'elect' [ἐκλεκτός] in Rom. 8:33; 16:13 (see also Col. 3:12; 1 Tim. 5:21; 2 Tim. 2:10 and Titus 1:1).

[294] Rom. 8:30; 9:24; 1 Cor. 1:9; 7:17-24; Gal. 1:6, 15; 5:8.

[295] Freedom—Gal. 5:13; fellowship—1 Cor. 1:9; peace—1 Cor. 7:15; see also Col. 3:15; worthy lives—1 Thess. 2:12; 4:7; see also Eph. 4:1; 2 Tim. 1:9.

into the kingdom and to glory.[296] Therefore according to Paul, God's call brings the individual all the benefits and blessings of the gospel. Second Thessalonians follows this same pattern, for the believers were called by God when the gospel was proclaimed (2:14). In 1:11 the author prays that they may be considered worthy of God's call, focusing on the future result of God's call. Paul, too, saw that the call of God was directly linked to the future, 'for those he called, he also justified; those he justified, he also glorified'.[297] Therefore the future consequence of the call of God found in 2 Thessalonians 1:11 is like the consequences Paul draws for the future in his undisputed letters.

C. *Conclusion on Soteriology*

Because the problems addressed by the author of 2 Thessalonians have to do primarily with eschatology and imitation, he does not focus upon soteriology. However, when the letter is read carefully, it is clear that the author does not present a doctrine of a merited kingdom, nor does he change the definition of 'faith' from that normally found in the undisputed letters of Paul. Instead, he assumes that salvation is a gift of God's grace (2:13-14) which is received by all who believe (1:10). There is a focus on the future consequences of salvation, but this is to be expected in a letter addressing the eschatological problems that 2 Thessalonians expounds. These future consequences are also found in the undisputed letters of Paul. Therefore even though these doctrines are not the focus of 2 Thessalonians, the inclusion of these doctrines strengthens the case for the authenticity of the letter.

V. Doctrine and the Authenticity of 2 Thessalonians

This study of the doctrinal content of 2 Thessalonians has primarily focused on eschatology and imitation. Although these subjects are the focus of attention, two other doctrinal themes permeate the letter: Christology and soteriology. Disputers have seen the hand of a pseudepigrapher formulating these doctrines in 2 Thessalonians, yet an examination of each doctrine reveals that the author of 2 Thessalonians is entirely consistent with Paul yet shows no slavish or mechanical dependence on any letter of Paul.

The primary objection raised by disputers concerning eschatology in 2 Thessalonians is the teaching about the parousia—its delay, its being preceded by preliminary signs, and the absence of joy in referring to it. However, as we have seen, 2 Thessalonians is not based on a theology of delay, it does not present a list of preliminary signs that would enable one to calculate the time of the end, nor is it devoid of all joy. While it is true that 2 Thessalonians does not focus upon the death and resurrection of Christ as Paul does in other

---

[296] 1 Thess. 2:12.
[297] Rom. 8:30; 1 Thess. 2:12.

eschatological passages (e.g. 1 Thess. 4:14 or 1 Cor. 15:3-12, 20-28), this is simply because of the nature of the problems discussed in each passage. The problem in 1 Corinthians 15 concerns whether the dead will be raised (15:12), and the problem in 1 Thessalonians 4 is grief for believers who have died (4:13, 18). The problem in 2 Thessalonians concerns suffering (1:4) and the false teaching that the day of the Lord has arrived (2:2). It requires a different answer, with more focus on the parousia of Christ and the final defeat of the forces of evil, yet even in 2 Thessalonians the readers are directed toward the perseverance of Christ (3:5). As he persevered in suffering, so must they. The eschatology of 2 Thessalonians shows a day when Christ will return to save his people and to judge Satan and all the forces of evil. At that time, unknown and incalculable, the believers will receive rest and give praise (1: 7, 10). This teaching is consistent with that found throughout Paul's undisputed epistles.

The teaching concerning imitation is also consistent with Paul's own teaching. The focus on following the example of the missionaries is also found in Paul's letters, and Christ himself is to be emulated in his perseverance (3:5). Elsewhere Paul refers not only to his work (1 Cor. 4:12) but to his whole life as an example to be followed (Phil. 4:9). The disorderly behavior or idleness in 2 Thessalonians 3 did not arise from eschatological enthusiasm but was a problem anticipated by the missionaries that had become more severe since the writing of 1 Thessalonians. The idea that the command to imitate Paul would have developed only at a later time does not match what is explicitly found in Paul's undisputed letters. Furthermore, it is much easier to imitate someone who has recently been known than someone who has been dead for a number of years.

The Christology of 2 Thessalonians is also like that found in Paul's undisputed letters. Although 2 Thessalonians uses the term 'Lord' more often than the other letters in the Pauline corpus, it is used consistently with the way Paul uses the terminology. Because Paul always uses terminology for Jesus Christ that applies to the particular topic he is addressing, each letter exhibits a numeric peculiarity dependent on the topic Paul is addressing, and this is exactly what is found in 2 Thessalonians. Paul also displays the same tendency to transfer the attributes of Yahweh to Jesus Christ in eschatological contexts as does 2 Thessalonians. Therefore a thorough examination of the Christology of 2 Thessalonians and of Paul strengthens the case for the authenticity of the letter.

The soteriology, although not central in the letter, shows a gospel of grace which is received by all who believe. It does focus upon the future aspects of this salvation, but not in an unpauline manner.

The major teaching in 2 Thessalonians, which concerns eschatology and imitation (1:5-10; 2:1-12; 3:6-15), is entirely consistent with Paul's teaching in his undisputed letters. The Christology and soteriology throughout the letter are like Paul's, yet the author's content and style both show that he did not merely copy these ideas from Paul's other letters. Therefore the eschatology, imitation, Christology, and soteriology in 2 Thessalonians actually strengthen the case for authenticity.

Chapter 5
The Literary Character of 2 Thessalonians

The starting point for nearly all of the modern challenges to the authenticity of 2 Thessalonians has been the perceived literary dependence of 2 Thessalonians upon 1 Thessalonians. In addition to this perceived dependence, disputers have noted a number of literary peculiarities which distinguish 2 Thessalonians from the undisputed letters of Paul. This chapter will show that the literary peculiarities and the structure of 2 Thessalonians as a letter are best understood if the document is an authentic epistle from Paul.

I. The Overall Structure of 2 Thessalonians

As was seen in the first chapter, three possible explanations for the overall literary character of 2 Thessalonians are feasible: (1) the author of 2 Thessalonians had a copy of 1 Thessalonians and imitated it in writing 2 Thessalonians (Wrede); (2) Paul reread a rough draft of 1 Thessalonians before writing 2 Thessalonians (Zahn);[1] and (3) a few months after writing 1 Thessalonians, Paul received more information about problems in Thessalonica and sent a brief supplementary letter (2 Thess.), the similarities of which are due to the kerygma, apostolic paraenesis, and epistolary genre (Rigaux). Because the second possibility is impossible to defend from the letter itself, the only defendable options are (1) and (3). Because Wrede's argument that 2 Thessalonians is literarily dependent on 1 Thessalonians is the starting point for most of the disputers, it is necessary to examine his argument in detail to see if literary dependence is probable. His argument depends not only on individual parallels but also on the structure of 2 Thessalonians as a whole; therefore it is beneficial to begin by examining the structure of 2 Thessalonians.

A. *Rhetorical and Epistolary Analyses of 2 Thessalonians*

In recent years a number of specialized studies focusing on epistolary and rhetorical analyses have shown that 2 Thessalonians must be viewed as a literary unit in its own right. Although these two forms of analysis are not as free from subjectivity as some of their proponents claim,[2] they do contribute to

---

[1] On the use of rough drafts see also John L. White, *Light from Ancient Letters* (Philadelphia: Fortress, 1986), p. 217.

[2] Jewett, *Correspondence,* p. 68, stressing the advantages of rhetorical analysis, says, 'outlines of Pauline letters that seek to reveal logical or thematic developments suffer from theological biases that are difficult to control', and 'the difficulty with studies of epistolary form is that the component parts are difficult to relate to each other'.

understanding the literary features of 2 Thessalonians.

The benefit of rhetorical analysis is that it helps to determine the purpose of a particular writing and to explain the flow and development of the argument used by the author. At the time of Paul, many handbooks of rhetoric were readily available, and rhetoric was taught throughout the Roman Empire. George Kennedy compares rhetorical education at the time of Paul with secondary school education today.[3] Thus it is probable that Paul not only knew rhetorical techniques but also made use of them. Three types of rhetoric have been distinguished which could be applied to all forms of discourse: (1) *judicial*—in which an author attempts to persuade his audience to make a judgement about events in the past; (2) *deliberative*—in which an author attempts to persuade his audience to take some action in the future; and (3) *epideictic*—in which the author holds or reaffirms some point of view in the present, such as celebrating or denouncing some person or quality.[4] The difficulty in assigning a document to one of these categories is that it is possible to have elements of one type of rhetoric within a document of basically another type.[5] The weakness of rhetorical analysis is that it can too easily ignore grammatical detail in order to fit all the appropriate categories into a particular document.

Epistolary analysis is also helpful because it focuses on grammatical characteristics and forms common to all letters. Whereas rhetorical analysis focuses on the flow of the argument and the type of argument, epistolary analysis focuses on the structure used to convey the argument. Its weakness is that the purpose and manner of argument may be obscured by concentrating on the form of the letter, and thus the two techniques are best used together to enhance the understanding of a letter. In order to understand 2 Thessalonians as a unit and yet not be limited by the weaknesses of using only one methodology, it is helpful to outline 2 Thessalonians using both rhetorical and epistolary analyses. The following outlines, which apply both methodologies to 2 Thessalonians, show that 2 Thessalonians has clearly defined epistolary and rhetorical categories and that the author, whether Paul or a later pseudepigrapher, was skilled in using epistolary and rhetorical techniques.

---

[3]George A. Kennedy, *New Testament Interpretation through Rhetorical Criticism* (Chapel Hill: University of North Carolina Press, 1984), p. 9.

[4]Kennedy, *New Testament Interpretation*, p. 19.

[5]Kennedy, *New Testament Interpretation*, p. 45.

Rhetorical and Epistolary Analyses of 2 Thessalonians

Rhetorical Analysis
Exordium (1:1-12)

Epistolary Analysis
I. Salutation (1:1-2)
II. Thanksgiving (1:3-12)
   A. Giving thanks (1:3-5)
   B. Reason able to give thanks (1:6-10)
   C. Intercession (1:11-12)
III. Letter Body (2:1-3:16)

Partitio (2:1-2)
Probatio (2:3-14)

   A. Body opening (2:1-2)
   B. Body middle (2:3-17)
     1. Teaching section (2:3-14)

  First Proof (2:3-12)
  Second Proof (2:13-14)
Peroratio (2:15-17)

       a. The opponent (2:3-12)
       b. Thanks for Thessalonians (2:13-14)
     2. Situational application (2:15-17)
       a. Command (2:15)
       b. Prayer (2:16-17)

Exhortatio (3:1-16)

   C. Body closing (3:1-16)
     1. Prayer (3:1-5)
       a. Request for prayer (3:1-2)
       b. Words of assurance (3:3-4)
       c. Prayer wish (3:5)
     2. Problem of the *ataktoi* (3:6-15)
     3. Benediction (3:16)

Epistolary Closing (3:17-18)
IV. Letter Closing (3:17-18)[6]

Epistolary analysis shows that 2 Thessalonians is in fact a letter, not just a doctrinal tract. This conclusion is strengthened by the work of John L. White, who has shown that 'finally' [λοιπὸν] is a common transition word introducing the final major section in a letter body,[7] and thus the use of 'finally' in 2 Thessalonians 3:1 signals a new section. Outlines which ignore this transition,

---

[6] A number of detailed rhetorical outlines of 2 Thess. have been produced; my rhetorical outline is very similar to those by Hughes and Wanamaker. See Holland, *Tradition*, pp. 8-33; Hughes, *Early Christian Rhetoric*, pp. 68-72; Jewett, *Correspondence*, pp. 82-85; and Wanamaker, *Thessalonians*, p. 51. The categories for epistolary analysis were taken from John L. White, *The Body of the Greek Letter* (SBLDS 2; Missoula, MT: SBL, 1972).

[7] White, *Light from Ancient Letters*, p. 206. See also M. J. J. Menken, 'The Structure of 2 Thessalonians', in *The Thessalonian Correspondence* (ed. R. Collins; Leuven: Leuven University Press, 1990), p. 377.

whether rhetorical[8] or thematic,[9] are incorrect. This understanding of the structure of 2 Thessalonians is important in order to compare it to 1 Thessalonians and determine the literary relationship of the two letters, as will be shown in the next section.

Rhetorical analysis also helps to interpret the literary character of 2 Thessalonians. Although the details of each rhetorical analysis of 2 Thessalonians may differ, advocates of this approach recognize that 2 Thessalonians is an example of deliberative rhetoric.[10] Thus its rhetorical purpose is different from the rhetorical purpose of 1 Thessalonians, which is epideictic.[11] This helps to explain one of the major differences between the two letters: whereas 1 Thessalonians is often characterized as being warm and personal, the disputers claim that 2 Thessalonians is cool and distant. The section of 1 Thessalonians which is considered to be particularly personal is 1 Thessalonians 2:1–3:10, where Paul narrates the history of his relationship with the Thessalonians. In a rhetorical analysis of 1 Thessalonians, this section is identified as the *narratio*,[12] the purpose of which is to state the facts or background information necessary for the rhetorical argument of the writer.[13] The *narratio* was considered a necessity for epideictic rhetoric (such as 1 Thess.), but not always for deliberative rhetoric (such as 2 Thess.).[14] Consequently 2 Thessalonians gives the impression of being more impersonal because as a type of rhetoric different from 1 Thessalonians, it contains no *narratio*. If the *narratio* is removed from 1 Thessalonians, then as a whole it is seen to be no more personal and warm than 2 Thessalonians.

B. *The Structure of 2 Thessalonians and the Disputation by Wrede*

Wrede's argument that 2 Thessalonians is literarily dependent on 1 Thessalonians is still one of the major arguments used for denying the authenticity of 2 Thessalonians. In five different ways Wrede presents evidence that 2 Thessalonians is dependent on 1 Thessalonians: (1) an overview in which 2 Thessalonians is placed in parallel to 1 Thessalonians and all the words that Wrede views as dependent on 1 Thessalonians are underlined; (2) an outline showing how the individual parallels stand within parallel sections; (3) a list of

---

[8]See Jewett, *Correspondence*, pp. 82-85, who sees the *probatio* going from 2:3 to 3:5 and the second proof within this section going from 2:13 to 3:5.

[9]See Trilling, *Untersuchungen*, pp. 94-95, who also makes a section from 2·13 to 3·5

[10]Holland, *Tradition*, p. 6; Hughes, *Early Christian Rhetoric*, p. 55; Jewett, *Correspondence*, p. 81; and Wanamaker, *Thessalonians*, p. 50.

[11]Wanamaker, *Thessalonians*, p. 47.

[12]Wanamaker, *Thessalonians*, p. 49.

[13]Kennedy, *New Testament Interpretation*, p. 24.

[14]Kennedy, *New Testament Interpretation*, p. 24.

conspicuous parallels; (4) an examination of two particular parallels; and (5) a list showing the similar order of the parallels.[15] This evidence must be examined to see if it does substantiate Wrede's literary dependence hypothesis.

1. Wrede's Overview

Wrede's overview of 2 Thessalonians gives the impression that almost every word and phrase found in 2 Thessalonians has come directly from 1 Thessalonians and that the author of 2 Thessalonians has simply cut up 1 Thessalonians and pasted it back together to form the second letter. However, a careful examination of many of the so-called parallels reveals that they are not really parallel at all, or they are simply part of the structure of the letter. For example, following the salutation, the writer of 2 Thessalonians begins with a thanksgiving for all of the believers at Thessalonica. There is a similar thanksgiving in 1 Thessalonians; in fact, Paul begins nearly all of his letters with such a thanks to God.[16] What is unique about 2 Thessalonians is the introduction to the thanksgiving: the author makes the verb 'to give thanks' an infinitive and adds 'we ought . . .and rightly so'. This clearly is not copied from 1 Thessalonians or any other letter of Paul, yet Wrede includes this thanksgiving and the thanksgiving in 2 Thessalonians 2:13, which has the same peculiarities, as part of his list of dependencies. In a similar manner, Wrede includes the final grace (3:18) as dependent on 1 Thessalonians. Again, this final grace is found in nearly all of Paul's undisputed letters.[17] Furthermore, in 2 Thessalonians the grace is slightly different from 1 Thessalonians for it also includes the word 'all'. Therefore it cannot be claimed that 2 Thessalonians is dependent on 1 Thessalonians any more than on any other letter of Paul. A more plausible explanation is that Paul himself has simply followed his normal practice. Furthermore, most of the individual words and phrases that are underlined and not mentioned again by Wrede are merely examples of similar vocabulary. These examples, found in a variety of contexts within 2 Thessalonians and sometimes used in ways different from 1 Thessalonians, are so vague that Wrede is unable to use them in his categories of conspicuous or particular parallels. Most of this vocabulary is found in the undisputed letters of Paul as well. Furthermore, when all the words Wrede has underlined in 2 Thessalonians are counted, they comprise less than one third of the whole book. Thus, even using Wrede's own figures, more than two thirds of 2 Thessalonians

---

[15]Wrede's sections on literary dependence are found on the following pages in *Echtheit*: (1) overview, pp. 3-12; (2) individual parallels within parallel sections, pp. 18-20; (3) conspicuous parallels, pp. 20-23; (4) two particular parallels, pp. 27-28; and (5) order of the parallels, pp. 23-27.

[16]See Rom. 1:8; 1 Cor. 1:4; Phil. 1:3; and Phlm. 4.

[17]See 1 Cor. 15:23; 2 Cor. 13:13; Gal. 6:18; Phil. 4:23; 1 Thess. 5:28; and Phlm. 25.

is *not* dependent on 1 Thessalonians. Therefore, although Wrede's overview gives the initial appearance of proving literary dependence, it really proves nothing. A close examination of his parallels, taking into account the epistolary genre and remembering that 2 Thessalonians presents itself as a letter written soon after 1 Thessalonians and so addressing similar topics, shows that most of these parallels simply do not exist.

2. Individual Parallels within Parallel Sections

Wrede's second line of dependencies shows how individual parallels stand within parallel sections in the two books. He lists four sections from 2 Thessalonians and the corresponding sections in 1 Thessalonians which he believes show dependency. His method of identifying the parallels, however, is not based on epistolary analysis, and consequently the parallels are not always in parallel sections. Before evaluating his potential parallels, it is helpful to compare the structure of 1 Thessalonians to 2 Thessalonians using epistolary analysis.

1 Thessalonians	2 Thessalonians
I. Salutation (1:1)	I. Salutation (1:1-2)
II. Thanksgiving (1:2-10)	II. Thanksgiving (1:3-12)
A. Giving thanks for work, labor, endurance (1:2-3)	A. Giving thanks (1:3-5)
B. How the gospel came and its effects (1:4-10)	B. Reason for thanks (1:6-10)
	C. Intercession (1:11-12)
III. Letter Body (2:1–5:24)	III. Letter Body (2:1–3:16)
A. Body opening (2:1)	A. Body opening (2:1-2)
B. Body middle (2:2–3:13)	B. Body middle (2:3-17)
1. How the gospel was brought and received (2:2-16)	1. Teaching section (2:3-14)
2. Further relationship & visit (2:17–3:10)	a. The opponent (2:3-12)
3. Prayer (3:11-13)	b. Thanks for Thessalonians (2:13-14)
	2. Situational application (2:15-17)
	a. Command (2:15)
	b. Prayer (2:16-17)
C. Body closing (4:1–5:24)	C. Body closing (3:1-16)
1. Instructions on holy living (4:1-12)	1. Prayer (3:1-5)
2. Comfort for grief (4:13-18)	a. Request for prayer (3:1-2)
3. Waiting for Christ's return (5:1-11)	b. Words of assurance (3:3-4)
	c. Prayer wish (3:5)
4. Brief instructions (5:12-24)	2. Problem of Idle (3:6-15)
	3. Benediction (3:16)
IV. Letter Closing (5:25-28)	IV. Letter Closing (3:17-18)

(a) 2 Thessalonians 1:3-12 and 1 Thessalonians 1:2-8. The first parallel identified by Wrede is between 2 Thessalonians 1:3-12 and 1 Thessalonians 1:2-8.[18] We have already shown that Paul frequently begins his letters with a thanksgiving and that these thanksgivings typically use 'all' and 'always'.[19] Our rhetorical outline labels this the *exordium*. The purpose of the *exordium* was to obtain the attention and goodwill of the audience,[20] and so a thanksgiving for the recipients was an especially appropriate *exordium*. That he commends them for their love and faith in both letters is not surprising if they were written only a few months apart and addressed to the same audience. But it is also important to note the differences in order to determine if there is literary dependence. The writer of 2 Thessalonians uses a different form of the verb 'to give thanks', and he includes the phrase 'as it is right'. This form of thanksgiving is not distant or cool but is very personal, using Jewish prayer language which is especially appropriate to the problem of suffering.[21] Furthermore, the writer refers not just to the presence of love and faith but to their growth and development; he does not include 'all' to modify 'you' as in the first letter; and he focuses upon their present perseverance in affliction. Both letters speak about faith, love and perseverance, but in 1 Thessalonians 1:3 the three are clearly paralleled, whereas in 2 Thessalonians 1:3-4, faith and love are parallel (v. 3) and then perseverance and faith are parallel (v. 4). This does not look like literary dependence, but instead, like the addressing of similar topics. Furthermore, the 'prayer' in 2 Thessalonians 1:3-12 is in a separate subsection at the end of the thanksgiving, whereas the 'prayer' in 1 Thessalonians 1:2-8 is at the beginning of the thanksgiving. The terminology is different for each of these 'prayers'. The prepositional phrase 'to all the ones who have believed' (2 Thess. 1:10) uses an aorist participle and refers to all believers everywhere waiting for the return of the Lord, whereas the prepositional phrase 'to all those believing' (1 Thess. 1:7) uses a present participle and refers specifically to Christians in Macedonia and Achaia. The only affliction mentioned in 1 Thessalonians 1:2-8 refers to the conditions when the believers initially received the word, but affliction is the focus of attention in 2 Thessalonians 1:6-7. The closest parallel listed by Wrede in this section is 'work of faith', yet in 1 Thessalonians it is used as part of a list of three parallel phrases with articles, while in 2

---

[18] Wrede, *Echtheit*, p. 19, lists twenty-three Greek words from 2 Thess. 1:3-12 which find some kind of parallel in 1 Thessalonians.

[19] See Rom. 1:8; 1 Cor. 1:4; Phil. 1:3-4.

[20] Kennedy, *New Testament Interpretation*, p. 23.

[21] Roger D. Aus, 'The Liturgical Background of the Necessity and Propriety of Giving Thanks according to 2 Thess 1:3', *JBL* 92 (1973), pp. 432-38. Marshall, *Thessalonians*, p. 170, notes that Phil. 1:7 uses similar language: 'it is right for me to feel this way about all of you'.

Thessalonians it is without any articles and is qualified by 'with power'. The way the phrases and terms are used shows no sign of literary dependence; rather, it simply shows an author dealing with common themes in a similar situation within the opening thanksgiving of a letter.

(b) 2 Thessalonians 2:15–3:5 and 1 Thessalonians 3:11(8)–4:2. Wrede's second parallel is between 2 Thessalonians 2:15–3:5 and 1 Thessalonians 3:11 (8)–4:2.[22] In both letters these verses do not comprise a distinct section at all, but the end of one section and the beginning of the next section. Wrede recognizes this, for his next parallel section for 1 Thessalonians begins at 4:1. The first parallel claimed by Wrede here is simply the verb 'stand firm' [στηκέτε]. However, this does not show dependency because Paul uses this verb in the exact same form in Romans 14:4, 1 Corinthians 16:13, Galatians 5:1, Philippians 1:27 and 4:1, 1 Thessalonians 3:8, and 2 Thessalonians 2:15. The contexts of the two passages are unrelated to each other, so Wrede is unable to list any more words with it.

The second parallel identified by Wrede in this section is between 2 Thessalonians 2:15 ('the traditions which you were taught') and 1 Thessalonians 4:1-2 ('just as you received from us'). Neither of the words 'tradition' or 'teach' is found in 1 Thessalonians; the only similarity is the general idea of passing on tradition, which we have already seen is found throughout Paul's undisputed letters. Furthermore, Wrede includes this parallel from 1 Thessalonians not only in this section but also in the next section of parallels. It might be argued that the writer of 2 Thessalonians is dependent on the same section of 1 Thessalonians in more than one place; however, the purpose of this section of Wrede's argument is to show that the phrases are parallel in form *and* also fall within parallel sections of the two books. If one section of 1 Thessalonians is used in two different sections of 2 Thessalonians, then the parallels do not fall within parallel sections. As has already been noted, 'finally' was commonly used in letters of the time to introduce a new section in a letter.[23] In 1 Thessalonians, 'finally' is linked with a coordinating conjunction, whereas in 2 Thessalonians it is preceded by the neuter singular article, the most common usage found in Paul.[24] The statements about tradition in 2 Thessalonians 2:15 actually conclude the main doctrinal section, while the so-called parallel in 1 Thessalonians 4:1-2 begins the paraenetic section. Thus, the statements about tradition are not in parallel sections.

Wrede's parallel referring to 'what we command' is also very weak. In 2 Thessalonians 3:4, the verb is in the present tense, while 1 Thessalonians 4:2 uses the noun to refer to past commands.

---

[22]Wrede, *Echtheit*, p. 19, lists thirty Greek words from 2 Thessalonians 2:15-3:5 which find some kind of parallel in 1 Thessalonians.

[23]See 2 Cor. 13:11; Phil. 3:1; 4:8; also see 2 Tim. 4:8 and Heb. 10:13.

[24]1 Thess. 4:1 begins λοιπὸν οὖν; 2 Thess. 3:1 begins τὸ λοιπόν.

Wrede also identifies the verb 'to direct' as a parallel in this section. This verb is found in only three places in the New Testament;[25] in both Thessalonian epistles it is an aorist optative, expressing a prayer wish. But the similarities end there. In 1 Thessalonians the wish is for a literal visit to see the Thessalonians, whereas in 2 Thessalonians the wish is figurative for the hearts of the Thessalonians to be directed toward God's love and Christ's perseverance. Although this verb is rare in the New Testament, it is frequently used in the LXX, very often in prayers or to express the direction of someone's heart.[26] Therefore the usage in 2 Thessalonians is not unusual; in fact, the literal use is less frequent in the LXX. The use of the optative is also something which is far more common in the undisputed epistles of Paul than anywhere else in the New Testament.[27]

Wrede identifies one other parallel (between 1 Thess. 3:13 and 2 Thess. 2:17), which he also lists in his category of "conspicuous" parallels.[28] Other than this parallel and the verb 'to direct', which he also lists under conspicuous parallels, the rest of his so-called parallels in 2 Thessalonians 2:15–3:5 are merely typical Pauline expressions or standard practices of epistolary genre, or they do not exist at all. Wrede's examples do not prove dependency.

(c) 2 Thessalonians 3:6-12 and 1 Thessalonians 4:1-12. Wrede continues his individual parallels within parallel sections by focusing on 2 Thessalonians 3:6-12 and 1 Thessalonians 4:1-12. His parallels in this segment are actually limited to 2 Thessalonians 3:6-7, 10-12 and 1 Thessalonians 4:1-2, 10-12.[29] He parallels almost the entire contents of the two verses that introduce the respective sections, yet most of the content words are different forms, and even the formulas are different. Literary dependence is most likely to be proved if an author uses the same words, in the same forms, in the same order and in a similar context. Dependency cannot be proved simply because the same topic is addressed. Wrede's proposed literary dependency does not explain the differences in these sections. If the author were imitating 1 Thessalonians, any

---

[25]Luke 1:79; 1 Thess. 3:11; and 2 Thess. 3:5.

[26]See 1 Chr. 29:18; 2 Chr. 12:14; 17:5; 19:3; 20:33; 30:19; 32:30; Pss. 5:9; 7:10; 77:8; 140:2; Prov. 15:8; 21:2; 23:19.

[27]J. H. Moulton, *A Grammar of New Testament Greek,* vol. 1 (3rd ed.; Edinburgh: T & T Clark, 1908), pp. 194-96, says there are thirty-eight proper optatives in the NT, of these only nine are not in the Pauline corpus. The books using the proper optatives in the Pauline corpus include Rom., 1 Cor., Gal., 1 Thess., 2 Thess., 2 Tim., and Phlm. Fourteen of these are the phrase μὴ γένοιτο.

[28]The so-called parallel about the Lord himself establishing them will be dealt with when Wrede's conspicuous parallels are examined.

[29]Wrede, *Echtheit,* p. 19, lists thirty-seven Greek words from 2 Thess. 3:6-12 which find some kind of parallel in 1 Thess.

The Authenticity of 2 Thessalonians

differences in the wording would likely not seem smooth or natural. The words which are actually identical in form include 'brothers', 'you know', 'from us' and 'how it is necessary'. Virtually all of these similarities can easily be accounted for by recognizing the letter genre and the way in which Paul normally introduces traditional paraenetic material.

Although the parallels Wrede finds in 1 Thessalonians 4:10-12 and 2 Thessalonians 3:10-12 are real parallels, they do not show literary dependency. The word group most focused upon in this segment, 'idle' [*ataktoi*], occurs in different forms in the two epistles, and there is no evidence here that the writer of 2 Thessalonians was making use of a copy of 1 Thessalonians. The only word that is common in form in these verses is the infinitive 'to work'. What is exhibited is not literary dependence but a thematic parallel addressing a similar yet further-developed situation.

(d) 2 Thessalonians 3:1-3 and 1 Thessalonians 5:24-25. The final parallel segments Wrede lists are the similar prayers in 2 Thessalonians 3:1-3 and 1 Thessalonians 5:24-25.[30] The words which are the same in both sections are 'brothers', 'pray concerning us', and 'faithful'. However, it is not surprising for a request for prayer to be somewhat stereotyped. Even the writer to the Hebrews says 'pray for us' with exactly the same words.[31] This means, not that he was imitating either 1 or 2 Thessalonians, but only that he was making a common request. It must be noted that the order of these words is different in the two epistles, and faithfulness is attributed to a different person in each section.[32] Furthermore, the prayers are in different places in the two epistles: the one in 2 Thessalonians begins the exhortation section and is first of all a request for prayer *from* the Thessalonians, but the one in 1 Thessalonians is a prayer *for* the Thessalonians.

Thus in his section on individual parallels within parallel sections, Wrede's failure to take into account the epistolary genre or the structure of 2 Thessalonians leads him to incorrect conclusions. What he identifies as literary dependency is actually normal epistolary practice for Paul, for most of Paul's letters have similar opening thanksgivings. By not recognizing the epistolary structure of 2 Thessalonians, which clearly divides the body closing from the body middle with the word 'finally', he incorrectly parallels the statements about 'tradition' in 2 Thessalonians 2:15 and 1 Thessalonians 4:1-2. Thus Wrede's parallels do not demonstrate dependency at all but instead could be expected in many letters of that time and in any letter from Paul. Furthermore, Wrede ignores significant differences between the letters, even in his parallel

---

[30] Wrede, *Echtheit*, p. 19, lists ten Greek words from 2 Thess. 3:1-3 which find some kind of parallel in 1 Thess.

[31] Heb. 13:18.

[32] It is possible the prayer in 1 Thess. also includes καί, but the textual evidence is not certain.

sections. Dependency is most likely to be shown by an author using the same vocabulary in the same form and in the same word order. But in nearly all of the examples in this group of parallels, there are many differences in vocabulary, form, and word order. Even if all of the parallels listed by Wrede in this section were accepted, less than one eighth of 2 Thessalonians can be said to be dependent (only 100 words in Greek). A much more plausible explanation is that 2 Thessalonians was written by the same author, dealing with similar problems, at a slightly later date.

3. List of Conspicuous Parallels

(a) **2 Thessalonians 2:13 and 1 Thessalonians 2:13.** According to Wrede, the second thanksgiving in 2 Thessalonians 2:13 clearly parallels the second thanksgiving in 1 Thessalonians 2:13. He remarks that only these two letters in the Pauline corpus contain a double thanksgiving, that both stress the subject of the thanksgiving ('we'), and that the 'we' in the second letter is unnecessary and simply taken mechanically from the first letter. He also suggests that the thanksgivings appear essentially in the same place in the letter because the writer of 2 Thessalonians has inserted his new material (2:1-12) into the parallel section of 1 Thessalonians (2:1-12) and omitted 1 Thessalonians 2:17–3:10.

Wrede focuses on the double thanksgivings in the Thessalonian epistles in order to show literary dependence. However, an examination of the two letters reveals that the structure of the double thanksgivings is not as similar as he presents. In fact, 1 Thessalonians appears to contain three small thanksgivings (1:2-5; 2:13; 3:9-13),[33] with the first thanksgiving being part of the normal epistolary thanksgiving which introduces the topics to be dealt with later, and the other two being part of the main matter of 1 Thessalonians which concerns the relationship Paul has with the Thessalonians. This emphasis on thanks helps to show that the rhetorical purpose of 1 Thessalonians is primarily to praise the Thessalonians, thus making it an example of epideictic rhetoric.[34] Bjerkelund's study on the significance of *parakalo*-sentences, also sheds light on the differences between the thanksgivings in the two letters. The main verbs of the *parakalo*-sentences in 1 and 2 Thessalonians are 'to exhort' [παρακαλέω] or 'to ask' [ἐρωτάω]. The first *parakalo*-sentence in 1 Thessalonians begins at 4:1, whereas in 2 Thessalonians the first sentence of this type is found in 2:1.[35]

---

[33] Peter T. O'Brien, *Introductory Thanksgivings in the Letters of Paul* (NovTSup 49; Leiden: Brill, 1977), p. 141, building on the work of Paul Schubert and Carl Bjerkelund, makes the less likely suggestion that these are not really three separate thanksgivings but, rather, one extended thanksgiving covering from 1:3 to 3:13, making this the largest thanksgiving in the whole Pauline corpus.

[34] Wanamaker, *Thessalonians,* p. 47; Jewett, *Correspondence,* p. 71.

[35] Bjerkelund, *Parakalô,* pp. 109, 128-37.

This means that 2 Thessalonians has two distinct thanksgivings, whereas 1 Thessalonians has an initial thanksgiving followed by a theme of thanks throughout chs 2 and 3. Consequently, Wrede's so-called second thanksgivings in the letters actually occur in different places in the overall structure of the two books. The early use of the *parakalo*-sentence in 2 Thessalonians is similar to the pattern found in 1 Corinthians and Philemon.[36] In addition, it is very clear that the second thanksgiving in 2 Thessalonians does not imitate 1 Thessalonians, but instead, recalls the first thanksgiving in 2 Thessalonians. This is seen particularly in the identical form which introduces the two thanksgivings in 2 Thessalonians, 'we ought to thank God always', which is found only in 2 Thessalonians.[37] The 'we' in 2 Thessalonians 2:13 is in the emphatic first position in the thanksgiving, which is quite different from the position in 1 Thessalonians 2:13, where 'we' is the fifth word in the sentence. The pronoun is needed in 2 Thessalonians 2:13 in order to make a strong contrast between the authors, who are giving thanks for the Thessalonian Christians, and those who are followers of the opponent and 'have not believed the truth' (2 Thess. 2:11-12).

Thus in this very significant parallel between 1 Thessalonians 2:13 and 2 Thessalonians 2:13, Wrede has misunderstood the structure of both epistles, failed to take into account that the second thanksgiving in 2 Thessalonians intentionally recalls its first thanksgiving, and misinterpreted the importance the emphatic pronoun plays in this context.

(b) 2 Thessalonians 2:16 and 1 Thessalonians 3:11; 2 Thessalonians 3:16 and 1 Thessalonians 5:23. Wrede deals with the next two conspicuous parallels, both prayers, together:

1 Thess. 3:11 'Now may our God and Father himself and the Lord Jesus direct our way to you'	2 Thess. 2:16 'May our Lord Jesus Christ himself and God our Father... encourage and strengthen you in every good deed and word'
1 Thess. 5:23 'May the God of peace himself, sanctify you through and through'	2 Thess. 3:16 'May the Lord of peace himself give you peace at all times and in every way'

He draws attention to the similarities between the parallel passages: both parallels use the word 'himself' to stress the subject, and the verbs are in the optative mood, which is rare in Paul. He further observes of the first parallel that its location in both letters is similar and that the verb 'to direct', though not actually in 2:16, occurs only a few verses later (in 2 Thess. 3:5). Of the second

---

[36] Bjerkelund, *Parakalô*, p. 138.

[37] For more on the parallels of the thanksgivings in 2 Thess., see Sumney, 'Pauline Rhetoric Pattern', pp. 192-204.

parallel, he notes that the word 'peace' is found in both verses.

These two parallels certainly give the impression of being closer than many of Wrede's other parallels. The first parallel passages (1 Thess. 3:11 and 2 Thess. 2:16) do occur in parallel sections of the letters, the closing of the body middle. Yet there are also significant differences between these two passages. First, the prayers are focused differently. In 1 Thessalonians 3, the prayer follows a long narration of Paul's past relationship with the Thessalonians (2:1–3:10) and focuses on his desire to visit them again, whereas in 2 Thessalonians the prayer follows a teaching section and focuses on his desire that they will take his teaching to heart.[38] In order to make these sections parallel, Wrede must say that the writer of 2 Thessalonians has omitted the heart of 1 Thessalonians (2:17–3:10) and moved the eschatological sections. This need to rearrange the entire letter shows that the two Thessalonian epistles are not so parallel as he thinks. Second, Wrede implies that the use of the verb 'to direct' helps to make these verses parallel, when in fact the verb is not used until a few verses later in 2 Thessalonians (3:11), in a completely different section, making this so-called parallel unconvincing.

In the second parallel, Wrede points out the use of the word 'peace'. However, this use of the word is easily explained by the fact that these two passages (1 Thess. 5:23 and 2 Thess. 3:16) occur near the end of the two letters, both of which address churches which are 'unsettled' (1 Thess. 3:3; 2 Thess. 2:2), and that is one reason why the blessing of 'peace' is appropriate in both letters.[39]

The most significant similarity in these passages is the use of 'himself' as an intensive pronoun and the optative mood, but even here there are important differences, for 'himself' modifies a different subject in each of the parallels, and the verbs are different as well.

Wrede's argument about these parallels is inconsistent: when he identifies individual parallels within parallel sections, he parallels 1 Thessalonians 5:23 with 2 Thessalonians 3:1-3, yet in this section he parallels it with 2 Thessalonians 3:16. Again his parallels show only similarities in vocabulary, and therefore, the parallels he identifies at the letter closing are parallel only in form, not content. Since the particular form is appropriate for the place and manner of use in each epistle, these parallels do not show dependency but only similarity of form.

---

[38]Witherington, *Thessalonians*, pp. 24-27, 31, points out that deliberative letters do not require a narration, whereas epideictic letters do.

[39]For further discussion of the change from 'God' to 'Lord' in these verses, see ch. 4, the section on Christology.

The Authenticity of 2 Thessalonians

(c) 2 Thessalonians 3:1 and 1 Thessalonians 4:1; 2 Thessalonians 3:10-12 and 1 Thessalonians 4:10-12; 2 Thessalonians 2:1 and 1 Thessalonians 4-5. The last three conspicuous parallels which Wrede identifies are all very weak. It has already been shown that 'finally' (1 Thess. 4:1; 2 Thess. 3:1) was a common literary transition and that the form found in 2 Thessalonians is like the form most frequently found in Paul. It has also been shown that the parallel between 1 Thessalonians 4:10-12 and 2 Thessalonians 3:10-12 is simply a result of dealing with a similar topic, with really only one word in common. And the final conspicuous parallel concerns the similar language used to describe the parousia in 2 Thessalonians 2:1 and 1 Thessalonians 4-5. All this parallel amounts to, however, is that the word 'parousia' is used in both passages and that both passages contain the idea that God's people will be gathered to the Lord. It is difficult to see this as really supporting literary dependency.

4. Two Particular Parallels

The strongest case for literary dependency is found in the two examples which Wrede classifies as 'particular parallels': (1) the salutations (1 Thess. 1:1; 2 Thess. 1:1-2), and (2) the description of Paul's work (1 Thess. 2:9; 2 Thess. 3:8). There can be no question that these are genuine parallels.

(a) 2 Thessalonians 1:1-2 and 1 Thessalonians 1:1. Wrede notes that the salutations show three unusual similarities found only in these two epistles: (1) no mention is made of Paul being an 'apostle' or a 'servant' of Christ; (2) the recipients are identified by name ('Thessalonians') and not by place; and (3) the phrase 'in God the Father' is included in both. However, by focusing only on the Thessalonian epistles, Wrede fails to realize that there may be a reason other than dependency for these similarities. Other pairs of salutations within the undisputed letters of Paul show strong similarities to each other. For example, the salutations found in the Corinthian epistles share a number of characteristics not found in the other undisputed letters: only in these two letters is he said to be 'an apostle of Christ Jesus by the will of God'; only in these two epistles and in Philemon is a co-author referred to as 'the brother'; and only these two letters are addressed 'to the church of God being in Corinth'.[40] It is possible that the two Thessalonian epistles are addressed 'to the Thessalonians in God the Father and the Lord Jesus Christ' because the author(s) wanted to stress that the individual Thessalonian Christians were united to the Father and the Son. This may have been important because of the suffering experienced by the congregation and/or because of their doctrinal confusion. Thus to find the similarities stressed by Wrede in two letters to the same church is not unusual and in no way proves literary dependency.

---

[40]Rom. is addressed 'to all those being in Rome'; Phil., 'to all the saints in Christ Jesus which are in Philippi with the bishops and deacons'; and Gal., 'to the churches of Galatia'.

Wrede does not mention the differences in the two salutations. Although all of the salutation from 1 Thessalonians is contained in 2 Thessalonians, 2 Thessalonians also has the pronoun 'our' after the first 'God the Father' and following the 'grace to you and peace' has the prepositional phrase 'from God our Father and the Lord Jesus Christ'. What is unusual is not that 2 Thessalonians has this final phrase, but that it is absent from 1 Thessalonians, for the writer of 2 Thessalonians follows the consistent pattern of the rest of undisputed letters of Paul. Similarity in the salutations can be observed in other pairs of his letter. If all words in the salutation of 2 Thessalonians which are parallel to words in the salutation of 1 Thessalonians are expressed as a percentage of the total number of words in the salutation of 2 Thessalonians, then 67 % of the salutation is parallel. If all words in the salutation of Philippians which are parallel to words in the salutation of Romans are expressed as a percentage of the total number of words in the salutation of Philippians, then 65 % of the salutation is parallel. And if the same is done for 1 and 2 Corinthians, then 80 % of the salutation of 2 Corinthians is parallel to the salutation of 1 Corinthians. The similarities Wrede focuses upon in the salutations do not prove literary dependency any more than the similarities found between 1 and 2 Corinthians or Romans and Philippians.

(b) 2 Thessalonians 3:8 and 1 Thessalonians 2:9. Wrede identifies the second particular parallel as the most important parallel in the Thessalonian epistles.

1 Thess. 2:9 '. . . our toil and labor, working night and day in order not to be a burden to any of you'	2 Thess. 3:8 '. . . by toil and labor, working night and day in order not to be a burden to any of you'
τὸν κόπον ἡμῶν καὶ τὸν μόχθον· νυκτὸς καὶ ἡμέρας ἐργαζόμενοι πρὸς τὸ μὴ ἐπιβαρῆσαι τινα ὑμῶν	ἐν κόπῳ ἡμῶν καὶ μόχθῳ νυκτὸς καὶ ἡμέρας ἐργαζόμενοι πρὸς τὸ μὴ ἐπιβαρῆσαι τινα ὑμῶν

The wording 'working night and day in order not to be a burden to any of you' is identical in the Greek of both verses. In 1 Thessalonians 2:9, the words 'toil' and 'labor' both have articles, are in the accusative case, and are modified by the pronoun 'our'. In 2 Thessalonians 3:8, the words 'toil' and 'labor' have no articles, are in the dative case, and are objects of the preposition 'by'. However, literary dependency is not the only possible explanation for this one clear parallel between the two epistles.

First, this parallel is not as extensive as Wrede presents, for the first two phrases are common phrases in their own right. The first of these, 'toil and labor', is a common way for Paul to speak about his ministry, for this phrase is found not only in the two Thessalonian epistles, but also in 2 Corinthians 11:27. The form of the phrase in 2 Thessalonians 3:8 is almost identical to 2 Corinthians 11:27 (same order of words, no articles, no pronouns, same case) yet different from 1 Thessalonians 2:9. The context in 2 Corinthians 11 is Paul's defense of his ministry, just as it is in both Thessalonian epistles. This seems unlikely to be just coincidence; most likely it was a set expression Paul used to defend his ministerial practice.

The phrase 'night and day' is used not only in the Pauline corpus[41] but also throughout the New Testament to convey the idea of continuous activity.[42] The combination 'night and day' is also frequently found in the LXX, but usually in the reverse order.[43] Therefore this would be a very common phrase for Paul to choose, especially in a description of his working habits. Thus the first half of the parallel does not prove literary dependence, but only shows common terminology.

Second, Paul was in the habit of repeating statements. This is seen not only in his use of preformed tradition but also in his frequent use of certain Scripture passages[44] and extra-canonical proverbs.[45] For example, in Romans 3:20 and Galatians 2:16, Paul says, 'By works of the law no one will be justified', most likely taken from Psalm 143:2 (LXX 142:2).[46] Though the wording is quite different from the LXX, it is identical in the two Pauline passages.[47] Thus in his teaching Paul used certain set phrases.

A regular part of Paul's teaching included a defense of his ministry.[48] Paul desired that his ministry would not be burdensome to his hearers,[49] and in 1 Thessalonians 2:9 he implies that the Thessalonians knew this, for he introduces this sentence with 'don't you remember, brothers'. This priority which Paul stresses to his readers may have been influenced by his rabbinic background,

---

[41] 1 Thess. 2:9; 3:10; 2 Thess. 3:8; 1 Tim. 5:5; 2 Tim. 1:3.

[42] Mark 4:27; 5:5; Luke 2:37; 18:7; Acts 20:31; 26:7; Rev. 4:8; 7:15; 12:10.

[43] See 1 Sam. 25:16; Esth. 4:16; Isa. 34:10; Jer. 14:17. The reverse order 'day and night' is used nineteen times in the OT and seven times in the NT.

[44] Gen. 15:6 (Rom. 4:3, 9, 22; Gal. 3:6); Lev. 19:18 (Rom. 13:9; Gal. 5:14); Isa. 40:13 LXX (Rom. 11:34; 1 Cor. 2:16); Hab. 2:4 (Rom. 1:17; Gal. 3:11); and Ps. 143:2 (Rom. 3:20; Gal. 2:16).

[45] Both 1 Cor. 5:6 and Gal. 5:9 contain the proverb 'a little yeast works through the whole batch of dough'.

[46] F. F. Bruce, *The Epistle to the* Galatians (NIGTC; Grand Rapids: Eerdmans, 1982), p. 140.

[47] Ps. 142:2b in the LXX is οὐ δικαιωθήσεται ἐνωπιόν σου πᾶς ζῶν, while the wording in both Rom. 3:20 and Gal. 2:16 is ἐξ ἔργων νόμου οὐ δικαιωθήσεται πᾶσα σάρξ.

[48] See Rom. 1:5; 1 Cor. 4:1; 2 Cor. 10–12; Gal. 1:1; Phil. 1:12-14; 1 Thess. 2:1-13.

[49] 1 Cor. 9:1-18; 2 Cor. 11:9.

which required religious teachers to have a secular occupation.[50] Furthermore, this rabbinic attitude was to be taught, for 'he that teacheth not his son a trade doth the same as if he taught him to be a thief'.[51] Thus several factors—Paul's rabbinic background with its positive stress on the value of work, his setting up of himself as an example for his converts, his frequent defense of his ministry as part of his teaching, and his regular use of set phraseology—make it likely that he would use set phraseology to describe his work and that he would use it in two letters written to the same church within a few months of each other. Even Trilling acknowledges that if the two Thessalonian epistles were written within a few months it would have been possible for the same author to use the same sentence.[52]

Thus the one real parallel found in both Thessalonian epistles does not require that one letter be dependent upon the other. The author of 2 Thessalonians applies the statement in a new application with the freedom Paul has when he applies the same proverb to differing situations.[53] The writer of 2 Thessalonians refers it back to the original teaching given by Paul at the founding of the church, as does 1 Thessalonians 2:9.

In summary, five of the conspicuous and particular parallels between 1 and 2 Thessalonians are best explained, not by literary dependency, but by understanding both 1 and 2 Thessalonians as actual letters which follow certain literary conventions. Two more of these parallels show only that the same topic is being considered, without any sign of literary dependence. The last particular parallel, the only true parallel, is best explained, not as literary dependence, but as Paul applying set phraseology concerning his ministry to a particular problem.

5. The Similar Order of the Parallels

Wrede's section on the order of the parallels presents the same information that was found in the overview and in the parallels within parallel sections, the only difference being that in this section Wrede has excluded many portions of 2 Thessalonians that do not fit his parallels. He underlines the parallel words which occur in the same order in the two books—about 100 words from the Greek text, or less than one eighth of the book. As was already shown, many of these parallels are not real parallels, are only individual examples of similar vocabulary, or are simply appropriate to literary convention. In addition, if, as Wrede suggests, the parallels are in the same order in the two epistles, he must explain how the main topic of 2 Thessalonians came to be placed in the wrong

---

[50]Best, *Thessalonians*, pp. 103-104; F. F. Bruce, *Thessalonians*, pp. 31, 34.
[51]Neil, *Thessalonians*, p. 41.
[52]Trilling, *Thessalonicher*, p. 147.
[53]See the proverb found in 1 Cor. 5:6 and Gal. 5:9.

order. He does this by saying that the author of 2 Thessalonians has basically ignored the historical information from 1 Thessalonians 2–3 and inserted the eschatology into this gap. Yet if the heart of the letter is not in parallel position, can it really be said that the structure of the letter is parallel? When this discrepancy is linked with the facts that many of his parallels are really dependent on literary convention and not necessarily on 1 Thessalonians and that he has misinterpreted the structure of the thanksgivings in both Thessalonian epistles, then his whole interpretation of the relationship between the letters must be abandoned.

Therefore, although Wrede repeats his 'parallels' over and over again in a variety of ways, a close examination of those parallels with an appreciation for literary convention shows that literary dependency is unlikely. Furthermore, Wrede acknowledges that there are virtually no direct parallels to the sections which we have identified as preformed tradition.[54] The so-called parallels he finds in the sections we have identified as non-tradition do not show literary dependence but are due to a similar yet more developed situation, literary convention, and similarity of expression. These are the kind of similarities one could expect to find in a letter by the same author to the same audience with an intervening gap of only a short time. Thus a much more plausible explanation is that Paul, having received more information from Thessalonica, wrote 2 Thessalonians only a few months after he wrote the first letter. Because this second letter had a purpose different from the first letter, Paul used deliberative rhetoric instead of epideictic. As is common with deliberative rhetoric, the narration of events is excluded. In his second letter he incorporated preformed tradition, as was his custom, and this accounts for the distinctiveness of the tradition sections and yet the similarity of non-tradition portions of the letter.

II. Sentence and Internal Structure of 2 Thessalonians

Wrede and Trilling compare sections of the letters in an attempt to show that the author of 2 Thessalonians imitates 1 Thessalonians. More recently, stylo-statistical techniques and computer analyses of the New Testament have been used in an attempt to exhaustively search for grammatical and lexical patterns. These methods can be helpful to evaluate the question of authorship; however, they must be used with caution because they are not always as objective as some might claim.

A. *Embeds*

Daryl Schmidt, with the use of the computer, has attempted to substantiate the case for disputation by focusing attention on the sentence structure in 2

---

[54]Wrede, *Echtheit*, pp. 6, 7, 74.

Thessalonians 1. Commentators on 2 Thessalonians have always noted the extreme length of the sentence that begins in 1:3, but in addition to its length, Schmidt has added the information that this sentence is the most complex sentence in the Pauline corpus.[55]

Schmidt's analysis is based on examining the number of subordinate clauses, which he refers to as 'embeds', found in a sentence. The degree of complexity of a sentence is calculated by measuring the 'depth' of embeds, that is, the embeds within the embeds. Schmidt's examination of 1 Thessalonians reveals that the most complex sentence (1:2-10) has a total of ten embeds, but only has a depth at level five. However, when he examines the thanksgiving section of 2 Thessalonians 1, he finds twenty embeds to a depth of level fifteen. Schmidt believes that the length of sentence and degree of complexity, which are far outside the norms found in the undisputed letters of Paul, present an objective test showing that 2 Thessalonians is pseudonymous.

There are, however, some serious flaws with this argument. First, the length of the sentence does not go from v. 3 to v. 12, but from v. 3 to v. 10. Schmidt appears to be alone in not seeing a break in the sentence at the end of 1:10.[56] Consequently, the sentence actually only goes to a depth of twelve, not fifteen. Second, this sentence is clearly unusual even for the writer of 2 Thessalonians, whether Paul or a pseudepigrapher. The sentence found in 1:3-10 is 158 words long; the second longest sentence in 2 Thessalonians is only 57 words (2:8-10). There are twenty-seven sentences in 2 Thessalonians; if all the other twenty-six sentences are averaged together, the average length is less than 26 words. Therefore 1:3-10 is not only highly unusual for Paul but is just as unusual for the author of 2 Thessalonians. Schmidt believes this one unusual sentence shows the letter is pseudonymous, but that solution does not explain why the rest of the letter does not have any sentences so long or complex.

The best explanation for the length and complexity of this sentence is that the author has incorporated a piece of tradition right into his own sentence. Because it is a preformed piece, its grammatical characteristics are not those of the author. When the piece of tradition (1:6-10a) is removed from 1:3-10, it is seen that the author's own sentence is not so long, and it goes only to a depth of level five, the same depth found in 1 Thessalonians.[57]

Schmidt is correct in noting the nonpauline character of this sentence, but his test does not confirm pseudonymity; rather, it strengthens the case that 2 Thessalonians 1:6-10a is a piece of tradition, for the sentence is unusual not

---

[55]D. Schmidt, 'Authenticity', pp. 289-96.

[56]See UBS³. Frame, *Thessalonians*, p. 239, also notes that vs. 11 begins a new sentences and points out sentences beginning in this same way in Rom. 14:9 and 2 Cor. 2:9.

[57]For the structure of 2 Thess. 1:6-10, see the identification of tradition in 2 Thess. 1 in ch. 3.

only for Paul but also for the writer of 2 Thessalonians. And this tradition, as has already been shown, is consistent with what Paul taught.

B. *A-B-A Pattern*

Jerry Sumney has sought to develop a new understanding of the form of 2 Thessalonians.[58] He states that the most serious argument used to dispute the authenticity of 2 Thessalonians concerns its literary form, in particular the double thanksgiving. Sumney notes that J. Hurd has defended the integrity of 1 Thessalonians by finding a pattern of subject matter which he refers to as 'the sonata form', or more simply, an A-B-A pattern. This pattern is found frequently in Paul, especially in 1 Corinthians 8–10 (ch. 8 = A, ch. 9 = B, ch. 10 = A') and 12–14 (ch. 12 = A, ch. 13 = B, ch. 14 = A'). Sumney maintains that 'the second passage is not a slavish imitation of the first', but rather, it 'returns to the subject with a different point of view'.[59] Sumney believes this same rhetorical pattern is seen in 2 Thessalonians 1:3–3:5 (1:3-12 = A; 2:1-12 = B; 2:13–3:5 = A'). The rest of his article focuses primarily on the parallels between 1:3-12 and 2:13–3:5, discussing each section's perspective.[60] Following his examination of the parallels in these two sections, he briefly discusses 2:1-12 and 3:6-13. He follows Malherbe's suggestion on 1 Thessalonians that 'the disorderly have resigned their occupations to be teachers of their new faith (as some Cynics did)'. He then links this activity (or lack of activity) with the condemned realized eschatology of 2:1-12, for 'who could be better qualified as a teacher than one who has experienced the Parousia?'[61]

Sumney concludes that (1) the A-B-A pattern gives a positive argument for the integrity of 2 Thessalonians; (2) 2 Thessalonians 2:13–3:5 is one section and should not be broken at 2:16 or 3:1; and (3) it is unlikely that a secondary author would repeat this Pauline rhetorical pattern. Therefore, because the problem of the literary form has been solved, the only question concerning the authenticity of 2 Thessalonians arises from possible theological disagreements with Paul.[62]

Sumney's parallels at first appear very numerous for such small sections, but upon closer examination, many of the so-called parallels are weak or non-existent. The parallel between the beginning of the two thanksgivings has always been recognized (1:3; 2:13). The writer of 2 Thessalonians 2:13-14 does pick up the themes found in the first thanksgiving and in the first verse, and the necessity to remain faithful in the midst of persecution (1:5-8) can be linked to

---

[58]Sumney, 'Pauline Rhetoric Pattern', pp. 192-204.
[59]Sumney, 'Pauline Rhetoric Pattern', p. 194.
[60]Sumney, 'Pauline Rhetoric Pattern', pp. 194-201.
[61]Sumney, 'Pauline Rhetoric Pattern', p. 202.
[62]Sumney, 'Pauline Rhetoric Pattern', pp. 202-203.

obedience (2:15-17). This does not, however, prove an A-B-A pattern, but only that 2:13-17 is the closing of the first main section of the letter. Although there are some similarities between 1:10-12 and 3:1-5, they are not close enough or numerous enough to see the sections as parallel. The statements concerning the Thessalonians' acceptance of the gospel are used in two different contexts, and at best the other parallels are only words or names. Furthermore, Sumney's parallels do not take into account the words linking various sections. He says 'the thought [of 2:14] is broken off by comments about the necessity of obedience',[63] but this ignores the fact that the 'so then' [ἄρα οὖν] at the beginning of 2 Thessalonians 2:15 clearly draws a conclusion from what precedes it. Sumney's argument does not strengthen the case to link 3:1-5 with what precedes it rather than what follows it because the introductory word of 3:1, 'finally' [τὸ λοιπόν], makes a strong break in the argument that introduces the body closing. In addition, Sumney's identification of the 'disorderly' in 3:6-13 with the errorists condemned in 2:1-12 is not convincing because he presents no actual links in the text between the two sections. Therefore this idea must be seen only as speculation. However, Sumney does show that the links between 2:15-17 and 2 Thessalonians 1 are 'certainly more substantial than the verbal similarities with 1 Thessalonians that Marxsen and Trilling note'.[64] Therefore, although Sumney is not convincing on his major thesis, he does show that 2 Thessalonians is not simply copying the format of 1 Thessalonians.

C. *Scalometry*

George Barr desires to present an objective statistical model that can be used to determine the authenticity and integrity of the letters of Paul.[65] He calls his methodology 'scalometry'. His basic premise is that certain writers display very distinct patterns in the length of sentences throughout their writings as a whole. In particular, Paul's letters display a distinct pattern with longer sentences in the first portion (usually the theological section) and shorter sentences in the latter portion (the more practical sections).

Barr's primary methodology is to graph the cumulative sums of the length of the sentences on the vertical axis and each sentence in order on the horizontal axis. Barr believes these graphs show a unique rhythmic pattern for the letters of Paul. The cumulative sums are determined by three factors: (1) the previous cumulative sum $[S_{i-1}]$ of the preceding sentence; (2) the number of words in the particular sentence $[X_i]$; and (3) the average

---

[63] Sumney, 'Pauline Rhetoric Pattern', p. 197.
[64] Sumney, 'Pauline Rhetoric Pattern', p. 198.
[65] George K. Barr, *Scalometry and the Pauline Epistles* (JSNTSup 261; London: T & T Clark, 2004).

number of words in all the sentences [X_{ave}] in the total sample. Thus the first task is to determine the number of words in each sentence in the particular letter of Paul. Basically he uses the sentences which in UBS^3 conclude with a full stop.[66] The relationship of the three factors used to determine the cumulative sum is found in the following equation: $S_i = S_{i-1} + (X_i - X_{ave})$. Thus for 2 Thessalonians, there are 27 sentences containing 823 words. Therefore $X_{ave} = 823/27 = 30.48$ (rounded to 30.5). The graph always begins at (0, 0) and it always ends back on the horizontal axis. Therefore S_0 is a value of 0. The first sentence is 28 words long, so $S_1 = 0 + (28 - 30.5) = -2.5$. The second sentence is 158 words in length, so $S_2 = -2.5 + (158 - 30.5) = 125$. The following chart shows what the numbers would be for all of 2 Thessalonians.

Cumulative Sum Information for 2 Thessalonians

#	sentences	# of words [X_i]	$S_{i-1} + (X_i - X_{ave})$	#	sentences	# of words [X_i]	$S_{i-1} + (X_i - X_{ave})$
0			0	14	3:1-2	32	154
1	1:1-2	28	-2.5	15	3:3	13	136.5
2	1:3-10	158	125	16	3:4	13	119
3	1:11-12	49	143.5	17	3:5	18	106.5
4	2:1-3a	54	167	18	3:6	27	103
5	2:3b-4	40	176.5	19	3:7-9	48	120.5
6	2:5	10	156	20	3:10	17	107
7	2:6	13	138.5	21	3:11-12	29	105.5
8	2:7	15	123	22	3:13	6	81
9	2:8-10	57	149.5	23	3:14-15	27	77.5
10	2:11-12	27	146	24	3:16a	15	62
11	2:13-14	44	159.5	25	3:16b	5	36.5
12	2:15	17	146	26	3:17	14	20
13	2:16-17	37	152.5	27	3:18	10	-0.5

---

[66] Barr, *Scalometry*, mentions three adaptations he makes to following the full stops found in the UBS^3 text: (1) When there is a string of questions (as in Rom., 1 and 2 Cor., and Gal.), these small questions throw off the surrounding scale as a whole. Thus he groups the questions together in line with the surrounding scale (p. 34). (2) When faced with colons, he finds editors vary greatly on their use, but very little on the use of full stops. Thus he decided usually to ignore colons, or adjust to the surrounding scale (p. 36). (3) When one-word exclamations like 'amen' are used, he usually links them to the preceding sentence (p. 26).

Cumulative Sum Graph of 2 Thessalonians

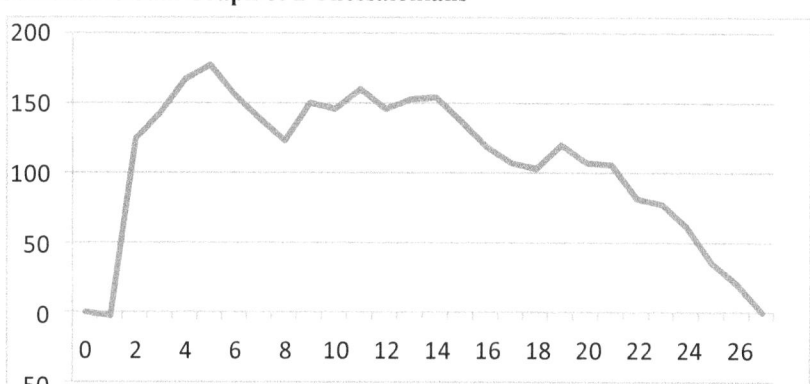

In this graph, the horizontal axis represents the twenty-seven sentences of 2 Thessalonians, and the vertical axis represents the cumulative sum of the sentences to that point. When the graph of this information rises, then that sentence is longer than the average, and when the graph declines, the particular sentence is shorter than average.[67] Thus it can be seen with 2 Thessalonians that basically the first half of the book has longer sentences, while the second half of the book has shorter sentences. This follows the basic pattern found most particularly in the undisputed letters of Paul, and also in rest of the epistles attributed to Paul in the New Testament.[68]

Barr has addressed some of the problems that have affected previous studies concerning sentence length. In particular he has been far more sensitive to where in a letter samples have been taken, and he also uses a somewhat more objective and external standard for sentence length (based on UBS³ full stops). He has also taken somewhat into consideration the nature of the argument, such as the series of short questions in Romans, 1 and 2 Corinthians and Galatians.

Second, Barr has shown that the mean sentence length in the Pauline corpus is similar in range both compared to present day authors and ancient authors.[69]

Third, Barr has also brought a new idea, that of 'scaling', into the discussion of authenticity. His broad comparisons with twenty modern and ancient writers give even greater weight to his findings.

---

[67] Barr, *Scalometry*, p. 28.
[68] Barr, *Scalometry*, pp. 86-88, 167.
[69] Barr, *Scalometry*, p. 31.

Fourth, Barr's methodology has also shown how most of the Pauline letters that have on occasion been viewed as multiple letters 'glued' together are actually letters with internal integrity. Barr believes his findings show that 2 Corinthians was originally two Pauline letters, and that 1 Timothy and Titus each contain insertions.

There are, however, some weaknesses with Barr's methodology. Because Barr must adjust some of the sentences, it could be argued he did this to make his graphs work.[70] Furthermore, although Barr does remove some quotations, it is possible that he should remove many more items of preformed material. For example, his samples from Romans include extensive quoting of Scripture, but because these do not seem to affect the scale, they are not removed. The question then arises, are the cumulative sums really indicative of a purely Pauline pattern? Finally, although his methodology does take into account more thoroughly where the sentences are in the argument as a whole, he still separates the statistical methods from exegesis.

Barr's methodology has added a new dimension to the discussion of authenticity. His very broad use of samples outside of scripture and his observation that there is a unique pattern and rhythm to the Pauline epistles is an important discovery. The fact that the eschatological sections of 2 Thessalonians are found in the first portion of the epistle, while the primary eschatological sections of 1 Thessalonians are found the second portion of that epistle, shows that the writer of 2 Thessalonians is clearly not just copying from 1 Thessalonians, for the scaling of his sentences remains appropriate for the section of each epistle. Barr's methodology shows that 2 Thessalonians has integrity as a letter, for its rhythm and scaling clearly put it within the Pauline pattern.

III. Vocabulary and Stylistic Features of 2 Thessalonians

In the past, both disputers and defenders of authenticity relied heavily on statistics about word frequency to determine authenticity. With the aid of computers these studies have been able to examine far more literature and more linguistic patterns than ever before. Yet like all other areas of study, the use of computers is dependent on the presuppositions of the programmer and on the manner in which particular questions are framed. Thus it is necessary to examine some methodologies being used, and their presuppositions, to see if some of these methods can be employed concerning the authenticity of 2 Thessalonians.

---

[70]See Adams, 'Review', pp. R31-34.

A. Word Ratios

One of the early statistical models used to evaluate authorship of the Pauline epistles was developed by K. Grayston and G. Herdan,[71] who used vocabulary to examine style in two separate tests.

After evaluating other methods, they present their first test, which relates to a ratio ('C') which is defined as:

C = [(words peculiar to a chosen part) + (words common to all parts)] (vocabulary of the chosen part)

'C' is then calculated for each of the Pauline letters. On the whole this ratio is very consistent for all the Pauline corpus (C = 31.0 – 34.8) except for the Thessalonians epistles (29.5) and the Pastorals (46.2). In reference to the Thessalonian epistles, they note that the two letters have 145 words in common with each other, and '*not fewer than sixty words common to both letters which are either* hapax legomena (in the true sense of the word occurring once in the letter) *or* dislegomena *in both letters, or* hapax legomenon *in one and* dislegomenon *in the other.* This clearly speaks for the partial identity of the two letters.'[72] As a result they suggest that the author of 2 Thessalonians copied 1 Thessalonians.

The second test, called a 'bi-logarithmic type/token ratio', compares the vocabulary of a particular letter to the total text length (**g** = log V/ log N, where 'V' = vocabulary of a particular letter and 'N' = the length of the text). This information is then placed on a bi-logarithmic graph. Ten of the Pauline letters are very close to the constant ratio, while only the Pastorals are not close to the rest of the Pauline corpus. Therefore, 1 and 2 Thessalonians fit this criterion for Pauline style, though Grayston and Herdan add that this does not prove they come from the same hand.[73]

Thus, with regard to the tests presented by Grayston and Herdan, only the first test can be used to dispute the authorship of the Thessalonian letters. When they conducted the test, however, the only examples Grayston and Herdan found not to fit the Pauline patterns (that is, the Thessalonian epistles and the Pastorals) were also the only samples for which they combined epistles to create the sample, thus distorting all the numbers in the equation. According to Grayston and Herdan, the total vocabulary for 1 and 2 Thessalonians is 471 words, with 58 words peculiar to them, and 81 words common to all the

---

[71] Grayston and Herdan, 'Authorship of the Pastorals', pp. 1-15.
[72] Grayston and Herdan, 'Authorship of the Pastorals', pp. 8-10.
[73] Grayston and Herdan, 'Authorship of the Pastorals', pp. 12, 14.

epistles. This means C = (58+ 81)/471, which is 29.5.[74] According to J. E. Frame, 1 Thessalonians has 362 words, with 42 words peculiar to itself, while 2 Thessalonians has 250 words with 26 words peculiar to itself.[75] Using the ratio suggested by Grayston and Herdan, for 1 Thessalonians C = (42 + 81)/362, which is 34.0, and for 2 Thessalonians C = (26 + 81)/ 250, which is 42.8. This would show 1 Thessalonians to be well within the 'Pauline' range established by Grayston and Herdan, and 2 Thessalonians to be well outside of this range. However, the number of 'words common to all letters' must also be called into question because neither the Thessalonian epistles nor the Pastorals are dealt with individually. This especially affects the equation for 'C' for a short letter such as 2 Thessalonians. The way the equation is set up, the 'words common to all letters' (81) overwhelms the other component of the numerator of the equation, distorting the ratio. This is seen when one realizes that 2 Thessalonians actually has a lower percentage of peculiar words (10.4 %) than does 1 Thessalonians (11.6%), yet the 'C' ratios are drastically different. In fact, only if 2 Thessalonians had *no* peculiar words would it fit the criterion set up by Grayston and Herdan (C = (0 + 81)/ 250, which is 32.4)—and then it would be identified as unpauline for its *lack* of peculiar words. Therefore, this test allows for no possible way for 2 Thessalonians to 'pass'. Any test that can only be failed, except by having the strangest peculiarities, is totally invalid for stylistic comparison, and thus the test by Grayston and Herdan is invalid in the case of 2 Thessalonians.

B. *Stylistic Peculiarities*

One of the sections in Trilling's disputation which appears most persuasive contains his numerous lists of non-Pauline characteristics in 2 Thessalonians. After concluding that neither Rigaux's analysis of style, nor the fact that 2 Thessalonians has more vocabulary in common with the undisputed letters of Paul than does 1 Thessalonians, allows one to make a judgment about authenticity,[76] he then makes his own list of stylistic peculiarities which he believes strengthens the disputers' case. He begins his listing under the heading of 'fullness of expression' (*plerophorie*), which includes compound words, the frequent use of 'all', difficult substantives, non-specific adjectives, parallel verbs with the same meaning, and noun-substantive parallels. The number and variety of these categories make it appear that 2 Thessalonians cannot possibly be Pauline; however, when each of these groupings is examined individually, many are seen to be subjective criteria.

---

[74]Grayston and Herdan, 'Authorship of the Pastorals', p. 9.

[75]Frame, *Thessalonians*, pp. 28-32.

[76]Trilling, *Untersuchung*, pp. 46-47, 57.

Trilling lists four compound words which he thinks are unusual for Paul,[77] yet A. Kenny's exhaustive computer study of all the letters in the Pauline corpus has shown that this characteristic cannot be used as a criterion for determining authorship.[78]

Paul's use of 'all' in the undisputed letters also shows that this cannot be used to show that 2 Thessalonians is pseudonymous. Paul does not use 'all' with any numerical consistency among his undisputed letters: it is used only 2 times in Philemon, 15 times in Galatians, and 18 times in 1 Thessalonians, but it is used 72 times in Romans, 111 times in 1 Corinthians and 33 times in Philippians. When this is compared to the 16 times that it is used in 2 Thessalonians, then it can be seen that Philippians uses 'all' *more* frequently than 2 Thessalonians, and the very long letter 1 Corinthians is nearly the same frequency. Therefore the frequency of 'all' in 2 Thessalonians actually places 2 Thessalonians within the limits of the undisputed letters of Paul. This is a very important point, because Trilling desires to show that 2 Thessalonians is not really a letter but a generalizing tract. Furthermore, the phrase 'in every way' (3:16) does not make 2 Thessalonians a general epistle for all situations, as Trilling says, but was actually a cliché that was frequently used in letters of that time.[79] The author of 2 Thessalonians does not generalize any more than the undisputed Paul.

The use of non-specific adjectives which Trilling identifies in 2 Thessalonians also has a high degree of subjectivity as a criterion for authenticity. The adjectives he mentions are 'righteous' in 1:5; 'eternal' in 1:9 and 2:16; 'good' in 2:16, 17; and 'wicked and evil' in 3:2. Although 'wicked' is used only here in the Pauline corpus and 'evil' is not used very frequently, 'righteous' is used seven times, 'eternal' is used six times, and 'good' is used twenty-one times in Romans alone. Such statements as 'the commandment is holy, righteous and good' in Romans 7:12, and the promise of 'eternal life' in Romans 2:7, reflect the same sort of use which Trilling isolates in 2 Thessalonians. Therefore this category also must be considered as being of little value in distinguishing 2 Thessalonians from the undisputed letters of Paul.

---

[77]ὑπεραυξάνει (1:3); ἐγκαυχᾶσθαι (1:4); καταξιωθῆναι (1:5); ἐνδοξασθῆναι (1:10), ἐνξασθῇ (1:12).

[78]Kenny, *Stylometric Study,* p. 88, shows that when comparing the compound verbs as a proportion of total vocabulary, 2 Thess. is the same as Phil. and has a higher proportion than Phlm., while a lower proportion than Rom., 1 and 2 Cor., Gal., and 1 Thess. The variance within the undisputed letters means this criterion is not usable to distinguish authentic from non-authentic letters. Neumann, *Authenticity,* p. 203, notes that it is not among the best variable sets, while O'Brien, *Introductory Thanksgivings,* p. 72, n. 32, comments on 2 Thess. 1:3 that Paul favors compounds with ὑπέρ.

[79]White, *Light from Ancient Letters,* p. 212. See also Rom. 3:2 and Phil. 1:18.

The Authenticity of 2 Thessalonians

Trilling lists three examples of substantives with similar meanings:[80] 'God or object of worship' in 2:4; 'in every good deed and word' in 2:17; and 'by labor and struggle, night and day' in 3:8. It is difficult to see how Trilling can stress that 'by labor and struggle, night and day' shows nonpauline style when Trilling himself believes this was probably copied from 1 Thessalonians 2:9. This parallel construction in which two related terms or phrases are objects of the same preposition is not unpauline. For example, 'in every good deed and word' appears very similar in form to 'against impiety and unrighteousness of men' (Rom. 1:18) and 'in all speech and in all knowledge' (1 Cor. 1:5).[81] Therefore the only peculiar example in this category is 'God or object of worship' in 2 Thessalonians 2:4.

When all the rest of the stylistic peculiarities are taken together, a very clear pattern can be discerned. This is seen most clearly in the following table, compiled from Trilling's lists, which shows the number and kind of peculiarities and where they are found in 2 Thessalonians.

Trilling's List of Stylistic Peculiarities in 2 Thessalonians

2 Thessalonians 1:

```
                       F    F
                       G    G
            F    G F   F G F S F
            X G  G G S G S G S G
Verse  1 2  3 4  5 6   7 8 9 10 11 12
```

2 Thessalonians 2:

```
                 F              G   F
            X N       F    X    G X G
            X V       X S F S S X S S    F F
Verse  1 2  3 4  5 6  7 8 9 10 11 12 13 14 15 16 17
```

2 Thessalonians 3:

```
       F
       G   F          G G F F   G V    X       X
Verse  1 2 3 4  5 6 7 8 9 10 11 12 13 14 15 16 17 18
```

In these charts each letter stands for one particular stylistic peculiarity: S = difficult substantives; V= parallel verbs with same meaning; N = noun-adjective parallels; X = conspicuous expressions; G = preferred word groups; and F =

---

[80] Trilling, *Untersuchung*, p. 60, 'Entsprechendes gilt für Substantive'.
[81] 2 Thess. 2:17: ἐν παντὶ ἔργῳ καὶ λόγῳ ἀγαθῷ; Rom. 1:18: ἐπὶ πᾶσαν ἀσέβειαν καὶ ἀδικίαν ἀνθρώπων; and 1 Cor. 1:5: ἐν παντὶ λόγῳ καὶ πάσῃ γνώσει.

parallel phrases. As can clearly be seen, the three largest groups of peculiarities are found primarily within the sections which were identified in ch. 3 as tradition (1:6-10; 2:3-4, 7-12). The only peak that does not fall within the tradition sections occurs at 1:11. One of the phrases Trilling lists as peculiar in this verse is 'work of faith in power', yet it is difficult to see how this shows nonpauline style, for Trilling follows Wrede's hypothesis of literary dependence, and the phrase 'work of faith' is one of the phrases Wrede believes is directly dependent on 1 Thessalonians (1:3). The phrase 'in power' is also found a number of times in the undisputed letters of Paul,[82] and thus this cannot be used as a sign of nonpauline style. Furthermore, the word group 'worthy' [ἄξιος, ἀξιοῦν] appears to be chosen specifically for the problem being addressed in 2 Thessalonians 1, suffering (1:3, 5, 11), and it likely arose out of Jewish prayer language.[83] Consequently the peculiarities that make this a peak do not really display such unusual characteristics as Trilling suggests.

Therefore these peculiarities do not show that the whole letter is nonpauline, but only that the preformed sections are. This same pattern is found in the undisputed letters of Paul as well: whenever Paul uses preformed material, it displays nonpauline characteristics. Consequently, Trilling's stylistic lists actually enhance the case that 2 Thessalonians is Pauline.

C. *Connectives*

A. Q. Morton has presented two stylistic tests to determine the authorship of the Pauline epistles.[84] His first test has to do with 'sentence length distribution'. Because this test requires a document to have at least fifty sentences, he was not able to include 2 Thessalonians, Titus, or Philemon in this test. The result of this test is that only Romans, 1 and 2 Corinthians, and Galatians are seen as Pauline. His second test, which evaluates the relative frequency of certain connectives ['and' (καί), 'but' (δέ), 'for' (γάρ), 'if' (εἰ)] yields similar results: only Romans, 1 and 2 Corinthians, and Galatians can be accepted as Pauline. Ephesians, Philippians, and Colossians are all isolated from each other statistically, but 1 and 2 Thessalonians are grouped together, as are 1 and 2 Timothy. Both Titus and Philemon are viewed as too short to evaluate by this test. He thinks that even Romans, although genuinely Pauline, has been adapted with the addition of between six and eight sentences to Romans 1.[85]

One major problem with Morton's statistics with reference to 2 Thessalonians is that they also negate the authenticity of 1 Thessalonians. If 1

---

[82] Rom. 1:4; 15:13, 19; 1 Cor. 2:5; 4:20; 15:43.
[83] See Aus, 'Liturgical Background', pp. 432-38.
[84] Morton, 'Authorship', pp. 165-83.
[85] Morton, 'Authorship', pp. 180-83.

Thessalonians is judged to be authentic, then by Morton's criteria, 2 Thessalonians must also be judged to be authentic because it falls into the same range. A second problem with Morton's statistics is that they do not take into account any contextual variation. This lack of exegetical concern on Morton's part means that a short letter with only a few topics is much more liable to fail his test simply because those particular topics may be dealt with in a style different from other topics. In addition, because Morton does not remove any quotes or traditional material, his comparison to a book such as Romans, with its numerous quotes, means that his standard for comparison does not display only Pauline stylistic patterns. David Mealand reexamines Morton's test for authorship by considering the use and position of the same four Greek particles ('and' [καί], 'but' [δέ], 'for' [γάρ], 'if' [εἰ]). In particular he examines the use of these particles at the beginning of sentences (first or second position) in order to see if this criterion distinguishes four letters (Rom., 1 and 2 Cor., Gal.), seven letters (adding Phil., 1 and 2 Thess.), or ten letters (adding Col., Eph., 2 Tim.) as from Paul.[86] He believes that Philemon is too short to be valid for this kind of examination. He uses the UBS edition of the Greek New Testament and defines a sentence as ending with a full stop, a question mark, or a colon. When he examines 'and' [καί] he finds that 2 Thessalonians is as close as Galatians to the undisputed Paulines, and that the seven letters as a whole cohere, with some question about 2 Thessalonians. In looking at 'but' [δέ] he again notes that the seven-epistle group coheres—in fact, the four-epistle group and the ten-epistle group are both less coherent than the seven-epistle group. When studying 'for' [γάρ] he comments on the great variety of usage among all the epistles: 'Were we to invoke different authorship alone that would lead us to assign even the four major epistles to different authors'. The usage of this particle probably depends on such variables as subject, situation and mood. The last particle, 'if' [εἰ], he finds to be a poor discriminator, and a four-epistle group shows no greater sign of unity than does a seven-epistle group. Therefore, Mealand concludes that if the use of positional tests of this sort are valid, then a seven-epistle theory fares better than a four-epistle theory.

Mealand's study is very limited in its scope, using only one test without attempting to prove whether this test is valid. However, his paper is of value in showing further weaknesses of Morton's arguments. It also is significant in that it links 2 Thessalonians stylistically to the undisputed Pauline letters.

D. *Independent Vocabulary and Grammatical Features*

Anthony Kenny has examined ninety-nine independent vocabulary and grammatical features of the Greek text to determine peculiarities and similarities

---

[86]Mealand, 'Positional Stylometry Reassessed', pp. 266-86.

The Literary Character of 2 Thessalonians

within the New Testament.[87] Of these ninety-nine tests, he was able to use ninety-six of them on the letters of Paul.[88] When he examines the Pauline letters he finds a greater difference between Romans and 1 Thessalonians than between the four Gospels. Using these ninety-six tests he then calculates the correlation between each epistle and every other epistle in the Pauline corpus. A perfect correlation would be 1.0. From this data he notes that only one book of the whole Pauline corpus stands out from the rest: Titus. Although he admits that the coefficients for the correlation of the epistles are not strictly additive, he does add them together to determine an order from the 'most comfortable to the least: Romans, Philippians, 2 Timothy, 2 Corinthians, Galatians, 2 Thessalonians, 1 Thessalonians, Colossians, Ephesians, 1 Timothy, Philemon, 1 Corinthians, Titus'. He concludes his chapter on the Pauline epistles, 'What is to be said of the authorship of the Epistles is in the end a matter for the Scripture scholar, not the stylometrist. But on the basis of the evidence in this chapter for my part I see no reason to reject the hypothesis that twelve of the Pauline Epistles are the work of a single, unusually versatile author'.[89]

Kenny rejects Morton's criteria of sentence-length and positional stylometry because the sentence length test is inherently subjective, for Morton's figures published in 1966 concerning Romans show a large enough divergence from his figures published in 1978 concerning Romans to imply a different author for the exact same book.[90] Morton's other tests can lead to the same kind of absurd results.[91]

Kenny's work is valuable for its exhaustive format focusing upon

---

[87]Kenny, *Stylometric Study*, pp. 123-24. The following list summarizes Kenny's tests:
Tests 1-2, the number of occurrences of 'and' [καί] and 'to be' [εἶναι]
Tests 3-22, the number and use of conjunctions and particles
Tests 23-35, occurrences of prepositions
Tests 36-45, occurrences of articles in various forms
Tests 46-57, occurrences of nouns in various forms
Tests 58-67, occurrences of pronouns in various forms
Test 68, occurrences of 'he', 'she', 'it' [αὐτός]
Tests 69-77, occurrences of different kinds of adjectives in various forms
Test 78, occurrences of 'all' [πᾶς]
Tests 79-82, occurrences of adverbs
Tests 83-99, occurrences of verbs in various forms

[88]Kenny, *Stylometric Study*, p. 124, notes that because of the limited number of non-standard adverbs, tests 80-82 were combined into one test. In addition, the pluperfect is never used in the Pauline corpus, so test 94 is not used.

[89]Kenny, *Stylometric Study*, pp. 95, 98, 100.

[90]Kenny, *Stylometric Study*, p. 108.

[91]Kenny, *Stylometric Study*, p. 115.

characteristics of style. However, it must be used carefully, for Kenny does not include any larger grammatical stylistic categories. Nor does he deal with any theology in his study, but only with the letters as a whole. He does not remove quotes, citations, or any other material from the text, possibly affecting some of his identified Pauline characteristics. Although this kind of examination can never prove a particular letter is Pauline, it can help to expose specious arguments and to demonstrate overall trends.

E. *Stylo-statistical Analysis*

Trilling's analysis of the style of 2 Thessalonians is not exhaustive in comparing it to the rest of the Pauline corpus, nor does he make sufficient comparisons to other known nonpauline writings or take into account any use of tradition within 2 Thessalonians. As a result, his findings are often subjective. In contrast to this, Kenneth J. Neumann's stylistic analysis shows a much more objective approach.[92] He first compares known Pauline material to other known Pauline material, and then, known Pauline material to known nonpauline material. From this he is able to judge which of his 617 indices could consistently be used to distinguish known Pauline material from known nonpauline material.[93] In choosing his samples he is also careful to remove quotes, salutations, and preformed traditions. Finally, he uses groups of tests together to see which group gives the most consistent identification of known samples. The two groupings which give 100% accurate identification of known Pauline samples he labels VARSET1 and VARSET2. VARSET1 has four indices: (1) the average word length in letters (not including *iota* subscript); (2) the number of relative and indefinite pronouns; (3) the number of initial *taus* (τ); and (4) the first noun-position in a modified full stop sentence. VARSET2 also has four indices; the first three are the same as VARSET1, and the fourth is the ratio of the percent of initial sentence connectors within the total number of modified full-stop sentences to the number of independent and major dependent clauses.[94]

When Neumann examines 2 Thessalonians, he finds it closer to Paul than to any other author but does not feel his criterion proves or disproves Pauline authorship. However, the one weakness of Neumann's work with regard to 2 Thessalonians is that in his effort to keep his sample size of 750 words, he does not remove any pieces of tradition. Because Neumann finds that if tradition is not removed, even a known Pauline sample could be improperly identified, it is

---

[92]Neumann, *Authenticity*.
[93]Neumann, *Authenticity*, p. 173.
[94]Neumann, *Authenticity*, p. 209.

$$\frac{\text{(number of initial sentence connectors/number of modified full stop sentences)} \times 100\%}{\text{number of independent clauses + major dependent clauses}}$$

therefore necessary to apply the five tests which make up VARSET1 and VARSET2 to 2 Thessalonians after the pieces of tradition have been removed. In order to do so, I applied the five tests to two samples from 2 Thessalonians, one containing only tradition and one with the tradition removed, to see if removing the tradition altered the results.

The following chart shows Neumann's mean results and standard deviations for the five tests that he found were the best for identifying Paul's letters. The samples Neumann used already had tradition and quotations removed, and his results are listed in the 'Undisputed Paul' columns. The figures in the '2 Thessalonians' columns compare my statistics from the tradition portion of 2 Thessalonians with the statistics from non-tradition portion of the letter. The statistics of the non-tradition portion of 2 Thessalonians can then be compared with Neumann's mean for each test on the undisputed Pauline letters.

Comparison of 2 Thessalonians and Neumann's Stylo-statistical Analysis of Paul's Undisputed Letters

	2 Thessalonians		Undisputed Paul[95]	
	Non-Tradition	Tradition	Mean	Standard Deviation
1. Word length	4.87	5.09	4.817	.12
2. Rel. and indef. pron.	17.82	16.74	11.125	4.29
3. Initial *tau* [τ]	86.38	127.23	95.125	9.11
4. First Noun Posit.	3.44	4.8	3.271	.195
5. Ratio of Sent. Conn.	.0909	0	.06444	.0522

In examining these results, it is first of all important to see that the tradition sections display significantly different stylistic characteristics from the non-tradition sections in 2 Thessalonians.[96] This again shows that the writer of 2

---

[95] Neumann calls this category 'Paul (all)'. The information for this category is taken from Neumann, *Authenticity*, pp. 207-10. The figures used are those which average all his samples, not just the original samples. Neumann's test samples are always 750 words in length; Phlm. is too short to use.

[96] I examined 2 Thess. 1:3–3:16 for my figures, which are listed under '2 Thessalonians' as 'Non-Tradition' and 'Tradition'. I chose this sample in order to include as much of the letter as possible, but to eliminate opening and closing greetings which are often stereotyped and do not necessarily display the author's normal style. Because the tradition and non-tradition sections are both shorter than 750 words, it was necessary on tests no. 2 and no. 3, which are dependent on the length of the sample, to adjust the numbers proportionally. In the sample made from 2 Thess. 1:3–3:16 there are 224 words of tradition and 547 words from the author himself. Therefore in tests no. 2 and

Thessalonians uses preformed material. Second, in all but one test (the number of relative and indefinite pronouns), the writer of 2 Thessalonians (non-tradition) is within the standard deviation of the undisputed letters of Paul, while in every case the tradition sections are outside the standard deviation. Neumann himself questions the validity of the second test (the number of relative and indefinite pronouns), for he notes that this index varies greatly for Paul, with 1 Thessalonians (having only 2 occurrences) in the third standard deviation. Thus 2 Thessalonians is closer than 1 Thessalonians to the Pauline mean in this particular test. Third, it must be remembered that Neumann's tests are not meant to be used individually but are considered conclusive only when used as a group. Four out of five tests which have been shown to correctly identify Pauline samples and to distinguish Pauline samples from nonpauline samples show 2 Thessalonians to be Pauline. In the case of the fifth test, which Neumann himself questions, 2 Thessalonians still is closer to the undisputed Paulines than 1 Thessalonians. Fourth, the nature of these tests precludes the likelihood that an imitator could have made his letter 'look like Paul'. It is hard to imagine an imitator counting the number of letters in each word, averaging them against known Pauline samples, and then consciously changing the average number of letters away from the Pauline mean in the tradition sections. The same is true with the other tests. The degree of sophistication required for an unknown author to use two distinct styles within the same piece of writing, to correctly imitate the style of Paul in the appropriate places, and to imitate with stylistic indices which are unlikely to be known—all without the aid of a computer—is beyond comprehension. Thus Neumann's methodology, when applied to 2 Thessalonians after the traditional sections have been removed, greatly strengthens the case for the authenticity of 2 Thessalonians.

In 1995, Mealand produced a much more sophisticated model than his previous study.[97] He was strongly influenced by Neumann's work.[98] He first removed clearly marked quotations and hymns, and then used a sample size of 1000 words. Because 2 Thessalonians has only 823 words and Titus, 659, he multiplied their statistics to make it up to sample size of 1000.[99] He first started with twenty-five variables, and after some initial studies this number was

---

no. 3, the numbers for 'non-tradition' were multiplied by a figure of 750/547, and the figures for 'tradition' were multiplied by 750/224. For test no. 2 there were thirteen relative and indefinite pronouns in the 'non-tradition' section, and five in the tradition section, while for test no. 3 there were sixty-three words beginning with τ in the 'non-tradition' section and thirty-eight in the 'tradition' section. The traditions in 2 Thess. are identified in ch. 3 of this book.

[97] Mealand, 'Extent of the Pauline Corpus', pp. 61-92.
[98] Mealand, 'Extent of the Pauline Corpus', p. 64.
[99] Mealand, 'Extent of the Pauline Corpus', p. 64

reduced to nineteen variables.[100] He then did a cluster analysis of these variables. His initial findings were that Romans, 2 Corinthians, and Galatians made a cluster, some of the samples from 1 Corinthians made another cluster, 1 and 2 Thessalonians, Philippians, and Colossians, another cluster. One of the Romans samples was also quite distant from the main Pauline cluster.[101] James also tended to cluster with Paul.[102] Eventually, with discriminant analysis, six of the nineteen variables were chosen which were most helpful in identifying groups. These variables are: word length, initial tau, 'for' [γάρ], relatives and indefinites, 'in' [ἐν] and 'not' [οὐ].[103] With reference to 2 Thessalonians he concludes his study by noting that 1 Thessalonians is more distant from the major letters of Paul than is 2 Thessalonians, and that after discriminant analysis 2 Thessalonians is definitely classed with Paul.[104]

F. *Further Vocabulary Analysis*

Gerard Ledger also used cluster and multivariant analysis in 1995, but focused entirely on vocabulary.[105] He began his study by breaking the entire New Testament into 1000 word samples. The only book under 1000 words which he examined was 2 Thessalonians, and he multiplied his results to make it comparable to other samples. This gave him 126 samples from the New Testament.[106] He used a total of twenty-nine variables concerning vocabulary. The first category he referred to as ALET. This concerned the percentage of words containing a particular letter in the Greek alphabet; thus there were potentially twenty-four ALETs. However, he noted that six of the letters in the Greek alphabet are rarely used, so he combined these six letters into one ALET, and thus had only nineteen ALETs.[107] The second category he referred to as BLET. This concerned the percentage of words ending in a specific letter. Because Greek words use a limited number of endings, every Greek word ends with only one of nine letters [α, ε, η, ι, ν, ο, σ, υ, ω]. The third vocabulary category was the type/token ratio (TTK). Because each sample has 1000 words, then there are 1000 tokens for each sample. The types are the number of different words in the sample. Thus if every word was only used once in the

---

[100] Mealand, 'Extent of the Pauline Corpus', p. 70.
[101] Mealand, 'Extent of the Pauline Corpus', p. 78.
[102] Mealand, 'Extent of the Pauline Corpus', p. 79.
[103] Mealand, 'Extent of the Pauline Corpus', p. 81.
[104] Mealand, 'Extent of the Pauline Corpus', pp. 82, 85-86.
[105] Ledger, 'Exploration of Differences', pp. 85-97.
[106] Ledger, 'Exploration of Differences', pp. 86, 97. Thus he excluded from his examination Titus, Phlm., 2 John, 3 John, and Jude.
[107] Ledger, 'Exploration of Differences', p. 86.

sample, the ratio would be 1. Because these types are orthographical entities, not lexicographic ones, any different form of the same word counts as a separate type. Thus he began with twenty-nine variables: nineteen ALETs, nine BLETs, and one TTK.[108]

He then examined multiple samples from Acts, Romans, 1 Corinthians and Revelation using multivariate and cluster analysis to see if the samples clustered into particular clusters. He found using the samples from these four books that the data created three distinct clusters: one cluster having both Romans and 1 Corinthians, one for Acts, and one for Revelation. This confirmed his hypothesis that studying these characteristics could potentially show differences in style and perhaps authorship.[109] When he ran these tests on all the New Testament epistles, he found two defined clusters.[110] The first cluster consisted of Romans, 1 and 2 Corinthians, Galatians, Philippians, and 2 Thessalonians. The second cluster contained Colossians, Ephesians and Hebrews. The books of James, 1 and 2 Peter, 1 Thessalonians, and 1 and 2 Timothy were all found at varying distances from the first cluster.[111] When he isolated the particular variables that separated the two main clusters, the two variables that stood out the most were BLET7 (words with a final sigma) and the type/token ratio.[112] He then examined some of the frequently used words with a final sigma, particularly in Romans and Hebrews. Although he acknowledges that statistics cannot prove authorship, he concludes 'that 1 and 2 Corinthians, Galatians, Philippians, 2 Thessalonians and Romans seem to form a core Pauline group, but that the authenticity of all the remaining Epistles as Pauline works must remain doubtful'.[113]

There are a number of possible weaknesses with Ledger's study. First, it is focused entirely on vocabulary, yet particular topics or congregational needs may require a different vocabulary. Second, although explicit quotes are removed, no other traditional material is removed from the samples. Third, in smaller epistles, especially in 2 Thessalonians, which is the smallest epistle he examined, the vocabulary directly associated with epistolary practices could carry a greater percentage weight than in a longer letter. Nevertheless, it is significant that 2 Thessalonians is more closely associated with the undisputed Paulines than even 1 Thessalonians.

---

[108] Ledger, 'Exploration of Differences', p. 86.
[109] Ledger, 'Exploration of Differences', p. 88.
[110] He excluded 1 John because the data could distort the more general results. Ledger, 'Exploration of Differences', p. 90.
[111] Ledger, 'Exploration of Differences', p. 90.
[112] Ledger, 'Exploration of Differences', p. 91.
[113] Ledger, 'Exploration of Differences', p. 95.

IV. Literary Character and the Authenticity of 2 Thessalonians

Recent disputation concerning the authenticity of 2 Thessalonians has stressed the literary character of the epistle, seeing its similarities to the undisputed letters of Paul as literary dependence on 1 Thessalonians and its differences from the undisputed Paul as the result of a later pseudonymous author. This argument has been based primarily upon Wrede's work on literary dependence and strengthened by Trilling's examination and such studies as Daryl Schmidt's. Yet each of these works has shown significant weaknesses.

Wrede's extensive parallels, which are repeated throughout his disputation, give the initial impression that the writer of 2 Thessalonians must have copied and imitated 1 Thessalonians. However, upon closer examination, the only parallels which are really of any value in determining whether Wrede's hypothesis of literary dependence is viable are his six conspicuous parallels and his two particular parallels. Wrede's examination of five of these eight parallels is deficient because he fails to deal with the epistolary characteristics of both Thessalonian letters and he ignores the significant differences between the two letters and the individual parts. Two more of the parallels show no sign of literary dependence at all, only topical identity; this is exactly what one would expect of a letter from the same author to the same audience a short period of time later. The one true parallel need not be explained as literary dependence but is fully understandable as an example of Paul's tendency to repeat certain phrases about topics he frequently discussed, such as a defense and presentation of his ministerial practice. Thus Wrede's case fails because he does not take into account the epistolary genre, the similarities of 2 Thessalonians not only with 1 Thessalonians but also with the other undisputed letters of Paul, and the similar situation which both Thessalonian epistles address.

Trilling's list of peculiarities, when carefully evaluated, actually shows that the writer of 2 Thessalonians uses tradition in the places the context indicates tradition is to be recognized. The use of epistolary and rhetorical analyses also show that 2 Thessalonians is a real letter, not just a doctrinal tract. Neumann's exhaustive stylo-statistical criteria show that the non-tradition portions of 2 Thessalonians display typical Pauline style.

Some of the earlier statistical analyses tended to show that 2 Thessalonians is different from the undisputed letters of Paul. However, the statistical analyses have developed more sophistication by (1) comparing known Pauline samples first with known Pauline samples and then with known nonpauline samples; (2) comparing 2 Thessalonians to all the undisputed letters of Paul rather than just to 1 Thessalonians; and (3) removing citations and preformed traditions before performing the analysis. Using these improvements, the studies have regularly shown 2 Thessalonians is to be numbered with the undisputed letters of Paul.

Thus, when the literary character of 2 Thessalonians is examined in the light of the use of preformed tradition, using statistical tests and the application of epistolary and rhetorical analyses, 2 Thessalonians is seen to show the style and character of an undisputed letter of Paul.

Conclusion
The Authenticity of 2 Thessalonians

In the years since J. E. C. Schmidt first wrote to question the Pauline authorship of 2 Thessalonians, the debate about its authenticity has become focused on three major areas: (1) the presumed literary dependence of 2 Thessalonians upon 1 Thessalonians, (2) the supposed theological differences between 2 Thessalonians and the undisputed letters of Paul, and (3) the alleged non-Pauline style of the writing. These arguments are frequently considered to have additive force, making the case for disputation unassailable. However, when each individual piece of the case for disputation is considered, the conclusion is far from certain.

The starting point for many modern disputers is the belief that because of the many similarities to 1 Thessalonians, 2 Thessalonians is literarily dependent on 1 Thessalonians and therefore must have been written at a later time by someone other than Paul. At the same time many disputers argue that the writing style and doctrine of 2 Thessalonians are too different from Paul to have been written by Paul. However, as we have seen, the differences between the two Thessalonian epistles are due in part to their different rhetorical purposes, and some of the similarities can be explained by their epistolary genre. The only clear parallels between the two letters are found in two places: in the salutation, which is the most stereotypical section of all the epistles, and in a proverbial statement which is used somewhat differently in the two epistles. The rest of the parallels involve occasional vocabulary similarities—exactly what one would expect in two letters written to the same audience. By focusing so much on perceived similarities to 1 Thessalonians, many of the disputers fail to do a thorough comparison of 2 Thessalonians to the rest of the undisputed letters of Paul. In fact, the actual vocabulary and syntax in 2 Thessalonians is actually closer to the undisputed letters than 1 Thessalonians is. Furthermore, the traditional portions of 2 Thessalonians display a different style from the rest of the letter, just as tradition does in Paul's other letters, explaining why these portions of 2 Thessalonians appear to be more impersonal. Thus a close examination of the literary character of 2 Thessalonians actually strengthens the case for authenticity.

Failing to compare 2 Thessalonians fully to the other letters of Paul also produces a wrong understanding of its use of tradition. The disputers argue that tradition in 2 Thessalonians is used in a nonpauline way which puts too much emphasis on Paul himself and not enough on Jesus and the cross, therefore exhibiting a later time in church history. However, our study of Paul's use of tradition shows that his letters contain more tradition than many commentators realize, and his use of tradition does not focus exclusively on Jesus but also includes practical exhortation to put into practice 'whatever you have learned or received or heard from me, or seen in me' (Phil. 4:9). Furthermore, the terminology used to refer to tradition and the volume of tradition in each letter are consistent with Paul.

The supposed theological differences between 2 Thessalonians and Paul are clarified by a careful consideration of the doctrine of 2 Thessalonians. The teaching in 2 Thessalonians concerning the return of Christ does not display a theology of delay which disagrees with Paul's teaching elsewhere; it simply reassures the believers that the day of the Lord has not yet happened because they have not yet been gathered to the Lord and because the final battle in which Christ conquers his ultimate enemy, Satan, has not yet happened. Nor is the command to imitate the life of Paul a later development, but rather, similar commands are found in Paul's letters to the churches that he personally established. Paul's gospel always includes not only the coming to faith, but also the living out of that faith; in the same way Paul's gospel presentation includes not only obedience to his words but also imitation of his life. The focus on Christ as Lord in 2 Thessalonians is not unusual for Paul, but instead, is especially appropriate in a letter focused on eschatology and obedience. Furthermore, salvation in 2 Thessalonians is not attained through meritorious suffering, but by believing the gospel (2 Thess. 1:10). Thus the doctrines in 2 Thessalonians considered by some to be unpauline are in fact consistent with the undisputed letters as they focus on the issues that troubled the church at that particular time.

The idea that 2 Thessalonians was written at a later time is also shown to be false when we consider the witness of the early church. As we have seen, the life and writings of Polycarp suggest that 2 Thessalonians was being used and recognized as Pauline when Polycarp was trained, at about AD 90 or before.
Based on this date, 2 Thessalonians must be Pauline because it would be highly unlikely for Polycarp or the churches in Macedonia to accept a pseudonymous letter as Pauline if it appeared so soon after Paul's death.

When carefully examined, each of these major categories—the early external attestation, the differences between the two Thessalonian epistles, and the similarity to the language, tradition, and teaching in Paul's other letters—authenticates this letter from the time of Paul which is consistent with Paul and was in fact authored by Paul.

Bibliography

Aarde, Andries G. van. 'The Struggle against Heresy in the Thessalonian Correspondence and the Origin of the Apostolic Tradition'. Pages 418-25 in *The Thessalonian Correspondence*. Edited by Raymond F. Collins. Leuven: Leuven University Press, 1990.

Adams, Sean. 'Review of *Scalometry and the Pauline Epistles*'. *Journal of Greco-Roman Christianity and Judaism* 2 (2001-2005): R31-34.

Adeney, Walter F. *Thessalonians and Galatians*. Century Bible. Edinburgh: TC & EC Jack, 1901.

Aejmelaeus, Lars. *Wachen vor dem Endem*. Schriften der Finnischen Exegetischen Gesellschaft 44. Helsinki: Finnish Exegetical Society, 1985.

Aland, Kurt et al., ed. *Greek New Testament*. 3rd corrected edition. Stuttgart: United Bible Societies, 1983.

Allison, Dale C., Jr. 'The Pauline Epistles and the Synoptic Gospels: The Pattern of the Parallels'. *New Testament Studies* 28 (1982): 1-32.

Apostolic Fathers. Edited by A. Roberts, J. Donaldson, and F. Crombie. Vol. 1 of Ante-Nicene Christian Library. 24 vols. Edinburgh: T & T Clark, 1867-1872.

Argyle, A. W. 'M and the Pauline Epistles'. *Expository Times* 81 (1969-70): 340-42.

———. 'Parallels between the Pauline Epistles and Q'. *Expository Times* 60 (1948-49): 318-20.

Arndt, William F., and Wilbur F. Gingrich. *A Greek-English Lexicon of the New Testament and Other Early Christian Literature*. Chicago: University of Chicago Press, 1957.

Aus, Roger D. 'Comfort in Judgment: The Use of the Day of the Lord and Theophany Traditions in Second Thessalonians 1'. Ph.D. thesis, Yale University, 1971.

———. 'God's Plan and God's Power: Isaiah 66 and the Restraining Factors of 2 Thess 2:6-7'. *Journal of Biblical Literature* 96 (1977): 537-53.

———. 'The Liturgical Background of the Necessity and Propriety of Giving Thanks according to 2 Thess. 1:3'. *Journal of Biblical Literature* 92 (1973): 432-38.

———. 'The Relevance of Isaiah 66:7 to Revelation 12 and 2 Thessalonians 1'. *Zeitschrift für die neutestamentliche Wissenschaft*. 67 (1976): 252-68.

Badcock, F. J. *The Pauline Epistles*. London: SPCK, 1937.

Bahnsen, W. 'Zum Verständnis von 2 Thess. 2:3-12. Ein Beitrag zur Kritik des 2ten Thessalonicherbriefes'. Pages 681-705 in vol. 6 of *Jahrbücher für protestantische Theologie*, 1880.

Bailey, John A. 'Who Wrote 2 Thessalonians?' *New Testament Studies* 25.2 (1978-79): 131-45.

Bailey, John W, and J. W. Clarke. 'The First and Second Epistles to the Thessalonians'. Pages 253-342 in *The Interpreter's Bible* 11. New York: Abingdon, 1955.

Baird, William. 'What is Kerygma? A Study of 1 Cor. 15: 3-8 and Gal. 1:11-17'. *Journal of Biblical Literature* 76 (1957): 181-91.

Bammel, E. 'Herkunft und Funktion der Traditionselemente in 1 Kor. 15:1-11'. *Theologische Zeitschrift* (1955): 401-19.

Barnard, L. W. *Studies in the Apostolic Fathers and their Background*. Oxford: Blackwell, 1966.

Barnouin, M. 'Les problèmes de traduction concernant 2 Thess. 2:6-7'. *New Testament Studies* 23 (1977): 482-98.

Barr, George K. *Scalometry and the Pauline Epistles*. Journal for the Study of the New Testament Supplement Series 261. Edinburgh: T & T Clark, 2004.

Barrett, C. K. *A Commentary on the First Epistle to the Corinthians.* 2nd ed. London: Black, 1971.

———. *The Epistle to the Romans.* London: Black, 1962.

Bartchy, S. Scott. *ΜΑΛΛΟΝ ΧΡΗΣΑΙ: First-Century Slavery and the Interpretation of 1 Corinthians 7:21.* Society of Biblical Literature Dissertation Series 11. Missoula, MT: Society of Biblical Literature, 1973.

Bartsch, H. W. 'Die Argumentation des Paulus in 1 Cor 15:3-11'. *Zeitschrift für die neutestamentliche Wissenschaft* 55 (1964): 261-74.

Bassler, Jouette M. 'The Enigmatic Sign: 2 Thess 1:5'. *Catholic Biblical Quarterly* 46 (1984): 496-510.

Batiffol, P. 'Polycarp'. Pages 242-47 in Vol. 2 of *Dictionary of the Apostolic Church.* Edited by James Hastings. Edinburgh: T & T Clark, 1918.

Bauckham, Richard. 'Pseudo-Apostolic Letters'. *Journal of Biblical Literature* 107 (1988): 469-94.

———. 'The Delay of the Parousia'. *Tyndale Bulletin* 31 (1980): 3-36.

Bauer, Walter. *Orthodoxy and Heresy in Earliest Christianity.* Edited by Robert A. Kraft and Gerhard Krodel. London: SCM, 1972.

Baur, F. C. *Paul, the Apostle of Jesus Christ, his Life and Work, his Epistles and his Doctrine: A Contribution to the Critical History of Primitive Christianity.* Edited by E. Zeller. Translated by A. Menzies. 2 vols. London: Williams & Norgate, 1876.

Beale, G. K. *1-2 Thessalonians.* IVP New Testament Commentary Series. Downers Grove, IL: IVP Academic, 2003.

Beare, F. W. 'On the Interpretation of Romans 6:17'. *New Testament Studies* 5 (1959): 206-10.

Beasley-Murray, G. R. *Jesus and the Future.* London: Macmillan, 1954.

Beasley-Murray, Paul. 'An Early Confession of Faith in the Lordship of Jesus'. *Tyndale Bulletin* 31 (1980): 147-54.

Berding, Kenneth. *Polycarp and Paul: An Analysis of Their Literary and Theological Relationship in Light of Polycarp's Use of Biblical and Extra-Biblical Literature.* Vigiliae Christianae Supplements 62. Leiden: Brill, 2002.

Best, Ernest. *A Commentary on the First and Second Epistles to the Thessalonians.* Black's New Testament Commentaries. London: Black, 1972.

Betz, Hans Dieter. *Nachfolge und Nachahmung Jesu Christi im Neuen Testament.* Beiträge zur historischen Theologie. Tübingen: Mohr Siebeck, 1967.

———, ed. *The Greek Magical Papyri in Translation: Including the Demotic Spells.* Chicago: University of Chicago Press, 1986.

Betz, Otto. 'Der Katechon'. *New Testament Studies* 9 (1963): 276-91.

Bjerkelund, Carl J. *Parakalô: Form, Funktion, und Sinn der parakalô-Sätze in den paulischen Briefen.* Bibliotheca Theologica Norvegica 1. Oslo: Scandinavian University Books, 1967.

Blass, F., and A. Debrunner. *A Greek Grammar of the New Testament and Other Early Christian Literature.* Translated and revised by Robert W. Funk. Chicago: University of Chicago Press, 1961.

Boers, Hendrikus. 'The Form Critical Study of Paul's Letters: 1 Thessalonians as a Case Study'. *New Testament Studies* 22 (1975-76): 140-58

Bornemann, Wilhelm. *Die Thessalonicherbriefe: völlig neu bearbeitet.* Göttingen: Vandenhoeck & Ruprecht, 1894.

Bousset, W. *The Antichrist Legend.* Translated by A. H. Keane. London: Hutchinson, 1896.

Branick, V. P. 'Apocalyptic Paul?' *Catholic Biblical Quarterly* 47 (1985): 664-75.

Braun, Herbert. 'Zur nachpaulinischen Herkunft des zweiten Thessalonicherbriefes'.

Zeitschrift für die neutestamentliche Wissenschaft 44 (1952-53): 152-56.
Bristol, Lyle O. 'Paul's Thessalonian Correspondence'. *Expository Times* 55 (1943-44): 223.
Brown, Colin, ed. *The New International Dictionary of New Testament Theology.* 4 vols. Grand Rapids: Zondervan, 1975-1986.
Brown, Francis, S. R. Driver, and Charles A. Briggs. *A Hebrew and English Lexicon of the Old Testament.* Oxford: Clarendon, 1975.
Brown, John P. 'Synoptic Parallels in the Epistles and Form-History'. *New Testament Studies* 10 (1964): 27-48.
Brox, N. *Falsche Verfasserangaben: Zur Erklärung die frühchristlichen Pseudepigraphie.* Stuttgarter Bibelstudien 79. Stuttgart: Katholisches Bibelwerk, 1975.
Bruce, F. F. *1 & 2 Thessalonians.* Word Biblical Commentary 45. Waco, TX: Word, 1982.
———. '2 Thessalonians'. Pages 1161-65 in *The New Bible Commentary: Revised.* Edited by Donald Guthrie and J. Alec Motyer. Grand Rapids: Eerdmans, 1970.
———. *The Epistle to the Galatians.* New International Greek Testament Commentary. Grand Rapids: Eerdmans, 1982.
———. *The Epistles to the Colossians, to Philemon and to the Ephesians.* Grand Rapids: Eerdmans, 1984.
———. *Romans.* London: Tyndale, 1963.
———. 'St. Paul in Macedonia: 2.The Thessalonian Correspondence'. *Bulletin of the John Rylands University Library* 62 (1980): 328-45.
———. *Tradition: Old and New.* Exeter: Paternoster, 1970.
Bultmann, R. *Theology of the New Testament.* Translated by Kendrick Grobel. 2 vols. London: Scribner's Sons, 1955.
Burkeen, William Howard. 'The Parousia of Christ in the Thessalonian Correspondence'. Ph.D. thesis, University of Aberdeen, 1979.
Burkitt, F. C. *Christian Beginnings.* London: University of London Press, 1924.
Cadoux, Cecil John. *Ancient Smyrna: A History of the City from the Earliest Times to 324 A.D.* Oxford: Blackwell, 1938.
———. 'Review of P. N. Harrison's *Polycarp's Two Epistles to the Philippians*'. *Journal of Theological Studies* 38 (1937): 267-70.
Calvin, John. *Commentaries on the Epistles of Paul the Apostle to the Philippians, Colossians, and Thessalonians.* Translated by John Pringle. Edinburgh: Calvin Translation Society, 1851.
———. *The First Epistle of Paul the Apostle to the Corinthians.* Translated by John W. Fraser. Edinburgh: Oliver & Boyd, 1960.
Campenhausen, Hans von. *The Formation of the Christian Bible.* Translated by J. A. Baker. London: Black, 1972.
Cannon, George E. *The Use of Traditional Materials in Colossians.* Macon, GA: Mercer University Press, 1983.
Charles, R. H., ed. *Apocrypha and Pseudepigrapha of the Old Testament in English.* 2 vols. Oxford: Clarendon, 1913.
Charlesworth, James H., ed. *The Old Testament Pseudepigrapha.* 2 vols. Garden City, NY: Doubleday, 1983.
Clement of Alexandria. *The Writings of Clement of Alexandria, vol 2.* Translated by William Wilson. Vol. 12 of Ante-Nicene Christian Library. 24 vols. Edited by A. Roberts and J. Donaldson. Edinburgh: T & T Clark, 1869-1871.
Collins, Raymond F. *Letters that Paul Did Not Write: The Epistle to the Hebrews and the Pauline Pseudepigrapha.* Good News Studies 28. Wilmington, DE: Glazier,

1988.

———. *Studies on the First Letter to the Thessalonians.* Bibliotheca ephemeridum theologicarum lovaniensium 66. Leuven: Leuven University Press, 1984.

Conzelmann, Hans. *1 Corinthians.* Hermeneia. Translated by James W. Leitch. Philadelphia: Fortress, 1975.

Cranfield, C. E. B. *Romans.* 2 vols. International Critical Commentary. Edinburgh: T & T Clark, 1975-1979.

———. *Romans: A Shorter Commentary.* Edinburgh: T & T Clark, 1985.

Cullmann, Oscar. 'Le caractère eschatologique du devoir missionaire et de la conscience apostolique de S. Paul'. *Revue d'histoire et de philosophie religieuses* 16 (1936): 210-45.

———. *The Early Church.* London: SCM, 1956.

Cyprian. *The Writings of Cyprian.* Translated by Robert Ernest Wallis. Vol. 8 of the Ante-Nicene Christian Library. Edited by Alexander Roberts & James Donaldson. 24 vols. Edinburgh: T & T Clark, 1867-1872.

———. *The Writings of Cyprian,* vol. 2. Vol. 13 of the Ante-Nicene Christian Library. Edited by Alexander Roberts & James Donaldson. 24 vols. Edinburgh: T & T Clark, 1867-1872.

Dahl, Nils. 'Der erstgeborene Satans und der Vater des Teufels'. Pages 70-84 in *Apophoreta, Festschrift für Ernst Haechen zu seinem 70 Geburtstag am 10 Dezember 1964.* Edited by Walther Eltester et al. Beihefte zur Zeitschrift für die neutestamentliche Wissenschaft. Berlin: Töpelmann, 1964.

Davies, W. D. *Paul and Rabbinic Judaism.* London: SPCK, 1948.

———. 'Reflections on a Scandinavian Approach to the Gospel Tradition.' Pages 14-34 in *Neotestamentica et Patristica. Eine Freundesgabe Herrn Professor Dr. Oscar Cullmann zu seinem 60. Geburtstag Überreicht.* Novum Testamentum Supplement 6. Leiden: Brill, 1962.

Denney, James. *The Epistles to the Thessalonians.* The Expositor's Bible. London: Hodder & Stoughton, 1892.

Dibelius, Martin. *Die Briefe des Apostels Paulus, II, an die Thessalonicher I, II, an die Philipper.* Handbuch zum Neuen Testament. Tübingen: Mohr Siebeck, 1911.

———. *Die Briefe des Apostels Paulus, II, an die Thessalonicher I, II, an die Philipper.* Handbuch zum Neuen Testament. 3rd ed. Tübingen: Mohr Siebeck, 1937.

———. *A Fresh Approach to the New Testament and Early Christian Literature.* Hertford: Nicholson & Watson, 1936.

Dio Chrysostom. Translated by J. W. Cohoon and H. Lamar Crosby. 5 vols. Loeb Classical Library. London: Heinemann, 1932-1951.

Dobschütz, Ernst von. *Die Thessalonicher-Briefe.* 1909. Reprint. Göttingen: Vandenhoeck & Ruprecht, 1974.

Dodd, C. H. *According to the Scriptures.* London: Nisbet, 1952.

———. *The Apostolic Preaching and its Development.* London: Hodder & Stoughton, 1944.

———. *History and the Gospel.* London: Nisbet, 1938.

———. *New Testament Studies.* Manchester: Manchester University Press, 1953.

Donfried, Karl P. '1 Thessalonians, Acts and the Early Paul'. Pages 3-26 in *The Thessalonian Correspondence.* Edited by Raymond F. Collins. Leuven: Leuven University Press, 1990.

———. '2 Thessalonians and the Church of Thessalonica'. Pages 128-144 in *Origins and Method: Towards a New Understanding of Judaism and Christianity. Essays in Honour of John C. Hurd.* Edited by Bradley H. McLean. Journal for the Study of the New Testament: Supplement Series 86. Sheffield: Sheffield Academic Press, 1993.

Doty, W. G. *Letters in Primitive Christianity*. Guides to Biblical Scholarship. New Testament Series. Philadelphia: Fortress, 1973.

Draper, Jonathan. 'The Jesus Tradition in the Didache'. Pages 269-88 in *The Jesus Tradition Outside the Gospels*. Edited by David Wenham. Vol. 5 of *Gospel Perspectives*. Sheffield: JSOT Press, 1985, pp. 269-88.

Dungan, David L. *The Sayings of Jesus in the Churches of Paul*. Philadelphia: Fortress, 1971.

Ellis, E. Earle. 'Paul and His Co-workers'. *New Testament Studies* 17 (1971): 437-52.

———. 'Traditions in 1 Corinthians'. *New Testament Studies* 32 (1986): 481-502.

———. 'Traditions in the Pastoral Epistles'. Pages 191-98 in *Early Jewish and Christian Exegesis: Studies in Memory of William Hugh Brownlee*. Scholars Press Honorary Series 10. Edited by Craig A. Evans and William F. Stinespring. Atlanta: Scholars Press, 1987.

Epstein, Isidore, ed. *The Babylonian Talmud*. 36 vols. London: Soncino, 1935-1952.

Ernst, J. *Die eschatologischen Gegenspieler in den Schriften des Neuen Testaments*. Biblische Untersuchungen 3. Regensburg: Pustet, 1967.

Eusebius. *The Ecclesiastical History*. Translated by Kirsopp Lake, J. E. L. Oulton, and H. J. Lawlor. 2 vols. Loeb Classical Library. Cambridge: Harvard University Press, 1926-1932.

Fee, Gordon D. *The First and Second Letters to the Thessalonians*. New International Commentary on the New Testament. Grand Rapids: Eerdmans, 2009.

———. *The First Epistle to the Corinthians*. New International Commentary on the New Testament. Grand Rapids: Eerdmans, 1987.

Ferguson, E. 'Canon Muratori: Date and Provenance'. *Studia Patristica* 18 (1982): 677-83.

Findlay, G. G. *The Epistles of Paul the Apostle to the Thessalonians*. 1904. Repr., Grand Rapids: Baker, 1982.

Finegan, J. 'The Original Form of the Pauline Collection'. *Harvard Theological Review* 49 (1956): 85-104.

Ford, Desmond. *The Abomination of Desolation in Biblical Eschatology*. Washington, D. C.: University Press of America, 1979.

Foster, Paul. 'Who Wrote 2 Thessalonians? A Fresh Look at an Old Problem'. *Journal for the Study of the New Testament* 35.2 (2012): 150-75.

Frame, James Everett. *A Critical and Exegetical Commentary on the Epistles of St. Paul to the Thessalonians*. The International Critical Commentary. Edinburgh: T & T Clark, 1912.

Fraser, J. K. 'A Theological Study of Second Thessalonians: A Comprehensive Study of the Thought of the Epistle and its Sources'. Ph.D. thesis, University of Durham, 1979.

Fuller, Reginald H. *The Formation of the Resurrection Narratives*. Philadelphia: Fortress, 1971.

Furnish, Victor Paul. *1 Thessalonians, 2 Thessalonians*. Abingdon New Testament Commentaries. Nashville: Abingdon, 2007.

———. 'The Jesus-Paul Debate: From Baur to Bultmann'. *Bulletin of the John Rylands University Library* 47 (1964-65): 342-81.

Gamble, Harry Y. *The New Testament Canon: Its Making and Meaning*. Philadelphia: Fortress, 1985.

———. 'The Redaction of the Pauline Letters and the Formation of the Pauline Corpus'. *Journal of Biblical Literature* 94 (1975): 403-18.

Gaventa, Beverly Roberts. *First and Second Thessalonians*. Interpretation: A Bible Commentary for Preaching and Teaching. Louisville: John Knox Press, 1998.

Gerhardsson, Birger. *Memory and Manuscript: Oral Tradition and Written Transmission in Rabbinic Judaism and Early Christianity.* Translated by Eric J. Sharpe. Lund: Gleerup, 1961.
Giblin, Charles Homer. '2 Thessalonians 2 Re-read as Pseudepigraphal: A Revised Reaffirmation of *The Threat to Faith'*. Pages 459-69 in *The Thessalonian Correspondence.* Edited by Raymond F. Collins. Leuven: Leuven University Press, 1990.
———. *The Threat to Faith: An Exegetical and Theological Re-examination of 2 Thessalonians 2.* Analecta Biblica 31. Rome: Pontifical Biblical Institute, 1967.
Gillman, J. 'Signals of Transformation in 1 Thessalonians 4:13-18'. *Catholic Biblical Quarterly* 47 (1985): 263-81.
Gloucester, A. C. 'The Epistle of Polycarp to the Philippians'. *Church Quarterly Review* 141 (1945): 1-25.
Gnilka, Joachim. *Der Philipperbrief.* Freiburg: Herder, 1969.
Goguel, Maurice. *Les Épîtres Pauliniennes.* Volume 4, part 1 of *Introduction au Nouveau Testament.* 5 vols. Paris: Leroux, 1922-1926.
Goppelt, Leonhard. *Theology of the New Testament.* Edited by Jürgen Roloff. Translated by John E. Alsup. 2 vols. Grand Rapids: Eerdmans, 1981-1982.
———. 'Tradition nach Paulus'. *Kerygma und Dogma* 4 (1958): 213-33.
Graafen, J. *Die Echtheit des zweiten Briefes an die Thessalonicher.* Neutestamentliche Abhandlungen 14. Münster: Aschendorff, 1930.
Grant, Robert M. 'Polycarp of Smyrna'. *Anglican Theological Review* 28 (1946): 137-48.
———, ed. *The Apostolic Fathers: A New Translation and Commentary.* 6 vols. New York: Nelson, 1964-1968.
Grayston, Kenneth, and G. Herdan. 'The Authorship of the Pastorals in the Light of Statistical Linguistics'. *New Testament Studies* 6 (1959-60): 1-15.
Green, Gene L. *The Letters to the Thessalonians.* Pillar New Testament Commentary. Grand Rapids: Eerdmans, 2002.
Gregson, R. 'A Solution to the Problems of the Thessalonian Epistles'. *Evangelical Quarterly* 38 (1966): 76-80.
Grimm, Wilibald. 'Die Echtheit der Briefe an die Thessalonicher: gegen D. Baur's Angriff vertheidigt'. *Theologische Studien und Kritiken* 23 (1850): 753-816.
Grobel, Kendrick. 'A Chiastic Retribution-Formula in Romans 2'. Pages 255-61 in *Zeit und Geschichte, Dankesgabe an Rudolf Bultmann zum 80 Geburtstag.* Edited by Erich Dinkler. Tübingen: Mohr Siebeck, 1964.
Gundry, Robert H. *The Church and the Tribulation.* Grand Rapids: Zondervan, 1973.
———. 'The Hellenization of Dominical Tradition and Christianization of Jewish Tradition in the Eschatology of 1-2 Thessalonians'. *New Testament Studies* 33 (1987): 161-78.
Guthrie, George H. *2 Corinthians.* Baker Exegetical Commentary on the New Testament. Grand Rapids: Baker Academic, 2015.
Hadorn, W. 'Die Abfassung der Thessalonicherbriefe auf der dritten Missionsreise und der Kanon des Marcion'. *Zeitschrift für die neutestamentliche Wissenschaft* 19 (1919-20): 67-72.
Hanson, R. P. C. *Tradition in the Early Church.* London: SCM, 1962.
Harnack, Adolf von. 'Das Problem des zweiten Thessalonicherbriefs'. *Sitzungsberichte der Preussischen Akademie der Wissenschaften zu Berlin* 31 (1910): 560-78.
Harrison, P. N. *Polycarp's Two Epistles to the Philippians.* Cambridge: University Press, 1936.
Harrisville, Roy A. *1 Corinthians.* Augsburg Commentary on the New Testament.

Minneapolis: Augsburg, 1987.

Hartman, Lars. 'The Eschatology of 2 Thessalonians as Included in a Communication'. Pages 470-85 in *The Thessalonian Correspondence*. Edited by Raymond F. Collins. Leuven: Leuven University Press, 1990.

———. *Prophecy Interpreted*. Lund, Sweden: Gleerup, 1966.

Hartog, Paul. *Polycarp and the New Testament: The Occasion, Rhetoric, Theme, and Unity of the Epistle to the Philippians and Its Allusions to New Testament Literature*. Tübingen: Mohr Siebeck, 2002.

Havener, Ivan. 'The Pre-Pauline Christological Credal Formulae of 1 Thessalonians'. Pages 105-128 in *SBL Seminar Papers, 1981. Society of Biblical Literature Seminar Papers 20*. Chico, CA: Scholars Press, 1981.

Hawthorne, Gerald F. *Philippians*. Word Biblical Commentary 43. Waco, TX: Word Books, 1983.

Hendriksen, William. *Exposition of 1 and 2 Thessalonians*. New Testament Commentary. Grand Rapids: Baker, 1955.

Hengel, Martin. 'Anonymität, Pseudepigraphie und "literarische Falschung" in der jüdisch-hellenistischen Literatur'. Pages 229-308 in *Pseudepigrapha I*. Edited by K. von Fritz. Vol. 18 of *Entretiens sur l'antiquite classique*. Geneva: Vandoeuvres, 1972.

Herford, R. Travers, ed. *Pirke Aboth.*. New York: Bloch, 1925.

Héring, Jean. *The First Epistle of Saint Paul to the Corinthians*. Translated by A. W. Heathcote and P. J. Allcock. London: Epworth, 1962.

Hilgenfeld, Adolph. 'Die beiden Briefe an die Thessalonicher, nach Inhalt und Ursprung'. *Zeitschrift für wissenschaftliche Theologie* 5 (1862): 225-64.

Hippolytus. *Irenaeus Vol. 2 and Hippolytus Vol. 2*. Volume 9 of Ante-Nicene Christian Library. Edited by Alexander Roberts and James Donaldson. 24 vols. Edinburgh: T & T Clark, 1867-1872.

Holland, Glenn S. *The Tradition that You Received from Us: 2 Thessalonians in the Pauline Tradition*. Tübingen: Mohr Siebeck, 1988.

Hollander, H. W. and M. de Jonge. *The Testaments of the Twelve Patriarchs: A Commentary*. Leiden: Brill, 1985.

Hollmann, Georg. 'Die Unechtheit des zweiten Thessalonicherbriefs'. *Zeitschrift für die neutestamentliche Wissenschaft* 2 (1904): 28-38.

Holmes, Michael W. 'Polycarp's *Letter to the Philippians* and the Writings that Later Formed the New Testament'. *The Reception of the New Testament in the Apostolic Fathers*. Edited by Andrew F. Gregory and Christopher M. Tuckett. Oxford: Oxford University Press, 2005.

———, ed. *The Apostolic Fathers: Greek Texts and English Translations*. Grand Rapids: Baker, 1999.

Holtz, Traugott. '"Euer Glaube an Gott": Zu Form und Inhalt von 1 Thess 1,9f'. Pages 459-88 in *Die Kirche des Anfangs: Festschrift für Heinz Schürmann*. Edited by Rudolf Schnackenburg, Joseph Ernst, and Joseph Wanke. Freiburg: Herder, 1978.

———. 'Traditionen im 1 Thessalonicherbrief'. Pages 55-78 in *Die Mitte des Neuen Testaments: Einheit und Vielfalt neutestamentlicher Theologie. Festschrift für E. Schweizer zum siebzigsten Geburtstag*. Edited by U. Luz and H. Weder. Göttingen: Vandenhoeck & Ruprecht, 1983.

Holtzmann, H. 'Zum zweiten Thessalonicherbrief'. *Zeitschrift für die neutestamentliche Wissenschaft*. (1901): 97-108.

Hughes, Frank Witt. *Early Christian Rhetoric and 2 Thessalonians*. Journal for the Study of the New Testament: Supplement Series 30. Sheffield: JSOT Press, 1989.

Hughes, Philip E. *Paul's Second Epistle to the Corinthians*. The New International

Commentary on the New Testament. Grand Rapids: Eerdmans, 1962.
Hunter, A. M. *The Epistle to the Romans*. London: SCM, 1955.
———. *Paul and His Predecessors*. Rev. ed. London: SCM, 1961.
Hurd, John C. 'First Letter to the Thessalonians'. Page 900 in *The Interpreter's Dictionary of the Bible: Supplementary Volume*. Nashville: Abingdon, 1976.
———. *The Origin of 1 Corinthians*. London: SPCK, 1965.
———. 'Second Letter to the Thessalonians'. Page 901 in *The Interpreter's Dictionary of the Bible: Supplementary Volume*. Nashville: Abingdon, 1976.
Irenaeus. *The Writings of Irenaeus*. Vols. 5 and 9 of Ante-Nicene Christian Library. Edited by Alexander Roberts and James Donaldson. 24 vols. Edinburgh: T & T Clark, 1867-1872.
James, M. R. *The Apocryphal New Testament*. Oxford: Clarendon, 1923.
Jenkins, Claude. 'Review of P. N. Harrison's *Polycarp's Two Epistles to the Philippians*'. *Theology* 35 (1937): 367-70.
Jeremias, Joachim. *The Eucharistic Words of Jesus*. Translated by Norman Perrin. London: SCM, 1966.
———. *Infant Baptism in the First Four Centuries*. Translated by David Cairns. London: SCM, 1960.
———. *Unknown Sayings of Jesus*. Translated by R. H. Fuller. London: SPCK, 1957.
Jewett, Robert. *The Thessalonian Correspondence: Pauline Rhetoric and Millenarian Piety*. Foundations and Facets. Philadelphia: Fortress, 1986.
Jewett, Robert, and Frederick Danker. 'Jesus as the Apocalyptic Benefactor in Second Thessalonians'. Pages 486-98 in *The Thessalonian Correspondence*. Edited by Raymond F. Collins. Leuven: Leuven University Press, 1990.
Jonge, Marinus de. *Christology in Context*. Philadelphia: Westminster Press, 1988.
Josephus. Translated by H. St. J. Thackeray et al. 10 vols. Loeb Classical Library. London: Heinemann, 1926-1965.
Justin Martyr and Athenagoras. Volume 2 of Ante-Nicene Christian Library. Edited by Alexander Roberts and James Donaldson. 24 vols. Edinburgh: T & T Clark, 1867-1872.
Kennedy, George A. *New Testament Interpretation through Rhetorical Criticism*. Chapel Hill: University of North Carolina Press, 1984.
Kenny, Anthony. *A Stylometric Study of the New Testament*. Oxford: Clarendon, 1986.
Kern, Friedrich Heinrich. 'Über 2. Thess 2, 1-12. Nebst Andeutungen über den Ursprung des zweiten Briefs and die Thessalonicher'. *Tübinger Zeitschrift für Theologie* 2 (1839): 145-214.
Kim, Seyoon. *The Origin of Paul's Gospel*. Wissenschaftliche Untersuchungen zum Neuen Testament 2. Tübingen: Mohr Siebeck, 1981.
Kittel, G. and G. Friedrich, eds. *Theological Dictionary of the New Testament*. Translated and edited by Geoffrey W. Bromiley. 10 vols. Grand Rapids: Eerdmans, 1964-1976.
Klappert, Berthold. 'Zur Frage des semitischen oder griecheischen Urtextes von 1 Kor. XV. 3-5'. *New Testament Studies* 13 (1966-67): 168-73.
Knibb, M. A. 'The Ascension of Isaiah the Prophet'. *The Old Testament Pseudepigrapha*. Edited by J. H. Charlesworth. 2 vols. London: Darton, Longman & Todd, 1983-1985.
Knox, John. *Marcion and the New Testament: An Essay in the Early History of the Canon*. Chicago: University of Chicago Press, 1942.
Koester, Helmut. '1 Thessalonians—Experiment in Christian Writing'. Pages 33-44 in *Continuity and Discontinuity in Church History: Essays Presented to George Huntston Williams on the Occasion of His 65th Birthday*. Edited by F. F. Church and

T. George. Leiden: Brill, 1979.

———. 'From Paul's Eschatology to the Apocalyptic Schemata of 2 Thessalonians'. Pages 441-58 in *The Thessalonian Correspondence*. Edited by Raymond F. Collins. Leuven: Leuven University Press, 1990.

Kreitzer, L. Joseph. *Jesus and God in Paul's Eschatology*. Journal for the Study of the New Testament Supplement Series 19. Sheffield: JSOT Press, 1987.

Krentz, Edgar. 'Traditions Held Fast: Theology and Fidelity in 2 Thessalonians'. Pages 505-15 in *The Thessalonian Correspondence*. Edited by Raymond F. Collins. Leuven: Leuven University Press, 1990.

Krodel, Gerhard. '2 Thessalonians'. Pages 73-96 in *Ephesians, Colossians, 2 Thessalonians, The Pastoral Epistles*. Proclamation Commentaries. Edited by Gerhard Krodel. Philadelphia: Fortress, 1978.

Kümmel, Werner Georg. *Introduction to the New Testament*. Rev. ed. Translated by Howard Clark Kee. London: SCM, 1975.

Ladd, George Eldon. *A Theology of the New Testament*. Grand Rapids: Eerdmans, 1974.

Lake, Kirsopp. *The Apostolic Fathers*. 2 vols. Loeb Classical Library. London: Heinemann, 1976-1985.

———. *The Earlier Epistles of St. Paul: Their Motive and Origin*. London: Rivington, 1911.

Laub, Franz. 'Paulinische Autorität in Nachpaulinischer Zeit (2 Thess)'. Pages 403-17 in *The Thessalonian Correspondence*. Edited by Raymond F. Collins. Leuven: Leuven University Press, 1990.

Lawson, John. *A Theological and Historical Introduction to the Apostolic Fathers*. New York: Macmillan, 1961.

Ledger, Gerard. 'An Exploration of Differences in the Pauline Epistles Using Multivariate Statistical Analysis', *Literary and Linguistic Computing* 10.2 (1995): 85-97.

Leenhardt, Franz J. *The Epistle to the Romans*. Translated by Harold Knight. London: Lutterworth, 1961.

Liberty, Stephen. 'Review of P. N. Harrison's *Polycarp's Two Epistles to the Philippians*'. *Church Quarterly Review* 247 (1937): 141-47.

Lietzmann, H. *Messe und Herrenmahl*. 3rd ed. Berlin: DeGruyter, 1955.

Lightfoot, J. B. *The Apostolic Fathers*. 5 vols. London: Macmillan, 1885.

———. *Saint Paul's Epistle to the Philippians*. 1913. Repr., Grand Rapids: Zondervan, 1953.

Lindars, Barnabas. 'The Sound of the Trumpet: Paul and Eschatology'. *Bulletin of the John Rylands University Library* 67 (1985): 766-82.

Lindemann, Andreas. *Paulus im ältesten Christentum: Das Bild des Apostels und die Rezeption der paulinischen Theologie in der frühchristlichen Literatur bis Marcion*. Beiträge zur historischen Theologie 58. Tübingen: Mohr Siebeck, 1979.

———. 'Zum Abfassungszweck Des Zweiten Thessalonicherbriefs'. *Zeitschrift für neutamentliche Wissenschaft* 68 (1977): 35-47.

Littleton, Harold E. 'The Function of Apocalyptic in 2 Thessalonians as a Criterion of its Authorship'. Ph.D. thesis, Vanderbilt University, 1973.

Loisy, A. *The Birth of the Christian Religion*. London: George Allen & Unwin, 1948.

Longnecker, Richard N. 'The Nature of Paul's Early Eschatology'. *New Testament Studies* 31 (1985): 85-95.

Maccoby, Hyam. 'Paul and the Eucharist'. *New Testament Studies* 37 (1991): 247-67.

Malherbe, A. J. 'Exhortation in First Thessalonians'. *Novum Testamentum* 25 (1983): 238-56.

———. '"Gentle as a Nurse": The Cynic Background to 1 Thess 2'. *Novum*

Testamentum 12 (1970): 203-17.

———. *The Letters to the Thessalonians*. Anchor Bible 32B. New York: Doubleday, 2004.

———. *Paul and the Thessalonians: The Philosophic Tradition of Pastoral Care*. Philadelphia: Fortress, 1987.

Manson, T. W. 'The Letters to the Thessalonians'. Pages 269-78 in *Studies in the Gospels and Epistles*. Edited by M. Black. Manchester: Manchester University Press, 1962.

———. 'St. Paul in Greece: The Letters to the Thessalonians'. *Bulletin of the John Rylands University Library* 35 (1952-3): 428-47.

Marshall, I. Howard. *1 and 2 Thessalonians*. New Century Bible. Grand Rapids: Eerdmans, 1983.

———. *The Gospel of Luke*. New International Greek Testament Commentary. Grand Rapids: Eerdmans, 1978.

———. *Last Supper and Lord's Supper*. Exeter: Paternoster, 1980.

Marxsen, Willi. *Introduction to the New Testament*. Translated by G. Buswell. Oxford: Blackwell, 1968.

———. *Der zweite Thessalonicherbrief*. Zürcher Bibelkommentare. Zürich: TVZ, 1982.

Masson, Charles. *Les Deux Épitres de Saint Paul aux Thessaloniciens*. Commentaire du Nouveau Testament 11a. Paris: Delachaux & Niestlé, 1957.

McKelvey, R. J. *The New Temple: The Church in the New Testament*. London: Oxford University Press, 1968.

McKinnish-Bridges, Linda. *1 and 2 Thessalonians*. Smith and Helwys Bible Commentary. Macon, GA: Smith & Helwys, 2008.

Mealand, David L. 'The Extent of the Pauline Corpus: A Multivariate Approach'. *Journal for the Study of the New Testament* 59 (1995): 61-92.

———. 'Positional Stylometry Reassessed: Testing a Seven Epistle Theory of Pauline Authorship'. *New Testament Studies* 35 (1989): 266-86.

Mearns, C. L. 'Early Eschatological Development in Paul: The Evidence of 1 and 2 Thessalonians'. *New Testament Studies* 27 (1981): 137-57.

Meeks, Wayne. '"And Rose up to Play": Midrash and Paraenesis in 1 Corinthians 10:1-22'. *Journal for the Study of the New Testament* 16 (1982): 64-78.

Meinhold, Peter. 'Polykarpos'. Pages 1662-93 in *Paulys Real-encyclopädie der classischen Altertumswissenschaft*. Edited by Konrat Ziegler. Zweiundvierzigster Halbband. Stuttgart: Druckenmüller, 1952.

Menken, M. J. J. 'The Structure of 2 Thessalonians'. Pages 373-82 in *The Thessalonian Correspondence*. Edited by Raymond F. Collins. Leuven: Leuven University Press, 1990.

Metzger, Bruce, M. *The Canon of the New Testament: Its Origin, Development, and Significance*. Oxford: Clarendon, 1987.

———. 'Literary Forgeries and Canonical Pseudepigrapha'. *Journal of Biblical Literature* 16 (1972): 3-24.

Milligan, George. 'The Authenticity of the Second Epistle to the Thessalonians'. *The Expositor* 9 (1904): 430-50.

———. *St. Paul's Epistles to the Thessalonians*. London: Macmillan, 1908.

Moffatt, James. *The First Epistle of Paul to the Corinthians*. London: Hodder & Stoughton, 1938.

———. 'The Interpretation of Romans 6:17-18'. *Journal of Biblical Literature* 48 (1929): 233-38.

Moore, A. L. *The Parousia in the New Testament*. Supplements to Novum Testamentum 13. Leiden: Brill, 1966.

Morris, Leon. *The First and Second Epistles to the Thessalonians.* New International Commentary on the New Testament. Rev. ed. Grand Rapids: Eerdmans, 1991.

———. *The First Epistle of Paul to the Corinthians.* London: Tyndale, 1958.

Morton, A. Q. 'The Authorship of the Pauline Epistles'. Pages 165-83 of *Literary Detection: How to Prove Authorship and Fraud in Literature and Documents.* Bath: Pitman, 1978.

Moulton, James H. *Prolegomena.* Vol. 1 of *A Grammar of New Testament Greek.* 3d ed. Edinburgh: T & T Clark, 1908.

Moulton, James H., and W. F. Howard. *Accidence and Word Formation.* Vol. 2 of *A Grammar of New Testament Greek.* 3d ed. Edinburgh: T & T Clark, 1929.

Mounce, R. H. 'Pauline Eschatology and the Apocalypse'. *Evangelical Quarterly* 46 (1974): 164-66.

Müller, Paul-Gerhard. *Der Traditionprozeß im Neuen Testament.* Freiberg: Herder, 1981.

Müller, Peter. *Anfänge der Paulusschule: Dargestellt am zweiten Thessalonicherbrief und am Kolosserbrief.* Abhandlungen zur Theologie des Altes und Neuen Testament. Zurich: Theologische Verlag, 1988.

Munck, Johannes. *Paul and the Salvation of Mankind.* Richmond: John Knox Press, 1959.

Murphy, Frederick J. *Apocalypticism in the Bible and Its world: A Comprehensive Introduction.* Grand Rapids: Baker Academic, 2012.

Murphy-O'Connor, Jerome. 'Tradition and Redaction in 1 Cor. 15:3-7'. *Catholic Biblical Quarterly* 43 (1981): 582-89.

Murray, John. *The Epistle to the Romans.* 2 vols. Grand Rapids: Eerdmans, 1959.

Neil, William. *The Epistles of Paul to the Thessalonians.* Moffatt New Testament Commentary. London: Hodder & Stoughton, 1950.

Neirynck, F. 'Paul and the Sayings of Jesus'. Pages 265-321 in *L'Apôtre Paul: Personnalitié, style et conception du ministère.* Edited by A. Vanhoye. Leuven: Leuven University Press, 1986.

Neufeld, Vernon H. *The Earliest Christian Confessions.* New Testament Tools and Studies 5. Leiden: Brill, 1963.

Neumann, Kenneth J. *The Authenticity of the Pauline Epistles in the Light of Stylostatistical Analysis.* Society of Biblical Literature Dissertation Series 120. Atlanta: Scholars Press, 1990.

Neusner, Jacob. *The Components of the Rabbinic Documents, from the Whole to the Parts, III, Ruth Rabbah,* Number 80. Atlanta: Scholars Press, 1997.

Nicholl, Colin R. *From Hope to Despair in Thessalonica: Situating 1 and 2 Thessalonians.* Society for New Testament Studies Monograph Series 126. Cambridge: Cambridge University Press, 2004.

———. 'Michael, The Restrainer Removed (2 Thess. 2:6-7)'. *Journal of Theological Studies* 51 (2000): 27-53.

Nielsen, C. M. 'Polycarp, Paul and the Scriptures'. *Anglican Theological Review* 47 (1965): 199-216.

Novum Testamentum Graece. Nestle-Aland. 26th ed. Stuttgart: Deutsche Bibelstiftung, 1979.

Nygren, Anders. *Commentary on Romans.* Translated by Carl C. Rasmussen. Philadelphia: Muhlenberg, 1949.

O'Brien, Peter T. *Introductory Thanksgivings in the Letters of Paul.* Supplements to Novum Testamentum 49. Leiden: Brill, 1977.

Oesterley, W. O. E. *The Books of the Apocrypha.* London: Robert Scott, 1915.

Ollrog, Wolf-Henning. *Paulus und seine Mitarbeiter.* Wissenschaftliche Monographien

zum Alten und Neuen Testament. Neukirchen: Neukirchener, 1979.
Orchard, J. Bernard. 'Thessalonians and the Synoptic Gospels'. *Biblica* 19 (1938): 19-42.
Origen. *Contra Celsum.* Translated by Frederick Crombie. Vol. 23 in Ante-Nicene Christian Library. Edited by Alexander Roberts and James Donaldson. 24 vols. Edinburgh: T & T Clark, 1872.
Orr, William F., and James Arthur Walther. *1 Corinthians.* Anchor Bible 32. Garden City, NY: Doubleday, 1977.
Oxford Society of Historical Theology. *The New Testament in the Apostolic Fathers.* Oxford: Clarendon, 1905.
Patrologia Graeca. Edited by J.-P. Migne. 162 vols. Paris, 1857-1886.
Paulsen, Henning. *Die Briefe des Ignatius von Antiochia und der Brief des Polykarp von Smyrna.* Tübingen: Mohr Siebeck, 1985.
Pearson, Birger. A. '1 Thessalonians 2:13-16: A Deutero-Pauline Interpolation'. *Harvard Theological Review* 64 (1971): 79-94.
Peterson, Robert J. *The Structure and Purpose of Second Thessalonians.* Th.D thesis, Harvard University, 1967.
Poythress, Vern. 'Is Romans 1:3-4 a Pauline Confession After All?' *Expository Times* 87 (1975-76): 180-83.
Prior, Michael. *Paul the Letter-Writer and the Second Letter to Timothy.* Journal for the Study of the New Testament Supplement Series 23. Sheffield: Sheffield Academic Press, 1989.
Quasten, Johannes. *Patrology.* Vol. 1. Utrecht-Antwerp: Spectrum, 1966.
Ramsay, W. M. 'Roads and Travel'. Pages 375-402 in *A Dictionary of the Bible,* Extra Volume. Edited by James Hastings. Edinburgh: T & T Clark, 1909.
Rensberger, David K. 'As the Apostle Teaches: The Development of the Use of Paul's Letters in Second-Century Christianity'. Ph.D. thesis, Yale University, 1981.
Richard, Earl J. *First and Second Thessalonians.* Sacra Pagina 11. Collegeville, MN: Liturgical Press, 1995.
Richardson, Cyril C., ed. *Early Christian Fathers.* Volume 1 of The Library of Christian Classics. London: SCM, 1953.
Richardson, Peter. '"I Say, Not the Lord": Personal Opinion, Apostolic Authority and the Development of Early Christian Halakah'. *Tyndale Bulletin* 31 (1989): 65-86.
Richardson, Peter, and Peter Gooch. 'Logia of Jesus in 1 Corinthians'. Pages 39-62 in *The Jesus Tradition Outside the Gospels.* Vol. 5 in *Gospel Perspectives.* Edited by David Wenham. Sheffield: JSOT Press, 1985.
Ridderbos, Herman. *Paul: An Outline of His Theology.* Grand Rapids: Eerdmans, 1977.
———. *Paul and Jesus.* Translated by David H. Freeman. Nutley, NJ: Presbyterian and Reformed, 1957.
Riesenfeld, Harald. *The Gospel Tradition and its Beginnings.* London: Mowbray, 1957.
Rigaux, Beda. *Saint Paul Les Épîtres aux Thessaloniciens.* Paris: Gabalda, 1956.
———. 'Tradition et Redaction dans 1 Thess 5:1-10'. *New Testament Studies* 21 (1975): 318-40.
Roberts, Alexander, James Donaldson, and F. Crombie, ed. and trans. *The Writings of the Apostolic Fathers.* Vol. 1 of Ante-Nicene Christian Library. 24 vols. Edinburgh: T & T Clark, 1867-1872.
Robertson, Archibald, and Alfred Plummer. *The First Epistle of St. Paul to the Corinthians.* International Critical Commentary. Edinburgh: T & T Clark, 1911.
Robinson, John A. T. *Redating the New Testament.* London: SCM, 1976.
Roloff, Jürgen. *Apostolat-Verkündigung-Kirche.* Gütersloh: Mohn, 1965.
Ross, G. A. Johnston. '"That Form of Doctrine": An Appeal'. *Expositor* 7th Series, 5

(1908): 469-75.
Russell, D. S. *The Method and Message of Jewish Apocalyptic.* Philadelphia: Westminster, 1964.
Russell, Ronald. 'The Idle in 2 Thess 3:6-12: An Eschatological or Social Problem?' *New Testament Studies* 34 (1988): 105-19.
Schmidt, Daryl. '1 Thess 2:13-16: Linguistic Evidence for an Interpolation'. *Journal of Biblical Literature* 102 (1983): 269-79.
———. 'The Authenticity of 2 Thessalonians: Linguistic Arguments'. Pages 289-96 in *SBL Seminar Papers, 1983.* Society of Biblical Literature Seminar Papers 22. Chico, CA: Scholars Press, 1983.
———. 'The Syntactical Style of 2 Thessalonians: How Pauline Is It?' Pages 383-93 in *The Thessalonian Correspondence.* Edited by Raymond F. Collins. Leuven: Leuven University Press, 1990.
Schmidt, J. E. Christian. 'Vermutungen über die beiden Briefe an die Thessalonicher'. Pages 159-61 in Wolfgang Trilling, *Untersuchungen zum Zweiten Thessalonicherbrief.* Erfurter Theologische Studien 27. Leipzig: St. Benno, 1972.
Schmidt, Paul Wilhelm. *Der erste Thessalonicherbrief neu erklärt: Nebst einem Excurs über den Zweiten Gleichnamigen Brief.* Berlin: Reimer, 1885, pp. 111-28.
———. *A Short Protestant Commentary on the Books of the New Testament.* Edited by Paul Wilhelm Schmidt and Franz von Holzendorff. Translated by F. H. Jones. 3 vols. London: Williams & Norgate, 1882-1884.
Schmithals, Walter. *Der Römerbrief.* Gütersloh: Mohn, 1988.
———. 'Die Thessalonicherbriefe als Brief-Komposition'. Pages 295-315 in *Zeit und Geschichte.* Edited by Erich Einkler. Tübingen: Mohr Siebeck, 1964.
Schoedel, William. *Polycarp, Martyrdom of Polycarp, Fragments of Papias.* Vol. 5 of *The Apostolic Fathers: A New Translation and Commentary.* London: Nelson, 1967.
Schütz, John Howard. *Paul and the Anatomy of Apostolic Authority.* Society for New Testament Studies Monograph Series 26. Cambridge: Cambridge University Press, 1975.
Schweizer, Eduard. 'Der zweite Thessalonicherbrief ein Philipperbrief?' *Theologische Zeitschrift* 1 (1945): 90-105.
Scott, J. Julius. 'Paul and Late-Jewish Eschatology—A Case Study, 1 Thess 4:13-18 & 2 Thess 2:1-12'. *Journal of the Evangelical Theological Society* 15 (1972): 133-43.
Scott, Robert. *The Pauline Epistles.* Edinburgh: T & T Clark, 1909.
Selwyn, E. G. *The First Epistle of Peter.* London: Macmillan, 1946.
Smith, Morton. 'A Comparison of Early Christian and Early Rabbinic Tradition'. *Journal of Biblical Literature* 82 (1963): 169-76.
Spicq, C. 'Les Thessaloniciens "inquiets" étaient ils des paresseux?' *Studia Theologica* 10 (1957): 1-13.
Spitta, Friedrich. *Zur Geschichte und Literatur des Urchistentums.* Göttingen: Vandenhoeck & Ruprecht, 1893.
Stanley, David M. '"Become Imitators of Me": The Pauline Conception of Apostolic Tradition'. *Biblica* 40 (1959): 859-77.
———. 'Imitation in Paul's Letters: Its Significance for His Relationship to Jesus and to His Own Christian Foundations'. Pages 127-41 in *From Jesus to Paul.* Edited by Peter Richardson and John C. Hurd. Waterloo, ON: Wilfrid Laurier University Press, 1984.
Stanton, G. N. *Jesus of Nazareth in New Testament Preaching.* Cambridge: Cambridge University Press, 1974.
Stephens, D. J. 'Eschatological Themes in 2 Thessalonians 2:1-12'. Ph. D. thesis, St. Andrew's University, 1976.

Stephenson, A. M. G. 'On the Meaning of e0ne/sthken h9 h9me/ra tou= kuri/ou in 2 Thess. 2,2'. *Studia Evangelica* 4 (1968): 442-51.
Stepien, Jan. 'Autentycznosc Listow Do Tessaloniczan'. *Collectanea Theologica* 34 (1963): 91-182.
Strack, Hermann L. and Paul Billerbeck. *Kommentar zum Neuen Testament aus Talmud und Midrasch.* 6 vols. Munich: Beck, 1922-61.
Strobel, A. *Untersuchungen zum eschatologischen Verzogerungsproblem auf Grund der spätjudisch-urchristlichen Geschichte von Habakkuk 2,2ff.* Novum Testamentum Supplement 2. Leiden: Brill, 1961.
Stuhlmacher, Peter. 'Jesustradition im Römerbrief?' *Theologische Beiträge* 14 (1983): 240-50.
Sumney, Jerry L. 'The Bearing of a Pauline Rhetorical Pattern on the Integrity of 2 Thessalonians'. *Zeitschrift für die neutestamentliche Wissenschaft* 81 (1990): 192-204.
Sundberg, Albert C. 'Canon Muratori: A Fourth Century List'. *Harvard Theological Review* 66 (1973): 1-41.
Tasker, R. V. G. *2 Corinthians*. Tyndale New Testament Commentaries. Grand Rapids: Eerdmans, 1963.
Taylor, Vincent. *The Epistle to the Romans.* London: Epworth, 1955.
Tertullian. *Against Marcion.* Translated by Peter Holmes. Vol. 7 of Ante-Nicene Christian Library. Edited by Alexander Roberts and James Donaldson. 24 vols. Edinburgh: T & T Clark, 1867-72.
Theron, Daniel J. *Evidence of Tradition.* London: Bowes & Bowes, 1957.
Thomas, Robert L. '1-2 Thessalonians'. *The Expositor's Bible Commentary* 11. Edited by Frank E. Gaebelein. Grand Rapids: Zondervan, 1978.
Thompson, Edward. 'The Sequence of the Two Epistles to the Thessalonians'. *Expository Times* 66 (1944-45): 306-307.
Thompson, Michael. *Clothed with Christ: The Example and Teaching of Jesus in Romans 12.1—15.13.* Journal for the Study of the New Testament Supplement Series 59. Sheffield: JSOT Press, 1991.
Thrall, M. E. *2 Corinthians 1-7*. International Critical Commentary. London: T & T Clark, 1994.
Thurston, Robert W. 'The Relationship between the Thessalonian Epistles'. *Expository Times* 85 (1973): 52-56.
Townsend, John T. '2 Thessalonians 2:3-12'. Pages 233-46 in the *SBL Seminar Papers, 1980.* Society of Biblical Literature Seminar Papers 19. Chico, CA: Scholars Press, 1980.
Trilling, Wolfgang. 'Literarische Paulusimitation im 2. Thessalonicherbrief'. Pages 146-56 in *Paulus in den neutestamentlichen Spätschriften: Zur Paulusrezeption im Neuen Testament.* Edited by K. Kertelge. Freiburg: Herder, 1981.
———. *Untersuchungen zum Zweiten Thessalonicherbrief.* Erfurter Theologische Studien 27. Leipzig: St. Benno, 1972.
———. *Der zweite Brief an die Thessalonicher.* Evangelisch-katholischer Kommentar zum Neuen Testamentum. Zurich: Benziger, 1980.
Trudinger, Paul. 'The Priority of 2 Thessalonians Revisited: Some Fresh Evidence'. *The Downside Review* 113 (1995): 31-35.
Tuckett, C. M. 'Synoptic Tradition in 1 Thessalonians?' Pages 160-82 in *The Thessalonian Correspondence.* Edited by Raymond F. Collins. Leuven: Leuven University Press, 1990.
Vander Stichele, Caroline. 'The Concept of Tradition and 1 and 2 Thessalonians'. Pages 499-504 in *The Thessalonian Correspondence.* Edited by Raymond F. Collins.

Leuven: Leuven University Press, 1990.

Vielhauer, Philipp. *Geschichte der urchristlichen Literatur.* Berlin: de Gruyter, 1975.

Vincent, Marvin R. *The Epistles to the Philippians and to Philemon.* International Critical Commentary. Edinburgh: T & T Clark, 1897.

Vos, Geerhardus. *The Pauline Eschatology.* 1930. Repr., Grand Rapids: Baker, 1979.

Walter, Nikolaus. 'Paul and the Early Christian Jesus-Tradition'. Pages 53-72 of *Paul and Jesus, Collected Essays.* Journal for the Study of the New Testament Supplement Series 37. Sheffield: Sheffield Academic Press, 1989.

Walvoord, John F. *The Thessalonian Epistles.* Grand Rapids: Zondervan, 1967.

Wanamaker, Charles A. *The Epistles to the Thessalonians.* The New International Greek Testament Commentary. Grand Rapids: Eerdmans, 1990.

Ward, Ronald A. *Commentary on 1 & 2 Thessalonians.* Waco, TX: Word, 1973.

Warfield, B. B. 'The Prophecies of St. Paul'. *The Expositor* 3rd Series, 4 (1886): 30-44.

Weatherly, Jon A. 'The Authenticity of 1 Thessalonians 2.13-16: Additional Evidence'. *Journal for the Study of the New Testament* 42 (1991): 79-98.

Wegenast, Klaus. *Das Verständnis der Tradition bei Paulus und in den Deuteropaulinen.* Wissenschaft Monographien zum Alten und Neuen Testament 8. Neukirchen Kreis Moers: Neukirchener Verlag, 1962.

Weima, Jeffrey A. D. *1-2 Thessalonians*. Baker Exegetical Commentary on the New Testament. Grand Rapids: Baker, 2014.

Weiss, Johannes. *Earliest Christianity.* Translated by Frederick C. Grant. Gloucester, MA: Peter Smith, 1970.

Wengst, Klaus. 'Der Apostel und die Tradition'. *Zeitschrift für Theologie und Kirche* 69 (1972): 145-62.

Wenham, David. 'Paul and the Synoptic Apocalypse'. Pages 345-75 in *Studies of History and Tradition in the Four Gospels.* Vol. 2 of Gospel Perspectives. Edited by R. T. France and David Wenham. Sheffield: JSOT Press, 1981.

———. 'Paul's Use of the Jesus Tradition: Three Samples'. Pages 7-38 in *The Jesus Tradition Outside the Gospels.* Vol. 5 of *Gospel Perspectives*. Edited by David Wenham. Sheffield: JSOT Press, 1985.

———. The *Rediscovery of Jesus' Eschatological Discourse.* Vol 4 of *Gospel Perspectives.* Sheffield: JSOT Press, 1984.

West, J. C. 'The Order of 1 and 2 Thessalonians'. *Journal of Theological Studies* 15 (1914): 66-74.

White, John Lee. *The Body of the Greek Letter.* Society of Biblical Literature Dissertation Series 2. Missoula, MT: Society of Biblical Literature, 1972.

———. 'The Introductory Formulae in the Body of the Pauline Letter'. *Journal of Biblical Literature* 90 (1971): 91-94.

———. *Light from Ancient Letters.* Philadelphia: Fortress, 1986.

Whiteley, D. E. H. *Thessalonians.* The New Clarendon Bible. Oxford: Oxford University Press, 1969.

Wilckens, Ulrich. *Der Brief an die Römer.* 3 vols. Evangelisch-katholischer Kommentar zum Neuen Testament 6. Zürich: Benziger Verlag, Neukirchener Verlag, 1978-1982.

Wilder, Terry. *Pseudonymity, the New Testament, and Deception*. Lanham, MD: University Press of America, 2004.

Williams, David J. *1 and 2 Thessalonians*. New International Biblical Commentary 12. Peabody, MA: Hendrickson, 1992.

Winter, Bruce W. 'Secular and Christian Responses to Corinthian Famines'. *Tyndale Bulletin* 40 (1989): 86-106.

Witherington III, Ben. *1 and 2 Thessalonians: A Socio-Rhetorical Commentary*. Grand Rapids: Eerdmans, 2006.

Wrede, W. *Die Echtheit des Zweiten Thessalonicherbriefs untersucht.* Texte und Untersuchungen zur Geschicte der altchristlichen Literatur 24:2. Leipzig: Hinrichs, 1903.
Wright, N. T. *The Epistles of Paul to the Colossians and to Philemon.* Leicester: Inter-Varsity Press, 1986.
Wrzol, Josef. *Die Echtheit des zweiten Thessalonicherbriefes.* Biblische Studien 19.4. Freiburg: Herder, 1916.
Zahn, Theodor. *Ignatii et Polycarpi.* Leipzig: Hinrichs, 1876.
———. *Introduction to the New Testament.* Translated by J. M. Trout et al. 3 vols. Edinburgh: T & T Clark, 1909.

Ancient Sources

Old Testament

Genesis
2:24 125
6:2 150
6:3 165
15:6 230
18–19 150
18:2 150
18:3 150
18:22 150
19:1 150
19:5 150
19:8 150
19:10 150
19:12 150
19:15 150
32:20 150
32:25 150

Exodus
15:3 151
31:14 166
32–34 13
32:13 167

Leviticus
6:16-18 126
6:26-28 126
7:6 126
7:8-10 126
7:28-36 126
19:18 230

Numbers
18:8-19 126

Deuteronomy
4:34 166
6:4 127
9:13 13
12:23 71
13:3 151
13:14 151
25:4 122
32 130

Joshua
1:11 167
22:22 154

Judges
3:19 158
13 151
13:3 151
13:6 151
13:8 151
13:9 151
13:10 151
13:11 151
13:13-21 151
19:22 151
20:13 151

1 Samuel
1:16 151
2:12 151
10:27 151
25:16 230
25:17 151
25:25 151
30:22 151

2 Samuel
1:9 167
16:7 151
20:1 151
22:5 151
23:6 151

1 Kings
13:1 104
13:2 104
13:5 104
13:32 104
21:10 151
21:13 151
21:35 104

1 Chronicles
15:15 104
29:18 223

2 Chronicles
12:14 223

13:7 151
15:8 167
17:5 223
19:3 223
20:33 223
29:19 154
30:19 223
32:30 223

Esther
4:16 230

Job
1–2 151
1:6 151
2:1 151
5:17-26 56
27:17 167
29:17 158

Psalms
5:9 223
7:10 223
17:5 151
27:1 107
68:37 167
72:12 167
77:8 223
85:9 (LXX) 35
85:12 (LXX) 35
88 147
88:18 (LXX) 91
88:23 (LXX) 147
112:4 107
140:2 223
143:2 230
142:2 (LXX) 230

Proverbs
4:18-19 107
15:8 223
21:2 223
23:19 223

Song of Songs
3:8 167

Isaiah
2:10 200
5:20 107
6:1 148
9:2 107
11:4 200
14 163
14:3-23 147
14:13 148
14:13-14 147, 148
24:15 35
28:16 200
29:13 82
34:10 230
40:13 (LXX) 230
40:22 165, 167
45:23 200
52:11 158, 166
57:2 166
59:17 108, 200
59:20 200
66:4-6 200
66:5 35
66:7 88
66:15 200

Jeremiah
2:19 154, 155
14:17 230
27:16 167

Ezekiel
11:23 158
28 163
28:2 147, 148
33:24 167

Daniel
7 167, 168
7:13-15 167
7:18 167
7:22 167
9:27 148
10–12 164
11 163
11–12 163
11:31 148
11:36 147
11:36-37 147, 163
12:1 164
12:11 148

Amos
5:18-20 107
5:25-27 77

Joel
2:32 200

Habakkuk
2:4 230

Zechariah
3 163
3:1 148
9:14 200
14:5 200

New Testament

Matthew
4:9 148
5:6 127
5:11-12 102, 127
5:32 121
5:44 102, 127
6:13 80
7:28 80
10:9-10 127
10:10 122
10:17-23 102
11:19 127
11:25-27 128
11:26 128
11:27 75
11:29 117
13:39 178
13:41 178
13:49 158, 166, 177
15 64
15:9 82
16:12 80
16:27 178
19 121
19:9 121
21:21 51, 128
22:33 80
23 99
23:31 99
23:31-37 99
23:32 99
23:33 99
23:34 99, 102

23:35-36 99
23:36 99
23:37 99
23:38 99
24 33, 34, 160, 171, 173, 174
24:1-2 173
24:3 173
24:4 173
24:6 173
24:9-13 102
24:11 34
24:12 172, 173, 174
24:12-13 173
24:13 34, 168, 175
24:15 148, 160, 173, 174
24:16 174
24:24 34, 173, 174
24:27 173
24:30 34, 172, 173
24:30-31 104, 175
24:31 34, 134, 171, 173, 178
24:34 160
24:36 173
24:36-39 107
24:42 34
24:42-43 108
24:42-44 107
25:1-13 108
25:3 178
25:6 104
25:14 75
25:20 75
25:22 75
25:31 172
26:41 80
26:61 123
27:40 123
27:60 113

Mark
1:22 80
1:27 80
1:36 172
4:2 80
4:27 230
4:29 75
5:5 230
7 64

7:1-23 64
7:3 64
7:4 69
7:5 64
7:7 82
7:8 64, 65
7:9 64
7:13 64, 75
8:38 178
10 121
10:11 121
11:18 80
11:23 128
12:29 127
12:38 80
13 173
13:1-2 173
13:5 172, 173
13:7 173
13:9-13 172
13:10 163
13:13 173
13:14 148, 172, 173, 174
13:22 172, 173, 174
13:23 172
13:26 172, 173
13:26-27 172, 175
13:27 171, 172, 173, 178
13:31 172
13:33-37 108
14:38 80
14:58 123
15:29 123
15:46 113

Luke
1:79 223
2:37 230
4:6 75
4:7 148
4:32 80
4:42 156
6:21-23 127
6:27-28 127
9:26 178
10:7 122
10:16 102
10:21 128
10:21-22 128

10:22 75
11:47-51 99
11:49 99
12:35-40 108
12:39-40 107
13:34 99
14:9 156
16:8 107
16:18 121
18:7 230
18:19 127
20:35 209
21:8 172
21:34 107
21:34-36 108
21:36 172
22:16 118
22:19 119
23:53 113
24:11 172

John
2:19-21 123
5:4 156
5:18 51
7:16 80
7:17 80
11:25-26 105
12:36 107
14:3 171
17:20 51
18:19 80
18:39 132
19:16 75
19:42 113
20:25 77

Acts
2:23 99
2:36 99
2:42 80
3:15 95, 99
4:10 95, 99
4:29 99
5:28 80, 99
5:30 99
5:41 209
6:14 75
7:43 77
7:44 78
7:52 99

8 96
9:16 102
10:39 99
13:10 60
13:12 80
13:27 99
13:29 99
14:22 102
14:26 75
15:26 75
15:40 75
16–17 60
16:4 75
17 15
17:4 15
17:5-14 160
17:19 80
17:33 158, 166
19:27 51
20:31 230
20:35 105
21:21 154, 155
23:10 158, 166
23:25 78
26:7 230
26:29 51
27:10 51
27:40 156

Romans
1-14 76
1:1 97
1:3-4 135
1:4 243
1:5 230
1:7 198, 205
1:8 118, 219, 221
1:8-16 196
1:17 230
1:18 156, 212, 242
1:18-32 179
1:25 212
1:32 51
2:2 72
2:3 168
2:5-10 179
2:8 212
2:21 68, 168
2:22 168
3:2 241
3:3 211

3:4 82	8:32 96	14:4-8 199, 204
3:19 72	8:33 212	14:6 168
3:20 230	8:35 204	14:9 233
3:29 89	8:36-39 102	14:11 203
3:30 89, 127, 136	8:37 204	14:12 82, 85
4:3 230	8:38 143	14:14 72, 105, 168, 207
4:8 203	8:39 185, 204	
4:9 230	9:5 206	14:15 95
4:16 145	9:6 81	14:18 168
4:16-17 51, 101	9:9 81	14:19 85
4:22 230	9:11 212	14:22 169
4:24 95	9:16 85	14:23 169
5:1 206	9:18 85	15:4 82
5:5 185, 204	9:24 212	15:11 203
5:6 95	9:25 204	15:13 243
5:8 95, 204	9:28 82, 203	15:15 193
5:8-11 96	9:29 203	15:15-16 101
5:9 179	9:33 168, 200	15:15-32 196
5:11 206	10:1 92	15:16 97
5:12 145	10:5 168	15:18 82
5:14 78	10:9 95, 103, 108, 206	15:19 243
5:18 85	10:11 200	15:29 72
6:1 77	10:13 200, 203	15:30 198, 206
6:3 77	10:16 203	15:33 205
6:3-22 77	11:1 193	16 49
6:6 129	11:2 72, 123	16:2-22 199
6:8 103	11:3 203	16:5 16
6:8-9 77	11:5 212	16:13 212
6:9 72	11:7 212	16:17 79, 80, 84
6:16 72, 77, 84, 123	11:13 193, 196	16:19 81
6:16-17 81	11:16 16	16:20 179, 180, 205, 207
6:17 75, 76, 77, 78, 79, 80, 84	11:19 193	
	11:25 134	16:22 17, 192, 194
6:18 76	11:26 200	16:25 134
7:2-3 127	11:28 212	
7:3 85	11:34 203, 230	**1 Corinthians**
7:5 113	12:1 210	1 128
7:6 156	12:7 68, 82	1–3 128
7:9-25 193	12:7-8 168	1:1 17
7:14 72	12:11 204	1:1-2 84
7:25 85	12:19 203	1:2 206
8:3 96, 210	13:1-7 159	1:3 198, 205, 206
8:9 89	13:2 168	1:4 219, 221
8:10 198	13:4 168	1:4-9 123, 128
8:12 85	13:8 168	1:5 82, 242
8:17 90, 102	13:9 81, 230	1:6 74, 88, 212
8:17-18 179	13:11 157	1:7 206
8:22 72	13:12 144	1:8 204, 206
8:23 179	14:1-2 168	1:9 205, 212
8:28 72, 185	14:3 168	1:10 206
8:30 212, 213	14:4 168, 203, 222	1:10-17 123, 128, 196

1:12-13 193
1:13 95
1:17 82
1:18 82, 128
1:19 135
1:18-25 128, 134
1:18-29 128
1:21 128
1:23 128
1:25 128
1:26 128
1:27-28 212
1:31 135, 203
2:1 74, 82, 212
2:1-4 193, 196
2:2 72, 88, 157
2:4 82
2:5 128, 129, 243
2:6 129
2:6-16 129, 134
2:7 129
2:8 161
2:9 135, 185
2:11 129
2:12 129
2:13 82, 129
2:14 128, 129
2:16 129, 135, 203, 230
3:1 129
3:4-5 193
3:4-12 196
3:5 204
3:16 72, 123, 134, 135, 137, 149
3:17 149
3:19 128, 135
3:20 135, 203
3:22 143, 193
4:1 134, 195, 230
4:2 205
4:1-21 193
4:4-5 203
4:5-6 179
4:8 179
4:8-21 196
4:9-13 188, 189
4:9-17 190
4:11-13 127, 134, 137
4:12 189, 197, 214
4:12-17 197

4:14 193
4:14-15 187
4:16 187, 197
4:16-17 68, 189, 193
4:17 68, 187, 189, 197, 205
4:19 82, 204
4:20 82, 243
4:21 196
5 196
5:1-5 124
5:2 158, 166
5:3 193
5:4 196, 198, 207
5:5 198, 204, 207
5:6 72, 124, 137, 230, 231
5:6-8 134, 137
5:7-8 124
5:9 68, 193
5:9-11 124
5:10-11 125
5:11 68, 193, 196
5:13 135
6 124, 125
6:2 72, 124, 134
6:2-3 137
6:3 72, 124, 134
6:9 72, 124, 125, 133
6:9-10 124, 134, 137, 210
6:10 124, 125, 133
6:11 125, 206
6:13 204
6:15 72, 125, 134
6:15-19 125
6:16 72, 125, 135
6:16-17 134
6:17 125
6:19 72, 123, 125, 134, 149
6:20 130, 134
7 121, 129, 130
7:1-7 130
7:1-16 129
7:1-40 201
7:2-7 120
7:8 120
7:8-9 130
7:10 73, 105, 120, 121, 120, 133,

134, 135, 137, 138, 193, 198
7:10-11 130
7:11 121
7:12 105, 121, 193, 198
7:12-16 130
7:15 120, 212
7:16 129
7:17 130
7:17-24 129, 130, 134, 137, 212
7:19 130
7:20 130
7:21 129
7:23 130, 201
7:24 130
7:25 105, 120, 121, 129, 138, 205
7:25-38 130
7:25-40 129
7:26 143
7:28 193
7:30 156
7:32 204
7:34 204
7:39 127, 135, 137
7:39-40 130
7:40 105, 138
8 234
8-10 234
8:1 72, 125
8:1-3 125, 135
8:3 185
8:4 72, 127, 135
8:4-13 125
8:5 90
8:6 127, 135, 206
8:7 132
8:11 95
9 66, 125, 126, 189, 190, 234
9:1-2 193
9:1-18 230
9:1-27 121, 193
9:5-6 122
9:6 181, 197
9:7-11 122
9:6-18 122
9:9 122, 126, 135
9:13 72, 125, 135

9:14 105, 120, 122, 133, 135, 138, 198
9:15 193
9:24 72, 126, 135
9:25 126
10 66, 119, 234
10:1 66, 126, 131
10:1-4 131
10:1-12 137
10:1-13 130, 135
10:1-22 131
10:6 78, 131
10:6-10 130
10:7 135
10:8 65
10:9 65
10:11 131
10:12 131
10:12-13 131
10:13 131, 205
10:16 65, 127, 135
10:17 65
10:22 65
10:23-33 65, 66
10:26 135, 203
10:29 65
10:29-11:1 66
10:30 65
10:31 188
10:32-33 188, 189
10:33 65
10:33-11:1 66
11 66, 119, 133
11–14 66
11:1 5, 65, 188, 189, 198
11:1-2 66, 67, 70, 131, 135, 197
11:2 65, 66, 79, 84, 138, 139, 156, 188, 189, 190
11:2-16 66
11:3 65, 66, 72, 131, 132
11:3-12 137
11:3-16 65, 131, 132, 135
11:5 132
11:6 132
11:7 132
11:12 132

11:13 132
11:13-14 132
11:14 68, 132
11:15 132
11:16 66, 131, 132, 133, 138
11:17 73, 116
11:17-34 116
11:18 116, 119
11:21 119
11:22 119
11:23 69, 79, 105, 118, 138, 206
11:23-25 117, 118
11:23-26 84, 110, 116, 119, 120, 135
11:24 119
11:25 118, 119, 120
11:26 118, 119, 120, 207
11:27 118, 119
11:27-32 119
11:28 119
11:29 119
11:30-32 209
11:31 119
11:33 119
11:33-34 119
11:34 119
12 127, 132, 234
12–14 201, 234
12:1 66
12:2 126
12:3 127, 135, 207
12:8 82
12:13 127, 135, 201
12:31 132, 133
13 132, 234
13:1-13 135, 137
13:2 72, 127
13:3 75
14 113, 132, 234
14:1 132, 133
14:6 81
14:9 82
14:19 82
14:21 135, 203
14:26 81
14:33 133, 138, 205
14:34-35 133, 135, 137

14:34-38 133
14:35 132
14:36 81, 133
14:37 133, 193, 198
14:37-38 68
15 110, 113, 114, 115, 116, 179, 214
15:1 70, 79, 110, 113, 114, 115, 116
15:1-2 140
15:1-11 110, 112
15:2 82, 110, 114, 115, 156
15:3 70, 79, 110, 113, 115, 117
15:3-4 115
15:3-5 70, 84, 112, 113, 114, 135
15:3-7 111, 113, 135, 138
15:3-8 111, 114, 116
15:3-11 110
15:3-12 214
15:4 110, 113
15:5 110
15:5-7 112
15:5-8 113
15:6 111, 113
15:6-8 110, 112
15:7 111
15:8 111, 112, 113
15:8-10 114, 115
15:9-11 193
15:11 110, 114, 115, 138
15:12 113, 114, 214
15:12-14 113
15:14 114, 115
15:14-19 113
15:15 90
15:16-17 113
15:17 113, 115
15:20 113
15:20-28 214
15:23 219
15:23-24 170
15:23-28 179
15:24 75
15:24-27 198
15:24-28 96
15:27 135

276

15:32 135
15:33 125
15:43 243
15:45 135
15:47 95
15:50 124, 210
15:51 133
15:50-57 133, 179
15:51-52 104
15:51-57 134, 135
15:52 134
15:53 134
15:54 81, 134, 135
15:54-55 135
15:55 135
15:57 134, 206
15:58 72, 114, 133
16:7 204
16:13 222
16:15 16, 126, 157
16:19-24 199
16:21 193
16:22 29, 128, 135
16:23 207
16:25 198

2 Corinthians
1:1 17
1:2 198, 205, 206
1:3 206
1:11 197
1:12 74
1:13 193
1:14 204, 207
1:18 82, 205
2 196
2:3 193
2:4 193
2:5-11 196
2:9 68, 193, 233
2:11 153
2:17 81, 196
3:1 196
3:16 96
3:16-18 199
4:1 196
4:2 81, 212
4:14 72, 207
5:1 72
5:2 95
5:5 72

5:10 179
5:11 72, 196
5:14 95, 204
5:15 187
5:19 82
6:3-13 196
6:7 82
6:10 156
6:14 206
6:14-15 178
6:15 152, 205
6:16 123, 149
6:17 158, 166, 203
6:18 203
7:12 193
8:7 82
8:9 206
8:13 145
9:1 193
9:2 157
9:7 204
10-12 193, 230
10:1 193
10:8 196
10:10 82
10:10-11 68
10:11 82
10:15 211
10:17 203
11 230
11:4–12:14 196
11:6 82
11:7 97
11:9 230
11:14 151, 153
11:27 230
12:1 105
12:3 157
12:8 204
13:10 193, 198
13:11 204, 205, 222
13:13 185, 204, 206, 219

Galatians
1 115, 116
1–2 193
1:1 95, 196, 230
1:2 17
1:3 206
1:4 113, 143, 144

1:6 212
1:6-9 195
1:8 95, 191, 196
1:9 70
1:11 115
1:11-12 84
1:11-17 116
1:12 68, 70, 105, 115, 116, 117
1:14 64
1:15 212
1:20 145, 193
2 116
2:2 84, 116, 126
2:4 145
2:5 212
2:6 116
2:8 193
2:9 116
2:14 196, 212
2:16 72, 230
2:20 95, 96, 204
3:6 230
3:9 205
3:11 230
3:20 127
3:26-29 15
3:27-29 127
3:28 130
4:4 96
4:8 72
4:9 96
4:13 72
4:14 196
5:1 222
5:2 193
5:6 130
5:7 212
5:8 212
5:9 124, 137, 230, 231
5:10 204
5:11 193
5:13 212
5:14 81, 230
5:21 124, 133, 179, 210
5:22 211
6:6 82
6:7 125
6:7-8 179
6:10 85

6:11 17, 193, 195
6:17 193
6:18 206, 219

Ephesians
1:1 205
1:2 205, 206
1:3 206
1:4 212
1:5 92
1:9 92, 134
1:13 82
1:15-16 153
1:15-19 153
1:17 153
2:1 113
2:14-17 205
2:19 85
2:21 123, 149
3:3 134
3:4 134
3:7 152
3:9 134
4:1 212
4:4-6 127
4:6 127
4:14 82
4:16 152
4:22 129
4:29 82
5:5 125, 133
5:6 82
5:8 107
5:12 132
5:20 206
6:8 72
6:9 72
6:14 108
6:19 82, 134
6:21 72, 205
6:23-24 206

Philippians
1:1 17
1:2 205, 206
1:3 219
1:3-4 221
1:3-5 40
1:6 204
1:7 221
1:10 204

1:12-14 230
1:12-15 101
1:14 81
1:15 92
1:16 72
1:18 241
1:19 72, 197
1:22 212
1:25 72
1:27 222
1:27-30 101
1:28 179, 197, 198,
    208, 210
1:28-30 208, 210
1:29 210
1:29-30 197
1:30 210
2:1 204
2:6-11 96
2:10-11 200
2:11 206
2:13 92
2:16 82, 126, 204
2:27 51
3:1 193, 222
3:14 126
3:17 78, 188, 189,
    190, 197
3:20 206
3:20-21 153, 198
4:1 222
4:1-5 199
4:5 144
4:8 222
4:9 70, 84, 138, 188,
    189, 190, 197,
    205, 214, 254
4:15 72, 82, 181
4:15-16 40, 60
4:17 82
4:23 206, 219

Colossians
1:2 205
1:3 206
1:5 82
1:7 69, 117, 205
1:14 113
1:25 81
1:26 134
1:27 134

1:28 68
1:29 152
2:2 134
2:6 70, 71, 83
2:6-7 68
2:8 64, 83
2:14 158, 166
2:22 82
2:23 82
3:9 129
3:12 212
3:15 205, 212
3:16 68, 82
3:17 82
3:24 72
4:1 72
4:3 82, 134
4:6 82
4:7 205
4:9 205
4:12 72
4:16 192
4:17 71, 83

1 Thessalonians
1–3 17, 95
1:1 16, 17, 206, 220,
    228
1:1-2:12 20
1:2-3 220
1:2-5 225
1:2-7 101
1:2-8 221
1:2-10 220, 233
1:3 206, 221, 243
1:3-3:13 225
1:4 157, 204, 212
1:4-6 101
1:4-10 220
1:5 72, 82
1:6 5, 6, 82, 139, 188,
    189, 198
1:6-7 197
1:7 78, 189, 221
1:8 82, 188, 204
1:8-9 13
1:9 96, 188
1:9-10 95, 96, 97, 108
1:10 96, 179, 198
2–3 97, 232
2:1 72, 97, 157, 220

2:1-12 97, 98, 109,
    139, 225
2:1-13 230
2:1-16 18
2:1-3:10 218, 227
2:1-5:24 220
2:2 72, 97
2:2-16 220
2:2–3:13 220
2:3 97
2:5 72, 82, 97
2:6 97
2:8 97, 189
2:9 5, 97, 137, 181,
    189, 190, 197,
    228, 229, 230,
    231, 242
2:10 189
2:11 72, 97
2:11-12 145
2:12 212, 213
2:13 20, 81, 82, 84,
    98, 117, 225, 226
2:13-16 100, 101
2:13–3:10 19
2:13–4:2 20
2:14-16 160
2:14 13, 188
2:15 98, 207
2:15-16 98, 99, 101,
    108
2:16 99, 100
2:17 99
2:17–3:10 97, 220,
    225, 227
2:18 13, 193
2:19 145
3 102, 227
3:2 16
3:3 13, 72, 102, 227
3:3-4 101, 108, 137,
    144
3:4 72, 102
3:6 19
3:8 222
3:8–4:2 222
3:9-13 225
3:10 230
3:11 20, 223, 226, 227
3:11-13 97, 220
3:11–4:2 222

3:12-13 198, 204
3:13 109, 200, 207,
    223
3:15 109
4 102, 104, 214
4-5 17, 179, 228
4:1 20, 70, 84, 102,
    117, 207, 222,
    225, 228
4:1-2 103, 139, 222,
    223, 224
4:1-12 102, 196, 220,
    223
4:1–5:24 220
4:2 72, 157, 207, 222
4:3 103
4:3-8 102, 108
4:3-12 108
4:3-5:28 20
4:4 72
4:5 72
4:6 102, 203
4:7 212
4:7-8 18
4:8 102, 103
4:9 102, 106, 193
4:9-10 102, 103
4:9-12 108
4:10 102
4:10-12 223, 224, 228
4:11 73
4:11-12 13, 102, 103,
    182, 201
4:12 102, 103
4:13 106, 201, 214
4:13-18 7, 18, 19, 103,
    141, 169, 220
4:13-5:11 179
4:14 103, 106, 108,
    200, 214
4:15 82, 106
4:15-17 104, 105, 199
4:15-18 200
4:16 106
4:16-17 106, 108, 134,
    138
4:17 106, 169, 171,
    198
4:18 82, 201, 214
5:1 193
5:1-2 13

5:1-3 106
5:1-10 106
5:1-11 19, 106, 108,
    198, 220
5:1-12 141
5:2 72, 124, 144, 169,
    204
5:2-3 108
5:2-10 108, 137
5:3 106
5:4 106, 107, 124
5:4-8 107
5:4-10 106
5:5-8 107, 108
5:6 85
5:6-7 108
5:8 108, 200
5:9 206
5:9-10 108
5:11 106, 108
5:12-22 18
5:12-24 220
5:14 13, 182, 201
5:21 156
5:23 205, 226, 227
5:23-24 109
5:24 205
5:24-25 224
5:25-28 220
5:27 16, 68, 192, 198
5:28 206, 219

2 Thessalonians
1 11, 24, 29, 87, 88,
    92, 93, 140, 171,
    233, 235, 242, 243
1–2 17, 93, 137, 181,
    183, 192, 217
1:1 92, 149, 190, 199,
    206
1:1-2 198, 220, 228,
    236
1:1-12 20, 217
1:2 92, 199, 205, 206,
    208
1:3 24, 92, 139, 192,
    195, 196, 199,
    211, 221, 233,
    234, 241, 243
1:3-4 195, 209, 211,
    221

1:3-5 88, 92, 139, 172, 217, 220
1:3-6 205
1:3-10 184, 197, 233, 236
1:3-12 24, 89, 217, 220, 221, 234
1:3–3:5 24, 234
1:3–3:16 247
1:4 39, 40, 42, 92, 186, 195, 199, 200, 211, 214, 221, 241
1:4-7 199
1:5 92, 168, 169, 197, 199, 208, 209, 210, 241, 243
1:5-8 24, 234
1:5-10 208, 209, 210, 214
1:6 90, 92, 170, 171, 184, 209
1:6-7 90, 93, 179, 190, 195, 197, 221
1:6-10 88, 89, 91, 92, 93, 94, 136, 138, 139, 140, 141, 169, 172, 177, 184, 198, 209, 212, 217, 220, 233, 243
1:6-12 200
1:7 88, 90, 92, 149, 164, 170, 171, 172, 173, 178, 179, 184, 200, 206, 214, 243
1:7-8 33
1:7-10 87, 91, 92
1:8 71, 72, 88, 92, 170, 206
1:9 92, 170, 172, 200, 203, 204, 241
1:10 29, 73, 88, 90, 92, 170, 171, 173, 179, 195, 200, 210, 212, 213, 214, 221, 233, 241, 254
1:10-12 24, 88, 235
1:11 92, 93, 211, 212, 213, 233
1:11-12 139, 172, 195, 217, 220, 236
1:12 35, 92, 198, 199, 206, 208, 210, 233, 241
2 5, 16, 33, 34, 66, 86, 87, 93, 142, 147, 150, 153, 155, 159, 160, 163, 168, 170, 171, 175, 198, 242
2:1 139, 143, 149, 169, 170, 173, 177, 196, 198, 206, 225, 228
2:1-2 86, 172, 217, 220
2:1-3 85, 139, 236
2:1-12 8, 11, 20, 24, 66, 84, 141, 142, 143, 166, 171, 192, 205, 211, 214, 225, 234, 235
2:1-3:16 217, 220
2:2 3, 7, 9, 15, 18, 82, 86, 141, 142, 143, 144, 146, 149, 173, 174, 178, 180, 191, 192, 195, 203, 204, 214, 227
2:2-12 169
2:3 11, 85, 86, 136, 145, 147, 149, 154, 155, 172, 173, 177, 195, 218
2:3-4 4, 85, 86, 93, 94, 136, 138, 139, 141, 145, 146, 147, 148, 149, 160, 169,236, 243
2:3-12 32, 85, 163, 217, 220
2:3-14 217, 220
2:3-17 217, 220
2:4 4, 6, 29, 33, 34, 145, 148, 149, 151, 153, 173, 174, 180, 199, 242
2:4-6 172
2:5 11, 66, 67, 72, 86, 166, 168, 169, 181, 190, 195, 236
2:5-6 85, 86, 139, 155
2:6 11, 71, 72, 85, 146, 149, 156, 157, 166, 168, 236
2:6-7 4, 145, 147, 155, 156, 158, 160, 162, 163, 167
2:6-8 166
2:6-10 4
2:7 11, 35, 86, 136, 149, 155, 156, 158, 159, 160, 161, 164, 165, 167, 168, 169, 171, 172, 173, 177, 236
2:7-8 157, 160, 166, 169
2:7-12 85, 86, 94, 136, 138, 139, 140, 141, 145, 243
2:8 11, 146, 149, 150, 151, 153, 155, 156, 173, 177, 200, 206
2:8-9 33, 145
2:8-10 140, 233, 236
2:8-12 172, 198
2:9 11, 34, 145, 149, 150, 152, 153, 155, 173, 174
2:9-10 149, 153, 155, 177
2:10 11, 85, 145, 149, 153, 173, 174, 175
2:10-12 154, 179, 192, 204
2:11 11, 153
2:11-12 85, 226, 236
2:12 85, 86, 150, 153, 159
2:13 15, 24, 41, 70, 85, 86, 139, 172, 192, 195, 196, 199, 204, 211, 212, 218, 219, 225, 226, 234
2:13-14 20, 24, 192,

195, 213, 217,
220, 234, 236
2:13-15 85, 86
2:13-17 24, 85, 139,
192, 235
2:13–3:5 24, 234
2:14 195, 199, 206,
212, 213
2:15 9, 12, 18, 24, 63,
64, 66, 67, 68, 82,
84, 85, 86, 139,
172, 191, 192,
195, 196, 217,
220, 222, 224,
236234
2:15-17 24, 32, 217,
220, 235
2:15–3:5 20, 222, 223
2:16 20, 24, 99, 185,
199, 204, 206,
208, 210, 226,
227, 234, 241
2:16-17 86, 139, 195,
199, 217, 220, 236
2:17 82, 198, 204,
206, 223, 241, 242
3 17, 29, 73, 87, 93,
180, 183, 195,
214, 242
3:1 24, 82, 86, 126,
139, 192, 196,
204, 205, 217,
222, 228, 234, 235
3:1-2 185, 197, 217,
220, 236
3:1-3 32, 177, 224,
227
3:1-5 24, 139, 192,
199, 217, 220, 235
3:1-15 139
3:1-16 217, 220
3:2 15, 211, 241
3:3 177, 204, 205, 236
3:3-4 217, 220
3:3-5 198
3:4 32, 72, 195, 204,
222, 236
3:5 35, 185, 186, 190,
195, 199, 200,
201, 204, 205,
206, 214, 217,

218, 220, 223,
226, 236
3:6 63, 64, 67, 70, 72,
84, 87, 117, 139,
182, 184, 192,
195, 196, 198,
206, 236
3:6-7 70, 223
3:6-10 84, 136, 137,
139, 181, 189
3:6-12 141, 181, 183,
186, 192, 223
3:6-13 5, 13, 184, 205,
234, 235
3:6-15 196, 214, 217,
220
3:6-16 20
3:7 67, 71, 72, 87, 94,
136, 181, 182
3:7-8 93, 183
3:7-9 67, 181, 195,
236
3:8 87, 181, 189, 228,
229, 230, 242
3:8-9 137
3:9 78, 87, 94, 136
3:10 32, 72, 87, 93,
94, 136, 181, 184,
195, 236
3:10-12 223, 224, 228
3:11 87, 182, 195, 227
3:11-12 236
3:12 72, 196, 206
3:12-15 195
3:13 139, 183, 196,
236
3:14 9, 72, 82, 184,
191, 192, 194, 195
3:14-15 184, 236
3:15 38, 139, 184, 196
3:16 195, 198, 199,
204, 205, 217,
220, 226, 227, 236
3:17 9, 18, 181, 190,
191, 193, 194,
195, 236
3:17-18 20, 217, 220
3:18 195, 198, 206,
208, 219, 236

1 Timothy
1:2 205
1:3 73, 82
1:8 72
1:9 72
1:10 124
1:15 82
2:5 127
2:6 74, 210
2:12 68
3:1 82
3:16 96, 113
4:5 81
4:6 82
4:9 82
4:11 68, 73
4:12 78, 82
5:5 230
5:7 73
5:17 82
5:18 122
5:21 212
6:2 68
6:3 82
6:4 206
6:13 73
6:16 134
6:17 73
6:20 82

2 Timothy
1:2 205
1:3 230
1:8 74
1:9 212
1:12 82
1:13 82
1:14 82
1:15 72
2:2 68
2:8 113
2:9 81
2:10 212
2:11 82
2:11-13 102
2:15 82
2:19 203
3:1 144
3:15 72
2:17 82
4:2 81, 82, 107

4:6 107
4:8 222
4:15 82

Titus
1:3 82
1:4 205
1:9 81
1:11 68, 132
1:12 107
1:16 72
2:5 81
2:7 78
2:8 82, 99
3:8 82

Philemon
1 17
3 206
4 219
9 193
19 193
21 72
25 206, 219

Hebrews
3:6 156
3:14 156
6:2 81
6:12 187
9:9 143
10:3 119
10:13 222
10:23 156
12:28 71, 83
13:7 187
13:9 81
13:18 224

James
2:1 129
2:19 127
4:4 123
5:11 186

1 Peter
1:6 102
1:21 95
2:6 123
2:23 75
3:13-17 102

4:7 80
5:3 78

2 Peter
2 79
2:21 79
3:9 163
3:10 107

2 John
9-10 81

3 John
11 187

Jude
1:3 79

Revelation
1:9 35
2:10 102
2:14 81
2:15 81
2:24 81
3:3 107
3:12 123
4:8 230
7:15 230
12 88
12:9 149, 153
12:10 230
14:6 163
16:15 107
20:3 149
20:8 149
20:10 149, 153
21:22 123

Apostolic Fathers

1 Clement
1.3 73
2.1 82
5.4 51
5.7 69
7.1 67
7.2 67, 83
13.1 69, 82
18.13 68
22.1 68
27.2 73

29.3 166
40.4 52
42.3 82
45.7 73
46.7 82
48.4 52
50.5-6 52
55.1 144
56.6-15 56
56.6-16 52
56.11-13 56
57.3 68

2 Clement
7.1 73
10.5 73
12.1 73

Ignatius
To the Ephesians
4.1 57
9.1 81
11.1 144
12.2 42, 44
15.1 68
21.1 58
To the Magnesians
3–7 57
3.1 57
6.2 81
8.2 82
9 32
15.1 58
15.2 82
To the Trallians
2.1 57
10–11 60
12.3 74
To the Romans
2.1 82
3.1 68
4.3 44
10.3 35
To the Philadelphians
3.2 57
4.1 57
6.3 74
7.1-2 57
10.1 56
11.1 82
10.2 52

To the Smyrnaeans
3.1 73
8.1–9.1 57
10.1 82
11.2 56
12.2 57
To Polycarp
1 55
2 55
3 55
4 55
5 55
5.1 73
6 55
7 55
7.1 55, 56
7:1-2 55
7.2 52
8 55
To the Antiochians
11 32

Polycarp
To the Philippians
1–12 48, 49, 51, 54,
   56, 59
1.1 53
1.1-2 58
1.3 73
2.3 52, 54, 69
3.1 54
3.1-2 58
3.2 41, 42, 43, 44, 52,
   69
3.3 54
4.1 54, 68, 73
4.6 54
5.1 73
5.2 53, 54
5.3 53
6.1 54, 73
6.3 43, 45
7 54, 59
7.1 59, 60, 74
7.2 45, 53, 54, 80, 83
8.1 54
8.2 186
8.2-9.1 58
9 48, 49, 50, 51, 53,
   54
9.1 43, 51, 53, 54

9.1-2 50
9.2 37, 49, 51
10.3–11.1 58
11 54
11.1 37
11.2-3 43
11.3 38, 39, 40, 41,
   42, 43, 52
11.4 37
13 48, 49, 50, 51, 52,
   53, 54,56, 58
13:1-2 55
13-14 48, 54
13.2 44, 48
14 49, 58

Didache
1.2 71
1.3 81
2.1 81
3.10 73
4.3 56
4.9 68
4.13 71
4.14 71
6.1 68, 81
11.2 68, 81
11.10 68
11.11 68
16.1 34, 73
16.2 34
16.4 34
16.5 34
16.6 34
16.8 34

Barnabas
1.7 144
2.1 35
4.1 144
5.3 144
5.7 49
5.8 69
8.3 74
8.4 74
9.3 74, 82
9.9 81
10.11 82
16.9 81
17.2 144
18.1 81

19.1 71
19.4 82
19.5 68
19.6 73
19.9 82
19.11 71
19.12 56, 71

Shepherd of Hermas
Visions
1.3.4 71
2.1.2 35
3.4.3 35
3.5.1 69
3.6.3 56
3.9.2 56
3.9.10 56
3.12.3 56
4.1.3 35
4.1.8 69
Mandates
2.3 56
6.2.7 81
Similitudes
1.1 73
2.6 73
5.1.3 68
6.2.6 71
6.3.3 71
8.6.5 81
8.7.2 56
9.19.3 68
9.25.2 69, 71, 82

Martyrdom of Polycarp
1.1 74
4.1 68
10.2 69
12.2 68
18.3 46
19.1 74
20 53
22.1 82

Diognetus
4.4 74
7.1-2 79
7.4 80
9.1 209
11.1 80

11.2 69, 82
11.3 82
11.6 83
11.6 67
11–12 67
12.9 69

Other Ancient Sources

2 Baruch
13.3-16 208

4 Baruch
9.18 33
9.20 33

1 Maccabees
2.15 154, 155

2 Maccabees
6.12-16 208
18.3 209

4 Maccabees
2.4-5 51
18.4 56

Achilles Tatius
Leucippe and Clitophon
2.27 158

Ascension of Isaiah
(Martyrdom and Vision of Isaiah)
2.1 177
2.4 177
2.7 177
3.11 177
3.13-4.2 32
3.13-4.22 177
4.2 177
4.7 177
4.11 177
9.13 33

Cicero
Att.
13.28 194

Dio Chrysostom
Discourse
32.11-12 97, 184

Diodorus of Sicily
2.60.3 209

Eusebius
Hist. eccl.
3.16.1 53
3.22.1 45
3.25.1-7 53
3.28.6 46
3.34.1-36.1 47
3.36.1-11 45
3.36-39 46
3.36.13-15 37, 48, 50
3.36.14-15 53
3.36.15 53
3.38.4-5 53
3.39.1 47
4.14.1 46
4.14.3 47
4.14.8 50
4.24.7 59
5.20.5-7 46
5.20.8 50
5.24.16 46
6.43.3 41

Greek Magical Papyri IV
2714 164
2724 164
2727 164
2730 164
2745 164
2768-72 164

Greek Apocalypse of Ezra
6.1-2 176

Irenaeus
Against Heresies
3.3 48

Josephus
Antiquities
4.281 209

Life
43 154

Jubilees
10.8 177

Judith
5.19 167

Justin Martyr
Dialogue with Trypho
32.4 32
110.2 32

Mishnah and Talmud
Pirke Aboth 75
Aboth 117
Baba Batra
16a 151
Berakot
4b 151

Oxyrhynchus Papyri
45 194
275 182
725 182

Philostratus
Vita Apollonii
5.33 99

Plutarch
Timoleon
5.3 158

Pompey
Att.
8.1 194

Psalms of Solomon
13.9-10 208
17.11-22 147
17.22 147

Pseudo Aeschines
Epistle
12.6 158

Qumran
1QM
1.1 107
1QS
1.9 107
3.13–4.26 107

Sibylline Oracles
5.14-25 176

Sirach
46.9 167
48.3 104
48.5 104

Tacitus
Historiae
5.5 99

Testament of Dan
3.6 177
6.1 177

Testament of Levi
6.11 99, 100

Authors Index

Adams, S. 25, 238.
Adeney, W. 15, 104.
Aejmelaeus, L. 107.
Allison, D., Jr 102,104,109, 120, 121, 138.
Argyle, A.W. 105, 122, 128, 134.
Arndt, W. and Gingrich, W. F. 43, 55, 64, 80, 97, 114, 154, 155, 164, 182, 211.
Audet, J.P. 33.
Aus, R.D. 88, 91, 92, 93, 147, 158, 165, 221, 243.
Badcock, F.J. 12, 13.
Bailey, J.A. 1, 2, 9, 30, 36, 141, 181, 198.
Bailey, J.W. 15, 105, 154.
Baird, W. 115, 116, 138.
Bammel, E. 112.
Barnard, L.W. 44, 48, 52, 53, 54, 58, 59.
Barnouin, M. 158.
Barr, G.K. 26, 235, 236, 237, 238.
Barrett, C.K. 79, 110, 118, 120, 122, 123, 128, 129, 132, 133, 144.
Bartchy, S. 129, 130.
Bartsch, H.W. 110, 111.
Bassler, J.M. 208, 209, 210.
Batiffol, P. 45, 46, 47.
Bauer, W. 43, 44.
Baur, F.C. 2, 3, 4, 8.
Beale, G.K. 16, 30.
Beare, F.W. 78, 79.
Beasley-Murray, G.R. 171, 172.
Beasley-Murray, P. 135.
Berding, K. 38.
Best, E. 14, 15 , 20, 29, 30, 33, 72, 85, 95, 96, 97, 98, 99, 100, 104, 106, 143, 145, 149, 150, 152, 154, 156, 157, 161, 162, 165, 167, 169, 177, 182, 185, 186, 191, 192, 195, 209, 231.
Betz, H. D. 187.
Betz, O. 159.
Bjerkelund, C.J. 20, 225, 226.
Blass, F., and Debrunner, A. 77, 90, 156, 168.

Boers, H. 100.
Bornemann, W. 27, 87, 140.
Bornkamm, G. 134.
Bousset, W. 142, 151.
Braun, H. 2, 3, 5, 6, 30, 198, 207.
Bristol, L. 12, 13.
Brown, F., Driver, S. R., and Briggs, C.A. 165.
Brown, J.P. 122, 135.
Bruce, F.F. 11, 16, 17, 65, 69, 77, 97, 98, 103, 118, 154, 158, 166, 186, 191, 192, 194, 230, 231.
Buchsel, F. 64, 75.
Bultmann, R. 64, 69, 75, 77, 116, 138.
Burkeen, W. 145, 158, 159, 161, 165, 170.
Burkitt, F.C. 17, 48.
Cadoux, C.J. 44, 46, 52.
Calvin, J. 114, 162, 163.
Campenhausen, H. von 43, 46, 48.
Cannon, G.E. 127.
Charles, R.H. 142, 176.
Charlesworth, J. 176, 177.
Clarke, J.W. 15, 105, 154.
Clement of Alexandria 30, 31, 62, 67.
Collins, J.J. 175.
Collins, R.F. 101, 104, 106, 107, 108, 144, 199, 201, 206, 207.
Conzelmann, H. 110, 117, 120, 121, 122, 123, 127, 128, 131, 132, 133, 144.
Cranfield, C.E.B. 76, 77, 78, 89, 90, 180.
Cullmann, O. 64, 69, 118, 138, 162, 163.
Cyprian 31, 62.
Cyril of Jerusalem 31.
Dahl, N. 60.
Danker, F. 7.
Davies, W.D. 102, 103, 109, 120, 122, 123, 133, 138.
Denney, J. 15, 154.
Delling, G. 69.
Dibelius, M. 14, 16, 87, 91, 92, 101, 140, 143.

Dobschütz, E. von 16, 104, 143, 145, 185, 186.
Dodd, C.H. 101, 110, 116, 121, 135, 138.
Donfried, K.P. 17, 97, 109.
Draper, J. 33, 34.
Dungan, D.L. 120, 121, 122, 125, 126, 138.
Ellis, E.E. 14, 16, 75, 94, 123, 127, 129, 130, 132, 133.
Ernst, J. 165.
Eusebius 31, 37, 41, 45, 46, 47, 48, 50, 53, 54, 59.
Fee, G. 16, 30, 66, 73, 74, 90, 112, 116, 117, 118, 119, 120, 121, 122, 123, 124, 125, 126, 127, 128, 129, 131, 132, 133, 144.
Ferguson, E. 31.
Findlay, G.G. 104, 143, 184.
Finegan, J. 44.
Fischer, J.A. 48, 49.
Ford, D. 171, 174.
Frame, J.E. 4, 9, 15, 27, 28, 31, 32, 85, 88, 102, 105, 107, 143, 144, 146, 149, 150, 154, 158, 161, 162, 186, 233, 240.
Friedrich, G. 96.
Fuller, R.H. 110, 112.
Furnish, V.P. 4, 104, 127, 133.
Gamble, H.Y. 44, 76.
Gaventa, B. 4.
Gerhardsson, B. 69, 75, 112, 117, 138.
Giblin, C.H. 71, 72, 85, 145, 146, 154, 157, 160, 161.
Gillman, J. 104.
Gloucester, A.C. 36.
Gnilka, J. 153.
Goguel, M. 14.
Goppelt, L. 78, 97, 127, 138.
Graafen, J. 18.
Grant, R.M. 36, 40, 43, 44, 45, 58.
Grayston, K. 10, 239, 240.
Green, G.L. 16, 30, 67.
Greeven, H. 184.
Gregson, R. 11, 13.
Grimm, W. 27.
Grobel, K. 135.

Gundry, R.H. 105, 166.
Guthrie, G.H. 178.
Hadorn, W. 12.
Hanson, R.P.C. 64.
Harnack, A. von 14, 15, 16.
Harrison, P.N. 40, 47, 48, 49, 50, 51, 52, 53, 54, 55, 56, 57, 58, 59, 60, 61.
Harrisville, R.A. 110, 117, 126, 132.
Hartman, L. 104, 105, 107.
Hartog, P. 38, 42, 43, 45, 47, 53, 59.
Havener, I. 95, 96, 103, 108.
Hawthorne, G.F. 153.
Hendriksen, W. 15, 154.
Héring, J. 110, 112, 117, 132, 133, 144.
Herdan, G. 10, 239, 240.
Herford, R.T. 75.
Hilgenfeld, A. 2, 4, 5, 63, 181, 191, 198, 207.
Hippolytus 31, 32, 62, 67.
Holland, G.S. 1, 3, 4, 5, 6, 30, 63, 139, 180, 195, 198, 199, 208, 211, 217, 218.
Hollander, H.W. 99.
Hollmann, G. 2, 3, 4, 5, 9, 142.
Holmes, M.W. 38, 40, 59.
Holtz, T. 95, 96, 103, 105, 106, 107, 108.
Holtzmann, H. 2, 8, 9, 191.
Hughes, F.W. 2, 3, 5, 180, 217, 218.
Hughes, P.E. 178, 191, 194.
Hunter, A.M. 77, 94, 102, 112, 113, 117, 128, 135.
Hurd, J.C. 11, 12, 13, 23, 129, 132, 234.
Ignatius 35, 42, 44, 45, 47, 48, 49, 50, 51, 52, 53, 54, 55, 56, 57, 58, 59, 60, 61, 74, 144.
Irenaeus 30, 31, 32, 41, 46, 47, 48, 49, 53, 59, 62.
James, M.R. 32.
Jenkins, C. 52.
Jeremias, J. 46, 70, 106, 110, 112, 113, 117, 118.
Jewett, R. 6, 7, 8, 20, 101, 182, 183, 215, 217, 218, 225.
Jonge, M. de 96, 99, 103, 105, 110, 117, 128.

Authors Index

Josephus 154, 209.
Justin Martyr 32, 62
Kennedy, G.A. 171, 216, 218, 221.
Kenny, A. 21, 22, 241, 244, 245, 246.
Kern, F.H. 3, 4, 8, 27, 30.
Kim, S. 68, 69, 116.
Klappert, B. 113.
Kleist, J.A. 48, 49
Klopper 27.
Knibb, M.A. 33.
Knox, J. 33.
Koester, H. 7, 100.
Kreitzer, L.J. 199, 200.
Krodel, G. 2, 3, 4, 5, 8, 9, 198.
Kümmel, W.G. 29.
Ladd, G.E. 69, 116, 117.
Lake, K. 14, 33, 35, 36, 39, 43, 45, 46, 47, 48, 50, 67, 71, 74, 80.
Laub, F. 2, 3, 5, 181, 198, 207.
Lawson, J. 44, 46, 57, 61.
Ledger, G. 25, 249, 250.
Leenhardt, F.J. 76.
Lietzmann, H. 117.
Lightfoot, J.B. 36, 40, 46, 47, 48, 51, 52, 53, 54, 107, 153, 159.
Lindars, B. 106.
Lindemann, A. 2, 3, 42, 180, 191, 192, 194.
Littleton, H.E. 2, 3, 63, 175, 208.
Loisy, A. 117.
Longnecker, R.N. 171.
Maccoby, H. 117.
Malherbe, A.J. 14, 16, 29, 97, 98, 234.
Manson, T.W. 11, 13.
Marcion 30, 33, 48, 49, 59, 60, 62, 76.
Marshall, I.H. 13, 15, 20, 29, 85, 98, 100, 102, 105, 107, 117, 118, 120, 139, 143, 145, 146, 149, 150, 154, 158, 159, 162, 163, 179, 182, 183, 184, 186, 194, 211, 221.
Marxsen, W. 2, 3, 5, 9, 15, 24, 181, 183, 235.
Masson, C. 15, 101, 106.
McKelvey, R.J. 148.
McKinnish-Bridges, L. 175.

Mealand, D.L. 22, 24, 244, 248, 249.
Mearns, C.L. 6, 104.
Meeks, W. 130, 131.
Meinhold, P. 46.
Menken, M.J.J. 217.
Metzger, B.M. 31.
Michaelis, W. 187.
Michel, O. 101.
Milligan, G. 15, 27, 28, 31, 32 , 104, 143, 144, 145, 149, 158, 182, 183, 190, 194, 210, 211.
Moffatt, J. 78, 79, 110, 120, 122, 123, 144.
Morris, L. 13, 15, 98, 106, 117, 143, 149, 150, 154, 158, 159, 182, 184, 191, 192.
Morton, A.Q. 10, 22, 243, 244, 245.
Moulton, J.H. 223.
Moulton, J.H. and Howard, W.F. 150.
Müller, P. 3, 4, 5, 63, 181, 196, 198, 208.
Munck, J. 95, 162.
Murphy, F.J. 175.
Murphy-O'Connor, J. 111, 112.
Murray, J. 76.
Neil, W. 15, 98, 105, 154, 156, 186, 194, 231.
Neirynck, F. 104, 122, 123, 128, 135.
Neufeld, V.H. 79, 127.
Neumann, K.J. 22, 23, 135, 246, 247, 248, 251.
Neusner, J. 164.
Nicholl, C.R. 18, 19, 163, 164.
Nielsen, C.M. 44.
Nygren, A. 76, 78.
O'Brien, P.T. 225, 241.
Oesterley, W.O.E. 33.
Ollrog, W. 16.
Orchard, J.B. 101, 105, 107, 108, 160, 171, 173, 174.
Origen 31, 62
Orr, W.F. and Walther, J.A. 66.
Paulsen, H. 40.
Pearson, B.A. 51, 100.
Pelt 27.
Peterson, R.J. 208.
Plummer 107.

289

Polycarp 30, 35, 36, 37, 38, 39, 40, 41, 42, 43, 44, 45. 46, 47, 48, 49, 50, 51, 52, 54, 55, 56, 57, 58, 59, 60, 61, 62, 74, 80.
Poythress, V. 135.
Prior, M. 17.
Quasten, J. 48.
Rengstorf, K. 68, 80.
Rensberger, D.K. 38, 40, 43, 44, 45, 59, 60.
Richard, E.J. 4.
Richardson, C.C. 45, 46.
Richardson, P. 120.
Richardson, P. and Gooch, P. 122.
Ridderbos, H. 116, 148.
Riesenfeld, H. 120, 138.
Rigaux, B. 15, 28, 30, 31, 32, 33, 34, 35, 38, 40, 41, 88, 96, 103, 106, 107, 108, 139, 154, 158, 215, 240.
Roberts, A., Donaldson, J., and Crombie, F. 32.
Robertson, A. and Plummer, A. 110, 123, 128, 130, 132, 144.
Robinson, J.A.T. 6, 33.
Roloff, J. 69, 75, 116.
Ross, G.A.J. 78.
Russell, D.S. 176.
Russell, R. 183, 184.
Schelkle, K.H. 101.
Schipper, R. 101.
Schmidt, D. 10, 11, 100, 101, 232, 233, 251.
Schmidt, J.E.C. 2, 3, 141, 254.
Schmidt, P.W. 2, 4, 6, 9, 207.
Schmithals, W. 19, 76, 79.
Schoedel, W. 36, 40, 41, 43, 46, 47, 50, 51, 58, 59.
Schoeps, H.J. 101.
Schubert, P. 225.
Schütz, J.H. 111, 114, 138, 139.
Schweizer, E. 14, 41, 42.
Scott, R. 17.
Selwyn, E.G. 17.
Smith, M. 138.
Spicq, C. 182.

Spitta, F. 17.
Stanley, D.M. 187.
Stanton, G.N. 122, 138.
Stephens, D.J. 143, 148, 165.
Stephenson, A.M.G. 143, 145.
Stepien, J. 28.
Strobel, A. 165.
Stuhlmacher, P. 104, 135.
Sumney, J.L. 23, 24, 226, 234, 235.
Sundberg, A.C. 31.
Tasker, R.V. 178.
Taylor, V. 77.
Tertullian 30, 31, 47, 62, 76, 159.
Theron, D.J. 31.
Thomas, R.L. 165.
Thompson, E. 12, 14.
Thompson, M. 136.
Thrall, M.E. 178.
Thurston, R.W. 12, 13.
Trilling, W. 4, 5, 9, 10, 16, 24, 30, 63, 84, 85. 86, 140, 142, 143, 149, 154, 156, 165, 181, 183, 184, 185, 186, 191, 192, 193, 194, 195, 196, 198, 218, 231, 232, 235, 240, 241, 242, 243, 246, 251.
Trudinger, P. 12, 13.
Tuckett, C.M. 99, 103, 105, 106, 107, 128.
Vander Stichele, C. 63, 84.
Vielhauer, P. 36, 40, 43, 44, 48, 49, 57.
Vincent, M.R. 153.
Vos, G. 150, 151, 152, 166, 167.
Walter, N. 104, 127.
Walvoord, J.F. 154, 165.
Wanamaker, C.A. 12, 16, 95, 96, 97, 98, 99, 100, 106, 143, 145, 147, 149, 150, 158, 159, 161, 162, 185, 186, 188, 192, 209, 211, 217, 218, 225.
Ward, R.A. 98.
Warfield, B.B. 143, 160.
Weatherly, J.A. 100, 101.
Wegenast, K. 76, 81, 100, 104, 114, 115, 116, 117, 118, 120, 121, 122.
Weima, J.A.D. 16, 30, 152, 169.
Wengst, K. 138.
Wenham, D. 104, 107, 120, 171, 173.

Authors Index

West, J.C. 11, 12, 13.
Westricks 27.
White, J.L. 215, 217.
Whiteley, D.E.H. 6.
Wilckens, U. 76, 77, 79, 101, 112.
Wilder, T. 21.
Williams, D.J. 29.
Winter, B.W. 144.
Witherington III, B. 20, 21, 227.
Wrede, W. 1, 3, 4, 8, 9, 30, 136, 198, 212, 215, 218, 219, 220, 221, 222, 223, 224, 225, 226, 227, 228, 229, 231, 232, 243, 251.
Wright, N.T. 65.
Wrzol, J. 18.
Zahn, T. 18, 36, 38, 39, 42, 47, 215.

www.ingramcontent.com/pod-product-compliance
Lightning Source LLC
Chambersburg PA
CBHW061432300426
44114CB00014B/1650